Dear Medora

Child of Oysterville's Forgotten Years

Sydney Stevens

Washington State University Press
Pullman, Washington

Washington State University Press
PO Box 645910
Pullman, Washington 99164-5910
Phone: 800-354-7360
Fax: 509-335-8568
E-mail: wsupress@wsu.edu
Web site: wsupress.wsu.edu

First printing 2007

The WSU Press gratefully acknowledges the support from Dick Hawes that helped make the publication of this book possible.

Library of Congress Cataloging-in-Publication Data

Stevens, Sydney.
Dear Medora : child of Oysterville's forgotten years / Sydney Stevens ; foreword by Willard R. Espy
p. cm.
Includes bibliographical references and index.
ISBN 978-0-87422-292-0 (alk. paper)
1. Espy, Medora, 1899-1916. 2. Espy, Medora, 1899-1916—Correspondence. 3. Espy, Medora, 1899-1916—Diaries. 4. Espy, Harry Albert, 1876-1958—Correspondence. 5. Espy family. 6. Teenage girls—Washington (State)—Oysterville—Correspondence. 7. Teenage girls—Washington (State)—Oysterville—Diaries. 8. Oysterville (Wash.)—Biography. 9. Oysterville (Wash.)—Social life and customs—20th century. I. Title.

F899.O9S74 2007 2007004947
979.7'0430922--dc22
[B]

Contents

For my mother, Dale Espy Little,
who began as the youngest and became the oldest.

Acknowledgments

My first thought was to present the correspondence between Medora and Mama without benefit of explanation, letting the story of "The Forgotten Years" be revealed, little by little, through the letters themselves. However, it became apparent that there were too many references and observations that would require background information on the part of today's reader.

Therefore, in addition to editing the letters I set about filling in the gaps so that the correspondence could be enjoyed from Mama and Medora's vantage point. Many people have assisted me in that endeavor and, for their insights and specialized knowledge of the people, places, and cultural mores of the early 20th century, I am deeply grateful. Any errors are in spite of their help and I claim them for my own—

The elders of my family, who not only shared their memories over the years but also, in so many cases, wrote them down. They provided a legacy that made this book a possibility—a legacy that I cherish beyond all telling.

Barbara Hedges Canney, for her years of meticulous work in the initial cataloguing of the Espy Papers. Her interest in the information and her continual look-out for Medora related materials were a great incentive in the very beginning stages of this book.

Larry Weathers (1948–2004), whose knowledge of early Pacific County, Washington, was without peer. Larry's generosity in sharing information, his meticulous reading of the many drafts of the book, and above all his unflagging encouragement were among the great pleasures of this journey.

Retired Washington State Senator Bob Bailey (1918–2005) was especially helpful regarding the political climate in Washington state as well as the geography and development of Olympia during the years Papa served in the legislature.

Dick Hawes, who believed from the beginning in the eventuality of *Dear Medora*. His generous support has helped me present her story more fully than I had ever dreamed possible.

The members of the erstwhile Shoalwater Bay Chapter of the Daughters of the Pioneers for continuing to gather together to share the history and stories of barely remembered years. Their combined knowledge is awesome indeed.

Bruce Weilepp of the Pacific County Historical Society and Hobe Kytr, Barbara Minard, and Joan Mann of the Ilwaco Heritage Foundation, for their enduring patience in answering my many questions about local conditions long ago.

Bobby Stevenson, my "Bay Area Connection," who more than once stormed the bastions of the California Historical Society in San Francisco on quests related to the material included in *Dear Medora.*

My late cousin, Barbara Espy Williams Geisler, who carted me around Portland visiting Medora's old haunts, some of which no longer exist. She helped me to see all of them thanks to her vivid descriptions of long-ago. Our treks even included lunch at the Multnomah Club! Medora would have been so pleased!

LaRee Johnson, for her expert assistance with clothing terms and early 20th century styles.

Michael Mathers, photographer extraordinaire, whose discerning eye and tender touch brought many of the old family portraits into the digital world of the 21st century.

Pat Krager, who read the manuscript at its earliest stage and who has been eagerly awaiting *Dear Medora* ever since.

Jean Stewart and Linda Johnson, whose insightful suggestions on reading the "final draft" helped me to rethink and reorganize yet again.

Thanks to them both for urging me to go that one last step.

The residents of Oysterville, particularly those who grew up and grew old here, for wondering with me about all the stories half remembered and photographs only partially identified. How many times we have all said, "If only we could go back in time for a day!"

The staff of WSU Press—in particular, editor-in-chief Glen Lindeman and marketing coordinator Caryn Lawton for their persistent belief in *Dear Medora* during the important concluding stages of this endeavor, and to designer Nancy Grunewald for her special attention to the "extras" and production coordinator Jean Taylor for her extraordinary talents of organization and hand-holding. Bravo, all!

My ever-patient husband, Nyel, for listening and listening and listening, and by so doing, helping me to hear those long ago voices more clearly. And my son Charles, for his wry humor and his way of seeing a path through all of the inevitable setbacks!

Archival and published sources of information for *Dear Medora*—

The Espy Family Archives, Espy family home, Oysterville, Washington, and the Washington State Historical Society Research Center, Tacoma, Washington.

Charlotte and Edgar Davis, *They Remembered, Volumes I–IV* (Ilwaco: Pacific Printing, 1981–1994).

Willard R. Espy, *Oysterville: Roads to Grandpa's Village* (New York: Clarkson N. Potter, 1977).

Velma Laakko, "History of Oysterville School District No. 1, Pacific County," *The Sou'wester* [Quarterly Publication of the Pacific County Historical Society] 13, no. 4 (1978).

Nancy Lloyd, *Observing Our Peninsula's Past: The Age of Legends through 1931* (Chinook Observer, 2003).

E. Kimbark MacColl, *The Shaping of a City: Business and Politics in Portland, Oregon, 1885–1915* (Portland: Georgian Press, 1976).

Charles Nelson, Native Son of Oysterville, "Shoalwater Bay: From Furs...To Firs...To Oysters," *The Sou'wester* 2, no. 4 (1967).

Terence O'Donnell and Thomas Vaughan, *Portland: A Historical Sketch and Guide* (Portland: Oregon Historical Society, 1976).

Marie Oesting, *Oysterville Cemetery Sketches* (Marie Oesting, 1988).

Guy Reed Ramsey, *Postmarked Washington: Pacific and Wahkiakum Counties* (Raven Press, 1987).

Washington: A Guide to the Evergreen State, compiled by workers of the Writers' Program of the Work Projects Administration in the State of Washington (Portland: Binfords and Mort, 1941).

FOREWORD
BY WILLARD R. ESPY

In 1814, Lord Byron took both England and America by storm with *The Corsair*, a narrative poem in heroic couplets. Its hero is the pirate Conrad—patterned, some say, after the real life buccaneer Lafitte. Among Conrad's few virtues, apart from courage, is his devotion to the beautiful Medora, whose love for him is as obsessive. Conrad is wounded and taken prisoner by Seyd, the Turkish Pasha. When he finally escapes and returns to his pirate island, he finds that Medora has perished from grief over a false rumor of his death.

The story was tailor-made for the young female romantics of America's southern states during the first half of the 19th century. It is no wonder that Ann Bullard Pryor, wife of Judge John Cannon Pryor, should have named their only daughter (born March 30, 1839, in Kentucky) Rachel Medora Pryor. The name has recurred in each succeeding generation of our family.

My great-grandmother—the great-great-grandmother of Sydney Medora Stevens, who has here so lovingly assembled and edited these letters—was that Rachel Medora Pryor, the first Medora in the family. Rachel Medora's daughter was Annie Medora Taylor. Annie Medora bore Helen Medora Richardson who, in turn, had Medora Espy, who before her death at 17 wrote these letters to her parents.

This Medora was my eldest sister, eleven years my senior, the first-born and my mother's strong right arm. I was just past 5 when she died in early 1916 and remember little more about her than her long double braids and the white shirtwaist she often wore. I do recall two stories that my parents used to tell around the nursery stove.

One day, after setting the table for supper, my mother left the room for a moment to replenish the wood in the kitchen stove. On her return, she heard the table grunting, and saw it pitching like a dinghy in a storm; with each tilt, the dishes slid to port or starboard, and glasses splintered on the floor. A hog was happily rubbing its back against the table's underside. Mama beat the rear of the beast with a broomstick, but it went on contently scratching. Fortunately, Medora, then aged 10, knew better than her mother how to handle a hog; she ran for a bucket of swill and waved it before the creature's nose. Eagerly grunting, it followed her back to the sty from which it had escaped—how I will never know.

And it was Medora, too, who seeing 1½ year old Edwin (my older brother) teetering on the edge of a second-floor window sill, slipped up behind and caught him around the waist before he could become alarmed and fall.

I remember Mama took to her bed following Medora's funeral and lay there for weeks, the shades drawn; she would let only Papa see her. Though the day came when she laughed again, she was touched for the rest of her life with melancholy.

One day I heard her murmur, unaware of my presence, "There is comfort in a grave."

New York City
(written March 1998)

Medora Espy, 1905.

Sydney Stevens.

Preface

"THE FORGOTTEN YEARS." That's what my mother, Dale, often calls that time when she and her brothers and sisters were growing up in Oysterville, Washington, from 1902 to 1925. Certainly, it is not because she or the other Harry A. Espy family members ever forgot those years or lost touch with the Oysterville of their childhood. For them, the tiny, tumbledown village on the shore of Willapa Bay and the gentle folks who were their friends and neighbors would remain forever etched on their memories. But to the outside world, which has "discovered" Oysterville more recently, it is the long-ago Oysterville of 1860–1890 that captures the attention and the imagination. That is the Oysterville that is "remembered" and, by contrast, my mother's Oysterville of the early 20th century is, indeed, "forgotten."

Oysterville—just a dot on the eastern side of the slender finger of land jutting north from the mouth of the Columbia River—is hard to find, even if you know where to look on the map. But that was not always true. Many years ago my grandfather Espy showed me the map of Washington State in a tattered copy of the 9th edition of the *Revised Encyclopedia Britannica,* published in 1891—a book that still sits on our library shelf. On that map the name Oysterville is in larger print than Seattle, a testimonial to both the size and importance of the village in the early days of its history—the days my mother contends are the only ones now remembered.

As the name Oysterville suggests, it was the acres of tiny, silver dollar-sized mollusks growing in Shoalwater Bay that enticed the first white settlers to the area in the 1850s. They were men intent upon making their fortunes by shipping oysters to the hungry miners converging on San Francisco during the California gold rush of the mid-19th century.

The Espy children in 1913—Dale, age 2; Willard, 3; Edwin, 5; Mona, 9; Sue, 10; Medora, 14. (Albert, born in 1900, had passed away in 1905.)

The very first to settle in the place that was to become Oysterville were my mother's grandfather, Robert Hamilton Espy, and his partner I.A. Clark. In April 1854, Nahcati, a leader of a local band of Chinook Indians, guided them to the rich oyster grounds on the west side of Shoalwater Bay. Within days, the two young men from the east had built a 10x12-foot log cabin a hundred yards behind the high tide line, and the years of prosperity began.

Demand was great for the succulent shellfish found in the briny waters off Oysterville's shore. Schooners came north from California at the rate of two or three a week to load up with as many as 2,000 bushel baskets of oysters. Ship captains paid a dollar per bushel, in gold, on delivery to the schooner. Each

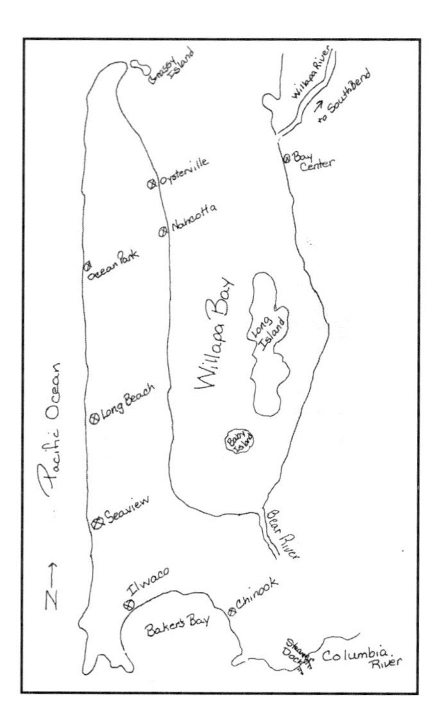

The North Beach Peninsula and Willapa Bay (not to scale).

basketful would receive ten dollars on the wharves at San Francisco.

The little oysters, dubbed "a taste of heaven locked between pearly shells" by San Francisco's carriage set, are said to have fetched a silver dollar apiece when served at gourmet restaurants in the earliest days of the gold rush. The first year alone, 50,000 baskets were shipped south; within three years the number doubled. Many a crew member jumped ship upon arrival in Shoalwater Bay, eager to settle in the burgeoning community and make a fortune in the oyster market.

In no time, Oysterville became a rowdy, lusty boomtown, the busiest coastal anchorage on the Pacific Coast north of San Francisco. Saloons, boarding houses, and boat works sprang up and, before the first year was over, the town became the Pacific County seat. On their northward voyage, schooners carried as ballast redwood lumber, fieldstone, and all the amenities of civilization that an oysterman could desire. Men soon sent for their families and, before long, a school, church, courthouse, and even a jail were built. In addition to the more practical appurtenances such as windmills, pitcher pumps, outhouses, and chicken coops, the gardens of the village homes were marked off with neat pathways of crushed, white oyster shells and rose-covered picket fences. Oysterville began to take on an air of permanence.

The thriving oyster business also must have seemed permanent. Out on the tide flats under shallow bay waters, the oysters grew reef upon reef as far as the eye could see. For centuries the Chinook Indians of the area had enjoyed a never-ending supply of the succulent bivalves. But it took only four short decades, following their discovery by enterprising whites, for the oysters to dwindle in numbers—too few to harvest commercially.

By my mother Dale's early childhood, seven decades after Oysterville's founding, the boom years were long over. No sooner had the oysters "disappeared" than most of the population left as well. The few who stayed did so because they were content to live a simple, uncomplicated life, a life marked by the rhythmic changing of the tides and seasons. By the early years of the 20th century, when the H.A. Espys were raising their family, you might say "there was nothing to write home about." But, oh, how wrong you would be! Letter writing was a major occupation among the Espys.

Due to family circumstances and also to Oysterville's somewhat isolated location, the Espys frequently were separated from one another for lengthy periods of time. During these times of absence, it was the daily correspondence between my mother's oldest sister, Medora, and her mother, "Mama," that kept the family informed and the household running smoothly. And it is their letters, carefully saved for three generations, that provide the link of nine decades between that time when my mother was the youngest and now, when she has reach the eldest age of them all.

My first awareness of Medora, at least that I can now remember, was in 1947 when I was 11. Along with my mother, I was staying with my Espy grandparents in Oysterville for my seventh-grade school year. (I am still unclear why my father remained in California—perhaps to sell our house or to change jobs. The three of us finally were reunited the following summer.)

While in Oysterville, mine was the large, north upstairs bedroom where there were (and still are) two big chests-of-drawers and a writing table, also with a drawer. The closet was miniscule, but the furniture provided ample bureau space for my needs, even though most of the drawers were filled with a little of this and a little of that—an old pair of pince-nez spectacles, assorted doll clothes, buttonhooks, hatpins, my grandfather's old collar box, and many other curiosities that had been tucked away in the "spare bedroom" and all but forgotten. I loved looking at these things and asking my grandmother about them—my questions inevitably led her to tell me about the long-ago days of my mother's childhood.

Shoalwater Bay Renamed Willapa Bay

During the 1890s, a group of businessmen in South Bend, Washington, felt that the name Shoalwater discouraged ship captains from entering the bay and sailing up the Willapa River to their community. They succeeded in having the name changed to Willapa Bay. The dream of maritime greatness, however, did not materialize.

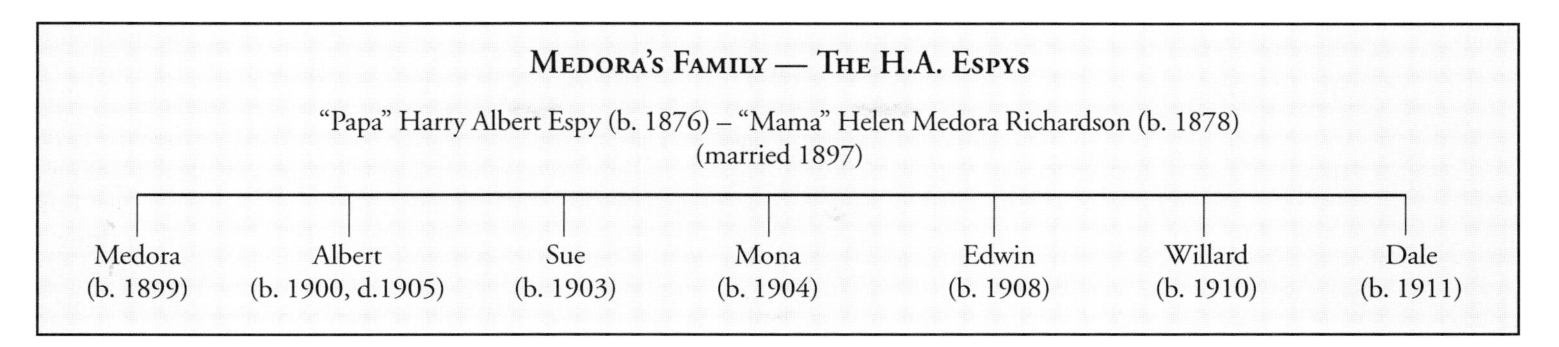

At one point in my rummaging, I ran across one of Medora's diaries. I was very interested because it was written in 1914 when Medora was 15, an age that from my preteen vantage point seemed magical indeed. I read and re-read it, and no doubt plagued my grandmother with questions about my aunt Medora, who had died at age 17 in 1916, twenty years before I was born. And for some reason, perhaps because my middle name was Medora, I began to worry that I, too, would die at 17. On my 16th birthday, I was presented with Medora's gold locket, which reinforced my rather morbid thoughts of an early death, and it wasn't until I had successfully passed that dreaded next birthday that I began to wear the locket, engraved with an "M" and enclosing a picture of Medora's "chum," Dorothy Strowbridge.

Medora's locket.

The years slipped by and my thoughts of Medora were few and far between until my Uncle Willard (Medora's youngest brother), while gathering information for his book, *Oysterville: Roads to Grandpa's Village* (New York, 1977), began questioning all of the family about Oysterville and our memories connected with it. He and I spent many pleasant hours comparing notes about our childhoods in Oysterville—mine, in contrast to his, spent mostly as a "summer kid," but with many of the same experiences at nearby woods, fields, and beaches, and in the dear old town that time seemed to have bypassed.

It was during these discussions that I confessed my desire to someday write about Medora. From that point onward, as Willard searched through the family papers, he set aside any letters from or to his sister Medora. Since his focus was on the Espy family's early generations, he graciously left the era of his own childhood to me.

The term "set aside" may be somewhat misleading. There are thousands of Medora letters! Boxes of them—letters to and from family members, distant relatives, friends, acquaintances, even strangers. (And these are actually a drop in the bucket when compared to all of the Espy family papers. When finally gathered together from the nooks and crannies of the house, they filled ninety large cardboard cartons.) The boxes containing Medora's correspondence and diaries were labeled "Medora Material" and turned over to me, awaiting a time when I could pursue my own writing project. That time didn't come until I retired from a 39-year career as a primary school teacher.

By then, I was living full-time in my grandparents' house—the home where Medora grew up. Much remains as it was in my childhood and as it was in Medora's time, as well. The furniture, china and silver, books and bric-a-brac—treasured keepsakes of the family and a bygone era—are now a part of my daily life. As I have used the dishes,

Willard R. Espy

The *New York Times* and the American Library Association recognized *Oysterville: Roads to Grandpa's Village* as a noted book for 1977. Willard "Wede" Espy (1910–1999) was an editor, radio interviewer, and public relations counselor in New York City, and a prolific author. Examples of his highly acclaimed books include *Omak Me Yours Tonight (or Ilwaco Million Miles for One of Your Smiles), The Game of Words, The Life and Works of Mr. Anonymous, An Almanac of Words at Play, The Garden of Eloquence,* and *O Thou Improper, Thou Uncommon Noun.*

In 1979, Willard received the Captain Robert Gray Medal, the highest award of the Washington State Historical Society given "in recognition of distinguished contributions to Washington State and Pacific Northwest History."

Harry A. Espy's wedding picture.

Helen Medora Richardson, ca. 1895.

dusted marble-topped dressers, and refilled kerosene lamps against the inevitable winter power outages, I have come to know a whole new dimension of the Espy family's life, albeit a century later.

As I began in earnest my own research concerning Medora, I found ever more intriguing bits and pieces of her short life. An old box, labeled "Crown Negligee Shirts, Size 13½," contained all the keepsakes from Medora's final school year—menus, notes written (apparently while in class) to and from schoolmates, theater programs, railway schedules, and much, much more. Among the volumes on the library shelves were her schoolbooks, many with notations in the margins or schoolwork tucked between the pages. Each new item shed more light on Medora, yet each created questions of its own. As Willard noted in his book, *Oysterville*: "Fragments from old letters are like a lightning flash on a stormy night, so brief that there is time for only a glimpse of the landscape before everything is blacker than before. There are references to unknown persons and events; to contexts that can only be guessed at."

Of most interest to me were the letters between Medora and her mother, "Mama." They corresponded, usually on a daily basis, each time they were apart. Through these letters one sees their bond grow as they exchange advice, share confidences, and keep one another informed about their slowly diverging lives. Indeed, Mama sometimes began her letters "My dear little Sister," indicating a mother-daughter relationship quite beyond the ordinary.

Originally, my desire was to prepare a full compilation—most likely several volumes—including every letter that Medora exchanged with her mother. It was a romantic and impractical notion that I eventually dropped. Instead, I have tried in *Dear Medora* to include enough letters and diary entries to keep the continuity of Medora's life intact and provide a complete accounting. In a few cases where appropriate, I have combined parts of letters for the sake of brevity, but all the words (and spelling) are those of Medora or Mama as they wrote them. To aid the reader, occasionally some brief information has been included within brackets. And I have added my own voice throughout, trying to give a picture of Medora's world as she found it those many years ago.

My research and writing has been enriching. At times, I have identified so much with "Mama" that I see her children (including my own mother) through her eyes. That, coupled with the fact that I now live in the house where Medora and my other aunts and uncles grew up has deepened my understanding of family, as well as my connection with the past. The years that my mother describes as "forgotten" have become fresh in my memory and I hope will become so for *Dear Medora* readers as well.

Sydney Stevens
Oysterville, Washington
April 2007

The indelible print that it left upon our hearts...

Oysterville, 1902

Medora and her family moved to Papa's hometown of Oysterville in the fall of 1902. She was 3½ years old, her brother Albert was 2½, and Mama already was planning for the arrival of Baby Suzita. They were the H.A. Espys, lately of East Oakland, California.

On a rainy November day, the young family took up "temporary" residence in town, just two blocks south down the road from "Grandpa" R.H. Espy's house. Grandma Julia had died the previous year and Aunt Dora and Uncle Ed, Papa's older sister and brother, had decided that Papa, of all the R.H. Espy children, was best suited to take care of Grandpa and to oversee the family's many Oysterville business concerns—for the time being.

The Espy Family in 1903—"Mama," Medora, Baby Suzita, Albert, and "Papa." Harry met Helen after he followed his brother Ed to Oakland College in California. They were married in November 1897.

Grandpa was, at 75 years old, a bit dotty according to some, and had an unmistakable eye for the ladies. He needed some serious "looking after" but, as Papa reassured Mama periodically, it wouldn't be for very long.

Papa fully intended to return to California at the earliest opportunity to complete his studies at Oakland College for a degree in mining engineering. He could then continue to oversee Grandpa's placer mine on the California-Oregon border and consider other opportunities that might arise. Meanwhile, for a $10,000 note to the Espy Estate Company,[1] Papa bought the family ranch and the R.H. Espy-owned parsonage across from the Baptist church and dutifully settled his family in, for however long should be needed. H.A. Espy family members have lived continuously in Oysterville ever since.

The Village

Oysterville had fallen on hard times in the previous decade. Not only had the Native oyster supply been depleted, but a long-promised narrow gauge railroad had stopped four miles short of town. This was a major blow to Oysterville and especially to Grandpa. He had invested $2,000 in his friend Lewis Alfred Loomis' train venture in the hope that reliable transportation would help bolster the flagging economy.

Even worse, there had been an election to move the county seat, with Oysterville losing out to South Bend across the bay. Oysterville

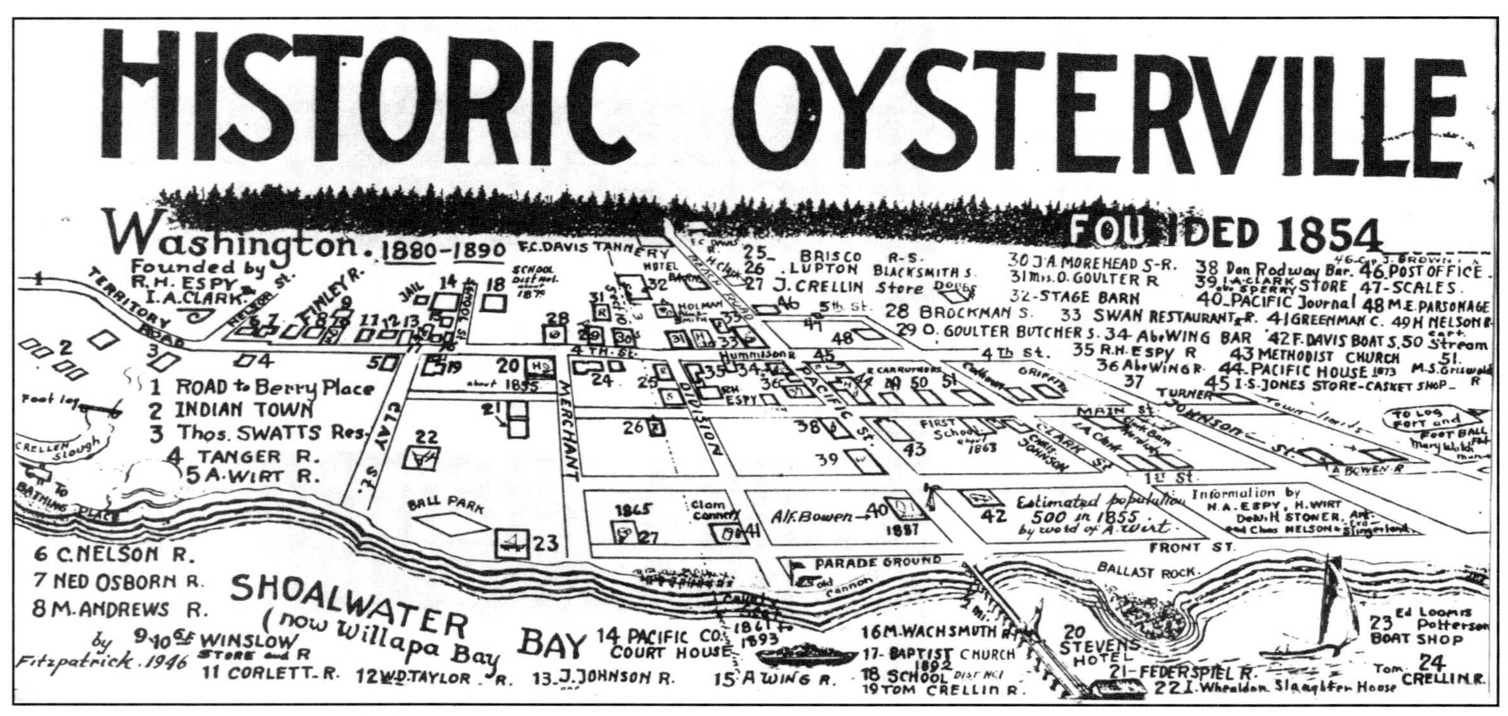

Oysterville in 1880–1890, during Papa's boyhood years. The H.A. Espys moved into the Tom Crellin house in 1902 (#19 on the map).

Medora, 1902.

residents went to court to protest, but, before a ruling was made, a group of "South Bend Raiders" settled the matter in 1893 by "kidnapping" the county records. Oysterville lost its status as Pacific County's political center.

Gradually, most of the population had packed up their belongings and moved on. They had left behind a motley and weathered collection of buildings huddled at the water's edge—the most northerly community on the bay side of the North Beach Peninsula (nowadays usually referred to, incorrectly, as the Long Beach Peninsula).

The North Beach Peninsula

Twenty-eight miles long and not more than two miles across at any point, this narrow peninsula of sand has been pushed northward by the outflow of the Columbia River. Water all but surrounds it. Though a fragile land bridge links the peninsula's south end to the mainland, visitors often refer to it as "an island," for that is how it feels. Locals call the peninsula "the beach."

According to a local Chinook legend, the first people arrived here in a canoe, anchoring the vessel to rocky Cape Disappointment at the Columbia's mouth. In time the canoe became the North Beach Peninsula, forming the bay. Of all Chinook possessions, canoes were the most valued. In a land of dense forests, freedom of movement was possible only along the many waterways.

As whites began to settle the coast country, they, too, found that the rivers, bays, and ocean provided the best transportation routes. Most of the early Oysterville families owned at least one skiff or sailboat, much as most families in later generations would own at least one automobile. Overland travel was mainly limited to the hard sands of the ocean beach, the only practical north-south land route, until 1889 when the narrow gauge railway went into service.

From W.R. Espy, *Oysterville* (1977).

The House

The house that Papa bought—facing the bay on the northeast corner of Clay and Fourth streets—most recently had been used as a parsonage, purchased for that purpose by Grandpa Espy ten years previously. Grandpa also had donated nearby land and $1,500 to build a Baptist Church (1892) on the opposite side of the road. Up to that time, the Baptists had been congregating at Grandpa's house two blocks north on Fourth Street—by far the most commodious home in Oysterville—where they held services and prayer meetings. The circuit-riding preachers (or in Oysterville's case, the circuit-sailing preachers) boarded there, as well, on their infrequent visits to Shoalwater Bay. When the Reverend Huff had taken up permanent residence—staying for twelve years and prepared to stay even longer, but he died—Grandpa had decided that a parsonage was in order.

Many Oysterville houses had been abandoned when the oysters failed and buyers were practically non-existent. The Espy family's new home originally had been owned by Tom Crellin, who left Oysterville early on to take up banking in San Francisco. Papa said the Crellins were the only people who came to Oysterville with money and left with even more, but, even so, Mr. Crellin had been glad to have a buyer. The house, constructed in 1869, consisted of four main downstairs rooms, four upstairs, and two add-ons—a washroom and woodshed. It was built from plans brought by the Crellin brothers from their native Isle of Man, and constructed of redwood lumber on a foundation of fieldstone—materials carried as ballast by the early oyster schooners.

As soon as Papa made the difficult decision to move north, he had written from East Oakland to his sister Susie in Oysterville, asking her to inspect the house and send him the particulars.

[Oysterville]
Sept. 9, 1902

Dear brother Harry,

Your letter reached me today. [Our brother] Will and I went up to the house right after dinner and obtained what we could of the information

Reverend Yeatman's chair.

you wanted. There are three double-bed steads and one single, one double wire mattress, one old-fashioned spring, 2 horrible shoddy mattresses and one very good hair, also one straw. One washstand, 2 small tables and several homemade dressers, 2 wash bowls, 3 pitchers and one soap dish. There are 10 chairs like those in the church, 4 bedroom chairs, 1 arm and 1 high chair, 2 old sofas (one with quite good cover but poor springs and the other just the reverse), 2 kitchen tables and the stove. This last looks as if it might be fixed but Mrs. Yeatman[2] *upon leaving said it just about done for. I would advise bringing your own.*

The measurements of downstairs rooms: Parlor, 17'3" x 17' with bay window 3½' deep; sitting room 17'3" x 17'4", bay 3½'; Bedroom 11'7" x 7'10"; Kitchen 11'7" x 12' Hall 11' x 7'; washroom 18' x 15'.

... if I were the one to live there and having the power to decide, also knowing what the conditions are here and the furniture etc. you have, I would have the kitchen as it is. The little room for a playroom (being right off the living room and next to the kitchen insures its always being dry. It's also on the south side of the house). The sitting room as a living and dining room and the parlor as a parlor.

Then either the N.E. or S.E. upstairs room for your bedroom (both these rooms can have a fire)—in time fixing both.

Let me say right here that there is one looking glass about 12 x 18 in. in the house. (This is the only mirror.) I would advise bringing all carpets, rugs, table-cloths, curtains etc. The matting probably is too old but the nursery carpet will come in handy. Bring all your dishes,

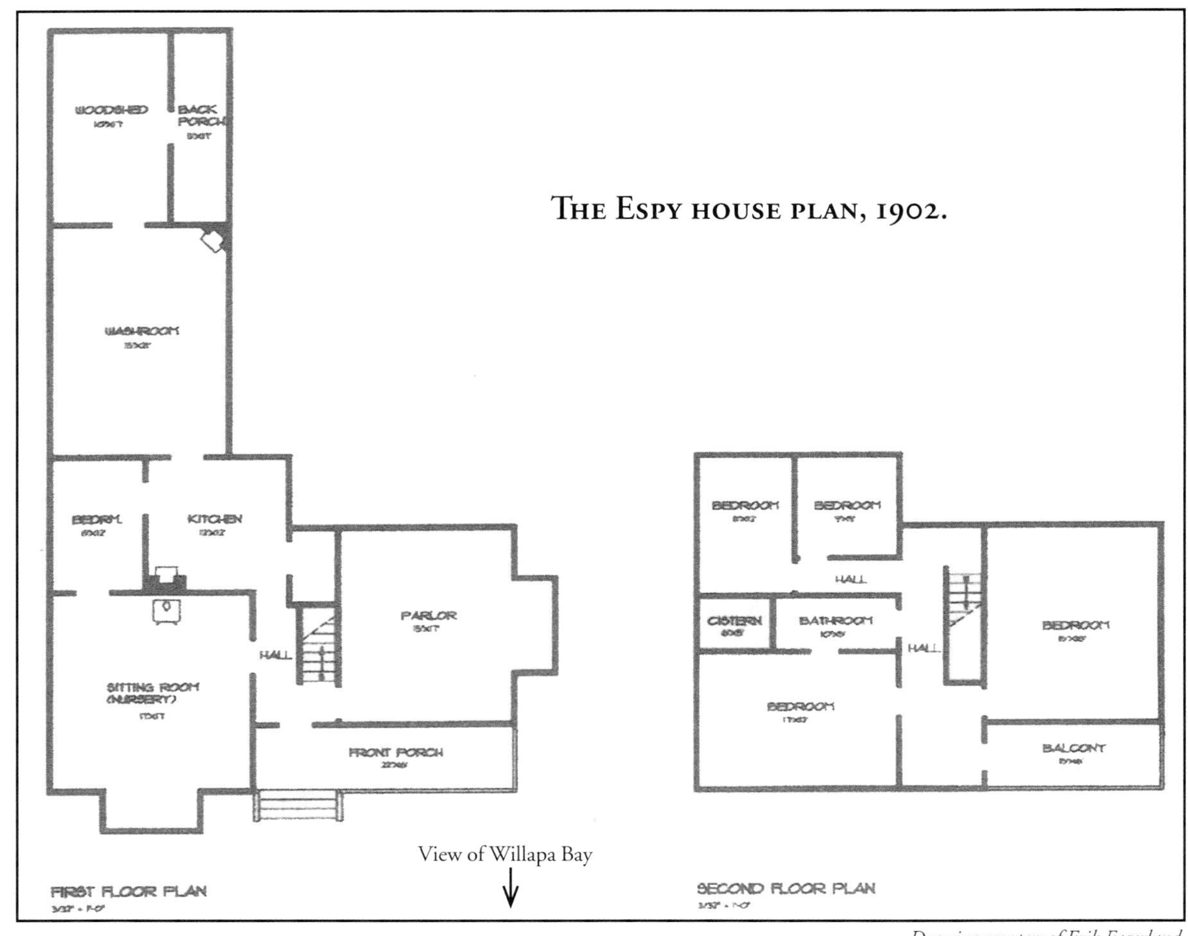

The Espy house plan, 1902.

Drawing courtesy of Erik Fagerland.

bedding (including pillows) nick-naks and rocking chairs; also one couch if you intend to furnish living room and parlor. But don't try to ship any bamboo furniture unless it is packed in a box. It might be feasible to put some of the small baskets or a small table in with the other things.

Beaver[3] *has not started work yet and most probably will not for a week or ten days to come. I'll try to have your directions carried out. I'll close now and write to Helen, not a repetition of this but a short note and the plan of the house with some of my views.*

Ever your loving sister, Susie M. Espy

Mama carefully followed Susie's suggestions. She packed up the bamboo furniture—a hall tree, two bookcases, a plant stand, and a whatnot shelf—and all the pictures painted by Great Aunt Cleora. The Haviland wedding china, Gorham silver, crystal goblets, kitchen utensils, and pots and pans were packed with sawdust in 50-gallon barrels, along with oil lamps, pitchers, washbasins, and other breakables. The trunks were filled with bedding, table linens, and family clothing. Mama felt even more strongly than Papa that their time in Oysterville would be brief, but she was determined that even a short stay would be a comfortable one.

Earning a Living

With the Native oyster supply depleted, those who stayed in Oysterville made their living by subsistence farming or as crafters, laborers, and tradesmen providing for the needs of their neighbors. They hired out as handymen, cut firewood for the railroad, or fished for salmon over on the Columbia. They did whatever was required.

Grandpa Espy was approaching his golden years by the time the oyster harvests failed, but leaving "his" village wasn't given even the remotest thought. He had diversified his interests early on and was, by the 1880s, "comfortably well off."

Storing hay in the "little barn," ca. 1910.

But for Papa, the matter of earning a living was a serious consideration. Over the next quarter century, he would support his growing family in a variety of ways. For a small yearly stipend, he continued as overseer of his father's mining interests in northern California; now and then he hauled wagonloads of clams from the beach to the local cannery; he served as the justice of the peace and, later, as a state senator. Primarily, however, he was a dairy farmer, selling cream to an Astoria creamery and occasionally increasing his earnings by marketing veal, pork, and eggs.

The ranch purchased from Grandpa consisted mostly of acreage—salt marsh, meadows, and forested uplands—ample space to raise hay and vegetables and plenty of pasture for two or three dozen head of cattle. There were two small barns—one across from the house that provided quarters for the horses as well as for "fresh" cows, and one a few hundred feet to the south that served for separating cream from each day's milking.

Not long after arriving in Oysterville, Papa negotiated with the county to buy the abandoned courthouse and its annex. He moved the courthouse a quarter-mile south of town, converting it into a large barn with an area for

The "big barn" at the ranch.

butchering.[4] The annex was dismantled and the lumber used to build a large, two-story house just across the road from the "big barn." Called "the ranch house" by the family, it provided accommodations for a series of hired men, who looked after the livestock and managed the dairy business when Papa was called away from the peninsula. Until his own sons were old enough to help out, a young local boy sometimes was incorporated into the family to assist with farm chores.

Household Management

Papa saw to it that Mama had help in the house, as well. Mama's own mother had been raised in the manner of her Kentucky forebears, when slaves or servants did all of the work in prosperous households. Young ladies were taught to direct servants, to cook, to embroider, and to arrange flowers—and little else. Though Mama was two generations removed from that lifestyle, she was reared according to her mother's strongly felt southern sensibilities.

In addition, East Oakland, where Mama had grown up, was an up-and-coming city with a trolley system, electricity, and even indoor plumbing. Mama was accustomed to the amenities of modern civilization. Arriving in Oysterville in 1902 was a rude awakening to this genteel and refined young woman of 23.

Papa was understanding of the trials of country living and the challenges facing his inexperienced wife. Accordingly, she was provided with help in the house whenever possible, most especially after each baby was born. Competent help was difficult to find. Sometimes an older woman in the community, whose own children were grown and gone, could be prevailed upon to stay at the house for short periods of time. Occasionally, a teenager would work and live in the house for room and board. At other times, Mama engaged a nurse or nanny from Portland or Olympia to come and stay with the family, especially when a newborn arrived. This latter scheme might have been ideal, except the lack of local amenities made housekeeping daunting. Help from the city tended to stay only a short time and usually was "not a satisfactory arrangement."

In August 1903, grandmotherly Mrs. Matthews from Ocean Park came to stay with the family when Mama went to Portland for Sue's birth. In December 1904, when Mona was born prematurely, Mama's sister Ruth took leave from Mills Seminary (the preparatory school for Mills College in Oakland, California) for several months to come north to help out. Papa's sisters, too, gathered around that winter, for the Espy family was going through an extremely difficult time. Scarcely six weeks after Mona's birth, little Albert died of a stomach ailment, probably colon cancer.

Years later Mama would write:

Little Mona, born the night Albert was taken ill—a two and a half pound wisp—had 75 convulsions in five days when five weeks old. Up she came, frail, unstable, completely dominated by Suzita's force and vividness. Twice during her fourth year she had pneumonia, and had to learn to walk all over again.

It was about this period that she used to sleep with her hands over her ears "to keep the dreams out." Always a pathetic hungry little creature unable to assimilate her surroundings. At four she used to sit by the hour perched on the fence accosting every passer-by with "Hellow what you goin' to do tomollow?"

And regarding her young son:

Albert was born talking or so it seemed. At fourteen months old he talked plainly and intelligently.

There was nothing of special note in his short life except the indelible print that it left upon our hearts.

All of the Irish ancestry culminated in this precocious child. True blue eyes of haunting beauty—the only blue eyes in the family, and the only child with his father's fair skin—a long upper lip and sensitive mouth, and stubborn straight fair hair that stood on end. "Happy Hooligan" we called him.

When less than two years old his uncle Ed and I had him on a street car and a Chinaman boarded. "What kind of a man do you call that" he astonished the passengers by asking. At the same period we had him at a zoo and he worried us by getting too near the cages so Papa took him in his arms, a baby figure in white coat and hood. We turned into an enclosed square where there was an elephant, and Albert exclaimed, "Well, I don't know—that beast might hurt me!" The bystanders lost interest in the elephant in amazement at the baby. Once when a little past two I asked him where he was going—"Going to call on Mrs. Wirt[5] *and God," he said.*

During his last illness we were watching children playing in the snow from the hospital window [in Portland]. I remarked that next winter he could play out with the boys, and he said, "Will they have snow in heaven?"

He had a marvelous head, the pride of his father's life, and when he died Papa had a cast taken—a tragic and futile effort to hold beauty gone. We none of us have ever seen it—yes, Papa did see it once, at first.[6]

Albert and Medora, 1903.

Notes

1. The Espy Estate Company, formed after Grandma Julia Espy's death in 1901, was comprised of Grandpa R.H. Espy and his wife Julia's assets. Shares in the company were held jointly by R.H. Espy and his seven children.
2. Mrs. Yeatman was the wife of the last pastor to occupy the parsonage.
3. Charles Beaver, a well-respected carpenter on the North Beach Peninsula.
4. Papa, perhaps, did not want to butcher in the "little barn" near home for the sake of Mama and the children.
5. Mrs. Wirt was the Espy's next door neighbor.
6. When the portrait of the Espy children was taken in 1913 (see page 1), Papa commented to Medora: "The picture of you children was fine…It shows very plainly tho' that one is missing. Dear little Albert! How nice it would be if he were with you. But God knows best and we must think as well as say, 'Thy will be done.'"

Grandpa R.H. Espy and his wife, "Aunt Kate."

Genealogy

"Papa's" Family—The R.H. Espys

"Grandpa" Robert Hamilton Espy (b. 1826) – "Grandma" Julia Ann Jefferson (b. 1851, d. 1901)
(married 1870)

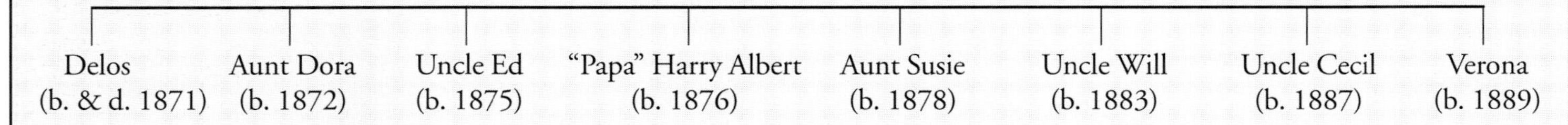

Second marriage; divorce settlement 1905.

Third marriage, 1907, to "Aunt Kate" Hulbert Miller Wichser (b. ca. 1836).

"Grandpa"; Robert Hamilton Espy—Not only the patriarch of the family, but patriarch of the village, as well. With partner Isaac A. Clark, Grandpa had founded Oysterville in 1854 and amassed a considerable fortune by shipping Native oysters to San Francisco. Early documents with his signature reveal he went by his middle name, Hamilton. However, after the Oysterville Militia was formed in 1860 and he was elected the ranking officer, he was called "Major Espy" by Oysterville and Pacific County residents, and referred to as "R.H." in print. In 1870, he married **Julia Ann Jefferson**, a 19-year-old schoolteacher from Salem, Oregon. At the time of her death in 1901, Julia had only two grandchildren, but through the years, eighteen youngsters would eventually refer to her as **"Grandma."** Not long after Grandma's passing, R.H. married a woman alluded to by the family as a "fortune-hunter" and upon whom his children settled the sum of $10,000 in 1905 in exchange for a divorce decree. In 1907, Grandpa was married for the third and final time to "Aunt Kate."

"Aunt Kate"; Kate Hulbert Miller Wichser Espy—She wore long black dresses, high buttoned shoes, and was proud that she could scrape the meat from an apple with her two remaining teeth. She was about 70 years old when she and R.H. married. Grandpa said she "cooked the long way of the flour," and my mother Dale yet remembers tossing Aunt Kate's caraway cookies into blackberry bushes on her way homeward after a visit. Aunt Kate had outlived two husbands—both Baptist ministers—and she would outlive Grandpa by a good many years. Once, when Uncle Cecil was in his nineties, my mother said to him, "I think Aunt Kate must be one of the few women who was married three times and died a virgin." "Not if you knew my father," was Uncle Cecil's reply.

"Aunt Dora"; Dora Jane Espy Wilson—Papa's oldest sister was born in Oysterville in 1872 and, after attending McMinnville College in Oregon and Bellingham Normal School in Washington, she taught school for two years in Pacific County, Washington. In 1895, she married **"Uncle King" (Alexander King Wilson)** and they eventually settled in Oswego, Oregon. Their children were **"Bob" (Robert Espy)**, born in 1899, **"Mary" (Mary King)** born in 1903, and **Julia,** who would join the family in 1906.

"Uncle Ed"; Robert Hamilton Edwin Espy—Just 10 months older than Papa, Ed as the oldest son was considered the "Crown Prince" of the R.H. Espy family. He had received his law degree from the University of California at Berkeley in 1898, practiced law in San Francisco, and was a member of the California state legislature. His untimely death from tuberculosis in 1906 was a great blow to the family.

"Aunt Susie"; Susie May Espy Christensen—Born in 1878, Susie was the fourth child and second daughter of Julia and R.H. Shortly after her mother's death in 1901, she left home and moved to Portland, taking her younger, invalid sister Verona with her. In 1910, Susie married a Danish immigrant, **Olaf Christensen**, and they had two children: **Robert** born in 1911, and **"Julia" (Julia Ann)** born in 1913.

"Uncle Will"; Thomas Willard Espy—Seven years younger than Papa, Will was perhaps the most opposite to him in temperament of all the siblings, with Will being as taciturn as Papa was loquacious. He married **"Aunt Minette" (Minette Phillips)**, valedictorian of the class of 1906 at Oregon State College where she starred on the debate team. They were to live most of their married life in the San Francisco Bay Area and had two children: **"Alice" (Alice Elizabeth)** born in 1908, and **"Jewel" (Julia Ann)** born in 1910.

"Uncle Cecil"; Cecil Jefferson Espy—The youngest of Papa's brothers, Cecil was born at Oysterville in 1887. It was while at home from the University of Oregon in the summer of 1909 that he met **"RuthieD" (Ruth Katherine Davis)**, who was visiting her childhood friend Ruth Richardson, who, in turn, was in Oysterville visiting her older sister, "Mama." Medora and her siblings were to witness the wedding of RuthieD and Uncle Cecil in 1910, for it took place in their very own living room, and Papa, as Justice of the Peace, performed the ceremony. Uncle Cecil became a banker, first in Donald and later in Portland, Oregon. He and RuthieD had four children: **"Cecil"** or **"Gussie" (Cecil Jefferson Jr.)** born in 1912, **"Katherine" (Katherine Ann)** born in 1914, **"John" (John Carroll)** born in 1916, and **Barbara** born in 1918.

"Verona"; Laura Ida Verona Espy—The youngest child of R.H. and Julia was born in 1889. She suffered from a disease similar to multiple sclerosis and was an invalid for most of her life. Verona resided in the Portland area, usually with one of her sisters or other relatives. In later years, she lived with a companion/nurse.

"Mama's" Family—The Daniel Richardsons

(Grandpa) Daniel Sidney Richardson (b. 1851) – Annie Medora Taylor (b. 1856, d. 1902)
(married 1876)

"Mama" Helen Medora (b. 1878)
Uncle Sid (b. 1881)
Ruth (b.1891)

Second marriage, 1903, to Eva F. Gaches (b. ca. 1874).

Daniel Gaches (b. 1909)

"Grandpa Richardson"; Daniel Sidney Richardson—Mama's father lived in East Oakland, California, where he served as Assistant Postmaster of San Francisco and also as American Secretary to the Japanese Consulate. In this latter capacity, he often was called upon to house and entertain visiting Japanese dignitaries, including members of the royal family. In 1903, just a year after the death of Mama's mother, he married Mama's best friend, **Eva F. Gaches**. The children called her **"Evie"** or **"Aunt Eva."** In 1909, they had a son, **"Dan" (Daniel Gaches)**.

"Uncle Sid"; Sidney Worth Richardson—Mama's brother was three years her junior. When his father married Eva Gaches (family members speculated Sid also was in love with her), he left the Bay Area for good. Uncle Sid married **"Aunt Bu" (Beulah Hunter)** and they lived for a time in Oysterville (growing cranberries) before settling permanently at Medford, Oregon, in the late 1920s. Their only child died in infancy.

"Ruth"; Ruth Richardson—Mama's younger sister was 12 when their father re-married. She boarded at Mill's College in Oakland, perhaps because she was "in the way" at home after her mother's death. During summer vacations, she resided in Oysterville with the Espys, helping out with the many household tasks that grew apace with Mama and Papa's ever-increasing brood. By ca. 1913, Ruth was an Oregon resident. Ruth married **"Uncle Hine" (Herman Alfred [Von] Hagedorn)**. Their only child, **"Joey" (Ruth Joan)**, was born in 1917.

Other Extended Family Members

Mary Bamford—Mama's second cousin.

Herbert Davis—RuthieD's younger brother, and a student at the Portland Academy. He carved his and Medora's initials "H.D. + M.E." on the shipwreck *Solano.*

"Aunt Ellen"—Mama's great aunt.

"Cousin Imogene" Jones—Mama's first cousin and daughter of Aunt Shae; her children**, Sherwood**, **Reed,** and **Ethel**, were Medora's second cousins.

"Aunt Hattie"; Harriet Jefferson Lacy—Grandma Espy's sister was married to a Methodist minister, who held pastorates at North Bend, Lebanon, Cottage Grove, Tillamook, Salem, and other communities in Oregon.

"Cousin Bob"; Robert Oliver—A cousin of Papa's on his father's side who lived in Oysterville for several years. He was a great favorite of the family.

Aubrey Pryor—Medora's third cousin living in Pacific Grove, California; daughter of Mama's second cousin Lida.

Frances Pryor—Medora's third cousin of about the same age and sister of Aubrey.

"Cousin Lida" Pryor—Mama's second cousin residing in Pacific Grove, California.

"Aunt Helen" Richardson—Grandpa Richardson's older, maiden sister, a recluse living with his family in East Oakland.

"Great Aunt Cleora" Richardson—Mama's great aunt by marriage; a California painter of some note.

"Aunt Shae"; Horatia Richardson Carlin Stein—Mama's aunt; Grandpa Richardson's younger sister.

Papa and Aunt Dora, ca. 1896.

Uncle Ed Espy.

The Espy aunts, Verona, Dora, and Susie, ca. 1905.

My dreams last night were all about babies...

Oysterville, 1908–1909

In Oysterville's early days, newborns usually arrived at home with the help of experienced female relatives or neighbors. The nearest doctor resided across the bay and, depending on weather and tides, a number of days often elapsed between the time a doctor was sent for and the time he arrived.

In the case of Grandma Espy in 1871, this had spelled disaster. After an extensive period of labor, her first child had to be delivered using "distressing methods," involving, it was whispered, dismembering the dead infant in order to remove him from the womb. After that first experience, Grandpa Espy saw to it that the doctor was sent for in ample time and remained on "standby" for each of Julia's seven subsequent deliveries.

Though he could ill afford it, Papa went a step further to insure that Mama's babies were born without incident. Mama "removed" to the city for six to eight weeks prior to the expected due date, and stayed for about the same amount of time after the precious bundle had arrived. Medora and Albert, of course, had been born in 1899 and 1900 in East Oakland, where doctors and up-to-date medical techniques were readily available. Sue, Mona, and Edwin were born in Portland, Oregon, in 1903, 1904, and 1908, with many local relatives to attend to Mama's needs. Willard and Dale were born at Olympia in 1910 and 1911, for they arrived during the years when Papa served as a state senator and when the family was headquartered there.

At the time of her marriage in 1897, Mama stood 5 feet 2 inches tall, and Papa could encircle her 19-inch waist with his hands, or so goes the family story. Within six years, she had borne four children, all girls except for the second, Albert, who died in his fifth year in 1905. It was thought that Mama needed

Medora, Edwin, Mona, and Sue in 1909.

Oysterville Friends and Neighbors

Mr. and Mrs. Bert Andrews—In 1912, Bert bought an automobile, the first in Oysterville. Their children included **Carl, Ruby, Ed, Mert,** and **Pearl.**

Mrs. "Mary Sam"; wife of Sam Andrews—So named to distinguish her from the other two "Mrs. Andrews" in town. Sam and Mary Andrews had two sons, **Vernon** and **Albert,** younger than Medora.

"Tom" (Thomas) and Katie Andrews, and daughter **Evelyn** and son **Ralph**—Tom owned and operated the Oysterville general store.

Asenath Barnes—A lifelong friend of Medora's. She eventually married a Mr. House, who took some pride in bringing her "from barn to house."

Mrs. Barnes—The mother of Medora's friend, Asenath. Mr. and Mrs. Barnes and their daughters resided on and off in Oysterville.

Miss Blair—Oysterville's school teacher, 1911–1912, who resided in a small house at the north end of town.

Anna (Bourke, Kistemaker, or **Nelson?)**—A neighbor that sometimes helped Mama with the housework.

Edie Bowen—Wife of Mrs. Wirt's son, **George.**

Marvin and **Wesley Bowen**—Mrs. Wirt's grandsons.

(The) Buells—Local residents.

Mrs. Eva G. Butler—Teacher in 1908–1909.

May Christy—Unknown.

Isaac A. Clark—Co-founder with Grandpa Espy of Oysterville in 1854.

(The) Cottles—A family living in the Oysterville vicinity.

John Crellin—An early Oysterville resident and Grandpa's business partner. House plans from his native Isle of Man were used by both his brother Tom and himself for their new homes.

Tom Crellin—Oyster merchant and first owner of the H.A. Espy house.

Mrs. Curry—Medora's piano teacher in 1911.

George Davis—A neighbor.

Mrs. Davis—A family friend.

Deats—A neighbor; probably a child.

"Brad"; Bradford Edwards—A boy from Long Beach, several years older than Medora, who worked for Papa in exchange for room and board.

Mrs. Myra Fisher—A neighbor.

Miss Katharina Friesen—In 1914, an interim teacher.

Dorothy Goulter—A neighbor and classmate of Medora's.

Mr. James Theophilus and Mrs. Maggie Goulter—Their children included **Edwin,** Dorothy, **Lester,** and **Helen.**

Mr. and Mrs. Heinrick—Sunday school and German teachers, respectively; daughter **Luella** was about Medora's age.

Mr. Holman—An elderly neighbor owning a cranberry bog at the north end of town that purportedly produced the most cranberries per acre of any bog on the peninsula. It was sold in the 1920s to Uncle Sid.

Mrs. Guy Hughes—A neighbor.

Miss Ethel Irving—A neighbor.

Mr. George Johnson—About Mama and Papa's age, he was a partner in the Johnson and Henry Store, first located in Oysterville and later moved to Nahcotta.

Mr. Cornelius and Mrs. Anna Kistemaker (a.k.a. **Kistemacher, Kistermaker**)—Mr. Kistemaker was a local handyman. Ruth called him "Kissy Cussy" because he liked to do both. The Kistemaker children included **Gladys** and **George.**

Mr. George and Mrs. Emma Lehman—Somewhat older than Papa, Mr. Lehman drove a mail wagon between Nahcotta and Oysterville. **Henry** and **Harley,** school mates of Medora's, were Mr. Lehman's step-sons.

Lloyd—Edwin's playmate.

"Mrs. M."; Mrs. Matthews—The H.A. Espys' housekeeper from Ocean Park.

Willie and **Ned Needham**—Mr. Wentworth's step-sons, and Medora's schoolmates.

Mr. Charles and Mrs. Anna Nelson—Parents of the "Nelson Boys," **Charlie, Harry, Herbert** and **Tommy**. Herbert and **"Lena" (Alena) Nelson** were parents of **Melvin, Ernest, Christie, Raymond, Gloria,** and **Catherine**.

Mrs. J.T. Owens—Teacher, 1914–1916.

Mrs. Parant—A neighbor.

Pete—Papa's ranch helper, handyman, and family friend.

Mrs. Rohrabeck—Teacher, 1912–1913.

"Dosie," or sometimes **"Dose"; Theodosia Sargant**—Medora's classmate and sometimes best friend.

Lillie Sargant—A school friend and playmate of Medora's.

Mr. F.L. and Mrs. Maggie Sargant—Their children included **William**, "Dosie" (Theodosia), **Fred,** Lillie, **Ed, Bob, Maisie, Mary, Frances, Alice**, and **Arthur.**

Miss Mary E. Siler—Teacher, 1914–1915.

Deane Stevens—An eighth grade classmate of Medora's.

Mr. DeWitt and Mrs. Ina Bourke Stoner—**Ed Bourke** and Anna Bourke were Mr. Stoner's grown step-children.

Mr. Meinert Wachsmuth —An across-the-street elderly neighbor.

"Tena"; Christina Wachsmuth—Meinert Wachsmuth's grown, unmarried daughter who cared for him.

Grace Walkowski—Occasional housekeeper for Mama.

Ida Walkowski—Occasional housekeeper for Mama.

John Walkowski (a.k.a. **Walkowsky, Walcowsky**)—A remittance man from England, living near the Wentworths with his wife and children, including **Albert, Louise, Frank**, Ida, Grace, **Leonard, Alvin, Kenneth, Rosy**, and **Virginia.**

Mr. "Len" (Leonard) and Mrs. Wentworth—A farming family located ¼ mile south of town. Their children included **Ethel, Imogene, Estelle, Geraldine**, and **Lorena.**

Mr. and Mrs. Winslow—The parents of **George** and **Clyde.**

Mr. and Mrs. Andrew Wirt—The next door neighbors, somewhat older than Mama and Papa.

Horace Wirt—The Wirt's grown, unmarried son.

Reverend and Mrs. Yeatman—Baptist minister and his wife who resided in "the parsonage" before Papa bought the house.

"building up" in order to conceive another, much desired boy, and with that goal in mind she went to Southern California during the winter of 1907–1908. Her sister Ruth, having completed her studies at Mills Seminary, accompanied Mama. Medora, already Mama's "strong right hand," went along as well. Suzita and Mona stayed in Oysterville with Papa and Mrs. Matthews from Ocean Park (who in the summer of 1903 had helped the family out when Mama gave birth to Sue in Portland).

The plan must have worked, for Mama and company returned to Oysterville in April and nine months later, on December 30, 1908, Robert Hamilton Edwin Espy was born. Late during the pregnancy, in October 1908, Mama with her sister Ruth as her companion took rooms at the Park Hotel in Portland and set up housekeeping. Papa visited as frequently as business demands in Oysterville permitted, often taking one of the little girls along. But it was primarily through daily correspondence with members of the Oysterville household that Mama managed to continue attending to the needs of her growing family. And, from the time she could read and write, Medora was Mama's most faithful and dependable correspondent.

[Oysterville]
Wednesday, Oct. 28, 1908

Dear Mama,

I have to run to get this in the mail. I am feeling fine. Mrs. M.[atthews] will be in Sunday. Take care of yourself Mama dear

Loving, Medora

[Portland]
Friday, Oct. 30th 08

My dear faithful little girl:

Ruth and I have been wishing you were here, for it is sadly lonesome with out any small girls around, and you are always such a comfort.

Were the waists large enough? I hope they are for you need to put one on right away.

Our quarters here are lovely. You will be pleased with the place I know but the babies would feel decidedly cooped up, as we are on the third floor.

I was sick after leaving Sue and Mona for they felt so badly, and made me feel worse than ever. However, it is a blessing to know that they are with dear Mrs. Matthews.

Espy Family Horses

Charlie
Coaly
Danny
Dolly
Empress ("Emp")
Fanny
Nick
Polly
Prince
Queenie

Family Cow

Daisy

Local Pets

Jack—Family dog
Patsy—Deats' dog
Rover—Wachsmuth's dog

The Weather

The North Beach Peninsula receives 80 to 100 inches of rain in an average year, with well over half falling from November through March. Before the advent of modern-day miracle fibers, "sou'westers" and rubber slickers were the outerwear of choice for Oysterville's inhabitants. Those who worked outdoors, particularly on the tide flats, added hip boots to their outfit.

Today—as in Medora's time, too—outside chores are curtailed only during the severest storms, when winds gust to 70 or 80 miles per hour. Locals describe the climate as "mild"—meaning that temperatures seldom fall into the 20s in winter or rise into the 80s in summer. But they admit that the rain is relentless.

It was an awfully desolate feeling to see Papa go last night. It always seems as tho the best part of my self had wandered off when your precious daddy disappears. Ask him to please mail us our kitchen door key, as the tradesmen now have to deliver at our "reception room."

Write often girlie, and tell me the news.

Ruth sends her love.

Our apartment is very comfortable. I wish you were here to enjoy the convenience of this gas stove. I had breakfast ready before fully dressed this morning and you know I don't get into my clothes slowly. A person with a gas stove is saved a big half of the usual standing around and fussing in the kitchen.

With love to all and many squeezes to the little ones I am devotedly,

Your Mother

Does Sue complain any more of head and back?

Papa's Sleeping Habits

Papa was a night person. The later it got, the more active he became. The quiet hours after the household was asleep was a time for him to work on his accounts, catch up on correspondence, visit a sick cow in the barn, or even repair shingles on the roof. Seldom did he retire until the bay was already streaked with the pinks and golds of the reflected sunrise.

When Mama was at home, she reminded Papa of the time as she headed up to the bedroom at 9 or 10 pm. Sometimes if she awoke in the wee hours and Papa was not in bed, she would call down to him again, hoping that by then he was dozing in his chair and could be roused to come up to bed for awhile, at least.

But usually she just carried on, secure in the knowledge that he didn't seem to need as much sleep as the rest of the family. And, too, by doing odd chores at odd hours, she could count on him to sit down with the family for dinner, and to spend the early evening reading aloud or telling stories to the children, helping the older ones with homework, and catching up on daily events.

When Mama was away, however, she worried a bit more about Papa's upside down clock. Perhaps she felt that he, as the only parent in the home, needed to see the children off to school. Or perhaps she felt he should try to coordinate his meal times more closely with those of the rest of the family to save extra work for the housekeeper-of-the-moment. Or perhaps she just worried about appearances. In any event, trying to change Papa's habits was an uphill battle.

[Oysterville]
Friday, Nov. 6, 1908

Dear Mama

Sue doesn't complain of any backacks or head acks anymore.

My waists are fine and large. They are just like I wanted.

I received 76 in arith test. I think I will get better in deportment too this month.

We hav bought a new clock. Papa sets the alarm for half past six. Papa and Brad go to the ranch at that time and then come down for breakfast. Papas gone to bed the latest ten o'clock.

I forgot to tell you that Aunt Kate is going to make are butter for us. I haven't tasted any butter since you left. Its so windy here and rainy I thought I'd be blown away when I went to Aunt Kates for Mrs. M. The plaster in my new bed room is all coming off by the rain.

The paper says [William Howard] Taft is going to be the president. Are you glad? I am. Almost all the people voted for him in New York.

Its awful hard to try to teach Sue her letters. She is very quick about her numbers but slow for everything else... Have you any thing to advise? I want to do right by her.

Do you think I had better have Mr. Holman make her a doll buggy. The dolls are so high I would have to pay a little to have a doll buggy.

I am reading the book called Dorothy Dean. Its awful good book.

Do you want anything sent to you for the apartment?

Mrs. M. got some pears from Mr. G. Johnson and we have sauce every meal.

Papa has killed three calves sinse you left. He bought down heads, tail, liver, tongue, and all the rest of the stuff except the hole outline of the beast.

I'll have to feed the pigs now.

Geog is a awful test. Arith is pretty easy and so is spelling but Lang is hard. I reseived (I can't spell that word.) 95 in spelling.

Pay Ruth the 20 cents you owe me. With the 15 cents she owes me I want some outing down flannel.

Papa sends love. So does Mrs. M. Mona and Sue and I send so much I can't tell how much. Brad would send his best regards if he knew I was writing.

Your loving, Medora E.

P.S. Send the card to Verona for me please.

Oysterville School

The one-room schoolhouse accommodated all of the children who lived within several miles of the village. Since it stood just a block west of the Espys' house, Medora could wait until the first bell rang before grabbing her books and coat and making a mad dash to avoid being tardy. Children began school when they were 5 or 6 years old, and attended through the eighth grade, when they were required to pass a state examination if they intended to enter high school. Those who failed could remain in elementary school and try again at a later time.

Student desks were arranged in rows, with the seat of one desk attached to the one behind. Smaller desks stood toward the front of the room. The teacher's desk and a recitation table were at the front of the class. A woodstove provided heat, with the wood box filled daily by the older boys, who carried armloads of alder or spruce from a woodpile out back. An American flag was displayed in one corner; a portrait of George Washington, a map of the United States, and several large blackboards hung on the walls.

A bucket of fresh drinking water with a dipper was located on the front porch, and the boys' and girls' privies stood behind the building near a covered play shed. In general, school was in session from September through May, with time off for holidays, Christmas vacation, and when the instructor was attending a teachers' institute.

Medora drew this at seven [illegible]

[Oysterville]
Sunday afternoon, Nov. 8

My dear Mama:

I'm all through "Dorothy Dean." It's a nice book.

I'll send Maud's [Mama's California friend] letter in with this.

My shoes are just awful. The soul is almost gone. I wish you could see them. I can't explain how it is. The leather is rolled back to where my heel begins. I wish you would send my shoes as soon as possible...

[Portland]
Monday, Nov. 9, 08

Dear little Sister:

Your notes each day are a very bright spot on the daily program and it's sweet of you to be so faithful.

You asked me about Sue's doll buggy. I have a suggestion to make. I intend to make one long baby dress and baby clothes for the doll and if you gave her a nursing bottle it would complete the outfit. These would cost five cents and would please Sue as much as a five dollar present. I could get it for you. What does Muriel [Mona] seem to want?

SCHOOL DISTRICT #1

Oysterville schoolhouse in about 1910, before a belfry was added.

School was held at various locations in Oysterville as early as 1860. In 1863, the school became the first in Pacific County to be supported by public taxation, and accordingly was designated as School District #1. The board of directors was made up of three community members; both Grandpa and Papa—in their time—served many terms. The school board's primary duties were to oversee maintenance, hold elections concerning school matters, and hire (and sometimes fire) teachers. These tasks were performed under the watchful eye of a county superintendent, who maintained an office in South Bend across the bay.

The first school building was built in the same year that District #1 was formed—a prefabricated structure made of California redwood and shipped north aboard an oyster schooner. When it arrived, the citizens declared a holiday and, with the aid of several carpenters, put the little one-room school together. The teacher's desk and a recitation table stood in the center of the 18' x 30' room. Two wide boards nailed to opposite walls (and extending along the full length of the room) served as student desks. Pupils sat with their backs to the teacher—boys facing one wall and girls the other. The first instructor was James Pell, followed by Norris Wirt, Julia Jefferson (Espy), Agnes Lowe, Miss Griswold, and W.W. Lilly.

The booming community soon outgrew the "little red schoolhouse," as it was called. In 1874, John Peter Paul, a master craftsman and the builder of the courthouse across the street, was commissioned to draft plans and construct a new building. Approximately 40'x 40', consisting of two rooms, and two stories high, it stood on a plot of land donated by Gilbert Stevens, "for school purposes." This has been the location of the Oysterville School ever since. When the two-storey building burned down in 1905, classes were held for a time in the Methodist Church and upstairs in the old courthouse. A third and final schoolhouse was built in 1907, ready for occupancy that fall as Medora entered the fourth grade.

Attracting qualified teachers to the remote little village was a challenge. Some years, when the search proved particularly difficult, school was delayed for several months until a suitable candidate could be found. In 1914, the salary was $80 per month, plus another $5 if the teacher was willing to perform janitorial work.

Today I made a cake for the first time and it took the layers twelve minutes to bake. A gas stove is a little touch of paradise.

I would like to get out more but can't as my back aches dreadfully when on my feet.

I am glad you did so nicely in the spelling test.

Ruth will see that you get your "outing down flannel".

There is no news and I must stop and write to the babies.

Lovingly, Mama

P.S. How about the pears Mrs. Bert Andrews was fixing for us

[Oysterville]
Wednesday, Nov. 11th, 1908

Dear Mama.

Your suggestion about the nursing bottle is fine. If you take five cents out of the money you owe me...

I can't find any number in my shoes, but you better send number 13 one half letter E or two EE.

Your loving, Medora

Compare both months' work. You saw last months but I ask you to compare them for me please.

	Last Month	This Month
Deportment	80	80
Arithmetic	82	80
Reading	92	92
Geography	88	90
Spelling	94	95
Writing	92	94
Lang	92	94
Scholarship	89+	90
Days Attendance	20	14
Days Absent	0	0
Times Tardy	0	1

[Oysterville]
Thursday, Nov 12th 1908

My dear Mama:

The teacher has made it a rule that if two children are out of their seats at once, there name will go on the board and we will have to stay in. It doesn't matter if we go to our class, then she doesn't put our name on the board then, but if we go up and ask her something when she is busy with a class, then our name is put on the board. I was trying not to have my name on the board but sure as I live it was there. I'm going to send a little poem that I have to learn, don't you think its pretty.

Harvest Song

Summer is gone, autumn is here
This is the harvest for all the year.
Corn in the crib, oats in the bin,
Wheat is all threshed, barley drawn in.
Carrots in cellars, beets by there side
Full is the hayloft, what fun to hide!
Apples are barreled, nuts laid to dry,
Frost on the garden, winter is nigh.
Father in Heaven, thank Thee for all,
Winter and springtime, summer and fall.
All Thine own gifts to Thee we bring
Help us to praise Thee, our Heavenly King.

With love from all, Medora Espy

Schoolmates

The school children were from sixteen families and ranged in age from 6-year-old Gladys Kistemaker to 17-year-old Harley Lehman. All eight elementary grades were taught in the 30' x 40' room.

As was common in rural schools of the time, children recited their lessons aloud to the teacher each day, being called to the front class by class. Students thus heard the recitations of their schoolmates on a regular basis. Those in grades above provided a "preview" of what was to come; those in the grades below provided a constant review for those in classes ahead.

Class sizes might vary from one to four or five pupils. Quite often, however, there was a grade or two with no children at all. In general, students progressed through the grades a year at a time, though very able children might proceed through several grades in a single year. Those who needed more time in a grade were held back, unless their families decided it was time for them to go to work rather than continue in school.

[Oysterville]
Sunday, November 15th, 1908

My dear Mama:

Up in my room I keep a bucket of water, my tooth brush, a towel, and a pan for a bowl—milk pan I mean.

Dosie won't let me in her play house. She writes notes about me.

Today I've had a fine time. To begin with I skated till breakfast then...I dressed the children so as to take them down to Aunt Kates... We played down on the beach. Dorothy played with us too. We went up to our old play house to get some dishes when Patsy (Deats dog) got caught in a trap. I ran to get Horace Wirt and Henry Lehman and they got him out. Sue and Mona were crying. Dorothy had her dog and Deats with her. She got her finger smashed in the trap and Patsy bit her finger. We went on with our play till Lester came crying saying that Maggie's niece (the one that was down here this summer) was dieing. Then we all went to dinner. It was a very nice one.

The stove smokes awful.

Brad likes his tie.

I haven't had my name on the board since Tuesday.

This is a heap of news isn't it?

Your loving daughter Medora Espy

Twenty-seven students labored under Mrs. Eva G. Butler's tutelage during the 1908–1909 school year—

Evelyn Andrews
Ralph Andrews
Asenath Barnes
Marvin Bowen
Gilmore Bowman
Willie Bowman
Darrel Clark
Earl Clark
George Davis
Lawrence Davis
Medora Espy
Dorothy Goulter
Edwin Goulter
Lester Goulter
Albert Kaedy
Gladys Kistemaker
George Kistemaker
Harley Lehman
Henry Lehman
Willie Needham
Dosie Sargant
Fred Sargant
Lillie Sargant
William Sargant
Everette Smith
Grace Walkowski
Clyde Winslow

Mama, Medora, and Ruth in 1907–1908, when Mama had gone to California "to build up."

My shoes fit very nice. I'm sorry [actually they] don't. I'll have to wear my new ones till Mr. Laymen [Lehman] fixs my old ones.

[Portland]
Wednesday, Nov. 18, '08

Dear Medora:

I was glad to get the standing of your report card the other day, and hope you will continue to raise in scholarship each month. Then too I was happy to know your name is staying off the board. We can not always understand our lessons, and it takes hard work to get them perfectly, but there is one thing every little girl can do and that is behave like a lady and not add to the trials of her teacher. Mama wants her little daughter to lead as the best example in behaviour like she stands for the highest in her lessons.

Do you remember that lot of collars and cuffs I bought three years ago when we were at Aunt Hattie's. They disappeared off my chair with other papers when I fainted that night and we searched the house for days afterwards but never found them. What do you think! Last night Aunt Hattie brought me the parcel just as it was even with the tag in it. She found it a few days ago where she had been keeping wrapping paper for years. She was "clearing out" and was finished when she noticed a corner of paper behind a rafter so she took a stick and after poking for a long time dislodged the package which proved to be my long lost collars. Isn't this odd, but I am glad to get the things even if it has been so long.

It is raining here and is probably doing the same in Oysterville...

Don't worry over the way Dosie and Dorothy act. Be sweet and good natured yourself and know in your own heart you are doing right, and then you cannot help but be happy. Content and happiness depend very largely on the thoughts and feelings we allow to dwell in ourselves. The time will come when you can have lots of girls to play with and enjoy, for we will not always be in Oysterville. I must lie down and scribble a note to dear Papa.

Lovingly, Mama

The Nursery

During the years when there were young children in the H.A. Espy household, the southeast downstairs sitting room served as a nursery and has been called that ever since. Each newborn spent the first year in Mama and Papa's room upstairs at night, but was placed in a cradle, and later a crib, in the nursery during the day. Each toddler and preschooler also slept in one of several cots along the nursery walls.

The nursery was the warmest room in the house, with a woodstove fire usually kept going day and night, especially during cold weather. It also was a place of refuge for the entire family during the darkest weeks of winter. By day, the nursery served as a playroom for the children and a work place for Mama. While sitting by the stove, she did mending, shelled peas, wrote letters, and, if the babies were napping, had a few luxurious minutes to herself, during which she generally read.

About the time they began school, the youngsters moved to upstairs bedrooms. Having a bedroom to oneself was a luxury, particularly as the family grew in numbers. There didn't seem to be much consistency as to who had which bedroom. Some years, Medora and Sue shared the largest room on the northeast side of the house. Later, it became Dale and Mona's room, and Medora and Sue each had a room to herself. Except for Mama and Papa's room, the upstairs bedrooms were not heated. On frosty winter mornings, even well into their teen years, all of the Espy youngsters gathered up their clothing and hurried down to the nursery to dress in the warmth of the nursery stove.

To this day, the nursery remains the headquarters for family living. There plans are made, bills paid, games played, and projects worked on, just as in past generations.

[Oysterville]
Friday, November 20, 1908

Dearest Mama:

Isn't it funny you have those collars and cuffs after all these months.

The outing down was fine. Just enough. Do you think it would be all right to ask Papa for a dollar? For Christmas...

I have the wash stand set that was in the north bedroom.

My rubbers won't go over my new shoes.

What time do you expect the baby?

Yours loving, Medora

P.S. I had the last letter you wrote me at school. Dosie & Dorothy got it away from me and read it. Dosie has been well good since but it made Dorothy mad. I'm kinder glad they got hold of it, aren't you?

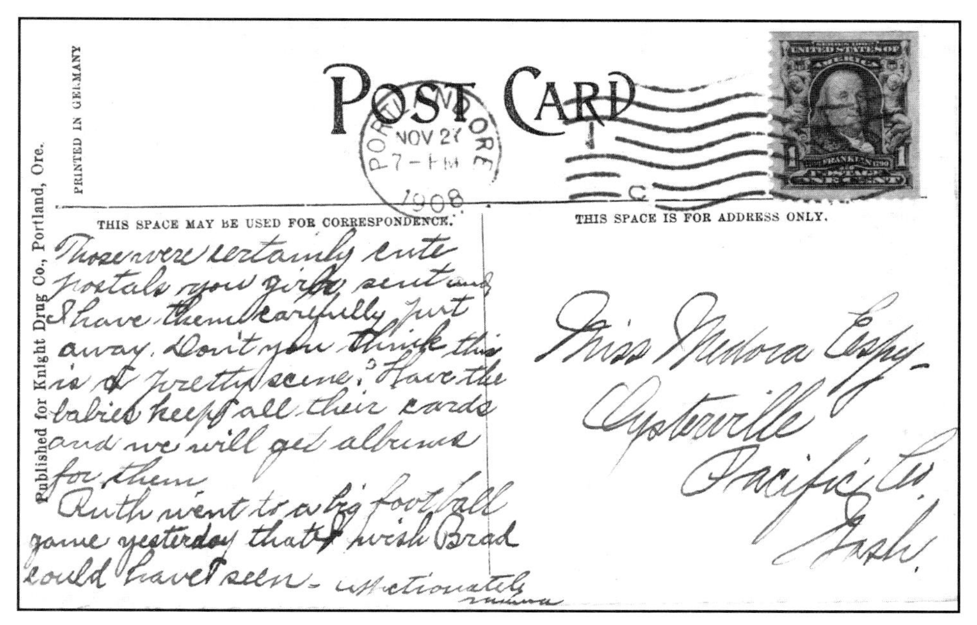

POST CARD

PRINTED IN GERMANY

Published for Knight Drug Co., Portland, Ore.

THIS SPACE MAY BE USED FOR CORRESPONDENCE.

Those were certainly cute postals you girls sent and I have them carefully put away. Don't you think this is a pretty scene? Have the babies keep all their cards and we will get albums for them. Ruth went to a big foot ball game yesterday that I wish Brad could have seen. Affectionately

THIS SPACE IS FOR ADDRESS ONLY.

Miss Medora Espy -
Oysterville
Pacific Co.
Wash.

Postcard sent from Portland, November 1908.

Postcards and Postals

Technically, a "postcard" is simply a card upon which a message can be written and sent without an envelope, and to which the sender affixes a stamp. A "postal card," on the other hand, is pre-stamped and officially issued by the postal service. Both were popular when Medora and Mama were corresponding, and the terms "postcard" and "postal" were used interchangeably.

The Espy family used them to save time and for sending brief messages when there was little to write about. They sent postal greetings to friends and family during holidays, especially Christmas, and sent souvenir postals when away on trips. During the years when the children were young (and money often was scarce), Mama and Medora sent photographic postals as presents. These became "all the rage" in 1906, when Eastman Kodak began selling an affordable "Folding Pocket Camera." It allowed the public to take black and white photographs and have them printed on postcards—a time known as the "Real Photo Postcard Era."

Apparently, the H.A. Espy family did not fit the purchase of one of these new cameras within their budget. Mama, however, saw to it that family members periodically visited a studio to have photos professionally taken and made into postals.[1]

Among postcard collectors, the years 1907–1915 are known as "The Golden Age" of postcards and it was during this period that collecting became a public addiction. Official U.S. Post Office figures for the fiscal year ending June 30, 1908, cite 677,777,798 postcards being mailed. At that time, the U.S. population stood at 88,700,000. Like many Americans, Mama and Medora did their share of postcard sending.

[Oysterville]
Sunday, Nov. 22, 1908

Dearest Mama,

My nice cape came yesterday. I like it very much. Thank you very very much indeed.

Since Dosie read the letter (from you) she hasn't been mad at all. Dorothy is mad at Dosie because she doesn't shun me.

Just think you've been away four weeks Tuesday. I hope Doctor sees fit for us to come up Christmas.

I'm going to write more after our three o'clock dinner.

Sunday evening—I wish you were home to help me out with the Christmas presents. I'll send you my list as far as I have decided. I thought of giving Papa a mail box but can't make it.

Mama—desided
Papa—don't know
Brad—shirt

Ruth—desided
Sue—doll bottle
Mona—don't know
baby—rattle
Asenath—don't know
Eva & grandpa—don't know
Mrs. M.—don't know
All my aunts & uncles & cousins & friends I'll give postal cards.

The next letter you write please tell me how to plan for Christmas.

I'm going to give Ruth a album to keep Lew's picture.

[Portland]
Nov. 26th, 08

My dear Medora:

You have asked me a number of questions, and I will try to answer them in this letter. As to when I'm coming home there is no telling. The sooner the better so far as I am concerned, but it may be a long time. I wish you were with me. I am going to the doctor's tomorrow and he may be able to tell me when baby is coming, but I know nothing definite to tell you, dearie, except that I don't feel as tho there can be much more of a wait. I think what you mentioned for Papa's Christmas would be very nice. Had not I better get it for you here? I will get what you want me to and we can settle the money question later. I am not doing anything for the friends or any one else except a little for the children in the family. I haven't decided what to get for Aunt Dora's little folks or Alice Elizabeth.

I hope you are getting along nicely, and feeling well. Be sweet to the little sisters…

I must change my occupation and get the kink out of my old back. Kiss the girlies for Mama.

When it is real stormy always wear your leggings with your cape, dear, because these wraps drip water into one's shoe tops. This was a ten year old size.

Lovingly, Mama

Mama's Butter-Scotch Recipe

Boil to a hard snap ½ cupful of sugar, ½ cup of molasses, ¼ cupful of butter, ½ tablespoonful of vinegar, ⅛ teaspoonful of soda, stirring sufficiently to prevent burning. Flavor to taste, after removing from the fire. Butter a tin and pour out the sirup in a thin layer. When nearly cold, check off in desired shape with a sharp knife. Wrap in waxed paper.

Keepsakes and Albums

When it came to paper items, most particularly those with writing on them, nothing was thrown out of the Espy household. Those that could be readily sorted and catalogued were kept in baby books, scrapbooks, photograph albums, and books designed especially for displaying picture postals.

Correspondence, both business and personal, was kept. Advertising circulars promoting the latest farm implements or laundering products were saved; even blotters, used or new, were kept. Boxes of "stuff" found their way to the spacious attic over the main part of the house, to a small attic above the kitchen, and to the root cellar, barn, and ranch house. Eventually, the accumulation became treasured keepsakes documenting the family's history.

Three generations hence, the "collection" would be turned over to the Washington State Historical Society Research Center (Tacoma)—a worthy record of life in the state's southwest corner during the first half of the 20th century.

[Portland]
Friday, November 27, 1908

Those were certainly cute postals you girls sent and I have them carefully put away. Don't you think this is a pretty scene? Have the babies keep all their cards and we will get albums for them.

Affectionately, Mama

[Portland]
Sunday, November 29,'08

Dear Medora,

Will you please look in that old dirty square note book that Mama has cooking receipts in and copy the Butter Scotch and Caramel recipes. They are off to themselves somewhere in the middle of the book at the top of a page. You may have a time finding them for the book is so battered, but they are there. I copied those recipes into that composition tablet the evening before you came to us, so I always want to keep it even tho worn out. I want to make some Butter Scotch for Verona, as she is so fond of homemade candy and does not get any.

Be careful of my girlie when she skates for what would we do if our "right hand man" became disabled. I never want to go off again without you dear. It is so lonesome.

Lovingly, Mama

[Oysterville]
Monday evening, Nov. 30th 1908

My dearest of all Mamas:

You don't need to worry about my skating as I am afraid to skate on skates when there's frost which adds just as well to my purpose. I know what dangeres things they are.

The recipe was torn out of the note book. I can't make it out either the butter sckotch or one of the words in the other one so I will send you the slip just as I found it in the bottom of the flour bin.

Your loving girl, Medora E

Christmas

In the Espy household, Yuletide was by far the biggest holiday of the year. Months went into planning and preparation, and family members spent many hours deciding what each would give and what each would receive. Mama, of course, was the initiator of the plans and festivities, involving each of the children as they grew old enough to participate. On the occasions that Mama was away—and there were several because Espy babies seemed to arrive in mid-winter—she directed events from afar with Medora serving as her avid co-conspirator.

The house was decked with holly from treess in the south garden and cedar boughs from the nearby woods. As the great day approached, Papa took the children out to select a tree, usually a spruce, to be placed in the parlor's bay window. A 10-foot tree fit comfortably under the 11-foot ceilings, leaving room for the star that always graced the top. Boxes of decorations were carried down from the attic, a ladder was placed by the tree, and the shades were drawn and the parlor door closed to all except Mama.

Over the next few days, she hung glass ornaments from Germany, clipped on holders with new red candles, and festooned the branches with garlands of tinsel and strands of glinting icicles. Last, she placed the gifts beneath the tree, leaving the children's toys unwrapped and beckoning.

On Christmas Eve, the family gathered for a traditional meal of baked oysters. Afterwards, in front of the library fire, Papa read the Christmas story according to St. Luke from the family Bible. Finally, when anticipation could rise no higher, the parlor door was opened and the days of waiting were over.

[Portland]
Monday, Nov. 30 '08

Medora dear:

Will you look in my "handy box" and send those little Christmas seals. You know those sticking plaster seals to put on packages. I think they are in a wee box. You can put them loose in your letter…If you know where the doll patterns are, send them…Will you please look in that telescope basket where Mama keeps scraps and get all the little "bits" of lace and embroidery, also send one of those white ruffles off of Eva's skirt. I think it has lace on the edge. I may have taken lace off but anyway send it. All of this is in the same basket. In the desk drawers you will find, I think, some wee scraps of ribbon like you made the pin holder out of. This all will make just a

Oysterville Baptist Church and congregation in November 1903. Medora, Albert, and Papa stand at far right.

tiny parcel. Put lace and ribbon in cloth, roll tight and mail. Don't send those wooden spools as they weigh. I want this stuff for doll clothes, as I have dolls to dress for the babies. Sue's is as big as Myrtle.[2] *I wish you enjoyed dolls for I would love to fix one for you but we will find things you do like so it will be all the same…*

The Baptist Church

As the town's population dwindled, the Baptist population declined as well, and, by the early 1900s, the synod could not in good conscience assign a full-time minister. Preachers visited the area intermittently over the next thirty years. When a man of the cloth was not available for Sunday service, Papa or another member of the congregation often preached, availing themselves of "canned" sermons from the old leather bound volumes in grandpa's library—books such as *Heavenly Recognition & other Sermons* by J.L. Campbell, D.D., published by the New York American Church Press in 1895.

In later years, Mama, too, walked across the street and took her turn in the pulpit when necessary. And, if the church needed attention—from sweeping or window washing, to re-shingling or painting—the Espy family naturally took care of it. Small wonder then, when in his dotage, Papa was asked by a passing stranger, "Do you belong to that church?" he answered, "No, young man. That church belongs to me."

Bells of Oysterville

The School Bell

Following a May 1912 school board meeting, bids were requested for adding a belfry to the Oysterville School, more than four years after the schoolhouse had been erected. A response—the only one—did not come until August. For $25, George Lehman agreed to provide materials and build the belfry in time for the start of the 1912–1913 school year.[3]

Presumably, the "big bell" to be installed in the belfry had been used in the two-story schoolhouse that burned down in 1905—in the ensuing years, teachers apparently had to wield a hand bell to call children to school. Where the "big bell" was stored during those intervening years is unknown.

Those who attended the Oysterville School prior to its closure in 1957 remember that the bell rope hung, tantalizingly, just inside the front door. Each day a student was chosen to pull it, signaling the end of recesses and the lunch hour. In the morning before class, it was rung twice by the teacher—the early bell alerting townspeople that it was time for students to be on their way, while the late bell signaled the start of lessons and informed stragglers they were tardy.

The Methodist Church Bell

In 1872, John Crellin offered a sizable donation toward construction when the Methodists built the first church in town. His only stipulation was that a steeple and bell be included, which wasn't part of the original design. The congregation was considerably short of funds. Since John Crellin had offered money and, if his Anglican sensibilities could be satisfied by including a bell, then so be it.

For the next forty-nine years, "John Crellin's bell" called worshipers to services. A gale blew the building down in 1921, with the bell ringing eerily as the steeple fell. Today, it is in service at the Methodist Church at Ocean Park.

Present view of the Baptist Church, from Medora's bedroom.

The Baptist Church Bell

Two decades after the Methodist Church was built, the Baptists were not to be outdone, adding an elegant steeple to their new, but smaller, church. It became an Oysterville hallmark—exhibiting three types of decorative shingles, ornamental cutwork with thirty-two pairs of hand turned finials, painted in alternating red and white stripes, and topped with a golden ball.

For years its bell served a dual purpose. In addition to calling the faithful to worship, the bell served as a fire signal. In the days when axe and bucket brigades were manned by every able-bodied person in the village, the continuous ringing brought men from the oyster beds and fields, women out of their houses and gardens, and children pouring out the schoolhouse door.

Years later, when the church no longer was regularly used and tourists began to flock to the newly created Oysterville National Historic District, pulling the bell rope was a temptation to curious visitors. Despite signs urging the contrary, people persisted in tugging the rope, each time giving the village old-timers a start. Eventually, the rope was tucked away out of sight, and the bell now is rung only on special occasions.

[Oysterville]
Sunday, Dec 6th, 1908

Dearest Mama,

Today there wasn't any church but Papa read one of Mr. Webster's sermons and a chapter out of the bible from the (14) fourteenth chapter of John.

I am always your daughter, M.E.

[Oysterville]
Thursday, December 10, 1908

My dear Mama—

There really isn't any news.

The bell rang when I was dressing. Have to run.

Sue is lacing my shoes. Mrs. M. is combing my hair while I write.

Yours loving, Medora

The Telephone

A black telephone on an oak fixture was mounted on the wall in the southwest corner of the kitchen. To speak into the mouthpiece, the shorter members of the family stood on tiptoe, while the tallest hunched over. The Espy's ring was a short, a long, and a short. By virtue of there being only one line in town, Mama or Papa could answer their ring when visiting a neighbor as well as when at home.

If the Espys were awaiting news that might be of interest to others in the community, any of the subscribers could pick up a receiver and listen in. The more listeners, however, the fainter became the voices on the primitive line. Even after a system update to automatic dial in 1950, members of the Espy family retained a habit of shouting when talking on the phone.

In 1903, J.A. Howerton installed the first telephone line on the peninsula, extending between Ilwaco and a (presumably stationary) fish-buying scow on the Wallicut River. Soon afterwards, Howerton installed a switchboard, and by 1907 his Ilwaco Telephone and Telegraph Company was connected to Astoria and the outside world. In 1930, however, there were only three telephones in the town of Long Beach, while by 1954 there were about a thousand telephones in use peninsula-wide.[4]

The records are largely silent in regard to Oysterville's telephones. From references in Medora's letters to Mama, however, it is clear there was a phone in the Espy household as early as 1908. Perhaps, Papa had made arrangements with Howerton and a line was run from Ilwaco to the village. Or, as my mother Dale has surmised, one of the enterprising members of Oysterville's Andrews family—always on the cutting edge of mechanical and electrical inventions for their times—might have somehow rigged a line. Whatever the means, the Espys were "connected" with the outside world from an early date.

[Oysterville]
Wednesday, December 16, 1908

Dear Mama

We are all well. Will send Papas mail.

Will you telephone when Baby comes.

Medora

[Oysterville]
Dec. 31frist 1908

Dear Mama:

The childrn and I had a big lunch over at Johnson's Hotel.

There has been a heavy storm out at sea and a lot of drift wood has come in.

I am at Henry's now.

Please excuse this awful scratch.

Tell Ruth what to say when she writes.

Has Robert Hamilton Edwin [b. 12/30/1908] been weighed yet?

How are you all.

Your loving daughter, Medora Espy

Skating Lake

A long strand of lakes, some large, some small, dot the center of the peninsula, parading north and south like so many mismatched pearls on a flapper's necklace. One of the largest was situated about a half-mile west of Oysterville. For years, it was the destination for great fun and excitement when wintertime was cold enough that the lakes froze.

Children, and those adults who were young at heart and physically agile, raced through the woods to Skating Lake, hauling sleds and skates if they had them, but content just to run and slide on the ice if not. As the shadows lengthened on those winter afternoons, bonfires were built on the banks, and lanterns placed around the perimeter on fence posts, so that the fun could continue well after dark.

"The *Alice* by Moonlight," ©1909 by H.J. Brown. Built at Bordeaux in 1901, the *Alice* was one of the largest vessels sailing under the French flag.

The lake was about 3½ miles long, and, when full, was 5 feet deep at the north end and 11 or 12 feet deep at the south. In summer, when the water level dropped, islands and high ground appeared here and there. It was a favorite place for duck hunting in the fall and more than one boy earned spending money running beaver trap lines at Skating Lake.

[Oysterville]
Monday, January 11, 1909

Mama, I wish you could see me. My cheeks are as red as my sweater. Skating yesterday, snowballing and sliding today. It has snowed all day long exsepting a little this evening. The weather here gets worse and worse all the time. Papa says it will soon be too cold to snow.

With whole stomack fulls of kisses (as Budge says in Helen's Babies) I am as ever,
Medora Espy

P.S. I received the Youth's Companion today.

The *Alice*

In the early hours of January 15, 1909, the graceful French sailing vessel *Alice* was blown onto the beach just north of Ocean Park. Salt water immediately catalyzed a cargo of 2,200 tons of cement into hard packets. Plans for salvage weren't even considered.

The ship had left London six months previously, with about two-thirds of a full load of pulverized cement in barrels. The *Alice* was bound for the Columbia, but when in sight of the river's mouth, a tugboat necessary for making a safe entry into the estuary couldn't approach due to heavy winds. A seaman named De Reugemond later described the plight of the ship and crew: "For a number of days it was just the same—in and off and hove to. It kept blowing pretty stiff, mostly from ENE, and it was chilly and disagreeable. It was often difficult making in on account of these winds."[5]

No sooner had the ship crashed on the beach than the alarm was raised by the

Wreckmaster

Dozens of ships have wrecked along the ocean shore of the North Beach Peninsula. At one time, a "Wreckmaster" was an elected position in Pacific County, as in all of Washington's coastal counties. The duty included protecting wrecks and cargoes from "seagulls," a local term referring to people who helped themselves to salvageable items and treasures littering a beach after a foundering.

Klipsan Beach

In 1889, due to the increasing number of shipwrecks along the peninsula, the federal government established a life-saving station on a two-acre compound at Klipsan Beach, three miles south of Ocean Park. A barracks and boathouse were built to accommodate a keeper, six-man crew, and two New Jersey style lifeboats. The peninsula's narrow gauge railroad offered a popular summer excursion to watch the lifesaving crew drill, with breeches buoys and horse teams trained for surf rescue.

Life boat drill at Klipsan Beach.

howling of a dog belonging to Willie Taylor of Ocean Park. Ironically, this dog had survived a shipwreck two years earlier when the *Solano*, a four-masted schooner, ran aground four miles to the north. Taylor quickly spread word, and the North Beach Life Saving Crew hitched up horses, put a surfboat on the beach cart, and proceeded toward the wreck.

Reaching the ship proved difficult, however, as the soft sand and adverse weather made the horses balky. Fortunately, all hands on the *Alice* had reached shore safely using their own lifeboat, but it was four days before the ship could be boarded. Several trips were made out to the vessel, which lay head-on to the beach, 300 yards offshore. All live animals aboard and portable articles of any value were salvaged.

[Oysterville]
Friday, January 15, 1909 at half past eight

Dearest Mama,

There was a ship come in last night at three o'clock. The crew consists of 27 men. They can't speak English. Bradford, Dorothy and I went to see the ship.

The ship is about a mile from Ocean Park. There was quite a number going from town. We didn't have any school after (12) twelve o'clock because we wanted to go see the ship.

Your loving daughter, Medora Espy

Oysters

When Grandpa arrived in the 1850s, an estimated 20,000 acres of Shoalwater Bay were covered with oyster "reefs"—clusters of bite-sized morsels considered a great delicacy by San Francisco gourmands. The shells of Native (or Olympia) oysters, found primarily in the Pacific Northwest, are about the size of a silver dollar. Like all oysters, they began life as free-swimming larvae. After several weeks, the larvae attach to a hard surface to continue growing, preferably next to other oysters—hence, the origin of the oyster reefs that the first settlers found in the bay.

Nineteenth-century epicures ate prodigious amounts of oysters, either raw on the half shell or in oyster cocktails. However, over-harvesting for the California market, in combination with disease and a series of freezing winters, severely depleted the oysters by the mid 1890s. Oystermen felt the business was no longer commercially viable in Shoalwater Bay.

About that time, a few oystermen attempted to revive the failing industry by experimenting with Eastern (or Atlantic) oysters, a larger variety with a thick elongated shell ranging from 2 to 5 inches across. The Eastern is considered ideal for serving on the half shell. When introduced to the West Coast, it achieved instant popularity. As the name implies, the Eastern is native to the Atlantic seaboard and the Gulf of Mexico.

When introduced at Shoalwater Bay, Eastern seed thrived and oysters reached harvestable size, reviving the industry for a few years. Papa, however, continued nurturing and occasionally harvesting Native oysters remaining on Espy tidelands. He was confident that conditions in the bay eventually would change and Native oysters would again dominate the market.

[Oysterville]
Saturday, Jan. 16th 1909

Dear Mama:

Papa got a word late last night telling him to take oysters up to N. [Nahcotta] so he couldn't write. Papa said he maint be up Saturday night...

Telegrams

Shortly after the completion of the railroad in 1889, the Ilwaco Railroad and Navigation Company erected a telegraph line from Ilwaco north to Nahcotta, situated a few miles south of Oysterville. This was the first "long distance" communication system on the North Beach Peninsula. With its business headquarters in Ilwaco, car shops in Nahcotta, and crewmen usually living in Nahcotta or Ocean Park, the telegraph system provided a communications link for the railroad's far flung operations.

In 1904, the newly established Ilwaco Telephone and Telegraph Company made connection with the Pacific Telephone and Telegraph Company. Real long distance service was soon established through Astoria via a cable under the Columbia River.

For residents of Oysterville and the north end of the peninsula, the Nahcotta train depot served as the terminus for incoming and outgoing telegrams. Until the telephone system was extended to Oysterville, telegrams were delivered by the mail wagon or, if a message seemed urgent, by a man on horseback.

[Oysterville]
Tuesday, January 19, 1909

Dearest Mama,

If Papa receives a telegram he will go up for you but doesn't know if he'll go or not if there isn't any word.

I have made sixteen valentines. We are going to have a Valentine box...I want to make a very pretty one for teacher (if I can).

Dosie, Dorothy, Lillie, and I have a club, (I forget the name). We are to sew for our dolls. I am secretary, Dorothy president, Dosie Vice President, and Lillie a member. We are to have badges. Don't you think that nice.

The Teacher is reading a dandy book named "The Midshipman" by Henty.

I am looking for you home Feb. 6th, 1909. Will you bring a work girl?

Your loving child, Medora Espy

PS The name of our club is Good Will Ben.

[Oysterville]
Thursday, Jan 21, 1909

Dearest Mama:

Has baby been weighed again, if so how much?

I have just finished reading "Phronsie Pepper" out of the library. I liked it first rate (I mean very much)...

I am collecting things (I mean pictures and products) of North America. Teacher asked me if I could get a Japanese lantern and fan to bring for the Asia Corner (that means she tacks a big piece of cloth on the wall and we paste our things on it.) We have a North America corner, South America corner, Asia corner and Europe corner.

Your lonesome girlie, Medora E.

The Tides

Since Oysterville's founding, residents had scheduled their lives more by tide tables than by clocks. Commonplace sights in most homes were hip boots in the mud room, long johns and boot socks drying by the wood stove, and breakfast on the table at 2 am. Neighbors—though often economic competitors—looked out for one another out on the bay. Many are the tales of lanterns hung high in upper-story windows to serve as beacons for a boat not yet accounted for during stormy weather.

Even those not directly involved in oystering, clamming, or fishing lived by the tides.

Oyster schooner *Louisa Morrison,* 1868.

Oystering. Courtesy of Tucker Wachsmuth.

Any news coming to or going from the peninsula was carried by boat and all vessels arrived or departed only when the tide was right. Since the train needed to meet a boat at either end of the line to receive and deliver mail, freight, and passengers, it, too, ran by the tide. Each day over a six day period, train departures were successively scheduled fifty minutes later to accommodate the tidal patterns; then, in a quick shift, the schedule was moved up five or six hours.

During winter storms, strong southwest winds over the Pacific seem to pile up ocean waters, forcing wave atop wave into the bay. Every few years when a hurricane force storm coincides with the highest tides of the winter, the bay overflows its banks, flooding meadows, lanes, and gardens of the village. For two or three hours, Oysterville becomes an eerie watery seascape dotted with protruding trees, houses, and picket fences.

Occasionally, a garden suffers the loss of a few plants, but, more often than not, the torrential rains leach out any ill effects of the salt water. Come spring, gardens flourish as usual. An extreme high tide becomes the highlight of a season—until the next such episode, the passage of time and events often is marked by it, as in "It was the year after that really high tide when the picnic table floated away."

[Oysterville]
Friday, Jan. 22, 1909

Dear Mama:

Today I saw Tommy and Herbert come as far as the pigpen, in a boat...

I certainly hope Papa will go up for you, and that you will be home by next Friday or Saturday.

Your loving daughter, Medora Espy.

[Portland]
Saturday, January 23, 1909

Dear Girlie—

I have enjoyed your letters but have not been able to write much in answer. Edwin weighs ten pounds and is growing very fast. I hope to have him home by the 29th. We keep very well but want Papa and you girls.

Be good -- Hoping to see you all soon I am as ever loving, Mama

Writing desk and chair.

Notes

1. This information was compiled from a variety of sources found on internet sites concerning vintage postcards and their collection.
2. "Myrtle"—Mama's childhood doll, and still today a "member of the family."
3. Records of the Oysterville School.
4. Research library records, Ilwaco Heritage Museum, Ilwaco, Washington.
5. D. Markham, "Able-bodied Seaman De Reugemond's Account of the Alice," *The Sou'wester* [Quarterly Publication of the Pacific County Historical Society]: Summer 1974.

Papa went to Olympia this morning...

Oysterville, 1911

Oysterville school children in 1911. Medora sits on the bench at far right, next to one of the Walkowski girls. The two tall girls behind Medora and slightly to the left are Dosie Sargant (wearing a dark sweater) and Dorothy Goulter. Sister Sue sits on the bench, third from left. Mr. Wachsmuth, at left, wears a bowler hat, while Wachsmuth's "Rover" sits on the ground next to Medora.

Papa was a people person. He enjoyed talking and swapping stories with neighbors and visitors alike. In fact, the expression "he never met a stranger" seemed coined especially for Papa, and Mama soon learned that any and all meals needed to be expandable in order to accommodate her husband's genial hospitality. Too, he was helpful by nature—almost too helpful, Mama sometimes thought. It wasn't unusual for family concerns to go unresolved because a friend's fence needed mending or a neighbor's stray cow needed finding. Perhaps it was the combination of these qualities, plus his innate sense of fair play, that prompted him to run for Justice of the Peace in 1902, a position he continued to fill for a number of years.

As Justice of the Peace, it was Papa's sworn duty to "administer summary justice in minor cases, to commit for trial and to administer oaths and perform marriages." Papa did all of these things, as well as witnessing numerous official documents, giving whatever legal assistance or advice he could, and writing letters for those who weren't fluent in English or not completely comfortable with "book learning."

The more he did for the community, the more he became aware of the need for better representation at the state level. It wasn't a surprise to anyone when he ran for the state senate on the Republican ticket in 1910.

Justice of the Peace

As Justice of the Peace, Papa met with concerned parties at the schoolhouse to settle legal disputes—no doubt to spare his family the possibility of hearing raised voices and blue language. On the other hand, it was his custom to perform marriages at the house, rather than in the church across the street. In *Oysterville,* Willard speculated that Papa "may have felt that, since he wasn't an ordained minister, it would have been inappropriate for him to officiate at a church ceremony."

One of the most memorable weddings that he performed took place on August 3, 1910. Papa's younger brother, Cecil, had asked him to do the honors, and the date was set. Shortly before the day approached, Papa, a candidate for the state senate, was summoned to Olympia for an urgent meeting. However, Cecil's bride, Ruth Davis ("RuthieD"), wouldn't change the date of the wedding, thinking it would be "bad luck."

Thus, the ceremony took place on the appointed date at one minute past midnight. This allowed Papa to catch the tide and row twenty miles to South Bend, where he boarded the 6:45 a.m. north bound train for Centralia. From Centralia, he took the 10:45 a.m. train, arriving in the town of Gate at 11:15 a.m. The final connection was at 2:05 p.m. from Gate, arriving in Olympia at 2:45 p.m. and getting Papa to the capital in time for the mid-afternoon meeting.

Cecil and RuthieD's Wedding

The children were put to bed early on the evening of August 2, 1910, so that they could be aroused and dressed in their finery to attend the midnight wedding. The family told this story so often that both Willard and my mother, Dale, neither of whom were yet born, had vivid "memories" of the event.

Uncle Cecil Espy.

Papa's campaign poster, 1910.

Olympia

The birth of the Espys' sixth child (Willard) was imminent that fall, and Mama lost no time in finding accommodations in Olympia as soon as Papa's election to the state legislature was announced. There she could be assured of the necessary medical attention, and could offer a helpmeet's support as Papa established himself among the ranks of the newly elected.

On December 10, 1910, Willard was born in the state capital, and on January 9, 1911, when the Twelfth Legislature convened, Papa took the oath of office as the state senator from the 19th district representing Pacific and Wahkiakum counties. For the next two years, the Espy household divided its time between Olympia and Oysterville.

Medora's seventh grade year, 1910–1911, was spent partly at the Oysterville School and partly at the Washington School in Olympia, a few blocks from the family's 5th Street rental house. There the family made its headquarters from January 9 through March 9, 1911, while the legislature convened. Since the next regular session wouldn't meet for almost two years, the Espys moved back to the peninsula where Papa could get on with his dairy business and the older children could continue their schooling in Oysterville's familiar surroundings.

For Medora, the 1911–1912 school year was the all-important eighth grade—at the end of which she had to pass a state examination in order to enroll in a public secondary school. Mama, meanwhile, returned to Olympia once more during 1911 for the birth of the seventh Espy child (Dale). It seemed a better choice than Portland, since Mama was pleased with the doctoring she had received during Willard's birth eleven months previously. Also, Papa frequently was called to the capital for meetings, and thus was on hand a good part of the time.

So that the home routine wouldn't be disrupted, Mama's sister Ruth once again was pressed into service to be with the children in Oysterville. But, increasingly, it was Medora to whom Mama turned for assistance with the myriad details that required attention in managing the large family of eight who were so often separated by a two-day journey.

[Oysterville]
Friday Evening 15 to eight o'clock
October 13, 1911

Dear Mama,

I am glad you are so comfortable... It is very lonely without you and dear little Edwin. We miss Papa, too, very much.

Suzita and I have quarreled only once since you left.

After I came home from school I practiced for a half hour, then helped George Kistemaker catch Danny. When he was caught I gave Mona a ride on him and then took a ride myself. I then ate dinner. After dinner I cleared the table and am now writing this note. I am sleepy.

Monday at about three thirty o'clock in the afternoon a bunch of cows broke in the lot in front of the school house, but I chased them out and then nailed the fence up again. A rotten post is the cause of the trouble.

Willard gets clear across the floor in the most remarkable fashion. He is put on the floor sitting up. He sees something across the room he wants. He deliberately falls back on his back, turns over, gets up on his hands and knees, lies down on his back again and rolls over once, twice, maybe three times, then gets up on his hands and knees and begins all over etc. etc.

Mona went to bed at seven at her own request. She is perfectly well. You know she is an early bird...

Did you hear [President] Taft? Did he ride on the same train with you? Tell us all about it when you write.

...Every time the telephone rings my heart leaps. Has it [the baby, Dale] come I ask myself...

I said in the letter rather note I sent yesterday that I forwarded nine letters but counted them wrong and I only sent eight. One was addressed Justice of the Peace but I scratched that out and put H.A. Espy. I am forwarding 3 letters, 1 advertisement.

Your lonesome little girl, Medora

P.S. Willard broke his bottle. If you can conveniently please send one. The bands and nipples are fine Ruth says.

[Oysterville]
Thursday, 5:30 o'clock, October 26, 1911

Dearest Mama,

...I am trying real hard to please Miss Blair in my studies and with some success, I think. She

Mama's sister, Ruth Richardson.

said she would put me ahead in Grammar and Deane also, but the other boys, especially Edwin, would have to study where they are. History I simply can't get. It's so hard to remember. The other studies I can get if I try. Teacher says she couldn't give us report cards until we get better marks. She said not a pupil in school has gotten higher than seventy in any study except spelling. She said she never was in such a shirky school. She said it was one of her brightest schools she had ever taught in but she said the trouble was we would not study. But I am going to. Miss Blair says my hardest subjects are History and Arithmetic, especially Arithmetic.

Pete has all of the four foot wood out of the street. He has everything sawed up except what's piled in north end of shed. I guess this has no meaning for you, Mama, but it will for Papa.

If Papa doesn't come home soon, please send stamp money, ten cents will be enough. Ruth hasn't a cent to buy anything with so the stamps are nearly gone. I am putting the last ones on this letter.

Asenath's mother is coming home tomorrow. She will have been away a week to the very day so Asenath came to ask if she could have Coaly. We said certainly.

With love and please write when you can.

Your loving little girl, Medora

If you have time send Mona a postal or a letter as she expects it. Thank you.

Mama's Flock

Because of the youngsters wide range in age, Mama and Papa often referred to Medora and Albert as "the children," Sue and Mona as "the girls," and Edwin, Willard, and Dale as "the babies." In later years, when Dale asked Mama which period of her life she had enjoyed the most, Mama said, "When the babies were little." Dale always believed she meant the time when the three youngest weren't yet in school and most of Mama's "flock" were still at home.

The Art of Writing

Of the thousands of letters that the Espy family members wrote to one another, only a few were written in ink. Occasionally, one of the letter writers apologized for this lack of formality. However, it was understood that writing in ink, though certainly preferable, was far too labor intensive for lengthy and frequent correspondence to one's nearest and dearest.

Writing in ink was difficult, mistakes could not be erased, and the newly developed fountain pen, though a vast improvement over a dip pen, wasn't always reliable and drips sometimes occurred. Care needed to be taken not to smear wet ink, and a blotter needed to be applied frequently. As irreparable mistakes mounted, it often became necessary to rewrite a letter or note again from the beginning. Understandably, the use of ink discouraged many from writing any more than what was absolutely necessary.

Corresponding in ink proved particularly daunting to the neophyte letter writers in the family, so in the interest of frequent communication, the etiquette of proper letter-writing was mostly overlooked. Pencils, not pens, were used in the Espy household.

[Olympia]
Friday, October 27, 1911

My dear Medora,

I have gotten every detail in readiness and there is nothing left to do, so this waiting around is very tiresome. I feel it especially on dear Papa's account.

I should write a lot of letters but can not sit up straight to a table with ink and there are very few to whom I want to write in pencil. Yesterday I wrote to Aunt Helen and Maud and plan a letter for Bess today. None of these will be shocked at my scrawl.

I had all of those photos framed and am well pleased with the result—Ruth's, Sue's and yours I had done in brown alike to group on the wall in our new brown living room. Mona's is in a square standard gilt frame and is lovely. The artist was enthusiastic over her photo and thought it was a "Jackson picture". Jackson is a famous child artist. Willard's I put into a ready made frame and took that sweet baby head of Edwin from the group of you girls and put it in a tiny black frame no larger than a dollar. That enlarged picture of Albert is in a black standard oval frame. The one [where he is on] on Prince is in gray to be hung. Now I have all my flock around me and a bonny group so thinks their mother.

Miss Tynen ["Tynie," the housekeeper] gets here tomorrow...

Did you get Sue's buttons fixed? Remember she is only a little bit of a girl even tho there are a half dozen younger than she in the family.

With much love to every one I am always devotedly, Mama

The Greater Community

Seemingly, interaction between communities on a 28-mile-long sandy peninsula could be accommodated with relative ease. Such has never been the case, however. Difficult terrain and isolation has caused each town to develop quite independently of the others. In time, residents took pride in and nurtured the factors making them distinctive from neighboring communities.

At first, Oysterville's only neighboring settlements were Ilwaco and Chinookville, located on Baker's Bay at the hilly Columbia River end of the peninsula. Overland travel north and south through the woods and the peninsula's marshy wetlands was extremely difficult. Most expedient access between the

North Beach Peninsula Friends—

(The) Allens—Seaview residents.

Charles Beaver—An area carpenter and house builder.

Bob—Summertime friend of Medora's from Ocean Park.

Bruce—Summertime friend of Medora's from Ocean Park.

Marguerite Dillon—Summertime acquaintance of Medora's.

(The) Giles—Family friends who lived in Chinook.

Helen Hazeltine—An acquaintance of Medora's.

Holland Houston—From Portland, and a bit older than Medora. The Houstons had a summer place in Ocean Park.

Lewis Koover—Summertime acquaintance of Medora's.

Lewis Alfred Loomis—Grandpa's contemporary, who built the peninsula's narrow-gauge railroad in 1889.

Dottie Mac—Summertime friend of Medora's from Ocean Park.

Mildred Mac—Summertime friend of Medora's from Ocean Park.

"Mrs. M."; Mrs. Matthews—An Ocean Park resident who sometimes took care of the Espy children and household when Mama was away.

Foster McGuire—An acquaintance of Medora's.

(The) McMasters—Summertime peninsula residents.

(The) Moreheads—A family residing in Nahcotta.

Deane Nelson—The wife of **Charlie,** the oldest Nelson son; she was a storekeeper in Nahcotta during Dale's childhood.

Dr. Paul—The only doctor on the peninsula during Medora's childhood.

"Don"; Donald Roberts—Summertime friend of Medora's from Ocean Park.

"Miney"; Meinert Wachsmuth Jr.—Mr. Wachsmuth's grown son living in Nahcotta.

Lew Williams—A member of Ilwaco's pioneer Williams family, and a suitor of Mama's sister, Ruth.

Rees Williams—Also from the large Williams family, and perhaps a suitor of Ruth.

North Pacific County Friends (Across the Bay)—

Mr. Lynn Bush—Papa's good friend living at Bay Center.

Mr. Cassels—The proprietor of Cassels' Hotel in South Bend.

(The) Holms—Family on the Naselle River.

Professor Angus Jack—Pacific County's superintendent of schools.

Mr. Payne—Lynn Bush's opponent in the 1912 county commissioner election.

(The) Priors—Family friends residing on the Nemah River. The large family included **Willie, Marion, Ethel,** and **Adam.**

Captain A.W. Reed—Owner of the Willapa Bay Transportation Company headquartered in South Bend.

Other Area Acquaintances—

Dr. Estes—An Astoria physician.

Mr. Scales—Family acquaintance in Centralia.

Ilwaco to Oysterville stagecoach, 1885.

Harvesting cranberries at Charles Nelson's bog, Nahcotta.

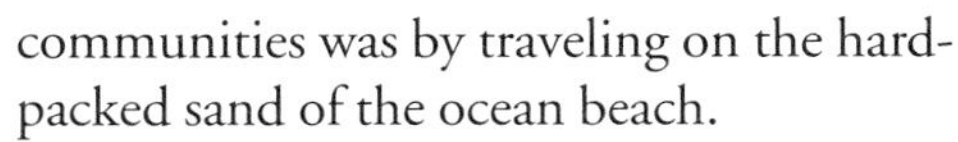

communities was by traveling on the hard-packed sand of the ocean beach.

Water transportation was preferable, and, for Oysterville, the communities across the bay and up the Willapa, Naselle, and Nemah rivers became more readily accessible than Baker's Bay. Business and professional services not found in Oysterville—such as banking, dentistry, and even clothes cleaning—often were available in South Bend, though Ilwaco and Astoria also remained commercially relevant to peninsula residents.

Papa's closest personal friend and associate, Lynn Bush, lived at Bay Center, almost directly east across the water from Oysterville. The Espys also visited regularly with the Holm family on the Naselle River, and the Priors on the Nemah River. The Espys, however, had few acquaintances on the peninsula outside of Oysterville.

Nahcotta

Nahcotta, located four miles south of Oysterville, was the only other community on the bay side of the peninsula. In 1889, this site was chosen to serve as the northern terminus for the Ilwaco Railroad. There, and only there, a deep-water channel came close to shore, thus providing the railway access to water transportation from all points on the bay; steamers brought passengers and mail from Raymond and South Bend several times a day. The port became the center of the peninsula's oyster business, and hotels, stores, and eating establishments flourished.

Oysterville citizens of Grandpa's generation watched Nahcotta's developing prosperity with some bitterness. They had invested heavily in the railroad, hoping it would come the additional few miles to Oysterville. That it failed to do so was cited as a major cause of Oysterville's slow decline into obscurity.

At Nahcotta, peninsula folks caught the steamer to South Bend, where they could make connections to Olympia and Seattle. Also at Nahcotta, north-end residents caught trains for points south as far as Ilwaco or Megler, where they could continue on by boat to Astoria or Portland. From Nahcotta, Papa shipped cattle, beef, or oysters; and at Nahcotta, the family met guests arriving by train or boat. For Medora and her family, Nahcotta was the gateway to the outside world.

Ocean Park

Ocean Park, a mile west of Nahcotta, was a "Johnny-come-lately" to the peninsula, at least by Oysterville standards. Platted in 1883 by Isaac Clark, Grandpa Espy's first partner in the oyster business, Ocean Park's 250 acres became a camp meeting place for the Methodist Episcopal Church of Portland. By the century's end, however, the summer meetings were discontinued and most of the property was sold to "outsiders," as vacationing Portlanders began building summer homes there.

During the years that Medora attended Portland Academy, a number of her Portland friends spent their summers at Ocean Park. The young people visited back and forth, making the short journey between Ocean Park and Oysterville by horseback, or "shank's mare."

Long Beach

Although a scant twelve miles distant, Long Beach seemed as remote from Oysterville as Coney Island and had the same tantalizing and somewhat risqué reputation. Railroad tracks ran right through the town's center; because people lined the right-of-way to watch the trains, this area was called "Rubberneck Row." Shops on either side of the tracks were scarcely an arm's length away and passengers leaned out windows to make purchases. With its resort hotels, natatorium, and carnival atmosphere, Long Beach was geared to tourists, and pretty much ignored by the Espy family and other full-time peninsula residents.

The town was the dream of Henry Harrison Tinker, who purchased a square mile of ocean front property in 1880. He laid out wide streets and alleys, set aside park and residential lots, and reserved areas for schools and entertainment activities. Tinker also helped develop East Side Camp, a tent city for hundreds of Portlanders arriving each summer.

He called his community "Tinkerville." Soon, promoters began referring to the resort town as "Long Beach," capitalizing on the many miles of drivable ocean sands a few steps away. Gradually, the entire North Beach Peninsula became popularly known as the "Long" Beach Peninsula.

Ilwaco

Ilwaco, on Baker's Bay, was to the salmon industry what Oysterville had been to the Native oyster industry. In addition to being the fishing capital of the area, it was a busy port town, boasted a sawmill, and for years was the southern terminus of the railroad, until the line eventually was extended to Megler.

It was in Ilwaco that Papa, as a state senator, often met with leaders of the fishing industry to ascertain views on needed or pending legislation. There, too, Papa had financial dealings with the Southwestern Washington Bank, and he negotiated with J.A. Howerton for telephone service to Oysterville. Ilwaco was the largest commercial center on the peninsula. Whatever business the Espys couldn't accomplish in South Bend, they could take care of in Ilwaco.

Seaview and Chinook

The Espys had little interaction with folks in Seaview, Chinook, or other smaller communities on the peninsula. As passengers on the railway, they paused at the stations in these towns when passing through in coaches, perhaps on the way to Megler to take the boat to Astoria. Only when a friend lived at or near one of these settlements did they have occasion to visit these communities.

Astoria

Astoria, Oregon, was a forty-minute boat ride across the Columbia River from Megler. Medical specialists, such as an eye doctor or a doctor who gave Mama treatments for female problems, were located there. The trip usually required an overnight stay—catching a train from Nahcotta to Megler, crossing the river by steamer, attending a doctor's appointment, and making the journey home again couldn't easily be accomplished in a single day.

South Bend

From the time in February 1893, when the "South Bend Raiders" stole the courthouse records from Oysterville and took them across the bay, all "county business" was conducted in South Bend. Papa, as a Justice of the Peace and also clerk of the school board, frequently had need to visit the new Pacific County seat.

Generally, he traveled across the bay and up the Willapa River on either the *Shamrock* or the *Reliable*, both owned by Captain A.W. Reed of the Willapa Bay Transportation Company. The little steamers carried mail, passengers, and freight, making alternate morning and evening runs between South Bend and Nahcotta, with stops at Raymond, Bay Center, North Cove, and Tokeland. When Papa's schedule could not be accommodated by steamer, he might sail across the bay with a friend, or row over in his dinghy.

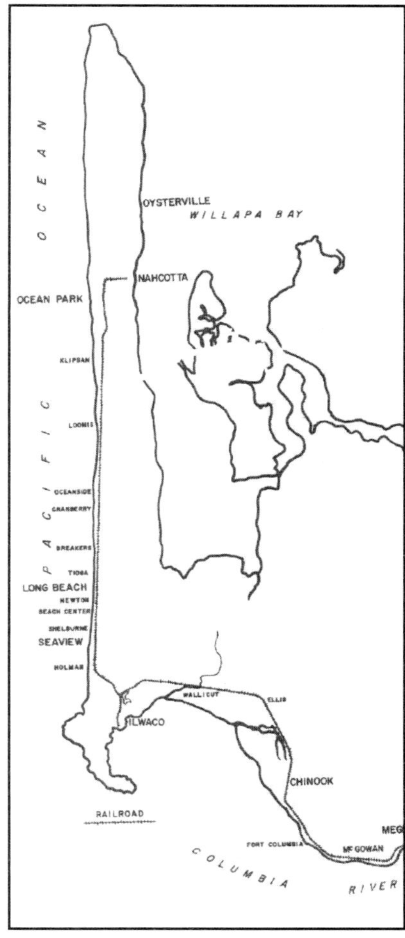

The North Beach Peninsula; map from Thomas E. Jessett, *Clamshell Railroad* (Pacific Printing, 1967).

[Oysterville]
Saturday 7 P.M. November 4th 1911

Dear Mama,

Edie Bowen went to Portland to be sick. She has a baby girl born Nov. 3rd. This baby is straight from the Lord. The boys came from the Devil.

Society is flourishing in Oysterville. By the following list you will think so too:

S.[ewing] Bee at Mrs. Stoner's Friday, Oct. 27th

Halloween Party Tuesday, Oct. 31st

Surprize party at Cottles tonight

Ruth's S.C. [Sewing Circle] afternoon Wednesday, Nov. 1st

Church tomorrow evening, Sunday

The girls have their circle meet at Mrs. Barnes Tuesday, Nov. 7th.

Mrs. Stoner gives a birthday party in honor of Ina on 6th, Monday

And Mrs. Barnes has an "at home" Wednesday, November 7th

The Ludwig upright piano.

I am sending the County papers. I haven't sent them the other times because I thought Papa would come home before they got there.

Has Edwin blocks, trains, and balls? I guess he is tired of toys, tho. Every time you say anything about how tired he is of it all, I wrack my brain for something I could do to amuse him. Does Papa take him with him around town? I imagine he gets pleasure out of the fishes in the park tho.

Ruth is putting the baby to sleep by "The Four Leaf Clovers." Isn't it beautiful?

Dorothy, Asenath, and I went riding today. We went to the cranberry marsh.

In Examination, we are examined in Reading Circle work as well as just reading. Miss Blair is going to find out what books are needed and if the District will buy them or county or what. We have to read three books out of school, that much she knows. If we have to buy them she is going to have Deane buy one and me buy one and Edwin Goulter buy one. We three are the only ones who will take the eighth grade examination. I don't know what books they are yet, even.

Willard grows cuter in his bath every morning. And everywhere else too.

Our laundry bill was $3.65 this week.

The snow has stayed on the ground all day. I fixed up that sled and hauled the children up the street.

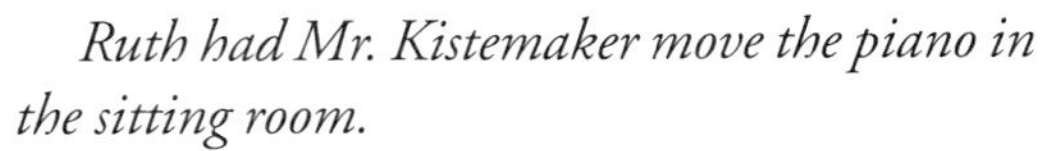

Ruth had Mr. Kistemaker move the piano in the sitting room.

George Davis, who is working at Ilwaco, came down to Nahcotta to push a boat off for Miney Wachsmuth and he called Ruth up and Ruth invited him down. He came and spent the afternoon here. George has grown lots since I saw him last which was two years ago when I went over to have my eyes attended to.

With much love, Medora

An Ear for Music

Mama was said to have perfect pitch. She played the mandolin and had a lovely contralto singing voice. During the years that Anna Brooks was teaching in Oysterville, she, with her clear soprano, along with Mama, occasionally sang duets at village functions. It was a great disappointment to Mama that none of her children were musical. In fact, the children often said—no doubt echoing Mama's own sentiments—that they couldn't carry a tune in a bucket! Mama said they took after the Espys in that regard.

All the Espys loved music, however, and most of them, including Papa, had loud, resonating voices. When the Espys gathered together at church each Sunday and raised their voices in song to make "a joyful noise unto the Lord," Mama painfully endured.

In 1908, when Medora was nine, Mama bought a piano—a Ludwig upright that was (and remains today) the centerpiece of the living room. Mama's sister, Ruth, an accomplished pianist, probably played the piano more during her stays in Oysterville than it was played in all the years since. The oldest Espy children dutifully took piano lessons and may have even enjoyed them, but the musical genes from the Richardson side of the family seemed missing. By the time the youngest children were of piano lesson age, Mama gave up the battle. Edwin, Willard, and Dale never learned to play the piano or any other instrument, and all were apologetic about their singing voices. So am I.

[Oysterville]
Wednesday Morning November 8th, 1911

Dear Mama,

How glad I will be when the great event happens [Dale's birth]. I am so lonely for Edwin I don't know what to do. I never have been so lonesome for anybody except when you were in Portland.

Willard is such a little imitator. He says "Mama" and "Papa" and then when Ruth starts to sing he begins to and when Sue, Mona or I start to make that noise we call singing, Willard imitates us exactly. He is talking to himself now and he reminds me of Edwin...

I am doing a simple duet with Ruth. It is whole notes for both hands and it's easy...

I am glad in a way you are having this rest. You will probably be much stronger when the time comes.

With love to all, Medora

[Olympia]
Thursday, November 9, 1911

My dear Medora,

We are going out to dinner in a moment and I will get a few words ready to mail. No news except that it snowed last night and has also whitened the ground a little today.

"Tynie" washed my hair this afternoon, another item of unusual occurrence but other than this time drags along as usual.

I am ever so glad you folks are having some social festivities. What does Ruth do for head gear for Willard? His coat and leggins are all right but that hood is a mile too big.

I wish you girls could have a big box filled with clean sand in the new woodshed by the time Edwin gets home. You can haul it in the little red wagon. He talks "yaud" all of the time, and I imagine the pile by the windmill will soon be a mud hole from the rains.

Edwin is restless to go out so I must close.

Dearest love to each one of you from,
Mama

Papa in ca. 1902, before major alterations were done to the west side of the house.

The Woodshed

When the Espys moved into "The Parsonage" in 1902, Mama considered it barely adequate for family needs. She immediately set about making improvements. Bit by bit, the downstairs living quarters were expanded to accommodate the family's growing numbers, and to provide space for the amenities that Mama felt essential—the Espy's library, the tea cart, and the piano were among the most important.

The large washroom and woodshed to the west of the original kitchen were converted into a living room and a dining room. The original back porch was expanded northward, becoming the new kitchen and woodshed. On the kitchen's north wall there was a door giving access to the woodshed. There was also a window located above the sink which provided a view into the woodshed. This gave Mama a convenient lookout where she could keep an eye on the youngsters as they played "outside" during the frequent inclement weather.

Village Streets

For years, Oysterville had five streets paralleling the bay, but by Medora's time, Fifth Street, the westernmost and a mere block in length, had completely disappeared. Unused for a generation or more, its short sandy length was reclaimed by blackberries and salal.

Also gone was Front Street, the most easterly, situated at the bay's edge and originally the location for boat builders, sail makers, and other marine occupations. Built on pilings, it had more or less "fallen in" once the businesses were abandoned. Territory Road, the one remaining north-south street through town, was once called Fourth Street and paved with planks. Between it and Front, there had been two other streets. Sharp eyes could pick out their erstwhile locations—just east of old fence lines that kept Papa's livestock confined in the meadows.

Mama's tea cart.

Territory Road (Fourth Street) in 1902, with the H.A. Espy house at right.

North/South Streets, ca. 1860–1895
Front
First
Main
Fourth (Territory Road)
Fifth

East/West Streets, ca. 1860–1895
Nelson
Clay
School
Merchant
Division
Pacific
Clark
Johnson

(see map, page 6)

Modern-day view of Clay Street, one of "the lanes."

Of the eight streets running east to west, only Pacific continued all the way from Willapa Bay to the Pacific Ocean. On the westerly outskirts of Oysterville at Davis Hill its name changed to Beach Road. Clay, Merchant, and Division, the grassy avenues leading to the bay from the Territory Road, generally were called "the lanes." Seldom did residents refer to streets by name. Instead, they identified locations by landmarks or in reference to where someone lived—e.g., "down by Stoners' place"—and nearly 100 years passed before numbers were assigned to houses and actual "addresses" were used.

[Oysterville]
Saturday, November 11, 1911

Dear Mama,

I received your letter today.

The snow gets deeper every minute. It hasn't drifted a bit. It is about 2½ inches thick. George K. hitched Charlie to Mr. Kistemaker's sled and we rode up and down the plank walk and when George went back to the ranch to put Charlie up I hauled the children (Sue, Mona and Gladys) up and down the street. I haven't snow balled all day.

Willard can really, truly crawl. He can say "bath," "by by," "Papa," "Mama," and tries to say "bottle." He was eleven months old today. Willard wears that stocking leg, knit waist length leggins and that new sweater and that bear skin coat. He loves the music rack.

Mr. Kistemaker has fixed the stalls in the barn across the street and put the colts and Dolly in there and he has the other horses in the big barn at the ranch. He gave the cows turnips.

I can't bring sand from the beach until the snow stops.

Sunday 15 to eight

At about half past five last night it began to rain and it is still doing so. The rain rained so hard that at bedtime a great deal of the snow was gone.

Mrs. Curry [piano teacher] came to dinner at four and stayed until seven. She is charming and Ruth enjoys her so much. Mrs. Curry regrets that she has never met you.

If Papa hasn't left by the time you get this, please have him send four dollars and fifty cents ($4.50) to cover six [piano] lessons. I have taken only five but by the time the money reaches here I will have had six lessons.

How did you enjoy "The Shepherd of the Hills?" I read it just about the same time you folks did. I enjoyed it very much and tried to read "Dan Mathews" but it's too deep. Those are the only storybooks I have touched since you left except [James Fenimore Cooper's] "The Pathfinder" and "The Prairie" which I have to read but I don't think they are a bit interesting. It took me two weeks to read "The Pathfinder" and I skipped everything except where the Indians were chasing the captain and that bunch. I have just looked at "The Prairie." I am memorizing snatches, rather quotations, from Longfellow, Whittier, Cowel, Bryant and Wordsworth. If I had any household duties, I don't know what I would do with practicing and all. I play at recess at school and if it is a good day Ruth lets me go at ten minutes to nine or one. On Saturday I put the nursery, dining room and my room in order. On Sunday I read, write, practice, study, and play with the children. Almost every Saturday I go horseback riding. Yesterday I went sleigh riding instead. Today Sue, Mona and I played paper dolls from five minutes to eleven until quarter of three. Then I dressed Mona for dinner.

My favorite quotation from Longfellow:

"Ah, how skillful grows the hand
That obeyeth Love's command!
It is the heart and not the brain
That to the highest doth attain

And he who followeth Love's behest
Far excelleth all the rest."
—from "The Building of the Ship"

I have learned it. Bed time—Good night, with love to all, Medora

[Oysterville]
Wed. 8 p.m. Nov 15, 1911

Dear Mama,

At recess yesterday morning Mona came over and said I had a baby sister [Dale]. She told me first and then Sue. You can imagine how tickled I was. Mona is tickled to death and insists that its name is Katherine. I haven't heard anybody's opinion on the subject.

Sue said yesterday "I think Daisy is going to have a calf," and Ruth said, "If you think Daisy is going to have a calf when she is walking around in the yard, can't you tell when your own mother is going to have a baby when you live in the same house with her"...

Ruth received a card from Papa written in Tacoma. He said he would be home Thursday. He said Edwin was with him. I guess Edwin was sound asleep thru the whole performance. I do hope you don't have the severe after pains.

Sue was promoted to the third grade Monday. I sent to Meier and Frank's for her books.

The three books we have to read out of school are Laura E. Richards' "Florence Nightingale," "Ethics of Success," and "David Copperfield." Mr. Sargant will buy "Ethics of Success" and I want to buy "David Copperfield" and "Florence Nightingale." I have to buy one of them...

Mrs. Guy Hughes had a baby girl Saturday, Nov. 4th and Mrs. Bowen Friday. Nov. 3rd and you yesterday. I guess we will hear of Aunt Susie's baby soon.

With love and a kiss for the dear baby,
Medora

The Library

As soon as the new dining room and kitchen were finished at the west end of the house, the vacated area was transformed into a library along with a separate office for Papa. Mama organized the library shelves, which included a children's section with works by Louisa May Alcott, Beatrix Potter, Booth Tarkington, and Gene Stratton Porter, among many others. A poetry section was well represented with prominent 19th century poets, and other shelves were devoted to Jack London, Mark Twain, Shakespeare, and the Harvard Classics. Papa's Greek and Latin books, along with mathematics and physics texts, took up one corner, while the works of Joseph C. Lincoln and Charles Dickens filled another.

The collection was extensive and unparalleled on the peninsula. Friends and acquaintances often borrowed books, and, in fact, Mama frequently urged works by her favorite authors on those local residents who expressed interest. Until the first public library facilities came to the peninsula in 1931, the Espys' books served as a welcome literary resource for Oysterville.

Papa's bookcase.

Children's corner of the library.

Milk Leg (Thrombophlebitis)

Following Dale's birth, Mama developed a condition called "milk leg"—a painful swelling of the leg that affects some postpartum women. Thrombophlebitis is caused by a sluggish flow of blood returning to the heart, due to the enlarged size of the uterus, and is compounded by a rise in female hormones that increases the tendency of blood to clot—ordinarily a protection for a mother during delivery.

Daily exercise such as walking, swimming, or bike riding can help prevent milk leg. If it occurs, however, the swelling does not go away quickly. Exercise can assist in a slow cure over a period of several years. For some women, the swelling may be permanent. In Mama's case, the difficulty lingered—she wore rubber stockings on and off for the rest of her life.

Mrs. Wirt with grandson Wesley Bowen, ca. 1909.

[Olympia]
Friday, November 24, 1911

My dear Medora,

I have meant to answer some of your questions before this, but have not gotten at it. Papa has probably told you that from present appearances it looks as tho you had better not come to Olympia just now. I hated dreadfully to disappoint you but knew that when you had all the reasons as detailed in my letter to Papa you would understand...

I am glad you chose "David Copperfield" to get. We need Dickens in the library...

I was so glad to know you are memorizing quotations. The mind is our most precious storehouse and you have no idea how much these thoughts gleaned from great hearts and brains will mean to you as years go on. The verses I learned...between your age and seventeen are such a comfort to me now when I have not the time to read. That stanza you quoted from "The Building of the Ship" is also one of my favorites.

Just think—Papa and I have been married fourteen years today. It does not seem possible. I do hope when you girls have been married this long you can look back over a vista of happiness such as I do today.

Give my love to each member of the flock and keep a big share for my dear first born.

Affectionately, Mama

Dale is a darling—no trouble at all.

Tell Ruth somebody is playing "The Rosary" in the other room and it makes me homesick. I always kind of resent having anyone but her play this anyway.

[Oysterville]
Thursday 3:45 P.M. November 30, 1911

Dear Mama,

Your postal came today while we were at Aunt Kate's and were much pleased that there was some chance of your getting home for Christmas after all and the telegram from Dr. Ingham to Papa coming this morning saying that your condition was not serious made us feel much relieved...

I am sending the November and December numbers of the "Success" thinking you might like to read them.

We had stewed chicken, beef roast, stuffing, potatoes, gravy, tea, beets, pickled cauliflower, jelly, coconut cake, pie (apple, I think), canned strawberries, sauerkraut, apples, cookies, and bread and butter. This was at Aunt Kate's. We had dinner at half past twelve. It was quite good but I wasn't very hungry.

Willard is beginning to draw himself up by chairs.

Everybody, (that's the whole town) are much interested in how you are getting along. Mrs. Wirt has been here twice and Mrs. Stoner called up to ask how you were.

With loads of love, Medora

[Oysterville]
December 3rd, 1911

Dear Mama,

Today is Sunday and no special event has taken place. I went to church and Sunday School this morning.

Rover Wachsmuth was run over and badly hurt Friday night. His leg was paralyzed. I don't know if he is dead or not. They (Mr. Wachsmuth) said they would have to shoot him because he couldn't live in that state. Yesterday when Asenath and I asked how Rover was Mr. Wachsmuth answered Asenath so gruff like and said "Awlright" and that was all. I heard a shot yesterday morning about six o'clock and it sounded like it was right under my window.

We are sending the old book of Tennyson as we don't want the good one to get damaged. If we knew what other poet you like especially we would send it too but we don't know so can't.

We are all well here. Pete sings Norwegian to Willard all the time. Prepare "Tynie" for Pete.
With heaps of love, Medora

[Oysterville]
Thursday 8:10 P.M. December 7, 1911

Dearest Mama,

Papa went to Olympia this morning so I guess you will get more news from him than me...

Willard will be a year old Monday, the eleventh, and Dale a month old the 13th, that's Wednesday.

We are all well but oh so lonesome, Medora

[Olympia]
Saturday, December 9, 1911

Medora dear,

I am so happy to have Papa. Am feeling better. Will surely be home Xmas unless something new happens.
Hastily, Mama

Toys

Even considering the numerous toys that the seven children owned, it seems surprising that so many of the Espys' playthings have survived for a century and still are part of the Oysterville household. Toys were cared for and cherished, not only because they were hard to come by, but because of respect due those who gave them.

Albert's 1899-style steam engine vehicle, with its large water tank, today is displayed on the nursery mantle in a place of honor—the driver sits up front at the steering wheel, as if negotiating through traffic. It was one of Albert's last Christmas presents, given to him by his adored Uncle Ed.

A wheelbarrow—a Christmas present from Mama and Papa to Willard in 1914—though rusty with age, waits on the porch as if ready for use. Tucked behind one of the bedroom doors is Medora's Old Mill Game with which she and cousin Bob whiled away many a rainy winter afternoon.

Mona's doll, "Little Flirt," given to her by Mama's friend Jenny, sits placidly beside "Myrtle," the doll that was Mama's a generation earlier. Both have been enjoyed by many Espy girls over the years. Though Flirt and Myrtle had to be re-strung recently, and though they have been re-clothed many times, their soft bisque complexions and bright glass eyes are as lovely as ever.

Even now I retain my little girl fantasy that, if only my hearing were a little more acute, they could share stories with me of their long-ago adventures.

[Oysterville]
Sunday, 20 to 4 December 10, 1911

Dear Mama,

Today Mona is seven years old. Yesterday we celebrated the occasion by a little party. Gladys and George and May Christy came. Mona received a nickel and perfume from Gladys, a box of candy and a large glass ball from George, a thing that you look in and see colors from Sue, a tablet and pencil from Ruth, a doll from Jenny, a bottle of perfume from Dorothy Goulter and three handkerchiefs from me.

The doll from Jenny is a beauty. It's about fifteen inches high, has brown curls and blue eyes that can twist any way. That's where she gets her name "Little Flirt." Jenny has dressed it beautifully—a white dress with blue ribbon run around the waist and elbow sleeves and a wide bow on her head. She has also made a beautiful white silk coat.

Tell Papa I put the nursery in order (I cleaned it out thoroughly) and it took three hours. It was in a worse mess than when he left as the laundry was dumped all over the room and Sue and Mona had the play things scattered in there

Albert's steam engine vehicle.

"Little Flirt."

Medora next to the clothesline in the Espy's yard.

as they had played with the dolls yesterday and hadn't put them away. I put the whole room in order all alone as I wanted to do it thoroughly.

Pete says he won't be here for Christmas.

What can I give Grandpa [Richardson] and Eva for Christmas? I never was more at my wits end about Christmas.

Mona is writing to everyone she knows on her new tablet. Pete and I have been playing The Old Mill Game on my game board. It is a very deep game.

With lots of love, Medora

Rover is dead.

[Olympia]
Monday, December 11, 1911

Dear Medora:

Edwin's gift (a long stick with horse's head and reins) was too awkward to send by Papa, so will pack in trunk. I will get something for Dale and bring. I think you had better give Asenath and probably Herbert photos.

I intend keeping that toy money for Mona. I hope you like the grinders and Willard's rattle. This is W's birthday. Bless him!

Mona must take care of Jenny's doll—not playing outdoors with it or leaving near boys—
Mama

I will get buggy for Mona for Papa to give her.

[Oysterville]
Monday, December 11th, 1911

Dear Mama,

Papa arrived today and we were all glad to hear all about you. We didn't expect such news from him at all.

My David Copperfield came today. I will wait until you come to read it.

Willard is a year old today, just think. He has learned a new word—"comeback." Pete is going to make a comeback for Willard…

Later—Papa says he has the children's Xmas presents in his grip but he's asleep so I guess I won't see them until tomorrow.

With love, Medora

Thank you for seals. They are very pretty.

[Oysterville]

Dearest Helen

I found them all getting along nicely tho' all much disappointed that you were unable to come with me. We all miss you much but I think I do more than any. No one can take the place of my own Dearest Helen.

Lovingly, Harry

[Oysterville]
December 13, 1911 Wednesday evening

Dear Mama,

Your letter to me came today and I was very glad to receive it.

The reason I didn't thank you for sending Willard's rattle is because I haven't seen it yet. I spoke to Papa a minute ago about it and he said he would get it for me tonight…

Dale is a month old today. I wish I could see her. I wonder if she looks like you described her two weeks ago, now.

I hope somebody gives me or somebody in the family a postal card album because we have lots of cards lying around getting dirty.

Ruth has been awfully spry since she heard how we may expect you Friday the 22nd.

Thursday Morning

Papa hasn't got that rattle yet. He says I surely believe in doing my Xmas shopping early and if he gave it to me now it would be broken before Xmas. I just wanted to wrap it.

With love, Medora

[Oysterville]
Thursday, December 14, 1911

Dear Mama,

We didn't receive any letter from you today so I don't know what to say.

Pete will go away for good Saturday. He is going to San Francisco.

When Papa shows me that rattle I will write and thank you at once.

We are all well,

With love, Medora

I have Papa's presents all made—one wrapped.

Dearest Helen,

...Have read the reverse side and found some news to me. Did not know Pete has set any day for going but was talking of it in general way. Am sorry as he will be away when I counted on his being here while I should be after you.

That rattle appears to be worrying Medora but she is inclined to want to spend the whole night wrapping presents. However, she and all are getting on fine.

Trust you are still improving and will soon be able to be with us.

Lovingly, Harry

[Olympia]
Saturday, December 16, 1911

Dear Medora,

I have some clothes on today for the first time and feel quite festive. My leg is behaving beautifully, tho it will be some time before I can get around. I put my weight on it this morning and the exertion did not increase the swelling so I feel that it will be all right. There is no news. We are positively so sick of the sight of trays and restaurant food that we can hardly stomach the stuff.

Dale is the brightest most active baby for her age that I have seen, except yourself. However, she does not look like anything unusual. She promises to be a blonde—is the only one of you children who ever had light lashes and brows. Her hair is lighter colored than the rest of you babies. She still is considerably wrinkled and speckled.

Much love to all from, Mama

[Oysterville]
Sunday, December 17, 1911

Dear Mama,

Papa will tell you all the news. Thank you for that lovely rattle.

With love, Medora

P.S. Grandpa's box came Saturday (yesterday). It's awful big, valued at $20. It weighs quite a bit, too.

Papa's Salary

Under the provisions of the Washington constitution, all elected state officials and legislators were allowed $5 per day when in session. Also, they were given a one round-trip mileage allotment, for each session, of 10¢ per mile from their home place to Olympia and back "on the most usual route."

When Papa stood for election in 1910, money was not an issue. His dairy business was adequate for family needs; indeed, he considered their finances secure enough to invest in a store in Nahcotta. However, the business failed several years later. Only Papa, of the three investors, felt morally obligated to pay off creditors, and, though it took him twenty years, he made good on every debt. No one, save the immediate family, knew the cause or the extent of their privation.

Papa at his desk in the senate, 1911.

H. A. ESPY.

PACIFIC AND WAHKIAKUM COUNTIES

Senate, 1911. Politics, Republican
Born, Washington. Age, 34. Occupation, Dairyman

He was born inside of Oysterville,
Where the oysters live and thrive.
He has slept upon an oysterbed,
He has eaten them alive.
He knows the kind of noise
That annoys an oyster.
He knows an oyster has a shell
And requires a lot of moisture.
With oysters 'round him every place
He lives in Oysterland.
Most anyone would think from this—
He was an Oysterman.
—But he is *not*—he is a Dairyman. And a good one.

From *The Twelfth Session of the Washington State Legislature and State Officials*, by Alfred T. Renfro (Seattle: Trustee Printing Company, 1911).

I would very much like a birthday party…

Olympia, 1912–1913

For Oysterville's eighth grade graduates, the logistics of attending high school posed a problem that families solved in a variety of ways. The nearest high school was in Ilwaco at the south end of the peninsula. Since the only north-south road was little more than a deeply rutted wagon road until the 1920s, the railroad provided the only convenient land link between the communities. Students residing in the Long Beach area rode the train to and from school if their families could afford it, but the passenger schedule did not readily accommodate youngsters at the north end of the peninsula.

When possible, high school aged students from Oysterville roomed with family or friends in Ilwaco, or even in Astoria, in order to attend high school. For a number of youngsters, completing grammar school was considered "good enough," and they immediately joined the work force. The Espys of Papa's generation had been sent to private boarding schools—the eldest children, including Papa, attended the Baptist Seminary in Centralia, and the youngest boys enrolled at the Portland Academy.

Portland Academy was also under consideration for Medora. It was decided, however, that her freshman year would be spent in Olympia so that she could be with the family for at least part of the year when they would all be in Olympia during the legislature's Thirteenth Session. Mama eventually would come to Olympia in late 1912 when the Espys rented a house from Mrs. DesGrange.

However, before and after Mama's stay in Olympia, Medora would board with a suitable family. Therefore, in August 1912, shortly before the school term began, Papa took her to the capital and arranged for her room and board at the home of Mrs. Eadie, who resided a few short blocks from Olympia High School.

Elizabeth Ayer, Marie Strock, and Medora in Olympia, 1913.

Olympia Friends and Acquaintances

Mr. Aiken—Principal of Olympia High School.

"Elizah Jane" (Elizabeth) Ayer—An Olympia High School classmate and lifelong friend.

Mrs. Baker—Medora's Olympia laundress.

Bertha—Olympia schoolmate.

Gladys Cline—A schoolmate and neighbor of Medora's from her earlier "seventh" grade stay in Olympia; a continuing correspondent and friend.

Mrs. Cline—Mother of Gladys.

Mrs. DesGrange—The Espy's Olympia land lady, late 1912–spring 1913.

Miss Dudley—Olympa High School Latin teacher.

Mrs. Eadie—Medora's "housemother" and owner of the boarding house where Medora stayed during the first part of her freshman year in Olympia, autumn 1912.

Dorothy Eadie—Mrs. Eadie's daughter, about Medora's age.

Emma Goldenberger—A well-known elocutionist.

Mrs. Lizzie Muir Hay—Wife of Republican **Governor Marion E. Hay** (served 1909–1913).

Dr. Ingham—Olympia doctor, who delivered Dale and cared for Mama following the birth.

Mrs. Mary Alma Thornton Lister—Wife of new Democratic **Governor Ernest Lister,** 1913.

Mr. and Mrs. Strock, and sons **Edgar, Howard,** and **George**—Parents and older brothers of Medora's Olympia friend, Marie.

Marie Strock—Olympia High School classmate and lifelong friend.

Miss Sylvester—Olympia High School algebra teacher.

Miss Torrey—A fellow boarder at Mrs. Eadie's, and Medora's math tutor.

"Tynie"; Miss Tynen—Woman engaged to help with the household and family chores after Dale's birth in 1911.

[Oysterville]
Monday, August 26, 1912

Dear Girlie,

You are probably speeding on your way, and my thoughts are with you every minute. It seemed to me last night was the stormiest we have had yet but maybe that was because you and Papa were away. This morning it is thundering and very dreary. Edwin says "some one in the sky must be shooting birds."

...Well the children want breakfast and there is no news in the few hours you have been gone.

Take every care of my dear little girl and remember that Mama has you constantly in her heart and in her prayers.

Lovingly, Mama

The "Eighth Grade Exam"

During the first quarter of the 20th century, Washington's students were required to pass an extensive eighth grade examination in order to advance into public secondary education. It was given in late spring of the eighth grade year, covering the entire curriculum taught in the public schools, and was anticipated with anxiety by both students and their families. Those failing only one or two parts were sometimes allowed to begin high school on a provisional basis, with the understanding that they must re-take and pass the failed portions within a proscribed period of time.

Much to the family's distress, Medora failed the arithmetic and physiology sections. Arrangements were made at Olympia High School, however, to allow her to enroll for the fall term. Medora had until mid-September to pass the arithmetic portion with a higher score, so that she could be officially enrolled.

Apparently, the school was not concerned about the low physiology grade.

[Oysterville]
Sunday, September 1, 1912

My dear Medora,

Papa has returned and has told me all about you and the house. Of course we are more than anxious that you should do creditable work these two weeks and pass your examination. Don't let anyone distract you from earnest, diligent work. Mama and Papa are doing all they can to make it possible for you to get through and I know you will repay them by doing your very best. Get a tutor at once—every day without one is lost...get one quick and conquer that arithmetic before it conquers you.

Remember, you are young, honey, and have lots of time for fun ahead of you. Mama intends to see that you have all the company and good times that any girl gets, but be willing to dig now and get a firm foundation so as to be able to enjoy play later. I know you will not disappoint us. We have absolute faith that you can and will make a good record for yourself. If you do thorough work this year I think you can count on going to Portland Academy next year, but don't say I said so yet...

Lovingly, Mama

Remember me to Mrs. Eadie.

Appropriate Apparel

Providing clothing for a family of eight in the isolated backwater of Oysterville was a constant challenge to Mama, especially since she was determined to have them attired not only appropriately, but in the most current styles. Mama, after all, had been reared in close proximity to the fashionable city of San Francisco. What's more, with her father's many associations with the near-royalty (and even royalty) of Japan, much of her girlhood wardrobe and all of her wedding trousseau had been fashioned of the finest silks and other exotic fabrics from the Far East. Not that she aspired to such impractical vestments for the H.A. Espys; she was far too sensible for that. But she was particular.

From the time that Medora left home for Olympia High School, a great deal of correspondence between mother and daughter was devoted to clothing. Not only did Mama "talk" with Medora about her eldest's own wardrobe, but she discussed and consulted with Medora regarding what the other children and Mama, herself, might wear.

Often their lengthy letters were concerned with what might be ordered from the National Catalog, or purchased from the Harris Company in Olympia, or Meier and Frank's in Portland. Too, Mama was an accomplished seamstress and, when time and energy allowed, she often sewed for her fast-growing brood. Relatives and friends, particularly the California connections, regularly sent "hand-me-downs" that could be re-worked or even used "as is." The task was never ending.

[Oysterville]
Wednesday, September 4, 1912

My dear Medora,

The express has come at last and I am greatly pleased with the things. All of the dresses were substitutes, as what we ordered were out but anyway the choice is fine. There is one bad thing tho, your dress is too long and I do not see how it can be shortened. I would not wear it if I were you unless there is some very special occasion. Then when I come up we can take it to a dressmaker and see how it can be shortened. It may not look too long with low shoes in the evening but with high shoes will reach the tops...

The white skirt to your middy was too short and I sent it back for a longer one...Go into Harris and see if you can get a separate white skirt to wear with your middy—something plain

Clothing Terms

Bloomers—Full loose trousers gathered at the knee, worn as an undergarment or for athletics.

Cambric—Fine white linen fabric.

Challie (challis)—Soft lightweight fabric made of cotton or wool.

Chambray—Lightweight fabric with colored warp and white weft.

Cheviot—A heavy, tough napped plain or twill fabric of coarse wool or worsted.

Corset—A close-fitting boned undergarment, often hooked and laced, that extends from above or beneath the bust or from the waist, to below the hips, with garters attached.

Dimity—Sheer plain weave fabric in checks or stripes, usually cotton.

Duck—A durable closely woven fabric, usually cotton.

Frock—Another term for dress, usually a daytime dress.

Galatea—Heavy cotton material for outing skirts and middy blouses.

Grimps—Probably "**guimpe**," a term for a chemisette of white batiste or tulle, designed to cover the neck of décolleté dresses and usually worn by young girls.

Indian Head—Trade name for a coarse, firm material used as a substitute for plain, heavy linen.

Jabot—A pleated frill of cloth or lace attached down the center front of a woman's blouse or dress.

Messaline—Soft lightweight silk dress fabric with a satin weave.

Middy—Loosely fitting blouse with a sailor collar, worn by women and children.

Moiré—A fabric with a wavy, watered appearance.

Pina—Lustrous transparent cloth of Philippine origin, woven with silky pineapple fibers.

Pique—A durable ribbed clothing fabric of cotton or silk.

Pongee—Type of silk, rougher than smooth refined silk, and usually a darker ecru in color, though some was dyed in color. Often used for undergarments or lightweight summer clothing.

Pumps—Slip-on shoes with a slight heel.

Rags—Absorbent cloths for menstrual blood.

Ripplette—A fabric with distinct horizontal ribs similar to poplin, but with more obvious weave.

Rompers—One-piece garment especially for young children, with the lower part shaped like bloomers.

Satine (sateen)—Medium weight, cotton-type fabric with a semi-lustrous appearance.

Scrim—Durable plain-woven cotton fabric for use in clothing or curtains.

Silkalene—Soft, light cotton fabric with a smooth lustrous finish similar to silk.

Union suit—One piece undergarment with long sleeves and ankle-length legs, and usually buttoned up the front and with a buttoned drop-seat.

Voile—A fine, soft sheer fabric used for women's summer clothing or for curtains.

Waist—A garment covering a girl or woman's body from the waistband upward; a blouse, bodice, or undergarment.

and suitable for school...I should not think it would or should cost more than two dollars for your whole middy suit only cost $2.25...At the same time get yourself three union suits part wool—you know the ribbed kind. Do not pay more than $1.75 or $2.00 a suit.

I decided to use my own judgement about your coat and dress so as to save time, so ordered them delivered direct to you and I surely hope you will be pleased. The coat was the best shown—cost $14.00—a black silk plush lined with tan satin. The hat a black beaver turned up in front. Then a brown corduroy soft hat to go with your storm coat. Your dress is a good quality brown corduroy trimmed with brown messaline and a large, lace collar. Do these sound all right? I sent for best of everything in your clothes.

The girls' dresses look very nicely on them. Sue's is much coarser than Mona's but very effective and at a distance does not show the difference in quality. Mrs. Parant has Sue's dress to work on. I have ordered satine for new bloomers for you and goods to match the girls' school dresses for bloomers.

I do hope you have your tutor and are getting along nicely. Work hard and pass your examination. Then we will have some good times when I get there.

Papa is getting his cattle ready for the scow. It is blowing up another storm...Anna comes to scrub and help in general tomorrow.

Edwin carried the postal you sent him all afternoon...School does not begin till Monday next and I am so glad for Sue is a great deal of help...

During bad storms I would wear woolen dresses but when it is nice, the cotton ones. Don't get all your clothes mussed at one time...

Devotedly, Mama

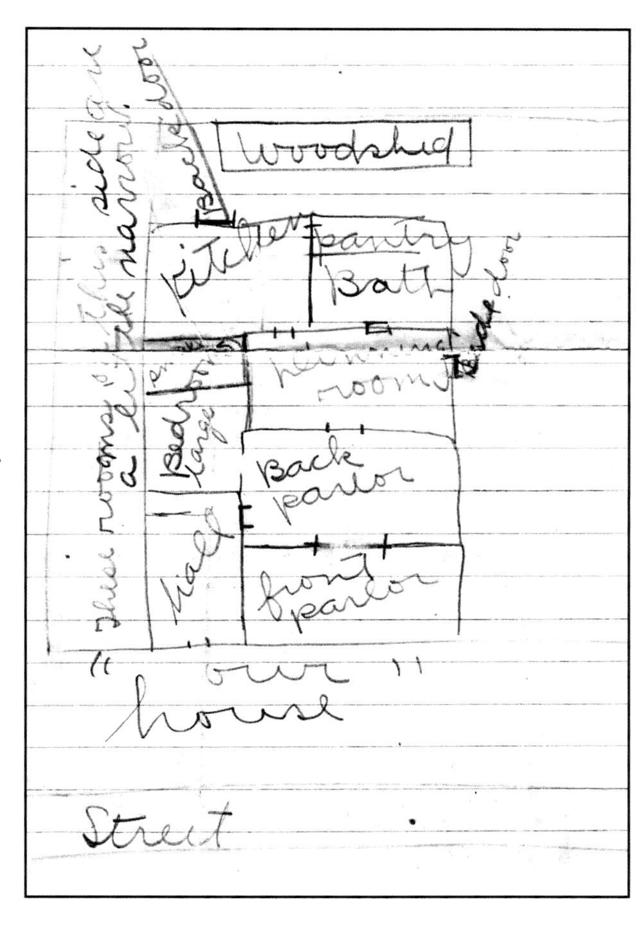

Medora's sketch to Mama of the family's soon-to-be occupied rental house in Olympia, owned by Mrs. DesGrange.

[Olympia]
Thursday, September 5, 1911

Dear Mama,

Our [soon to be rented] house has a large lawn which is just like velvet and has climbing white roses, fruit, and dahlias. There is a very small front porch, a large hall (not extremely large but about the size of our home one), a front and back parlor (It is locked so I couldn't see it, but judging from the size of the other rooms it must be quite large), a good sized dining room, bedroom with closet and small bed room adjoining, fine bath, pantry, large kitchen with gas and coal range, downstairs. Upstairs there is a tiny hall and two large bedrooms. The house is completely furnished, even silverware. The pictures are awful, also the mattresses. In the downstairs bedroom is a chest of 7 drawers.

...Yesterday we were down to Mrs. [Governor] Hay's all day.

...My shoes cost $6.00—the pumps $2.50 and school shoes $3.50 which makes a total of $6.00. The shoes are just like Asenath's were and my pumps patent leather.

I have been wearing my pink dress, but I think I will wear my white all the rest of the time...I tried on my lavender dot and it lacks three or four inches of fastening at the waist line.

Miss Torrey is Mrs. Eadie's other boarder. The teacher of the seventh grade in the Lincoln School. A very sweet girl.

I have 2 weeks to study in before my exam. Prof Aiken is hunting a tutor but he (prof) is very, very busy.

Oh! I have the best piece of news. I have just been speaking to Miss Torrey and she says she will be willing to tutor me for <u>nothing</u>. But I told her Papa would be perfectly willing to pay. We will begin tomorrow evening.

Love, Medora

The Vote for Women

In November 1910, nine years before the 19th Amendment to the U.S. Constitution extended the ballot box to all the nation's women, Washington became the fifth state to give females the right to vote. The amendment to the state constitution carried by nearly a two to one margin.

The early enfranchisement of women in the state followed a trend that began more than a half-century earlier. In 1854, at the first meeting of Washington's territorial legislature, Seattle's founder, Arthur Denny, proposed woman suffrage. His suggestion lost by a nine to eight vote, but in 1883 the territorial legislature granted women the right to vote, passing the legislation by a good majority. The victory was short lived, however. In 1887, the territorial supreme court ruled that the U.S. Congress had not intended to give territories the power to enfranchise women.

[Oysterville]
Wednesday, September 11, 1912

My dear Medora,

I wrote to Mrs. DesGrange and told her we would take the house at the rent she stated ($35) but told her you older girls were taking music lessons and I wanted you to continue so hoped she would leave the piano in…

Mrs. Wirt kept Dale twenty minutes yesterday so I could vote. Every vote counts and we were so anxious that a splendid man like Mr. Bush should not be beaten by a dissolute fellow like Payne. We do not know who won yet.

You have not told me how your velvet shoes look since the heels are fixed. Won't they be pretty with that plush coat? If we find your black beaver is too somber we can add a rose or I thought maybe set in a piece of gold braid around the black velvet just so a little edge would show. This would harmonize with the coat lining. We can tell better when it comes.

I have about decided on a cardinal cheviot for Sue trimmed with velvet and a large cardinal beaver hat.

Mrs. Rohrabeck is starting out well with the school…

Save enough money for your laundry each month.

After your arithmetic is over, I do not care if you go out once in a great while on a school evening provided Mrs. Eadie thinks it of enough importance. I want you to see and do all you can out of school days, but would prefer you would postpone everything until after that Arithmetic examination.

Be considerate of Mrs. Eadie and find your shaky places in that Arithmetic so as to get through…

We will certainly pay your teacher and appreciate her kind interest and thoughtfulness. It would be wrong to take her time unless she were recompensed. When your two weeks are up have her charge what it has been worth to her. Explain this or read these last two paragraphs to her.

We miss you dreadfully—but hope to be with you before many weeks.

What color is taupe? I do not know.

Devotedly, Mama

[Olympia]
Saturday 5 P.M. September 14, 1912

Dearest Mama,

This morning I cleaned my room, peeled some pears for Mrs. Eadie and helped Dorothy pick apples…

My exam comes off Tuesday or Wednesday… When you want to know how I feel about my arithmetic I can not say, it is so hard to tell. Miss Torrey and I have covered almost everything. Miss Torrey is away this evening so I will study by myself tonight.

My velvet shoes look fine since they were fixed but I am afraid I can't wear them as they pinch my big toe…

I went to a party last night at the club house. All the high school pupils were invited… The purpose of it was to let the freshmen get better acquainted with the faculty and with their fellow students… There was a short programme. Emma Goldenburger [sic] spoke and there were solos also. After the programme we ate. Ice cream, cake and candy were served. After the lunch everybody went upstairs and the seniors had rented an orchestra so there was dancing. All the popular girls danced but of course I didn't as none of the boys know me and then all the teachers have the impression that I am a hired girl, I mean that I am working for my board, but wait till January. I will show them a thing or two… I wore my blue dress.

I asked you on my last card to please send my cramp medicine as I might need it about the end of this coming week. Wasn't I foolish to send it home, but Papa left in such a rush I couldn't help it.

I am invited to Gladys' to dinner tomorrow. Mrs. Cline asked me.

Take good care of yourself, Mama, and have Anna come in often.

Taupe is a new color of gray about the color of moleskin—a sort of tannish gray.

King Wilson

Aunt Dora, Papa's oldest sister, had married Alexander King Wilson in 1895. She was 23 and King 31, making him more than eleven years older than Uncle Ed, the oldest of Grandpa Espy's boys. Since King was an attorney from Maryland, it undoubtedly seemed natural for Grandpa to seek his advice in business matters. Perhaps King even had an influence on Uncle Ed's choice to read the law a few years later. By the time of Grandma Julia's death in 1901, Ed and King worked hand-in-hand in advising Grandpa, particularly regarding money matters, and most especially respecting the financial interests of Grandpa and Grandma's minor children.

In June 1902, fourteen months after Julia's death, Ed wrote to his father: "King and I have both…always said that an undivided one-half of the community property went to you and the other undivided one-half to the children; and that the estate should be probated or the title would not become absolute until six years after mother's death; that is, after six years, creditors would have no right to proceed against the estate and the real property would become absolute in the heirs. As I say, both King and I have recognized this fact, and yet it did not seem necessary that the estate should be probated. The expense would be considerable, and as long as we are not selling property in any great quantities, it will be an unnecessary outlay."

It wasn't long before the older children—Papa and Susie—began lobbying Ed to stand with them against King, when they felt that King's position in regard to the minors, or even to themselves, was unfair. As time passed, there were whispers among all of the Espy's that King was too controlling with the estate.

When Uncle Ed died unexpectedly in 1906, whispers became murmurs as King tightened his grip on the family finances. Medora's generation grew up with vague feelings that King was a bit shady in his dealings with "the estate money," and there often were veiled remarks by their elders that led them to believe that any financial reverses could be traced directly to King's mismanagement of funds. But innuendoes never became direct accusations for, after all, family was family.

[Oysterville]
Wednesday, September 18, 1912

My dear Medora,

I am in the kitchen and will write to you while my "apple butter" cooks. There are so many apples that I could not resist putting up a few…

Your letter was just received, and I suppose today you are having your examination. I will be restless until I know the result.

One thing makes me decidedly disgusted, and that is how such an impression could exist that you are a "hired girl." You have a tongue and I hope enough sense to correct such an idea at once. If this mistake gets established it may follow you clear through school. I do not like it at all and do not want you to wait until January to get people set right. There is no disgrace in being a "hired girl" but seeing you are not one I do not care to have you pass for such, especially amongst your teachers. It is easy enough to let them know that you are boarding until the Legislature opens when your father and family will be there. It is not right to yourself or us either to allow such an idea to get established.

I am afraid that blue dress was pretty shabby to wear to a big gathering like that. Did you press it and what hair ribbons did you wear? Did you have your velvet shoes stretched? They can probably be fixed so you can use them for dress affairs. They will be pretty with your plush coat. I had my dress shoes stretched last winter and they felt like a different pair…

I am glad you are contented and hope you will be happy all the time you are there. We will probably come up the first of November. As usual it is the financial side of things that worries us. I wish King had stayed in the East never to return.

Let us know immediately the result of your examination.

Mona is doing splendidly at school. I am really surprised at the way she takes hold. The teacher has put Sue in Fourth Grade work entirely. She had her in the Third at first and says she does not belong there.

You had better go into Sawyer and Fillup and get some Viburnum right away. It is impossible to mail a bottle of fluid. Also ask them for our bill.

I hope and pray you passed your exam.

Lovingly, Mama

[Olympia]
Sunday A.M., September 22, 1912

Dearest Mama,

I am writing this in bed, as nobody is up and I am wide awake.

My clothes that came from the National are very nice. I don't care very much for the collar on my dress. It is pure white and I thot that eqru would be prettier. Everything else is very nice. I will not be able to wear my coat till you come as it is so very wintery. I do hope that the children's and your things come and are as satisfactory as mine are. I am glad every coat is a different color. You have such perfect taste, I know everything will be lovely.

I went to Priest Point Park with Gladys yesterday. The park has a very nice playground, all kinds of swings, teeters, bars, rings etc…They have a raccoon and three kinds of pheasants. I want to take Edwin out there as soon as possible after you come.

I have a lady do my washing who is very cheap. Mrs. Baker charged for 1 dress, 1 pr. hose, 1 panties, 6 hankies, one union suit—65c. Laundry charged: 1 dark blue petticoat, 1 pr hose, 1 union suit, 1 black bloomers, 6 rags, 4 hankies— 85c.

The dresses I have worn are:
1st wk—pink
2nd wk—white
3rd wk—light blue dot
4th week—dark blue dot

and next week I am going to wear my pink. I have worn my dark blue a week and it is still brand clean.

There was a football game between Olympia and Shelton yesterday. Olympia beat…I don't think I will play basketball. Do you think I had better?

Ask Papa if he remembers Edgar Strock, page in the Senate? I have been going with his sister, a very nice girl…

Poor Miss Torrey the doctors are afraid has tuberculosis…Her folks are clear in Maine.

Is Papa very worried these days? Has he paid any on that mortgage yet? I wish he could have some settled business…Is it possible that Gov. Hay could give him a good political position? I don't know why but I have worried a good deal about finances. I will try and keep mine down. Tell me what you think I shouldn't have bought when you read my account. I have only spent one 5 center for candy, pop corn, gum etc. and that time it happened to be popcorn (my failing).

Do write and tell me if Edwin has forgotten me yet…

I saw the governor's baby today. It is awfully sweet and funny.

I haven't gone downtown for any medicine yet as I didn't want to get it unless I needed it and I have felt so fine...

...I would very much like a birthday party with a cake and fourteen candles because I have never had a birthday cake...

The night I wrote that crazy letter that I was thot a hired girl, I guess I was pretty blue or crazy. I'll tell you whatever gave me that impression. The first day almost I walked home with three girls from school who were Freshies (except one) like myself. I had not met them before but by chance they happened to be in my roll room and I walked home with them. One said to me, "Where are you staying?" I said "Mrs. Eadie's." Bertha—"Does she make you work very hard?"

Another thing that made me say I was thot a hired girl by the teachers too was: One Friday evening at Algebra class Miss Sylvester said (I had missed a good many problems): "Will you be able to make this up or have too much work to do or are you going out home for the weekend?" I said I was staying in town with Mrs. Eadie and that I had nothing to do so I could make it up easy enough. And one day in Latin Miss Dudley said, "Why don't you get your Latin? Have you too much outside work to do?" I said I was preparing for an examination in arithmetic. And so just because five persons suggested that I was working out I got it into my fool head that everybody thot so...I see now that I made a mountain out of a mole hole.

Mrs. Eadie always introduces me as Sen. Espy's daughter which sounds very snobbish to me. So I hope you will see that it was all <u>*my mistake*</u>*,* <u>*not theirs*</u>*.*

Please...don't work too hard putting up fruit. You know we don't eat much anyway of that kind of stuff.

Mr. Aiken said I passed with the highest marks of any pupil yet who had had my same experience, that is failing in the state exam. He said my average was very good. You see, he took my average for my high school subjects and my

Willapa Harbor Pilot
South Bend, Washington, Friday, September 20, 1912

Oysterville Rancher Makes Threats to Kill

When 15-Year-Old Son Is Hurt, Father Loses Temper and Threatens to Kill C. Kistemacker and Own Family. Arrested and Charged with Insanity.

F. Kistemacker of Oysterville was in the city last Monday to make complaint against a neighbor, John Walcowsky, who is alleged to have made threats to kill Kistemacker and members of the Walcowsky household. Walcowsky is alleged to have been driven to his threats because of the accidental injury of Walcowsky's 15-year-old son...in an accident last Thursday week on the Espy estate while hauling hay.

Senator Espy and his father had been called to Portland on business connected with their estate, and Kistemacker who is a neighbor, agreed to superintend the putting away of some hay. Young Walcowsky had been engaged to help. He was driving a team hooked to a load of hay when accidentally the rack struck a gate post, demolishing the rack, giving fright to the team and the latter ran away. The boy was thrown under the wagon, and but for the fact that a skull of a cow lay in the track of the wagon wheels which one of the wheels struck lifting the wheel away from the lad's body, he would have been crushed to death.

He was picked up quite badly injured about the abdomen. When the father of the boy heard of the accident, it is alleged he became violent and blamed Kistemacker for the accident and threatened to kill Kistemacker, Senator Espy, Mrs. Walcowsky and then himself. Kistemacker did not at the time pay any attention to the threat, but hitched up a horse to a single rig and hurried the boy to Nahcotta where the steamer was boarded and the injured boy taken to an Astoria hospital, where he is now reported as doing nicely.

Walcowsky raced after the rig and also went to Astoria. He made a demonstration upon the wharf at Nahcotta, and is alleged to have made his threats so emphatic that Kistemacker and Walcowsky's family feared for their lives. Kistemacker came to South Bend and started out last Monday afternoon in a special launch with the sheriff for Oysterville to have Walcowsky arrested.

When Sheriff T.J. Stephens, who went to make the arrest, arrived at the Walcowsky ranch with Kistemacker, Walcowsky started after the complainant when the complaint was read to him, Sheriff Stephens had to restrain his prisoner. The sheriff says he believes Walcowsky's violent temper makes him almost an insane man under such spells, but that he believes him sane otherwise. Walcowsky has been charged with insanity. Sheriff Stephens arrived home with his prisoner Tuesday morning at 6 o'clock.[1]

Eighth Grade Exam—Revisited

To her parents' great relief, Medora had at last officially passed the eighth grade examination. Later, ironically, Papa would write to Mama with news about Medora's initial tests, which had been re-evaluated: "You and she [Medora] will both be glad to know at this late date, that I yesterday saw Miss Bode, & she said Medora passed in both Arithmetic and Physiology. She recently discovered that [the] man who went over papers marked on basis of ten questions whereas there were only seven (or 8 possibly in one). She therefore received good marks. Pretty system "(aint)" isn't it? She will issue her a diploma. Might be well for her to tell Prof. Eaken [Aiken]."

grade in my Arith. and added and then took the average of that sum, which gave me a very good grade, he said. And so I have passed.

By the way, we owe Miss Torrey a dollar and a half. For tutoring for ten lessons only $1.50. I was dumbfounded but awfully glad.

I hope Mr. Klousky doesn't go after you folks.

Give Papa a good big squeeze and kiss the children for me.

With dearest love to each one and don't work too hard, little mother, for you are going to have lots of good times when you come up.

I am awfully glad Sue's made the 4th grade. I hope she works hard and can go into the 4th grade up here.

With love, Medora

[Oysterville]
Wednesday, September 25, 1912

Dearest little daughter,

Your good long letter just came and to say that we were happy that you had passed your examination only half expresses it. The tears would come when I read the glad tidings. Papa was at Nahcotta and I called him up to tell him and he too was delighted...

Don't think for a minute that Kluskie is after us. Anyway, if he were he is safely in jail now. Everyone thinks Kistermaker just as demented as Kluskie only [he] never gets violent. It is going to be a funny mess in court "the pot calling the kettle black."

I still hope to be with you the first of November if the flies do not eat us up first. They are a fright!

Dale is in my lap and wiggling so that I can hardly write. She gets clear across the room and no one can tell just how. She is reaching the dirty stage and I suppose by the time we go to Olympia will be an animated mop...

Ida is here—has been here for the most of two weeks and is fine help. She goes home tomorrow and then will go to Olympia with us later. She would be more satisfactory away from her people as they hang around. I feel sorry for the girl as she has no future ahead and has the making of a good woman.

Remember me to Mrs. Hay and Mrs. Eadie.

The court declared that Walkowski was not insane

Lovingly, Mama

[Olympia]
October 1, 1912

Dearest Mama,

I am not so very homesick yet, but I wish you were here...

Mrs. Eadie and I were over at the [rented] house today... There are loads of dark red dahlias, some brown ones, pink ones and a few white ones; then some nasturtiums and roses. There are grapes and winter apples in the yard...

Wednesday A.M.

Next time you write if you have time, write at length about Mona's and Sue's school. Does Willard say any new words? Is Edwin still so funny and is Dale growing?

With love, Hastily, Medora

[Oysterville]
Tuesday, October 1, 1912

My dear Medora,

Yesterday I had a lovely letter from Mrs. Eadie which, however, upset me completely. I am so sorry you said anything to her about what I said concerning that "hired girl" business. I should have thought you would have known better. Do you often read my letters aloud?

I want you to keep the contents of this letter absolutely to yourself, as Mrs. E. would think me betraying her confidence to write, as she asked me not to let you know she had written about it. That is she says she is not strong and is so tired many times that even making up one extra room is almost more than she can do and she wants you to leave your bed made and room in order every morning before you go to school.

I was very much hurt and surprised to think you ever failed to do this, as it was understood from the start that you should care for your own room. I had counted so much on Mrs. Eadie's friendship and surely if she thinks we can not keep our word, and are inconsiderate, she will not care to know us.

Such untidiness is a dreadful reflection on me, as she will lay it to your raising. When you have no household duties, there is no excuse for your room being unmade before school. Even if your bed only airs while you are dressing, make it. Never mind any sanitary notions when you are in another's home and they wish order. You must remember it is a privilege to be allowed in the home of one like Mrs. Eadie, and you should appreciate it and not make her extra work by requiring her to do your room work.

Now, for my sake and for the sake of Mrs. Eadie's regard for yourself, make up in this next month for your neglect of the past. I would rather you were late to school than have you let her make your bed another time. Be sure it is done before school. She does not want it to wait until noon. I hate to scold but feel dreadfully to think Mrs. Eadie should have any complaints.

Now remember, do not let her know by word, look or deed that I told you she had said anything as she will then surely be disappointed in us, as her letter was written me in confidence.

Make your room your business on week days and if you can be of any help Saturdays and Sundays, do so. There is only a month left and you want them to love you and miss you, not be glad when you are gone. We want to be happy in Olympia.

Lovingly, Mama

Aunt Cleora's "apples" watercolor.

[Olympia]
Thursday, October 3, 1912, 8:30 A.M.

Dearest Mama,

I am so glad Papa is coming that I can hardly wait. I do hope he will have at least a half day here so he can visit school and talk to the teachers about me, ask them what I should study most and why it is I get just fair grades. I know the fault lies with me but I am anxious to know the very best way to correct and the quickest way to correct it too so I won't be at the foot of my class...

I suppose you know by this time that Mrs. DesGrange had to leave the house suddenly and go to Seattle but she will be back soon. The windows are washed and the house is swept but she isn't through putting it in order.

The parlor just is bare nothing in it yet. I hope she gets a decent carpet, not a gorgeous one. The pictures are awful, great big brass frames and pictures of fancy dressed little girls. I think you better bring pictures for the dining room, living room and parlor. The rooms are small so if you bring your fruit pieces[2] *and four or five paintings I think it will be a plenty. I hope you won't forget the pennants so I can make a den out of the room upstairs. There is only one room upstairs but it is the only large room in the house. I wish Sue, Mona and I could have that room and Ida have the tiny bedroom off the kitchen.*

My there is more <u>drawer</u> room in that house—two seven-drawered chiffoniers, two three-drawered bureaus, a buffet and something else, I forget what.

Do tell Sue to write. I want to know all about school.

With love, Medora

Please examine this carefully

ACCOUNT

From the time check came Sept 17th, 1912

school dues	*50*
church	*10*
stamps	*10*
cards (one cent)	*10*
jewelry fixed	*50*
laundry (1st wk.)	*85*
listerine	*25*
purse	*25*
Mrs. Baker wash (2nd wk)	*1.00*
stamps	*05*
Mrs. Eadie	*10*
laundry (3rd wk)	*65*
tablet (pencil)	*10*
one large writing tablet	*10*
one small writing tablet	*05*
car fare	*05*
church	*10*
S.S. [Sunday school]	*05*
stamps	*10*
	$5.00

if you send me five dollars I will use $2.50 right away.

See how!

$1.50	*Miss Torrey*
.75	*Anc. History*
.25	*Merch of Venice*
$2.50	

Maybe— 50c School Paper

$5.00–$3.00 = $2.00 left for Laundry, stamps and church

Medora

Bert and his first truck in front of the garage, ca. 1913.

Bert Andrews' Oysterville Garage

The Andrews family, or at least the men of the family, were mechanically inclined. In fact, it was pretty much the prevailing sentiment in Oysterville that the Andrews were mechanical geniuses. Especially Bert.

He acquired the first "automobile truck" in town. It seemed to require a lot of tinkering, special tools, and, in not too long, a barn-cum-garage. As soon as other "machines" appeared in the area, owners began taking them to Bert for fine-tuning and repairs.

[Olympia]
October 7, 1912

Dearest Mama,

I have been thinking about going home a good deal. It would cost about ten dollars to go home and it would only cost five to stay here. Anyway, as I think of it, I am afraid of changing there at Centralia. And if you would be up here so soon anyway I guess we could both stand waiting a few days longer. But if you think I would be any help to you to come home, I would gladly do so.

Mrs. Eadie very often speaks of you. She thot your letter was so nice. She said that I am very fortunate to have such a lady for my mother <u>and</u> I am too. That's what makes me love you so, Mama, the fact that you are my own mother *and such a sweet, loving mother. Like I tell the girls, I never think of my mother as a person who will take a stick to me if I do wrong but as an ideal. Don't you know, little Mama, that I am trying to tell how good and great you are but I get all mixed up in trying to express myself without seeming "fickle."*

When is Papa coming? Soon, I hope.

With love, Medora

Does Bert still run his auto or does it break down every time he starts out.

[Oysterville]
Tuesday, October 8, 1912

My dear Medora,

Papa says yes you had better come home for your vacation. It will surely be joyous to have you home again.

Papa will probably be in Olympia on Sunday as he must be in Seattle on Friday.

I would rather you did not wear your good coat and hat to school, unless there was some especial reason. Be sure you wear this outfit home, however, as we will have Mr. Scales meet you at Centralia and Mr. Cassels at South Bend, and will want to tell them how you are dressed so they can spot you quickly.

Hastily, Mama

Enclosed find check

[Oysterville]
Thursday, October 10, 1912

My dear Girlie,

Did Mrs. Eadie get my check? I have wondered as Edwin mails the letters often lately and being so little he might drop one. Did you get my letter regarding the care of your room? Answer these questions!

...We have a month's rent paid on the house so it is ours. I had a nice letter from Mrs. DesGrange. Will I need to take any bedding or table linen? I think I will bring the latter anyway. Shall I take more sofa pillows? How many couches are there?

Are you sure you can get home safely? I want you to promise not to go one step with man or woman on any ground what so ever. If you must ask questions, ask someone in authority. At Centralia there is a woman who guides and directs all young girls. Unless they have changed, she is a gray-haired rather heavy-set person—very kind. Don't you remember her? I speak of her in case Mr. Scales does not meet you...

Lovingly, Mama

[Olympia]
Friday, October 11, 1912

Dearest Mama,

Yes, Mrs. Eadie received your letter some time last week and the check also. Isn't dear little Edwin growing up? The idea! He seems so little but he is so independent.

Yes, I received your letter and am following your instructions about my room.

I am quite sure I can get home safely and will be very careful and not to talk to any one, will take a book or something to read or study, so no one will notice me if I am quietly reading... Oh! When you tell Mr. Cassels and Scales to meet me you can tell them that I wear my hair down my back either in one braid or two curls...

Tomorrow is Saturday... I don't know about the bed linen yet but will find out tomorrow morning. I thot Mrs. DesGrange sent you a list of all dishes, linen etc. There is only one couch in the house that I know of. I think if you bring a few of those bigger pillows we could put a cot in the parlor and put them on it. The couch in the back parlor is a leather one, quite dilapidated.

Mama, 1913.

My stock of information is growing low so I will stop now.

Love, Medora

Chicken pox is very popular. Are you not glad we have had it?

[Olympia]
Wed. 6:15 A.M. Oct. 16th 1912

Dearest Mama:

I didn't write yesterday as Papa was here and as he is going straight home I knew you could hear more directly from him. Papa took me to see "The Old Homestead." I enjoyed it very much. It was played very well.

Professor Aiken said the other day that I was doing 6 work in Latin which is the lowest I can get without failing, B work in Algebra, English and Ancient History which is between 84 and 89. He said I must raise my standard at once so I am very anxious for you to come so as to help me. Mrs. Eadie says "concentrating" is all I need. I don't mean to worry you but I feel that you ought to know my exact standing. If we only have time when I am home we can go over everything that I have gone over so far and get it perfect...By Christmas if possible I want to raise my grades to A that is between 90 and 95. Please don't let Mrs. Wirt or the children know my grades as I don't want them floating all over town.

Papa said Mona was getting along very nicely in school. I am so glad. It will be very much better if Mona gets to High School at fifteen with good grades (nothing below 90) than at fourteen or thirteen with poor grades (nothing above 90) like I have done. If I can't enter the sophomore year better than I did the freshman I will simply take the whole freshman year over. I have summed it up and I think all I need is somebody to say "study, learn to concentrate." Just because I have always gone to school in Oysterville amongst a bunch of block heads and been at the head of my class is no reason for my doing the same here. I, as an older sister to Sue & Mona hope that you and I will say to them, study see what Medora has gone through because she didn't study. I have learned that reading my lesson over two or three times is not studying, it is not "knowing" so the first thing for me to do is to learn to study, dig. I do hope that it will be possible for Sue and Mona to go to a city school for the last two grades of grammar school and then be at the head of the class. I have learned that you can not judge your brightness or capability by a country school. I do hope that when Sue & Mona are old enough to understand that they will take my experience for a lesson. Please do not think that I am blaming you because I am not. If I had studied during the 7th and 8th grades, I wouldn't have been in the fix that I am now. I think that, well I am quite sure that I will come home Sunday arriving in Oysterville Monday. I will wear my plush outfit.

With love to each one, I am your
affectionate girlie, Medora

From Olympia to Oysterville

Like any journey to Oysterville from almost anywhere, the trip from Olympia to the peninsula was arduous and time consuming. When Elizabeth Ayer and Marie Strock, two of Medora's Olympia High School friends, visited Oysterville in the summer following their freshman year, Elizabeth wrote this account to her mother:

[Oysterville]
July 10, 1913

Dear Mamma [Mrs. Ayer],

...Mr. Strock bought our tickets. Also a life insurance apiece. They were for one day and $25.00. Well we got aboard baggage, cherries, candy and all. Made a very slow trip to Tenino. It seemed to me that we crossed the new railroad

about every half hour. Marie immediately dived into a novel, the characters of which eloped in the second chapter, while I gazed out of the windows. Some of the workers waved at us. In Tenino we had to wait about 20 minutes. In which time Marie read and I asked about 50 questions at the office concerning our trip. From Tenino to Centralia the trip was quite uneventful. Very nice depot at Centralia. Here we deposited our baggage preparatory to a good rest. I then inquired about the train to South Bend and found that it was at the end of the station. Then we made a rush for the train, got into the parlor car…so we got off the car to take another. We were about 3 hr. getting to South Bend. There were only about 10 babies in our car and they all made as much music as they could. At South Bend we deposited our baggage while I inquired about the boat to Nahcotta. The man at the window said it was at the wharf and that we would have to hurry. Then he rushed out, grabbed our baggage, and told us to follow. He led the way across the tracks and through grass past our knees. Soon as we came in sight of the boat, our guide yelled to the captain that he had a couple of passengers for him. Then the Captain met us and took the baggage. He wasn't much more than a boy. The captain took our suitcases down below and the boat started…As we neared the ocean, the water grew very much rougher and it became impossible to stand alone. I went down and got my raincoat and then we staggered forward and clung onto the gangplank and the water washed over the front and soaked our legs. (It was great.) Finally, Marie wanted to go down and read and I wanted to change my hat so we waited until the boat was tipped to suit our fancy. Then we made a dash for a ladder, got ahold of it and after half an hour managed to fall downstairs and finely got my suitcase and after much work got out my hat. I spent most of the 3 hours up in front. One time when I was leaning over the rail reading a notice concerning corked boots, the captain leaned out of the window and inquired if my pal was sick. She was leaning on the pilot house. We ate our lunch about 3 o'clock.

Don't know when the stage goes so will give the most important part of my letter. I have left in the way of funds the money to get my ticket back and 50 cents beside of which I owe Medora 20 cents for postals and intend to put the 30 cents in on films. So that will leave me without a cent. And have just discovered that we will have to stay over night in South Bend which will be 50 cents beside meals so need more money.

We met Medora half way up the wharf. She is the same goodnatured goodfornothing that she was last winter. We took dinner at the Bay View Hotel, Nahcotta. Had a three minute steak. Everybody stared at us…The hotel is kept by a family of 14 or 16 all of whom dressed up in honor of our presence. Medora said it was the first time in her life she had seen them dressed up. Drove to Oysterville behind Coaly…

[Oysterville]
Friday, October 18, 1912

Dear Medora,

Papa says to take the 9:40 train from Olympia which will land you in Centralia about noon. Mr. Scales may not be there but anyway by daylight you can make it all right. There is a Porter at Centralia and a woman—at any rate ask as you step on to your train, "Is this for South Bend?" You will arrive in S.B. at 3:30 and had better look Mrs. Davis up as there will be nothing to do on Sunday. Go right to Cassels' and get your room first.

I hope this reaches you before you leave. I had missed my calculations and was thinking you were to be a week later.

Ask some one to see you off on Sunday so as to get started right. You change at Tenino. Be sure to take the 9:10 by way of Tenino. Ask if you are on train for Centralia when you make change.

If you should miss at Centralia, call up Scales.

Lovingly, Mama

Mama's Eyes

Mama's eyes troubled her from an early age. She loved to read and write, but too much of it, particularly by the light of a kerosene lantern, caused severe eyestrain and much discomfort. Too, she was a fine seamstress, but even in the early years of marriage Mama lamented that she could only sew for a short time before her eyes gave her grief. She encouraged the children to read and study in good light, and was diligent in seeing to it that they had regular eye examinations. But it was Mama herself who eventually lost her sight.

Mama's sewing lamp.

Long before her Golden Wedding Anniversary, Mama was diagnosed as "legally blind." She suffered from both glaucoma, for which she faithfully used prescribed eyedrops, and cataracts, for which there was not yet a reliable cure.

In the early 1940s, when realizing she soon would be blind, Mama taught herself touch typing. Her children pooled their resources and bought the smallest typewriter then on the market—the Underwood Standard Portable. Without the lid to the case, it weighed 7½ pounds and sat comfortably on Mama's lap while she typed. In this way, she was able to sit in her easy chair close by the nursery fire and write to each of her children and many far-away friends. Each day at mail time, Papa went to the post office, exchanging the outgoing mail for the incoming. He then joined Mama near the wood stove and read each letter aloud, pausing to chuckle at something that tickled his funny bone or to discuss a point of interest. Thus, Mama continued to keep in touch with her loved ones.

She also "read" as voraciously as ever, listening to Talking Books from the Library of Congress. The books—on phonograph records—arrived in the mail packed in sturdy brown cardboard boxes with protective metal corners and fastened together with a webbing strap. Current titles often were recorded in the voices of the authors themselves. Mama took great pleasure in listening to them, and later in discussing the books with friends and family, who had read them in the traditional manner.

In 1949, Mama and Papa flew to New York where Mama underwent one of the earliest cataract surgeries and lens transplants. Both eyes were done while she remained in the hospital for almost a month. Each eye was operated on separately. Following each surgery, her head was made immovable for ten days by the placement of sandbags to either side—a grueling ordeal that Mama suffered gladly in the hope that her precious eyesight could be restored. When the bandages were finally removed, she found herself face-to-face with the doctor's tie, which she thought amazingly colorful and bright—far different from the somber-colored ties she had last seen clearly years before.

On the homeward-bound trip, they flew into San Francisco, the beloved city of her girlhood, and she saw the Golden Gate Bridge (completed in 1937) for the first time. Her memory of San Francisco Bay was the way it looked in long-ago days, when she and Papa were courting and traveled by boat from San Francisco to Marin County, taking along a picnic lunch and their own golden dreams for the future. Though she had visited the Bay Area several times since the bridge was built, her vision had been too poor to glimpse it. Seeing the bridge from the air in 1949 was a sight she remarked upon again and again in the years that followed.

[Oysterville]
Monday, November 4, 1912

Medora dear,

I have been doing so much writing for Papa the last few days that my eyes won't stand much today so I am just sending a line to let you know that we are fine.

It is storming terribly.

Take great care not to get the lining of your coat mud splashed as it will be a long time before we can get another expensive coat.

Is your hat becoming? The picture looked as tho it was especially meant for you.

What were your grades?

Much love, Mama

[Olympia]
Wednesday Evening, Nov. 6th, 1912

Dearest Mama,

I received your letter of Tuesday today. I am very sorry that it will be impossible for you to come before another week but I guess it can not be helped...

I menstruated last Thursday and I am well now. Sunday evening I went to bed with a sick headache but besides that everything went fine. I have caught a cold yesterday and now my nose is all stopped up...I am drinking lots of water, took a quinine pill and some physic...

Isn't it awful that the Democrats have won all over the U.S.[—]Wilson president, [Ernest] Lister governor and 294 Democrats in Congress, 125 Republicans and 16 Progressives. I have been wearing a Bull Moose pin but since the election my pin is put safely away where I shall keep it and show my grandchildren the badge the progressives wore the first year of the Progressive Party.

I am finding Marie Strock such a dear friend. I hope her friendship will be long and strong and I do hope our friendship is not one of those quick and flaming friendships and then in a little while nothing but ashes.

With love, Medora

I am anxious to know the County returns. What is good for Hay Fever? Ans: Listerine

Theodore Roosevelt and the Bull Moose Party, 1912

Due to his disenchantment with President William Howard Taft, "Teddy" Roosevelt was determined to run again for the presidency in 1912. At the Republican convention in Chicago, however, the political bosses saw to it that the pliable Taft, not Roosevelt, was re-nominated.

Roosevelt, who had served as the nation's chief executive in 1901–1908, still retained a large and loyal following. Immediately, he was nominated by the Progressive Party, headed by Robert M. LaFollette of Wisconsin. The Progressives were dedicated to needed social and political reforms as America was becoming increasingly industrialized and urbanized in the early 20th century.

Because Roosevelt often boasted about feeling as strong as a bull moose, the Progressives became known as the Bull Moose Party. Papa, an alternate delegate to the convention that year, took some pride in being part of the rump group that nominated Roosevelt on the Bull Moose ticket. The national election became a three-way race between Taft, Roosevelt, and Woodrow Wilson, the Democratic Party candidate.

Electricity

Electrical power wasn't universally available on the peninsula until 1940, two years after Pacific County's Public Utility District No. 2 was formed. For several decades before that time, only small private generators were in use at various peninsula locations. By the late 1920s, even some citizens of isolated Oysterville had sporadic power supplied by a generator owned by Bert Andrews. When the "electric" was turned on, the houses on "Bert's Line" were tenuously illuminated by light bulbs on cords dangling from high ceilings in Oysterville's Victorian houses. It would be years before electric appliances, small or large, were even a remote possibility.

However, in the state capital, as in other up-and-coming cities across the region, there was electricity as early as 1905, but it, too, was limited. Gas lamps still illuminated city streets at night, and electric lights were available only for certain hours at the harbor. Electricity was supplied by a dam at Tumwater on the Deschutes River. During seasonal slacks in stream flow, folks complained about the dam's weak output. During these periods, the electric railways sometimes didn't have sufficient power to climb hills.

Still, even basic, bare light bulbs must have seemed luxurious to the Espy family when they finally moved into the rented house in Olympia in late 1912. At least for the duration of Papa's legislative session, the girls' daily chores of washing lamp chimneys and trimming wicks could be put on hold, as could eye strain when reading and writing by lamp light.

Raymond Herald

Mrs. H.A. Espy Entertains in Olympia

February 14, 1913—Mrs. H.A. Espy entertained today at her present home in Olympia, Mrs. Governor Lister, Mrs. Howard Taylor and the ladies of the Senate.

Miss Emma Goldenberger, one of Olympia's popular elocutionists, rendered a few selections, and the ladies were requested each to make a speech rivaling their husband's in the Senate.

After a vote the prizes were awarded to Mrs. Sutton and Mrs. Iverson for the best addresses.

Refreshments were served and the remainder of the afternoon was spent in becoming better acquainted.

[Olympia]
Saturday Morning, November 9, 1912

Dearest Mama,

A week from today I hope you will be here.

Please pack some blotters. I need so many; one for my Anc. History notebook, one for my English notebook and one for correspondence. And each blotter gets used up in a week...

I received your letter of Wednesday last night. It is just the fourth letter I have received from you since I came back.

It has been raining here for almost ten days steady; that umbrella comes in handy. There has been no wind at all with the rain—just rain, rain. I wish I were home so as to enjoy the high tides and storms. I have not minded the rain here so far at all. I think when people complain of the weather they just have nothing to say and want to say something...

With love, Medora

P.S. There won't be any fire in the kitchen range, any electric lights, water or wood there the day you arrive. Because I have to pay to have each one of those things turned on. (There will be a fire in the living room however). So you had better plan to eat at Doanes or else send me ten dollars to get wood, groceries, turn on water and lights. Wood would cost $3.00; groceries the same; light I don't know; water $2.17. I think between Mrs. Eadie and me if we had the money we could have everything cosy for you when you come, but if you would rather attend to those things yourself when you come it will be alright.

Olympia Nabobs, February 1913

Mama settled into the duties of "a Senator's wife" with pleasure. Not since leaving East Oakland ten years previously had such social opportunities been available to her. In February she hosted a reception for the wives of the leading politicians in state government. The guest list included: Mrs. Mary Alma Thornton Lister, wife of the new Democratic governor; Mrs. Howard Taylor, wife of the speaker of the house from Seattle, District 19; Mrs. W.J. Sutton, wife of the president pro tem of the senate from Spokane, District 5; and Mrs. Peter Iverson, wife of the senator from Mason, Kitsap and Island counties, District 23.

In addition—as indicated by acceptance notes among Mama's keepsakes—other attendees included Mrs. John Sharpstein, wife of the senator from Walla Walla County, District 12; Mrs. Ralph Nichols, wife of the senator from King County, District 31; and Mrs. Frank C. Jackson, wife of the senator from King County, District 37. Presumably, most of the senators' wives living in Olympia attended if they were able to do so.

Of the forty-five or so state senators, perhaps thirty of their wives resided in Olympia during the legislative session. Because of their husbands' erratic working hours, wives needed to be flexible about household routines and mealtimes. They often were left on their own while the men were busy with early and late committee hearings, in addition to their duties on the legislative floor. The women themselves established informal social groups, meeting regularly for lunch at a local restaurant or in homes on a certain afternoon each week. The wives, of course, were included in the dinner invitations issued several nights a week by leading lobbyists in Olympia. Such dinners were informal and unscheduled, and most of the dining activity took place at the town's hotels.

The big event of any legislative season was the Inaugural Ball in election years, or, in the alternating off years, the Governor's Ball. It was attended by the governor and all state elected officials, legislators, supreme court judges, and their wives—all of whom were in the receiving line. These events were arranged and sponsored by Olympia's citizens, and hundreds of tickets were sold to the general public, which helped cover expenses. Usually, large contingents came from all over the state. Many legislators' wives, who didn't accompany their husbands to Olympia for a legislative session, would come to town for the event—the social highlight of the season.

Teenage Trials

Medora and Mama had chafed at their periods of enforced separation during the start of the autumn 1912–1913 school year, and were happy to be reunited when Mama and the family finally came to stay at the rented house in Olympia. However, their relationship was not without the usual mother-daughter trials.

Late in the spring of 1913, when Mama and the family had been ensconced in Olympia for almost six months, Papa (home to check on things at the ranch) wrote to Mama:

...I know you are mistaken about Medora enjoying boarding better. She will not and she knows it. Her attitude about things around the house is disconcerting and very trying—still I am convinced she is doing that for your sake—strange as that may seem—i.e. she is so very solicitous about what people may think of you that she is overly particular... Remember she is but a child... and working and worrying hard...

Mama's chocolate set.

Notes

1. *Willapa Harbor Pilot* newspaper article in the files of the Pacific County Historical Society.
2. The half-dozen fruit still-lifes—watercolors painted by Aunt Cleora—still adorn the walls of the Oysterville dining room. For some reason, only the oils by Aunt Cleora were referred to by the family as "paintings."

Portland Academy, from Medora's copy of the November 1913 issue of *The Troubadour,* the school's literary publication.

I feel perfectly at home here...

PORTLAND, 1913–1914

In spite of the fact that Portland was not easily accessible from the peninsula and had a quarter-million inhabitants—a sharp contrast to Oysterville's one hundred—it still was the logical choice for Medora's final three years of high school. Olympia no longer was an option, as Papa hadn't run again for the senate. Family finances (or lack thereof) and Grandpa's deteriorating health demanded Papa's full-time attention in Oysterville.

Since both Uncle Cecil and Uncle Will had attended the Portland Academy, the family felt there was an established "connection." Furthermore, with a number of relatives living in and around the city (including Ruth, who had recently moved there), Medora would not be totally isolated from her loved ones. Portland also was the nearest bit of "civilization," at least by Mama's standards, and Medora could readily avail herself of numerous cultural opportunities, thereby giving an additional polish to her education that no amount of school attendance could provide.

Under the best of circumstances, Portland was a full day's journey from Oysterville. By boarding the morning train at Nahcotta, crossing the river at Megler, and catching a steamer at Astoria, one could arrive at the Ash Street dock in Portland at 6:00 a.m. the following morning. It also was possible to travel by train from Astoria to Portland, rather than by boat. When the children were little, however, Mama preferred to book a stateroom on the steamer *Hassalo*, putting them all to bed for the night. This made the trip easier by far.

In Portland, Medora resided at "The Hall," a boarding establishment managed by Miss Colina Campbell.

[Portland]
Thursday—September 11, 1913

Dearest Mother:

...Papa took me over to Portland Academy yesterday morning and I am so pleased with everything I could jump up and down for joy. At the dorm I have a lovely room opening right onto a porch. Miss Campbell is adorable. She is over sixty. She says I can visit Auntie Ruth any time providing I am not neglecting anything—that is at the weekend.

I went to the oculist with Ruth last afternoon. He said my eyes were very bad. He is just lovely and is only putting weak lenses on me at first, for he says my eyes are too weak for strong ones.

Lovingly, Medora

THE MAIL RUN

The arrival and departure of red-whiskered Mr. Lehman's rattly mail wagon were focal points of daily life in Oysterville. Mail was the connection to the outside world and, to Mama especially, an essential link with family and friends. From the time she arrived in Oysterville and until her death more than a half-century later, Mama corresponded several times a week with any of the children that were "away," and with numerous friends, acquaintances, and relatives.

Portland Friends and Acquaintances

"Alec"; Alexander Bell—Medora's first serious "case."

Billie—Rosetta Klocker's pen pal from Victoria, B.C.

"Marge"; Margaret Bronaugh—Portland Academy friend.

"Pete"; Anne May Bronaugh—Marge Bronaugh's younger sister.

Elizabeth Bruere—Portland Academy classmate and friend.

"Miss C"; Miss Colina Campbell—Owner of The Hall where Medora resided in Portland.

Harry Clair—Portland friend whose family had a summer home in Ocean Park.

Dorothy Collins—Two years ahead of Medora at the academy.

Dorothy Connell—Portland Academy friend; family had a summer place in Ocean Park.

Marge Connell—Portland Academy friend and Ocean Park summertime friend.

Ruth Connell—In class ahead of Medora at the academy.

Helen Davidson—Two years ahead of Medora at the academy.

"Helen D."; Helen Dunne—Portland Academy friend.

Mr. Ewing—Portland Academy principal.

Ardis Fischer—A student boarder at Miss Campbell's.

James Gamble—Portland Academy friend.

Anastasia Hague—Medora's first roommate at The Hall; younger than Medora.

Mary Irving—Portland Academy classmate and good friend.

"Kinks"; "Mary K."; Mary Kingsbury—A year ahead of Medora at the academy; Medora's roommate at Miss Campbell's during the 1914-1915 school year.

"Bunch"; Rosetta Klocker—Medora's housemate and friend at the academy.

Mrs. Klocker—Rosetta's mother.

"Mal"; Malvina—Portland Academy friend.

Margaret—Portland Academy friend.

Helen Miller—Portland Academy friend.

Helen Morgan—Portland Academy friend.

Mrs. Morgan—Helen Morgan's mother.

"Jean"; Jeanie Murdock—Portland Academy friend in the class ahead of Medora.

Dr. Herbert Nichols—Portland physician.

Elizabeth Richardson—Portland Academy friend.

Mrs. Richardson—Elizabeth's mother.

Russell Sewall—Portland friend and occasional escort.

Harry Stevens—Medora's escort to the prom.

"Dote"; Dorothy Strowbridge—Portland Academy friend.

Mrs. Strowbridge—Dorothy Strowbridge's grandmother.

Eloise White—Portland Academy classmate.

Lester White—Portland Academy friend and occasional escort.

"Carl"; Charles Pearson Wilson—Portland Academy classmate and occasional escort.

Both isolation and geographical features made the mail route to Oysterville an interesting one. Before the arrival of whites, Indians had traveled along a route between the mouth of the Columbia River and Puget Sound by way of Shoalwater Bay and Grays Harbor. As whites began to settle the coast country, they used the same route to carry mail and supplies. For the first three years after Grandpa Espy and I.A. Clark founded the village, mail came and went by oyster schooner, and also was hand-carried by those stalwart few who ventured into or out of the area by canoe or sailboat following the Indian trails and portages.

By 1857, a short one-mile road across the peninsula connected Oysterville on the bay with the ocean beach to the west. Though not far, it involved climbing Davis Hill and the primary dune at the beach—both formidable enough in good weather, but a muddy stop-and-go business when it was stormy. Nevertheless, "the mail must go!" and Isaac Whealdon of Ilwaco assured that it did. He carried mail and passengers along the length of the peninsula by wagon three times a week—the major portion on the hard sands of the ocean beach. It was said that the mail driver had to be a first class navigator on the beach run, handling the reins in all kinds of weather and, when the tide was high, avoiding drift logs surging back and forth in the swells.

In 1874, two years before Papa was born, a peninsula sheep farmer, Lewis Alfred Loomis, acquired the mail contract for the route between Astoria and Olympia. Mail destined for Oysterville and points north and east of Shoalwater Bay were sent via Astoria—from there, the steamer *General Canby* took freight and mail across the Columbia River to Ilwaco, where it then was hauled north by the Loomis Stage Line, traveling directly along the "weather beach" to Oysterville.

Mail continuing on was transported across the bay from Oysterville to Bay Center, South Bend, Riverside, Woodard's Landing, and North Cove. At North Cove, passengers and mail were again transferred to a stagecoach run to Peterson's Point, now known as Westport. The fifth leg of the journey, from Peterson's Point to Montesano, was again by water on the little stern-wheeler *Montesano.* The sixth and final leg of the trip was by stage line from Montesano to Olympia. Total time for the mail run—sixty hours!

By 1902, when the H.A. Espy family arrived back in Papa's native Oysterville, the railroad from Ilwaco to Nahcotta had been operating for thirteen years, and mail now was hauled most of the length of the peninsula by train rather than stagecoach. Mama and Medora could count on next day delivery between Oysterville and Portland if they posted their letters in time.

In Oysterville, outgoing mail was picked up by Mr. Lehman in his wagon (which my mother Dale remembers being pulled by a mule and a mare) about 8:30 a.m. each day of the week, except Sunday. According to the carrier's contract with the postal service, mail was to arrive in Nahcotta, four miles distant,

Medora's friend Asenath Barnes and the mail wagon in front of Tom Andrews' store.

in 1½ hours or "fines will be imposed for every failure...unless such failure is satisfactorily explained."

Oysterville and Nahcotta were connected by a difficult, poorly maintained, sand road. Willard later recalled that the gravelling of that road was "an outstanding event" of his boyhood. As he explained: "Barges brought the gravel from Long Island, in the bay above Nahcotta. Volunteers (I think this was done without pay, but I may be wrong) shoveled it into wagons on the tide flats. The wagon beds consisted of loose, longitudinal planks; when the wagons arrived at the spot on the road where the gravel was to be deposited, the workmen simply pulled the planks out at the rear of the wagon."

Mr. Lehman delivered his mail sacks to the Nahcotta post office, from whence it was dispatched on the first train heading south. The time of departure varied each day, for the railroad waited for the arrival of either the *Shamrock* or the *Reliable*, the little steamers that took turns plying the waters between South Bend and Nahcotta twice a day. The vessels' schedules, of course, depended upon the tides (the bay is pretty much devoid of water at low tide). The railroad took pride in

Postage

In 1913, the price of sending a first class letter of one ounce or less was 2¢. The cost went up to 3¢ in 1917, and, rather surprisingly, back to 2¢ in 1919. In 1932, the rate returned to 3¢ and has been rising steadily ever since.

its unusual timetable that ran according to the tides in accommodating boat connections at either end of the line.

By the time Mama and Medora resumed their daily correspondence in the fall of 1913, the railroad had been extended to Megler. The 25-mile run from Nahcotta to the Columbia took about three hours. There, mail sacks were transferred to a launch for the 40-minute trip across the river to Astoria and to a steamer that proceeded up the Columbia to the Ash Street dock on the Willamette River in Portland—another six-hour journey. If Mama wrote to Medora on a Tuesday, she could count on Medora's answer in Thursday's post—if Medora answered promptly.

[Oysterville]
Friday—September 12, 1913

My Dear Medora,

It seems ages since you left and nothing of importance has occurred. It is about two o'clock now, and thus far I have been picking up the pantries and washing an accumulation of pans. Also scrubbed the kitchen. All the while looking for a lost spoon as usual. I am going to get some tin spoons, and they can get lost if they want to. It keeps me worn to a frazzle hunting silver.

...I am anxious about your eyes. Take care of them. Always read in a good light, and study with the light falling over your left shoulder. More than one person has had to give up school entirely because of abused eyes, and what is worse, blindness is often the result. It does not take any more time to take care than it does to suffer the result of carelessness.

I am delighted that you are so pleased with the dormitory. If you are worthy of Miss Campbell's confidence and never take advantage in the least degree of the privileges she allows you, you will undoubtedly have a very happy time. The girl who adheres rigidly to the rules always has the most fun in the long run. It is such a comfort to us to know that you can be trusted and we need not worry about your behavior.

Don't go to Ruth's every Saturday. Once in two or three weeks is plenty. Remember, too, that one of Ruth's failings is being behind time and you will have to watch the clock for yourself. When you are supposed to be home for dinner, get there—better early than late. Another thing, don't stay over night at Ruth's even when you go those Saturdays. This would interfere with your church attendance.

Let me know the color and what you have to get for a gym suit.

Where is my gold chain? I can't find it. Is it with your things?

Where do you suppose I found the lost brown darning cotton? In the bottom of the bread box.

[Portland]
Monday—September 15, 1913

Dearest Mother,

There are only five of us girls here at Miss Campbell's. Anastasia Hague is my roommate. She is a little girl in the 4th grade. I have the largest bureau and am mistress of the room...

I went to the Dentist and he said my teeth weren't bad. Dr. Herbert Nichols said my adenoids were a little larger than natural, but that I had very little catarrhal trouble and three or four treatments would prevent me from having any sort of cold all winter. Should I take the treatments?

Miss Campbell lets the girls have lots of freedom. They go down town or anything providing they have their lessons and they know where they are going.

It's getting late. Lovingly, Medora

[Oysterville]
Tuesday—September 16, 1913

My dear Medora,

Yes, certainly you may take the treatments of which Dr. Nichols speaks... Unless Miss Campbell objects to your going alone, we would prefer that you do not bother any of the relatives to take you. Our girl is "tried and true" and I know she will not loiter. In fact, Medora, I feel you can do your errands more promptly alone for the different aunties have so many things to look after that they are apt to be an unintentional cause for tardiness—delaying you, see?

Your letter received today is a comfort in its assurance that you are so pleasantly situated. Do not fret over having a little girl for a room mate. This need not bar you from comradeship with the older girls, of the age you are accustomed.

Lovingly, Mama

The Two Ruths

In 1902–1907, when Mama's sister Ruth Richardson attended Mills Seminary, she met Ruth Davis of Millbrae, California, and they became great friends. To distinguish them from one another, classmates began calling Ruth Davis "RuthieD," the name by which she always was known to the Espys.

Both girls had somewhat unusual family situations causing an even closer bond. Ruth Richardson had enrolled at Mills Seminary not long after her mother died, and her father was courting Eva Gaches, shortly to become his second wife. Similarly, Ruth Davis' father had died and her mother had remarried. While Ruth Richardson was the youngest child and soon would be involved in helping care for her older sister's brood, Ruth Davis was the eldest and early on took responsibility for her younger brother, Herbert.

The two Ruths' lives had become forever intertwined in the summer of 1909, when "RuthieD" visited Ruth Richardson in Oysterville and met Papa's younger brother, Cecil. A year later, they were married by Papa—the Justice of the Peace—shortly after midnight on August 3, 1910, in the Espy house. Both Ruths eventually became Portland area residents.

[Portland]
Thursday Evening—September 18, 1913

Dearest Mama,

Your letter of Wednesday a.m. arrived this morning.

All the girls go home weekends except me. Mary, a very quiet girl goes out past Oswego; Helen to Hood River (Helen is a senior, a very nice girl); Dorothy only lives three blocks from here; and Anastasia lives at the Multnomah. The girls can go anywhere after school without asking. Boys are allowed to see the girls on Friday nights. I won't ever stay over night but I would like to go for all day Saturday as I will get lonesome doing nothing.

Ruth is so irritable that I simply can't get along with her. She keeps remarking about how much "horse sense" I have. It's just because she's so shallow about some things. RuthieD is perfectly lovely, just like she always was, and she is so much deeper than Ruth that I can talk about my hopes and schoolwork and anything without being laughed at. RuthieD says Ruth's views of things haven't changed at all since she left Mills. I'm just awfully fond of Ruth but...

I understand about the church attendance. I will be sure to go every Sunday.

Miss Campbell said my father was a very bright man. (I already knew it.)

I am sure I don't know anything about your chain. I haven't seen it since that time I lost it in Olympia and found it again. Miss Campbell says P.A. is very much harder than Public School. She says I'll probably never get higher than 78 because nobody she knows of ever has. This is my daily program

Ruth Richardson, ca. 1910.

"RuthieD"

8:45 French
9:35 Study Hall
10:20 English
Chapel
11:25 Lunch
12:20 Algebra
1:10 Study Hall
2:00 Latin

Then I go home. I won't have Freehand Drawing till next week. I have Gym on Tuesdays and Thursdays.

Do you remember Jean Murdock who I used to correspond with? I was introduced to her sister and Jean came up to me in Study Hall and asked if I wasn't Medora Espy. She's attending P.A. now.

I have cramps today. Isn't that interesting. First time in my life.

The girls almost all wear their hair down their back, dresses to the floor, and shoes flat on the ground; if any heel at all it is so low you wouldn't know it. Such Fads?

Lovingly, Medora

Mama's Recipe for Pickled Pears

Peel and core 3# pears

Boil 1½ quarts of water; put pears in water. Cook until tender.

Add bouquet garni of 6 cinnamon sticks, 2 T cloves, 2 t whole ginger.

Add 2 C sugar.

Cook 5 min.

Add 1 C white vinegar. Simmer 3 min.

Discard bouquet garni

Pack in jars; cover with syrup and seal.

Pickled Pears

The pear tree still stands in the garden of the H.A. Espy house, and, in spite of a honeysuckle that embraces its entire height—forty feet at least—it continues to produce a fine crop of pears each summer.

Fine for pickling, that is!—for they are so hard when they fall "ripe" from the tree, even birds pay them little heed. But once they are pickled using Mama's recipe—Ah! Ambrosia!

[Oysterville]
Thursday, September 19th, 1913

My dear Medora,

There is nothing new. I put up more pears yesterday; also, a box of peaches pickling the latter as I do the pears.

If you show symptoms of measles call the doctor—exposure or cold might mean your death.

I am perfectly willing you go out Saturdays, providing it is customary. Go every week if you want to seeing Miss Campbell does not object, but don't stay over night unless some especial occasion should arise.

Do you know the way to the doctor's office? Don't be foolish about asking someone to show you... They are not apt to think of it unless you ask them. After you once are shown the way downtown you will get along alone. It is not too far to walk. In fact, Papa says it is a nice walk. You can see and learn more on foot, besides saving carfare, which soon runs into money. But take care in crossing streets.

I would go to one Ruth's one week and the other Ruth's the next, not the same place every week. You will find Ruth more agreeable if you don't see her every week. After you get acquainted go see the girls once in awhile—after school if you wish. You know I have no objections to your going. I am simply anxious for you to abide by Miss C's wishes.

I hope you bought sensible heels, but not flat ones on your shoes.

Don't read books. Your eyes will have all the work they should with your studies. Next semester I hope you can take music. If you study hard at first and get a good start your work will go smoothly the rest of your time there. With all the time from two o'clock on you should make excellent daily lessons. I know you will do your best. I want Papa to feel that the expenditure is bringing full returns so he will never be sorry he put you into P.A.—a little against his inclination.

Lovingly, Mama

I am glad you met the Murdock girls. Papa knows their mother. It may be pleasant for you having them there.

[Portland]
Tuesday—September 23, 1913

Dearest Mother,

I received your most welcome letter today. Those pickled pears and peaches are probably delicious.

The Chinaman said 25c a week, but I only sent 1 nightie, 2 pr of hose and 1 combination suit. This week I sent 1 nightie, 1 shirt, 1 dress, and 6 pr of hose.

I know the way to all the relatives, but get all mixed up when I go downtown. I wouldn't think of going with Dorothy, because she always goes with a boy generally in a machine. But I wouldn't mind going with Mary or Helen. Saturday I go to the dentist again for the third and last time. I know the way to church, too, and as soon as I can get around downtown I will feel satisfied.

My shoes are just like my last year school shoes. I would hate to shuffle around on no heels...

I am just crazy to take music and I never will be able to have any fun dancing because I can't dance. So as soon as possible I must take dancing lessons.

Could you please have Papa send me a check for a dollar. I have to get a book price 80c or could get along without it. "Les Miserables" is at the Heilegg and I'm crazy to go. I have the 25c.

Lovingly, Medora

Literary Connections

When he was a young man, Grandpa Richardson taught school and wrote for newspapers and magazines. In 1874, as a reporter, he went to Mexico City, where he eventually served at various times as consul, charge d'affaires, and secretary of the American legation. In 1879, several years after his father's death, he returned to California in order to care for his sisters and a young brother. Accompanying him was his wife, Annie Medora Taylor, whom he had met and married while in Mexico City, and their one-year-old daughter, Helen Medora (Mama).

For many years, in addition to his duties as Assistant Postmaster in San Francisco and as American Secretary to the Japanese Consulate, Daniel S. Richardson served as the secretary-treasurer of the Astronomical Society of the Pacific (for 16 years). Throughout his life, he gravitated toward companions with bookish interests, especially writers. Grandpa Richardson was a contemporary and friend of California's early literary leaders, including Bret Harte, Ambrose Bierce, Joaquin Miller, and Charles Warren Stoddard. He also wrote poetry and was an early contributor to the *Overland Monthly*, and in 1908 wrote a small book of verse, *Trail Dust*.

San Francisco Chronicle

January 3, 1909—Californians and others who have enjoyed the occasional poems of Daniel S. Richardson will welcome the opportunity to secure a collection of them between book covers...bearing the title of *Trail Dust*.

Loving California and San Francisco, this quiet man, whose life has been one of patient service, and whose dreams have been snatched in the midst of a busy life, has in few words painted one of the most vivid descriptions ever made of sunset at the Golden Gate:

"The sun sinks low and his crimson locks
Trail after him down the west;
They weave the day into trembling bars
Just over the ocean's crest.
They build the clouds into golden harps
Where the day has gone to rest."

Grandpa Daniel S. Richardson.

[Oysterville]
Thursday, September 25, 1913

My dear Medora,

Papa is mowing. We are having a few warm days. The kind that come before a storm...

Grandpa sent me some of his books yesterday and I sent one to Mrs. Higginson and one to

Mrs. Rohrabeck. The latter, by the way, is in a sad condition, hopeless I guess. She has a well developed cancer in her side, and has only recently learned of it. I was shocked when I heard it, for nothing can be worse.

How are your eyes? Do you have as much head ache?

Lovingly, Mama

Enclosed is check. See "Les Miserables" if you can.

Measles

"Measles is a contagious disease, characterized by a preliminary stage of fever and catarrh of the eyes, nose and throat, and followed by a general eruption on the skin...The disease begins like a severe nasal catarrh with fever. The eyes are red and watery, the nose runs, and the throat is irritable red, and sore, and there is some cough, with chilliness and muscular soreness...The preliminary period, when the patient seems to be suffering with a bad cold, lasts for four days usually, and on the evening of the fourth day the rash breaks out."—From Mama's copy of the *Home Medical Library*, Vol. I (Review of Reviews Company, ca. 1907).

[Oysterville]
Friday, October 3, 1913

My dear Medora,

The children all have terrible colds. About two weeks ago they all developed every symptom of measles—even to sore throat and sensitiveness to light. We thought, of course, it was the real thing. On the fourth day all but Sue broke out with a faint rash on the face but none of them were sick. All felt a little dull and dumpy. I had the same thing. We all stayed indoors and kept warm a few days but nothing further developed. Yesterday the girls went back to school after losing nearly two weeks. It was undoubtedly a very light form of measles and we were fortunate to "get off" so easily—however, I don't think this will protect us from getting the real red measles another time if exposed.

Papa always is right—you are not in a regular boarding school and consequently are not getting the advantages of boarding school life. A few girls like that of such assorted ages do not make up a dormitory. I think Miss Campbell shows good sense not to have a lot of rules and regulations for a half dozen girls, most of whom live a block from the school. A month should be time to at least form some acquaintances. I wish you had gone to McMinnville.[1] *This is like the school we attended and we have something to show for it—friends.*

I must see to dinner. Do you enjoy the fare where you are? I would go up for treatments soon but simply have not the money. Everyone is hounding us and it costs to turn around...I hate to talk money so much, but only yesterday Papa borrowed from the Ilwaco bank to meet a few driving bills. Before you are through school I am sure you will find money comes easier, and when it does you shall have all possible to make up for all this stinting. Things will change because they have to. It can't go on indefinitely like this and I can't believe we will have a complete crash.

...I wish we could talk dearie. My heart goes to you like a tree in the wind, and all my thoughts are loose leaves that fly after you while I remain behind.

Lovingly, Mama

Portland Academy

The academy was founded in 1889 by two college professors from Iowa. Their purpose in coming to the Pacific Northwest was to establish a college preparatory school of high academic standards. It opened with three instructors and forty-two pupils.

By the time Medora entered, the staff included sixteen instructors. According to the *Twenty-Fifth Annual Catalogue of Portland Academy* for the 1913-1914 school year, the curriculum offered Latin, Greek, Mathematics, Chemistry, Physics, Geography, French, German, English, Rhetoric, Music, History, Bible Study, Drawing, and Physical Training. The school year (comprising thirty-seven weeks) was divided into two terms, with tuition at $60 per term. Listed at the back of the catalogue were the number of former students who had gone on to college or advanced schools of technology—forty-six institutions from coast to coast reflecting the pursuits of 374 academy graduates.

From its first year, the institution struggled financially and couldn't meet its operating expenses from tuition revenue alone.

Fortunately, several prominent Portland citizens, among them W.S. Ladd and H.W. Corbett, took a lively interest in the academy and provided substantial gifts so that it could enlarge its quarters and meet financial obligations. Rumors persistently circulated in the city that the continuation of the school was doubtful. Finally, at the end of Medora's senior year, Portland Academy closed its doors and was absorbed by St. Helen's Hall (an Episcopal school that continues to thrive today).[2]

[Portland]
Monday, October 6, 1913

My dear Mama and Papa,

I never felt happier in my life. Portland Academy is the sort of a school I had always dreamed about. I feel perfectly at home here and like it so very much.

I am just home from Gym. I like it better each time. There is a great deal of dancing in it. Just as soon as possible I want to take dancing. Four dollars for eight lessons.

I like my drawing very much. It requires no preparation and counts half a credit. Gym is the same. So if I take both for three years I will have three credits and feel very much accomplished.

Papa, don't worry about paying Miss C. Helen hasn't paid yet. And the other girls pay on the installment plan.

Lovingly, Medora

[Oysterville]
Thursday Evening, October 9, 1913

My dear Medora,

It is an awful day. The bay is lashing in foam and the wind howls and there is all winter ahead of us. It is wintry enough now so that we keep a fire in the bedroom all of the time and in the fireplace a part of every day.

I was glad to get your explanatory letter regarding P.A. and am glad you are satisfied…

About your dancing, couldn't you manage to save four dollars. I simply can not ask Papa for that much just now when he is so worried. There have been some unforeseen things occur that make money even in small amounts unobtainable. The bank has called for a payment of a certain note that Papa had not expected to meet so soon and he is distracted. This is confidential. Don't say a word to the Ruths or any one else. Can't you save on your laundry? Do your own stockings, bloomers, handkerchiefs etc. and an occasional slip put into Ruth's wash. Tell her what you are trying to do and she would gladly help you. Then when you have the money saved, pay it down in advance for your lessons. Where is it you get these eight lessons for four dollars?

I turned the rug over in the living room but Papa wants me to turn it back. He says it spoils the room. I told him it looked as tho we might never get another rug and we had better preserve that one. He said if that was so, we had better enjoy that one while it lasted!

I am reading "The Little Shepherd of Kingdom Come" and tho it is fine, I think it most too sad to be enjoyable.

My leg has been so "gimp" that I have had to sit down off and on through the day, so am doing more reading than usual—so far have read just essays and famous authors, which I greatly enjoy. Yesterday picked up "The Little Shepherd" and am in it now. Did you read "On Christmas Eve" by the same author?

I have ordered ingredients for chili sauce to put up next week. It is going to be a task, but we all enjoy it so much that it is worthwhile. The pears are all gone. I have three crocks of pickles…I made my first doughnuts yesterday and they turned out fairly well for a first attempt.

It is nearly ten o'clock and I want to get up reasonably early to do some needed cleaning tomorrow. The kitchen floor will have to be gone at with a hoe.

Academies and High Schools

In 1892, the entire state of Oregon had only one fully accredited four-year "public" high school, as did Idaho, while Washington had but three. Consequently, "private" academies and seminaries necessarily played a key role in providing high school age youngsters with a college preparatory curriculum. Thereby, students gained the skills needed to qualify as freshmen at the region's denominational colleges and in the expanding state-run higher education systems.

Colleges and universities also often organized "preparatory" departments—with essentially a high school senior year course—to provide students as young as 14 with the training needed to enter college freshman classes.

By the 1910s, however, the increasing number of "accredited" public high schools in many Northwest communities were displacing the former reliance put on private academies and preparatory departments.

Take good care of your dear self. I wish you were here for a good night kiss.

Lovingly, Mama

The Julia Anns

Shortly after Grandma Julia Ann Espy died in 1901, Grandpa Robert Hamilton Espy offered an enticement of $2,000 to his offspring if they would give the name "Julia Ann" to any newborn granddaughter. Although Papa and Mama had five more children subsequent to this proposal, three of whom were girls, they chose not to take him up on the offer. Three of Grandpa's other children did, however, and Dora, Susie, and Will each named a daughter after their mother.

Interestingly, there was only one Robert Hamilton among the male grandchildren—Robert (pronounced Rōbert) Hamilton Christensen, Aunt Susie and Uncle Olaf's son. Aunt Dora and Uncle King's son, Bob, was "Robert Espy Wilson," and Mama and Papa's Ed was "Robert Hamilton Edwin Espy" in memory of Papa's oldest brother. Although it seems likely that Grandpa made a similar monetary offer with regard to a namesake of his own, it is probable that only grandson Rōbert met the required nomenclature.

[Portland]
Saturday, October 12, 1913

My dearest little mother,

Your long letter started Thursday evening just received…

I have been thinking about saving and I will. I could do all my winter washing except corset covers, nightgowns and union suits; that oughtn't to be more than 35c. I could save four dollars between saving on my laundry and carfare.

The dancing hall is just a little ways from here. The most beautiful carpets and palms, and then a lovely floor.

I enjoyed "The Little Shepherd of Kingdom Come" very much. I never read anything else by him tho I am crazy to read the "Trail of the Lonesome Pine."

I am sorry to hear about your leg. You surely should come up to have those treatments.

Aunt Susie's baby that arrived yesterday a.m. at 7 is another Julia Ann.

Feel fine, Lovingly, Medora

Verona says Aunt Susie got along fine.

I forgot to tell you Dorothy took me to "Quo Vadis" last night. It was wonderful, positively. I can't see how they get such wonderful reels. We didn't get home till eleven but I felt as tho it was worth seeing. Every little detail was perfect.

My grades were

French	*87*	*Average*
English	*90*	*Average*
Caesar	*76*	*Average*
Prose	*82*	*Average*
Algebra	*90*	*Average*

Have not asked about drawing or gym yet.

Lovingly, Medora

[Oysterville]
Sunday, October 19, 1913

My dear Medora,

We were disappointed not to have but one letter from you all week.

You know how careful we have always been about having vessels of water around. Well, it has rained hard lately and the tub across the street filled up. The babies are seldom in the street since school opened and none of us gave that far-away tub a thought. The day Papa fixed the pens back of the barn, all of the children went over to watch. When through, he went into the barn to hitch Nick and I went to the gate and called the boys and told them to bring Dale. She was near the tub, apparently on her way to where they were watching the pigs. I went right in to pour Papa's coffee. In a moment something occasioned Papa's coming out of the barn, and looking toward the tub he saw only Dale's dear little feet. She had fallen head first and was struggling like mad. If Papa had not just happened to be there she would certainly have drowned, for I probably would not have called the boys again before the table was set. It unstrung the whole family. Poor little Dale was not well for two days after. The tub is bailed out now and Papa says water shall be carried so long as there are babies around. Don't, for goodness sakes, tell the relatives, as it sounds like pure carelessness. I will be more afraid than ever of water now.

Dale talks considerably more than when you left. She always asks "what he say" when I go to the phone, and never fails to ask me "what doin" when I am busy. She could not be cunninger—just think of the precious little mite being nearly drowned.

Mona is doing splendidly and is a great favorite with her teacher. I think Sue is doing work too hard. She should not have gone into the fourth grade last winter.

Lovingly, Mama

Dearest Medora,

Opened this letter to put in enclosed check for $3.00. Hope it will cover what you need.

How did your marks compare with others? Some of them seemed low for you.

Must rush to get this in the mail.

Lovingly, Papa

Grandpa's Notions

In his dotage, Grandpa's "eye for the ladies" occasionally became a problem, particularly to the women of the family. His grandfatherly hugs were just a bit too amorous; his grandfatherly pats a bit too lingering. As long as he was in Oysterville under the watchful eye of Aunt Kate, he behaved himself.

However, if he was feeling up to a journey to Astoria or Portland, perhaps to do some doctoring or take care of a little business, family members quickly spread the word. The girls and women made themselves scarce or, if necessary, enlisted one of the male relatives to do escort duty.

[Oysterville]
Sunday, November 9, 1913

My dear Medora,

It is dreadfully wet here and the days are so short and dreary. Have you your flannels on? I have asked you this before. I don't want you wearing those thin summer underclothing any longer this year…

I haven't seen Grandpa so well for years. He always gets so full of notions when he has an energetic streak…

The girls are rushing the dishes so as to get to church. Last night Sue asked me if you were a Christian and Mona spoke up with, "Of course not. Medora is a Baptist."

Sue is in constant trouble at school, but fortunately not with the teacher. The children seem to pick on her.

Be sure not to sit up late. With all the afternoon at your disposal you should always be in bed by 9:30. Health is the greatest blessing this world can bestow. Without it money and education can be of little good. Many a person has ruined his health acquiring wealth, and then would give all his money to have his health back again.

Good night girlie. I wish you were not so far away from home.

Lovingly, Mama

Just heard [Grand]Father is going to Portland. Don't "go out" with him at all. Have a previous engagement or have to study—anything but do not go.

[Oysterville]
Monday, December 15, 1913

Dear Medora,

Enclosed find check. I wish it were bigger but is the best we can do. I want to be sure it gets to you in time to buy your ticket and berth. This money business is about reaching a climax. I don't see what we are going to do. However, when things are as bad as they can be, they of necessity must improve...

[Holiday vacation, Oysterville]
Diary, Saturday, January 3, 1914

Woke up about seven...Mama told me to come down, and I was never more surprized than when she said "Happy Birthday" and handed me a book by John Fox Jr. "The Trail of the Lonesome Pine". As I intended to leave for Portland, I went down to say "Goodby" to Aunt Kate & Grandpa...Papa drove me up with Fanny...

The California Connection

For years after her arrival in Oysterville, Mama believed that Grandpa was not long for this world, and she remained confident that her young family's stay would be short. She continued to refer to East Oakland as "home," and maintained close contact through regular correspondence with friends and relatives.

Every few years, she and the children would go for a visit, and the Californians, in turn, occasionally braved the rigors of a three-day ocean voyage and two-day train trip for a vacation in Oysterville. Presents were exchanged at Christmas and, as the Espy family grew and the need became greater, hand-me-down clothing was gratefully accepted. Meanwhile, Grandpa Espy hung on tenaciously.

By the time of Grandpa's death in 1918, the H.A. Espys were well ensconced in the community; in fact, not only locally, but at the county and state levels, as well. In the intervening years, Mama had discovered that Oysterville was home after all. As she aged, she sometimes likened herself to Byron's "Prisoner of Chillon," who grew to love his prison cell and even to prefer it to the outside world.

[Oysterville]
Tuesday, 3:30 January 27, 1914

Dear Little Sister,

It has been impossible to write because I have one of my weepy, blurry colds—only worse than usual. This A.M. have my face all done up in flannel—am a beauty. Have neuralgia due to having partially dislocated my jaw last night—I bit a cough drop. It was hard and slipped, wrenching my face. I will attempt a letter tho you may find it muddle-headed.

I guess too much vanity gave me my cold. The buggy came from grandpa when I was in a hot kitchen baking. I was so delighted with the "looks" of it that I ran out into the cold and rain to see closer. It is the nicest looking buggy on the Peninsula—just what I wanted—a low, high-backed seat phaeton—rubber tired, roll back top. Eva told me it was dilapidated but there is nothing wrong except a piece out of one tire. It is not so shining new looking as the big buggy but it looks like the city and home to me...

Willard...has been having three days of slight fever and croup. He is not in bed but looks wilted. Dale has one of her wracking bronchial coughs and so has Mona. In fact, every member of the household barks until we sound like a kennel.

Mrs. Wirt made an awful scene in church Sunday night. We had a fine speaker from Los Angeles. Beth grew fussy and Mrs. W. took her into the vestibule. There was a great commotion and pretty soon in came Mrs. Wirt "right out in meeting" with, "Papa, papa I can't make that child come home. She won't budge. You will have to come take her." The minister stopped preaching

Train at Nahcotta, August 1913.

and Mr. Wirt went in back for a lantern and handed it to Mrs. W.—then calmly took his seat. This was not enough. Mrs. W. spied Wesley who was peacefully sleeping and she trots over, stands him up, shakes him, yells at him—he acting all the time like Sue does when we try to get her awake. She finally managed to haul him out and the three of them thundered out…

There certainly is a lot of dignity about our church. The minister attended S.S. [Sunday School] in the morning and, as usual, they sang without an organ. An hour later at church, he sat down and played, himself, and if Mrs. Bowman did not blurt out, "Well why in the world didn't you say you could play at Sunday School?" He must have thought it a disorderly crowd. We are to have a resident Baptist minister come next month. Poor man!…

Parcel Post

Although an international parcel-post system was established as early as 1878 and various countries quickly established both domestic and foreign services, the United States delayed instituting a domestic system until the Parcel Post Act of 1912. Up to that time, peninsula residents had used the railroad's freight services for sending and receiving packages and parcels.

[Oysterville]
Monday, February 9, 1914

My dear Medora,

Enclosed you will find some stamps Aunt Kate sends. You must write and thank her.

Aunt Dora will be here tomorrow to spend Grandfather's birthday with him.

We are all some better of our colds.

I am taking things as easy as possible. The girls have been fine about doing their regular work without being told. They dress themselves within fifteen minutes in the morning, then Sue dresses Willard and Mona Dale in fifteen minutes. I have not had to prompt them in regard to this since you left. They have been ideal for weeks and so we are getting along nicely. Of course they are gone so much of the day that they have but little time to help but they are doing their best.

I believe books can be sent by Parcels Post now, so I wish you would send "The Trail of the

Lonesome Pine." Bob wants to read it. Keep close track of our books...

Lovingly, Mama

[Oysterville]
March 1st, 1914

My dear Medora,

The tribe is just home from Sunday School. There is a new minister installed in the Bullard house and this was his first Sunday. I have not seen him yet.

What caused Ruth to move so suddenly? I hope she is on the West side.

The best plan for your sewing is to get materials, patterns and so on, and bring home at Easter. Then hire Mrs. Wirt at $1.00 per day. She cuts, fits and sews nicely. Of course, she has no style or ideas, but with our own patterns she would be fine. She said she would bring her machine and work by the day.

Instead of a satine dress, why could we not have the corduroy coat you want also a skirt of same material. This would serve as suit until Fall, and then the coat could do for evening, or extra over winter dresses. We could make it nicely. The coat would be nice over summer dresses or the skirt with waists. Then we can make a white duck or Indian head skirt—for middy waists—I sent for that plain waist (1.49) at the National. This with your nice white lengthened and my white French knot fixed, should be enough until school opens in August.

The sewing circle can not do much toward regular dress making. Straight ahead work is what they can do. I had them work button holes last time and they did lots...

Sue and Marvin and Wesley are making candy in the kitchen. Those boys live here Saturdays and Sundays.

I am puzzled about the girl's clothes. They never had less in their lives and I do not want to get any more than absolutely necessary because of needing so much the next summer. I like catalogue and store dresses better than any made by dress maker or at home. They have a "something" you can't make—but I suppose I will have to be content with what I can manufacture myself.

You must not get discouraged. "It is a long lane that has no turning."

Much love from Mama

Don't be too familiar with that cat. They are common carriers of disease—especially scarlet fever and diphtheria.

[Portland]
Wednesday Evening, March 4, 1914

Your letter arrived yesterday A.M. and I was very glad to hear your suggestions. Mrs. Wirt would be the very thing. But I don't think a corduroy suit would be very practical for summer wear, and then they wear the suit coats so beastly short I couldn't wear it over a dress but I think a white linen suit as enclosed. Dorothy designed this after the suits we saw in at Barthalemews the other day. Don't you love it? It is so essentially girlish and simple, no drapes to fuss with and you can pleat beautifully for you know these pleats are just a little smaller than the ordinary ones in youngsters dress. Not accordion pleated like my other dress. The heavy black line represents the blue moiré ribbon through back of coat ending in large bow in front of coat. Three quarters sleeves are all the vogue this year. The only thing possibly extreme about this costume is the collar, which if you object to can easily be replaced by a turn down one.

Enclosed you will also find a list of my dresses which must be repaired or made anew. You will notice that I have not put down the challie as I won't need it or the French Knot one. But you can readily see how I would be in desperate need of a coat, but if you make my suit while I am home at Easter and Ruth makes my hat (Alice blue moiré) with the aid of Dorothy's I could do very well without till the end of May, or as I think about it till the end of school, but I will need it during the summer months if I keep up with the P.A. girls on the beach. I don't mean keep up in the sense of clothes, for the six girls whom I admire and enjoy have just a few nice things. For red sash I mean...I can't explain very fully on paper but have tried my best. I believe I have planned so as to save quite a bit. Don't despair about the coat for Dot will probably get a new one before May and gladly turn hers over to me. Possibly I could bribe or buy it from her for a very small sum.

Elizabeth R. was over yesterday afternoon. We played cards and ate. Had an awfully good time. She is the sweetest girl, very athletic. She's going to take me to the Multnomah some Saturday morning to play tennis. All these girls are regular sharks at swimming, tennis, golf, dancing etc. so you can imagine how I feel. But I am going to show them something. I am bound I shall row every high tide all summer till I am an expert for some of them are very good at that. Please don't let me forget this resolution and urge me to it all summer or I will forget it sure.

Ruth moved suddenly because they all decided they wanted to be together.

...RuthieD's report of Uncle Cecil's impression of our children rather surprised me. He says Dale ruled both the boys and that she was a close second to Gussie in strength but much quicker. That Sue was getting very good looking and Mona lanky and awkward. Willard was too pretty for a boy and Edwin the same as ever. She made me homesick with the descriptions of everyone, but I only have six more weeks to wait. Soon I will be home and Oh! How happy I will be.

Lovingly, Medora

[Oysterville]
Monday, March 9, 1914

My dear Medora,

I am getting kind of sick of the subject of clothes, especially as we keep going around in a circle...

I think we are beginning to see daylight about your spring clothes.

1. *Buy your best wash suit—not to exceed $10, less if possible*
2. *Clean white coat of D's*
3. *Send East for white wash skirt—$2.00*
4. *Make 2 shirtwaists*
5. *Lengthen last summer's dresses*
6. *Extra dress—white—for school and shopping*

Be careful not to get your dresses too long. You have plenty of time to grow old in...

Mama

[Easter vacation, Oysterville]
Diary, Saturday, April 11, 1914

Awakened at quarter to six. I cleaned the yard, that is picked up twigs and tore down the play house. In the afternoon I washed the pantry then read Peg O' My Heart. Cousin Bob was in. He is lots of fun. The children were busy decorating the church. They are real expectant about the program. Sue had to go to the woods for ferns and flowers. Mama made rocks.

Correspondence

By the spring of 1914, when she was fifteen, writing letters was second nature to Medora. It was a given that she would correspond with any of the immediate family when separated from them for more than a day or two. She wrote most regularly to Mama, of course, but often enclosed a note or wrote separately to Papa, and to her little brothers and sisters.

Mama's Rocks

2 cups brown sugar
½ cup butter
3 eggs
salt
1 pound chopped nuts
1 pound raisins
1 ts. Soda in ⅓ cup boiling water
1 ts. Cinnamon
½ ts. Cloves
Flour to make stiff (about 2½ cups)
1 ts. Nutmeg
Mix and drop in spoonfuls on greased pan
Bake at 350 for 15 min.

A bundle of Medora's letters.

In addition, she kept up a lively correspondence with relatives, her friends in Olympia, and chums from Portland Academy. She also wrote to former teachers from her Oysterville school days, and to family friends in California. And they all wrote back. Medora kept each and every letter—hundreds of them—in their original envelopes, often grouped by year and tied with ribbons. On most she put a notation indicating the day they were answered.

[Easter vacation, Oysterville]
Diary, Monday, April 13, 1914

Papa didn't come home today from Portland. I was busy all day—washed the pictures in the dining room and the paint in the kitchen—made a blotch of the ceiling. Finished "Peg O' My Heart." Mailed a letter, note I mean, to Dorothy this a.m. Mama cooked, baked and made salad dressing. The girls telephoned to say that Mary had sprained her ankle so they couldn't walk down as planned on Wednesday. I will go for them. Rec'v'd a letter from Dote.

Grandpa's Treatment

Grandpa Espy suffered from an enlarged prostate that eventually blocked the urethra and made it difficult for him to urinate. Treatment choices were few, and relief generally was provided through catheterization.

Each day after the milking was done, Papa went over to "give Grandpa his treatment." Villagers told of Papa's coffee consumption while there. Some said twelve cups at a sitting, and some said more. He generally stayed for dinner—the noon meal—his excuse being that he didn't want Mama to have to stop everything to fix him something. But in reality, he enjoyed visiting with Aunt Kate and Grandpa, and undoubtedly relished the daily respite from the constant demands of home and ranch.

[Easter vacation, Oysterville]
Diary, Wednesday, April 15, 1914

We didn't start till quite late as Papa had to give Grandpa his treatment. I wanted to take one pair of colts and the hay wagon as there is one too many for the surrey but we ended up with Polly and Empress. As it was, Emp acted up on our way home. The girls seemed to have a pretty good time on the Bay but managed to get real wet. It seemed so good to have a bunch of girls around the house again. On our return trip to the Park nothing happened. The girls sang and I was supremely jubilant listening. Coming back it was pitch dark so Papa wouldn't let me go to sleep as Emp might act up. He had me walk through the grove. I walked home from the ranch asleep.

[Oysterville]
Friday, April 24, 1914

My dear Medora,

I was glad to get your letter and know that you are having such a nice time. I don't care how much fun you have so long as your school record stays good.

Sue has been miserable with a pain in her side ever since Monday morning. She has been out of school two days and I am getting quite anxious. I have been wishing you were home so I might question you and see if her trouble is similar to any of yours at her age. The pain lies in the left side rather low in front and runs up across the small of her back. It seems to be worse when she moves. She shows so many signs of the coming change that I am wondering if this is one or whether there is some real malady. She is not sick, just uncomfortable...

Mama

[Portland]
April 27, 1914

Dearest Mother,

Your most welcome letter received this morning,

I am so sorry about poor Sue. As I remember, I just had those pains when I had waited, then very severe so at times I could hardly stand up. The two that I remember particularly... the first one which I had when Mrs. Mathews was there. I simply doubled up then; and the one when you told me about Willard. I had been sweeping and then came this awful pain. It was always a sharp pain not an ache. I never had them after I was sick. I also had continual stomach aches which chamomile helped a great deal...

Shoalwater (now Willapa) Bay

On a voyage of discovery in 1788, British adventurer John Meares named the bay "Shoal Water" for good reason. At mean high tide, water in the bay encompass 140 square miles, but at mean low tide, just half that much (70 square miles). When the tide is out, it is possible to walk a full mile out on the muddy bottoms to the main channel. On summer days, the exposed mud flats bake in the sunshine, and the water grows warm as the tide creeps in toward shore.

My mother remembers that the village children played by the hour along the sandy beach and in the bath temperature water. However, most never learned to swim, for at high tide it was necessary to wade out a hundred yards or more before the water reached waist level. Swimming seemed superfluous. In Oysterville, the bay was considered a benevolent playground for children.

[Oysterville]
Wednesday, May 6, 1914

My dear "Sister,"

It is about eleven o'clock, and as the work was fairly "done up" I came down to the bay with the children. Sue is still out of school and I doubt if she goes back this term. I feel anxious, and yet she seems to feel fairly well in general. I have feared her spleen might be enlarging but yesterday borrowed a good "manikin" and found the spleen located quite a bit higher than the seat of her pain. This relieves me greatly. There are not organs low on the left side except the ovaries. It must be a strain or because of her developing.

I can not write very connectedly as the children keep finding wonders in the sand, and it is "look Mama" "see Mama" every moment.

It is a lovely morning—most too warm for Oysterville, but nice here on the beach. The babies look so cunning paddling around in the water. Dale doesn't venture in but she digs in the wet sand. This certainly is an ideal spot for little children.

Last night I was finishing "Via Crusi" (have you read it?) and Dale had evidently been asking some question and I had not noticed her for pretty soon she was looking up in my face and saying "Miss Espy, O, say Espy, where my Mama gone?"

On Friday the preacher had the children meet at church. About quarter past three the bell began to ring, and I thought it early, but it kept

Dale at 2 years, 11 months.

Medora with friends at Miss Campbell's, "The Hall."

right on ringing until the teacher got nervous and dismissed school. The youngsters all rushed in haste into church and Mr. Heinrick was not even there, but Edwin was serenely pulling the bell rope.

Yesterday Papa hung a splendid swing in the cypress tree. It is heavy boat rope, new. Cousin Bob worked up so high we feared he would turn over the limb. Any one can swing in safety. Papa and I got in, but Papa says he prefers going in a boat to get seasick. He also hung two others. One of light trunk rope, safe only for the babies, and the other medium that Mona can use if the large one is occupied. I am so glad to have this amusement right in the yard.

It is years since I have read anything that was so true to life and beautifully natural as "Mother"...I shed the first tears over "Mother" than any book for ages has brought forth. Papa and I read it together and think it splendid. I wish all young girls and women might read it. Fortunately Papa has not some of the failings of "daddy" and unfortunately Mama falls short of "mother."

Be careful in the water, dearie. I have not learned yet whether you swim alone or not.

I am getting tired of the sun on my neck and am about ready to go home. I brought "Ivanhoe" down here to read but have not read much.

Much love from Mama

[Portland]
Wednesday, May 13

Dearest Mother,

...I am so glad that you enjoyed "Mother." I certainly did. You don't fall short of "Mother" at all. I think you are her superior because you haven't forgotten how to dress and to care about dress, and our table generally is better than theirs even though you don't have a maid...

[Donald, Oregon]
Sunday, May 17, 1914

Dear Mama and Papa:

I am out at Uncle Cecil's and RuthieD's, as you probably know if my card reached you.

On the train I didn't settle down and look out the window because I couldn't understand the conductor and every station we passed I stretched my neck to see the name on the depot. Also I strained my ears listening. Finally, in desperation, I asked the conductor who said we wouldn't be in Donald for an hour yet...

Uncle Cecil met me with the buggy. It was a beautiful drive out here. Everything smelt so sweet. Ruthie D. and baby Gussie were waiting for me at the gate. We had dinner right away. In the evening Uncle Cecil turned on the victrola for my edification. I think it a wonderful invention! Then Ruthie D. showed me her new house.

It is a lovely little place, perfectly plain but so fresh. There is the big bedroom and a bathroom; and a large closet with shelves clear to the roof on one side and a rod for hangers on the other with a shelf for hats at one end. The bathroom fixtures haven't arrived yet, but they are going to have a cesspool for the toilet with a gasoline pump for pumping of the water...

Mama, I think we had better plan on a blue suit for winter so that we can have the gray squirrel furs put on it as they would make a cheaper suit look expensive and would also be very becoming to me. Then I could have the plush coat cut into a large muff and get some fur to put on the edge to wear with a new long coat—if they wear them.

Papa, so far this month I have done very well in school. My English grades are 9, 10, 9. I haven't asked about the others but know they aren't very low. I didn't skip a single class all week and wasn't scolded for being late or anything else so have really been better than I have for a month.

Thursday the girls and I went to see "Tess O' the Storm Country" at the Peoples. It was very good—a five reel film with Mary Pickford starring. She is adorable. I wept through the whole performance but it can't be helped. That evening I played one game of tennis and was beaten flat, and then Mrs. Richardson took a bunch of us driving in her machine. Next week I am going to have the girls over at the house but I am sure I don't know what they'll do and what I will feed them. Sandwiches and chocolate I guess...

Lots of love, Medora

Tennis Attire for Girls

"Clothing, light of weight, should be worn, enabling one to move freely. There should be no restriction at the neck, and as little as possible at the waist. To further this, it is wise to substitute for the corset, some good corded waist, or a boned brassiere, the stockings to be supported from the waist or shoulders. The use of round garters is worse than foolish—it is often dangerous, leading to the formation of varicose veins. The sleeves should not extend below the elbows and the skirt should be wide enough to permit of a broad lunge and not longer than five inches from the ground. The best shoe is of soft canvas with a flexible, not too heavy, rubber sole. If there is a tendency toward fallen arches, a light-weight leather support should be worn inside the tennis shoe."—From Medora's copy of *Tennis for Girls* by Miriam Hall (A.M. Robertson Publishers, 1914).

[Oysterville]
Tuesday, May 19, 1914

Dear Little Girl:

Your delightful letter written at RuthieD's is just here, and I am glad you had such a pleasant trip.

I have been putting in elastics, making button holes, and hemming napkins today, besides getting a big baking done. My bread has been delicious lately. I make ten loaves twice a week.

I wish you had said what day the girls would be with you. I would love to send you some "eats" if you will let me know and send me ten cents worth of oil paper, such as they use to wrap sandwiches

Blue would be nice for your winter suit but not trimmed with my furs—I want them my own self. Fur will probably not be used anyway as it has had two winters run. You will need a long coat. They are always worn in winter. A woman's wardrobe is incomplete without a long wrap.

I am ever so glad you are playing tennis. Even if you never become more than a medium player it is nice to know how, and if you stay at it, you are bound to become lighter on your feet and more flexible in all your movements. There is nothing like it for grace except dancing. Whenever there is an opportunity to dance with the girls, try. This gives confidence and practice that no number of lessons possibly can. You have to blunder a little at first. Don't be self-conscious. It will cut you out of lots of fun. Papa says it would be nice for you to skate too, but I am afraid to see you on such an uncertain underpinning. How is the swimming progressing? I am getting anxious to hear that you can really swim.

Papa says keep up the good work in your lessons. Dearie, you have the best, most unselfish father in the world and it is worthwhile pleasing him. Let me know right away about cooking for you. How I wish I were with you so as to be able to do things of this kind for you.

Yours with ever abiding love, Mama

[Portland]
Wednesday, May 27, 1914

Dearest little Mother,

So tomorrow is your birthday. I hope you have a pleasant, happy day for I know you can't have an exciting one. May you see many, many more birthdays, Mama. I didn't know what

PORTLAND ACADEMY — Occasional Report

Report of Medora Espy

for 2 weeks, ending May 20 1914.

STUDIES	DAILY	TERM	REMARKS
English	70		
Chemistry	67		
History	95		
Cicero	74		
French	90		

Assistant Principal

J. R. Wilson, Principal

NOTE—This report is sent because the student is below grade in one or more subjects as shown above. We ask your cooperation in the improvement desired. 70% is the grade required for passing and college recommendation.

on earth to give you except perhaps a book as I know that you have everything for the table that I can afford, unless some crepe napkins. When I go downtown this afternoon I will send you something.

I am going over to Asenath's this week end. She made me promise to so as I might get the full benefit of their strawberries.

I meet strawberries every place I go and am taking full advantage of it for I do love them so. I suppose you poor folks haven't even seen any yet. I wish I could send you some. Apricots and cherries are on the market here, also string beans and peas, though they all are quite expensive…

Lovingly, Medora

[Oysterville]
Thursday, May 28, 1914

My dear Medora,

Well, the box was sent this morning and I hope it reaches you in good condition. You can pretend you are having my birthday party. Yes, this is my birthday—always a depressing date to me by contrast, I think, to the pleasant day it was so long as my mother lived. You are the only person who knows it is my natal day. It is of no importance anyway.

I must tell you of the day I put in yesterday. The day before I had fixed the nuts for the cookies, and had everything in readiness so there need be no confusion when I baked, but the Fates were against me. I was in the midst of the cookies (had the oven full) and was feeling all serene, when in came Papa saying he had to leave for South Bend in twenty minutes and the girls had better go with him to get their teeth fixed.

I was simply paralyzed for it seemed out of the question to get them ready, and, too, I was vexed. It seemed as though I might have had the possibility of the trip suggested sooner. Anyway, I yanked the pan off the nail and ducked Mona's head in before she knew she was standing still. She went off like a drowned rat but I suppose her hair dried before she reached Nahcotta. In twenty-five minutes both youngsters were on their way—clean to the skin, but maybe you think I wasn't a wreck, and the house couldn't have looked worse if someone had picked it up by the chimney and whirled it around their head. Of course, the cookies burned up and my bread rose mountains high. It was impossible to stop and get order out of chaos then, so I proceeded to bake. Things were going along as well as could be expected in my nerve-shaken state until I began frosting the cake. Dale came running in and made headlong for one of the chairs and in her rush leapt clear over the seat onto her head. It was an awful bump. I immediately deluged her with water, but was alarmed that her color did not return so put the smelling salts to her nose. In some unknown manner she threw her head back and spilled the ammonia in her mouth. Of course it burns and is poisonous. Well, on the table were the stiff beaten whites of eggs ready to put in the salad dressing, so I poured them down the poor baby and made her drink milk. Again, my cooking suffered but Dale recovered sufficiently to pour the vinegar off of the sweet pickles and over the eggs when I was stuffing them later. I certainly hope the food does not taste of trouble.

Devotedly, Mama

[Portland]
Saturday, May 30, 1914

My dearest little Mother:

Well, mother dear, your things were absolutely delicious, and the girls enjoyed them so much, each one wishing they had a lovely mother to send them things. Honestly, I never tasted anything so delicious as those deviled eggs. They were simply "scrumptious." You are certainly the sweetest mother a girl could wish for. I simply roared, it seemed so like a storybook when I read your letter, though I know you must have felt like swearing. Still I can see you laughing in spite of it all. Dear, darling little Dale. I wish I had her here to simply squeeze.

My Algebra teacher has smallpox, so I don't know how I will come out on the honor list. This is the last week, too. Oh, I love Portland Academy, Mother dear, just love it!

With lots of love and kisses
XXXXXetc. Medora

[Oysterville]
Saturday, May 30, 1914

Girlie,

It was sweet of you to send the book. I know I shall enjoy it. Papa began it at eleven o'clock last night and kept me disturbed until one o'clock chuckling. Thank you, dearie. A book is always such an acceptable gift to me...

Hastily, Mama

Smallpox

"Smallpox is one of the most contagious diseases known. It is extremely rare for anyone exposed to the disease to escape its onslaught unless previously protected by vaccination or by a former attack of the disease...In the absence of a physician, vaccination may be properly done by any intelligent person when the circumstances demand it...The special treatment of an attack of smallpox is largely a matter of careful nursing...The patient should be quarantined in an isolated building, and all unnecessary articles should be removed from the sick room, in the way of carpets and other furnishings...All clothing, dishes, etc, coming in contact with a patient must be boiled, or soaked in a two-per cent carbolic-acid solution for twenty-four hours, or burned. When the patient is entirely free from scabs, after bathing and putting on disinfected or new clothes outside of the sick room, he is fit to reenter the world."—From Mama's copy of the *Home Medical Library*, Vol. I (Review of Reviews Company, ca. 1907).

A Life of Their Own

Over the years, there were few references made by Mama and Papa to the burdensome conditions inherent in living just a few hundred yards from the formidable Espy paterfamilias. As the days sped by and the expected "year or two" in Oysterville blurred into permanence, Grandpa's growing eccentricities were an accepted part of daily life.

If Mama and Papa spoke of their disrupted plans and shelved dreams, it certainly was never in front of the children. And if either of them resented the demands made upon them by R.H., they kept those thoughts to themselves. Mostly.

[Oysterville]
Monday, June 1, 1914

Dear Medora,

Sue went for a walk with Tena and returned with a severe pain in her right side, in the same position as it had been on the left. Only this time she had a temperature and her pulse was up. I was much alarmed as it all spelled appendicitis. I think yet she had a mild attack. She stayed in bed all day yesterday, and her temperature was normal.

Last night Papa said there was a possibility of his going to Portland on business this morning so I hoped he would go and take Sue. This morning I gathered everything together to pack if he did go. So a little later when he said "get ready" I dressed Sue and packed her grip, really glad she would go and be examined. She was all ready, coat etc. when Papa came (he had the buggy out and the horse ready) and said they wouldn't go because "Father was not agreeable to it." It provoked me terribly as I get so tired of having Papa live according to Grandpa's whims. We have a life of our own...

Lovingly, Mother

[Oysterville]
Tuesday, June 2, 1914

My Dear Medora:

This surely has been a bemuddled day.

Sue killed a rat tonight and Willard has been after me ever since to "cook it." I have explained in every possible way that rats were not meant for human consumption, but at all my talk of their being dirty he says "well wash 'im clean, den."

I helped the girls carry a couch down to the playhouse. That is I helped them as far as in front of Wachsmuth's barn, where I came within an ace of stepping on a snake. For all I know the couch is where I dropped it. I have had delirium tremens ever since.

Have all the pupils been exposed to small pox? How near were you to the poor plague stricken professor? Portland Academy seems to have kind of a fondness for small pox. If you should get such a thing, have your hands tied or your head in a cast! I don't want your pretty face to be transformed into the likeness of a colander or sieve!

"Peg O' My Heart" is fine. It did not take me long to read it. Did you read "Pollyanna?" It is one of the sweetest child's stories I have read in years. Sue has nearly finished it.

Lovingly, Mama

[Portland]
Diary, Wednesday, June 3 1914

No one can imagine how surprised I was this morning when Papa arrived with Sue. I took her to Algebra. Then Rosetta took charge of her. I stayed home this afternoon and washed Sue's hair. Then Rosetta and I took her to the doctor's. From there we went to Ruth's. Poor Sue was very carsick. Ruth is going to Oysterville for a few weeks and I am so glad for Mama's sake.

Priorities

No matter how poverty-stricken the family might feel, Papa was uncompromising in two major areas of expenditure—eating fully, and taking advantage of any cultural or educational opportunities that might be available. During the winter of 1907–1908, when Mama, Medora, and Ruth were in Los Angeles, he wrote to Mama:

...The statement you made in letter of Sunday...just received tonight that you do not eat fruit because you can get along without it altho'

Papa's rolltop desk.

you want it, for the reason that it costs money. What is money for? You better spend it on something to eat than save it for your funeral which will surely be not long delayed if you starve yourself. A person can get along without many things and do well and be healthy, but they can not do well with out food. Get it, plenty of it—lots of it—all you want of it—and enjoy it, without thinking of the cost but just thinking of how good it is. Remember this will be economy in more ways than one, for if you stuff yourself on good fruit there where it is cheap you will probably not want much poor stuff when you get here where it is dear...

Later that winter he admonished Mama again:

Don't skimp yourself, particularly in eating and sight-seeing. The latter you want to be sure of because you will always be sorry to have been all winter right alongside the famous "shrines" and "beauty-spots" around Los Angeles & not to have seen them. Go to the beaches and different resorts of gayety. Write me how much clothes they wear in bathing there & if my overalls would be "just the thing" when I come down to bathe—in the dim future... Do not let cost stop you from having what will do you most good, either eating, going, or wearing...

[Oysterville]
Thursday, June 11, 1914

Dearest little Sister,

It is a joy to hear you will be home even three days sooner than we expected. We will send check so you can leave the sixteenth.

Be sure to bring all of our things, books and pictures especially.

I will enclose a list of things for you to get. Try to charge all at M & F's[3]*...*

Ruth is helping me greatly and it is lovely having her with us again.

Papa says if there are any school "doings" after the 16th, you had better stay and see it through. He wants you to see all you can...

Love, Mother

Please ask Mrs. Strowbridge to allow Dorothy to come down on July 1st as you know how much Harry and I want her. I would write to Mrs. Strowbridge only I haven't time. Please ask her and beg her to tell Dorothy to come because Sue and you and I are all so fond of her.

Notes

1. McMinnville, Oregon, located not far southwest of Portland, and today the site of Linfield College, which traces its roots to an institution established by the Baptists in 1849.
2. St. Helen's Hall was combined in the 1970s with another school and today they are the Oregon Episcopal School. The name St. Helen's Hall is no more.
3. Meier & Frank's—a well-respected department store in Portland.

Medora's diaries, begun in January 1914.

We all slept under the stars...

Oysterville, Summer 1914

The summer months in Oysterville always were busy. For the Espys, as for other full-time residents, numerous fair weather chores had to be completed—roofs to re-shingle, wood supplies to replenish, haying to be done, fruit to put up, and many other preparations to be made for the cold, stormy months ahead. And, of course, there were the visitors.

Throughout each summer a parade of relatives arrived, many from Portland and from other points east and south, as well. Friends and acquaintances also chose the summer months to visit, perhaps even arranging to stay for a while. Summer was, after all, a time for getting together and it seemed to make sense to gather at the beach. Oysterville families managed to be gracious hosts, with impromptu picnics and outings, even as they worked hard at completing summer chores. Children were pressed into service, weeding beet rows and stacking firewood, but there always was time for a bonfire at the bay or an excursion up one of the nearby rivers.

Now that Medora was attending the academy, her circle of friends had widened—a surprising number of her classmates had connections to communities on the beach, especially to nearby Ocean Park. Summer in Oysterville took on a whole new dimension for Medora, and, without the necessity of writing to Mama every day or so, she turned to her diary to record her summer adventures and thoughtful observations.

In 1914, from left to right, Sue, Mona, Edwin, Willard, and Dale on "Danny," with Medora petting "Jack."

Diary, Wednesday, June 17, 1914

I was so glad to get home. Unpacked my trunk, a big job done. Ruth and Mama put up the curtains in the dining room. Ruth and I slept together. I share my room with her while she is here.

The Sewing Bee, ca. 1914. Back row: Ruth, Mama, and Aunt Minette, second, third, and fourth from left. Middle row: Aunt Kate in center.

The Troubadour, a quarterly publication of the Portland Academy, served as a literary magazine, news periodical, and class yearbook. The June 1914 issue included a "Class Poem" by Medora's friend, Dorothy Collins. Among the senior portraits were several students whose families had connections to the North Beach Peninsula.

The Sewing Circle

Oysterville's women, calling themselves "The Sewing Circle" or sometimes "The Sewing Bee," met on an irregular basis in one another's homes, mending, darning, or working on other needs of the hosting household. Female visitors coming to the village were included at the get-togethers, and each session concluded with refreshments provided by the hostess.

In the mid-1920s, they organized themselves more formally by founding the Oysterville Women's Club and electing Mrs. Stoner as the first president. They continued to meet weekly or bi-weekly, and, while they spent some time at each meeting on sewing projects, their endeavors by then included fund-raising for school equipment and acting as guardians of community needs.

By the early 1940s, the group called themselves "The Oysterville Improvement Club" and devoted a major part of their attention to the home front effort during World War II. They volunteered as airplane observers; collected and sold scrap metal and fat, giving the profits to the Red Cross; knitted afghans, lap robes, and sweaters for "soldier kits"; and took Red Cross First Aid classes. Meanwhile, they continued raising money for school and town projects by holding rummage sales, dances at the Community Hall, and public dinners where they raffled off quilts and other handmade items donated by members.

Mama maintained an active membership in the group, even in her later years. She undoubtedly would be pleased to know that "The Sewing Circle" continues to meet today under the name, "The Oysterville Community Club." She might be amazed that the group now includes men and that her grandson-in-law has even served as president.

Diary, Thursday, June 18, 1914

We flew around all morning... The sewing bee met here in the afternoon. It consisted of Mrs. Heinrick, Mrs. Stoner, Mrs. Davis, Mrs. Wirt, Mrs. Myra Fisher, Miss Ethel Irving, Ruth H., Mama and I. Dale went to sleep behind the door, Willard behind Mama's back in her chair. I slept with Sue tonight. Mrs. D. slept with Ruth.

Diary, Monday, June 22, 1914

This morning I intended to clean the upstairs as a whole, but just as I got a basin of water and Bon Ami and started upstairs Papa announced that we might expect the Priors. The children reported their progress up the street. We sat and talked, showed the Troubadour *and my album to Willie and Marion. Ruth played for them by request. Then we played whist, Willie and I winning. They stayed to lunch...*

Diary, Wednesday, June 24, 1914

Today Mama and I cleaned the library—worked hard, consequently finished it by dinner. Papa and I shook the rug. We had lots of fun joking. He is certainly the darlingest Daddy... Ruth sewed again all day but helped us hang the pictures in the library. Mama found a silver spoon in back of the books.

Diary, Thursday, June 25, 1914

Today I did the kitchen work, then washed about a three weeks accumulation of my clothes. It took me a good while on account of the inconveniences of carrying water...

Diary, Friday, June 26, 1914

This morning Ruth, Mama and I cleaned the pantry (kitchen) paint. Then Papa painted the ceiling immediately upon returning from Grandpa's. We three continued to paint the walls etc., but I seemed to get the most in my hair and on the floor... Bob and Papa hoed Buell's garden in between the two coats on the ceiling.

Diary, Sunday, June 28, 1914

After Sunday School I came leaping into the living room. I was certainly startled to see Rees Williams calmly sitting there... I related the doings of the A.M. at S.S. Then we discussed machines. Rees took Ruth and I and the three babies to Ocean Park in his Ford. I had a dandy time but was jolted to pieces.

Summer Fun

After the dark, rainy months, Oysterville's residents reveled in the long, warm days of summer. Families fortunate enough to have sleeping porches moved bed and bedding outdoors for the season, tables and chairs were taken out into yards, and impromptu bonfires and crab bakes were held down at the bay. Youngsters spent hours picking blackberries and gathering mud clams—activities so pleasant, and providing such tasty morsels, that they weren't looked upon as chores at all.

A designated picnic ground west of town near Skating Lake was indicative of the importance the villagers placed on outdoor entertainment. Here, the community gathered for speech-making, races and contests, and lunch basket socials. Get-togethers were held throughout the summer when the weather cooperated, and always—rain or shine—on "Celebration Day," the Fourth of July.

Diary, Saturday, July 4, 1914

This morning we all got up early. After the children were ready I started in on the kitchen. When two thirds of the way through Papa announced that we must hurry, so about eleven we started for the picnic grounds. Everybody was there from all around. After the program (Papa orated) I served lemonade. I was very genial to all especially to the youngsters (funny thing to say). When the races began we left. I rushed home, then to Nahcotta for Dorothy. Polly was very slow, consequently I arrived late... After dinner we went to the bonfire at the bay but only stayed a short time. Came home and talked with Ruth and let Mama and Papa go.

Camping on the Nemah River

Medora's *Camp Cookery* booklet (1902) described how to build a "practical" camp fire, dress a deer, bake fish without an oven, and perform other outdoor skills. Also included were recipes and helpful hints for cooking clams (in chowder, stew, fritters, and roasted), fish (fried, boiled, planked, skewered, salted, and scorched), soup (mock terrapin, bean, pea, vegetable, and Scotch broth), and that old standby, pork and beans.

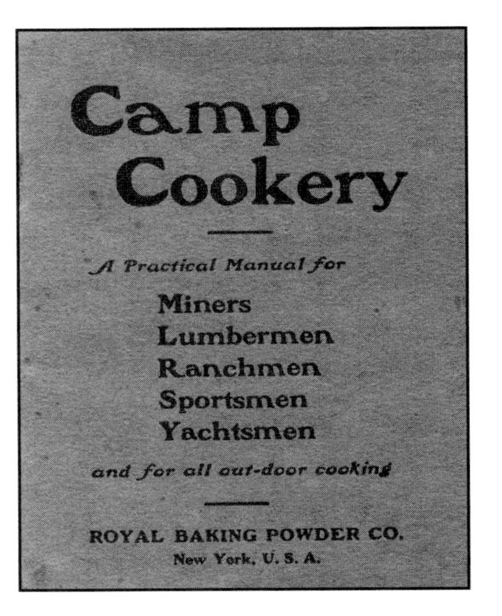

Fourth of July parade in Oysterville.

Fourth of July Picnic Schedule, 1914

10 A.M.—Parade
11 A.M.—Speaking
12 Noon—Lunch
After lunch—Singing and Music
2 P.M.—Races

- Horse Race (1st Prize, $2.00; 2nd Prize, $1.00)
- Foot Race for boys under 10 (1st Prize, 50 cents; 2nd Prize, 25 cents)
- Peanut Race for boys and girls under 8 (50 cents)
- Running Broad Jump for boys under 15 (50 cents)
- Foot Race for girls under 14 (1st Prize, 50 cents; 2nd Prize, 25 cents)
- Sack Race for boys and girls under 16 (1st Prize, 50 cents; 2nd Prize, 25 cents)
- Foot Race for ladies of all ages (1st Prize, 50 cents; 2nd Prize, 25 cents)
- Fat Woman's Race (1st Prize, 50 cents; 2nd Prize, 25 cents)
- Potato Race for boys under 16 (50 cents)
- Foot Race for men (1st Prize, 50 cents; 2nd Prize, 25 cents)
- Hop, Step and Jump for men (50 cents)
- Egg Race for young ladies under 21 (1st Prize, 50 cents; 2nd Prize, 25 cents)

8:30 P.M. FIRE WORKS ON THE WATER FRONT

Diary Tuesday, July 7, 1914

This morning we had to rush terribly to get our camping outfit on the stage. Bob fixed the camera. It had had lots of sand in it. Papa took us to Nahcotta in the lumber wagon drawn by the colts (Emp and Queenie). The bumps were awful. We fooled around Moreheads' till about one. Holland Houston came down from the Park with Ruth C. and Marge. The ride over to the Nemah in the launch Edna was wonderful. Dote and I sat up in front, rather lied. Ruth Hag. was our chaperone. Upon arriving at Prior's landing was much surprised to find the whole family there except Ethel who is a week old bride. Priors helped us pitch camp. Adam was down to dinner. Had a bonfire. Slept on the ground in the tent. Rather uncomfortable. Gene W. is attractive.

Diary, Wednesday, July 8, 1914

Gnats woke us up early. Had fish for breakfast. Ruth C. and I spent the A.M. gathering hay for tonight's beds. After lunch Marge and I went fishing with Willie. He looks as if he would blow away. We went through miles of underbrush. I caught the largest fish. Marge nearly broke her arm falling under a log. Her arm hurt all afternoon. I fell in the river; got sopping wet but enjoyed myself... We all slept under the stars. Very comfy.

Campsite at the Nemah River.

Back Home in Oysterville

Diary, Friday, July 12, 1914

Immediately after breakfast Mona, Willard, Edwin and I went for wild blackberries. Between us we only got a half bucket. Willard and Edwin took the wheelbarrow home. They did look so cute trudging through the sand wheeling the barrow. After lunch I read "A Fighting Chance," then helped Mama pick some berries. I made

Postcard photo of the Nemah River.

three black berry pies which turned out pretty good. My first ones too. After dinner Bob was in. He got to joking and fell back in his chair. That sure did make him laugh. Spent so much of the evening talking to Cousin Bob that we had to leave the dishes. Sue played croquet. One of the little chickens we have been nursing died. I have been home a month.

Diary, Saturday, July 18, 1914

About eleven we (Mama and I) took the children to the bay for their Saturday bath. The tide was too far out so we brought them back and put them in the tub...I read almost all afternoon. I have been quite lazy the last few days. Idle days always make me irritable.

Diary, Monday, July 20, 1914

After lunch I tried to find something interesting to do, but didn't succeed. Read while Mama bathed and prepared for her trip. About four o'clock Dorothy Connell and Marguerite Dillon dropped in. Mother served tea. After that we had to rush. I washed Willard's head and helped Mama finish packing.

The *Reliable.*

The Family Horses

The Espy children rode from the time they could manage to sit astride a horse, their short little legs akimbo on the gentlest (and seemingly largest) of the family's many horses. By the age of 10, each child had a horse of his or her own. In addition, there were horses to pull the farm wagons and a team for Mama's buggy. Many did "double duty" as both riding and work horses, but Papa's "Nick," the friskiest of the lot, was "off limits" to the children and usually the only mount that ever was saddled. The children rode bareback; Papa thought saddles were dangerous.

A favorite family story concerning a riding "incident" involved Edwin, who, at about age 10, had ducked down as his horse went under a tree but caught his overall straps on a branch. The horse continued on, while Edwin "hung" back, quite literally, until his cries for help were heard by a passing neighbor.

Later, when Dale was in eighth grade in the 1920s, Mama and Papa decided that she should attend the Nahcotta School. "They must have thought that I would have trouble passing that eighth grade exam," my mother said in later years. "They felt that Mrs. Brooks was the best teacher in the county. She had been my teacher in the primary years, but by the time I was in eighth grade she was teaching at the Nahcotta School. I rode the four miles on horseback every morning that it wasn't too stormy. At school, I'd take off the bridle, give the horse a slap so he'd go home and then, in the afternoon, I'd catch a ride back to Oysterville on Mr. Lehman's mail wagon. On rainy days, I'd have to leave an hour earlier to go with Willard and Ed in the Model T, which they drove to get to high school in Ilwaco. [There was no school bus in those days.] I'd spend that extra hour with our friend Deane Nelson who worked at the store in Nahcotta."

When Papa needed to visit South Bend on business, which occurred frequently, the entire family became involved. The smaller children were posted up in the attic, where Papa had fashioned a "crow's nest" with a window providing a good view of the bay. The watchers waited until a little steamer, either the *Shamrock* or *Reliable,* reached a certain point in its voyage from South Bend to Nahcotta. At that crucial spot, the children called down to Papa—generally trimming his whiskers—and he would dash to the door where Mama held his cup of coffee at the ready. Outside, one of the older children already had Nick saddled and bridled by the gate. On Papa would leap and, with coffee cup in one hand and reins in the other, he'd head out for Nahcotta.

A 2006 view of the east side of the H.A. Espy house. Long ago, the original front door visible here had become the barely used "east door."

The timing was impeccable. By the time the bridle and coffee cup were tied to the saddle and Nick headed homeward, deckhands were slipping the hawsers off the stanchions at the dock and Papa was jumping aboard. Papa was never late, nor was he ever early—a fact remarked upon frequently by those who knew him.

Diary, Wednesday, July 22, 1914

...did the kitchen work, swept the living room and library. Also wrote Mother a letter. I had everything done by noon. Then I dressed Edwin and Dale to go with me to the Picnic at Giles Grove...I drove Coaly up. Connells and McMasters from Ocean Park and Allens from Seaview were all there. I got there too late for the bathing. We had a most delicious lunch with fruit which tickled me for we can't get any here in Oysterville. We five girls and two boys spent the afternoon target shooting. Left about four. I had one rip-roaring time with Coaly. He wanted to start home. Then he refused to go. I never saw any animal so stubborn. When I finally arrived home, discovered that Sue was feeding the town at a supposed sewing bee.

Front and Back Doors

The H.A. Espy house, like most Oysterville homes, had been built facing east toward the bay, though several hundred yards separated the front door from the high tide line. Originally, there had been north-south streets running between the house and the bay, but by the time the young Espy family arrived in 1902, these streets were fading into obscurity. In fact, the only remaining north-south village thoroughfare was Fourth Street, situated on the west side, or behind, the Espy property. People calling on the Espys, however, still

The H.A. Espy house in Medora's time.

came to the front door on the east side of the house. To get to it, they had to approach from east-west running Clay Street on the south of the house, and walk through an orchard.

On the other hand, family members and close neighbors—such as Tena Wachsmuth and Mrs. Wirt—often used a south side-door, situated closer to Fourth Street. It was easier to get to and a covered porch provided protection from the elements while waiting for a knock to be answered—though not many actually knocked. A person familiar enough to use the south door generally just walked in—a common village custom that Mama never really got used to. By the time the youngest children started school, this more convenient south door would become the "front door," and the original front door, "the east door," which afterwards was not often used. And so it is to this day.

There were other outside entrances—a west door behind a large roller door leading into the woodshed, and a back door on the north side of the house leading from the living room to a little kitchen garden. This back door was seldom used. However, Papa frequently used the west doors—a wagon load of wood could be pulled right up for easy off-loading into the woodshed, and it was but a step or two through the woodshed into the kitchen pantry for depositing groceries. The west door also was most convenient when entering the house with dripping slickers and sou'westers to be shed.

[Oysterville]
Friday, July 24, 1914

Dearest Mama:

Was rather disappointed not to hear from you today, but know you are very busy in Portland. I am in the kitchen writing this while drying my feet. I got them wet while carrying water to the cows. The children are at a crab bake down at the bay and Papa is getting in a wild cow.

This morning we had a late start but it didn't seem to matter very much. I scrubbed the kitchen floor and washed the pantry and milkroom shelves extra. After lunch I went up to Mary Sam's and sewed up those two aprons and made some doll clothes for Sue and Mona. Came back at 2:45 and was glad to get home. She makes me sick. I get so tired of having her complain about Edwin doing this or that to Vernon. Sewed then till four when I prepared a lunch for Papa. Then got dinner. Since dinner I have carried water, talked to Mrs. H., chased cows, put the babies to bed and set bread. I followed the directions minutely, even to stirring ten minutes. I hope it turns out well.

Luella H. awakened us yesterday A.M. by pounding on the south door with a stick. I would like to stick her!

Everything has gone very nicely here so far. Sometimes I get very put out with the girls and intend to remember the incident but always forget by night which shows how trivial it is. My blackberry pies were pretty good. Sue was sent to pick some more today, but didn't come home with enough to make a turn over. The oven isn't baking very well. I cleaned it out well today so that I can bake bread tomorrow. The children brought home three crabs. I wish you were here to help us eat them. We have no oil and I haven't a recipe so guess I can't make any mayonnaise. Papa isn't going to finish mowing this week as planned. He has had these two fresh cows to attend to, and there is always something extra. Last night it was Judge Steven's horse.

Dale is very good, sleeps well, but the first two mornings she called me "Mama" and then was startled to find it me. She doesn't cry for you nor run away, so I consider her very good. She is just as cunning as ever.

You have only been gone a few days, Mama, and it seems months. Don't overdo and get all tired out. Everything is getting along fine and you aren't needed at home so stay longer if necessary.

Lots of love, Medora

The No. 3 Ansco

Earlier, in April 1913, several letters had been exchanged between Medora and Papa on the subject of Mama's birthday. Toward the end of that month, Papa wrote: "Enclosed you will find c'k of $10.00 which you may use to get something for mamma as a present from you and me together...If you can get a good kodak with that am't I believe it will please her more than anything else."

The camera Medora chose, costing $7, was a No. 3 Ansco box camera—5¼ x 6 x 7¼ inches in size, weighing 33½ ounces, and covered with "genuine seal grain leather." It had a fixed lens, a shutter for fixed and instantaneous exposures, and a diaphragm with three different sized openings. "Six Exposure 4 x 5 Film" cost 45 cents.

According to the accompanying manual, "the chief advantage and benefit of the Ansco camera is as a means of education and a source of enjoyment for old and young alike." This certainly proved true for the H.A. Espy household. Despite the brand name, the Espys referred to it, and any other camera, as a "Kodak."

[Portland]
Friday, July 24, 1914

My dear Medora,

Your two postals came yesterday and were welcome. Willard was delighted to hear but much concerned that he had not gone in bathing "too."

I am sending a box of the photo supplies. It is complete. Don't overlook the small box that has the finder in it for the Kodak. Please don't use all the large film as I want to take some especial pictures when I get home.

Give Dale the doll and tell her Mama sent it. Bless her dear curly head. I wish I was home. The handkerchiefs are all defective but maybe the children will not notice it. I will try to bring them each a token.

Yesterday a letter came from RuthieD urging me to visit them but I have not decided as I hate to spend the money. My glasses have cost me more than I expected so I want to shave off elsewhere.

I have new rubber stockings on and they feel fine. They asked me to wear them a couple of days and then be sure to bring them back in case of any defect or discomfort. These hot days are a strenuous test.

Tomorrow we hope to get Willard's picture taken. Ruth is making him a dress. I tried to buy him one but was staggered at the prices so got sixty cents worth of material and he will have a cunning romper I hope. It is white poplin—no starching required. While I remember, don't let Dale get hold of these poisonous photo chemicals.

Must help Ruth. Let Papa see this. I am due at the doctor's soon.

Lovingly, Mother

Diary, Sunday, July 26, 1914

We had all the work finished and the children ready by ten. The whole family went to S.S. It does seem so lonesome without Mama and Willard. About nine Cousin Bob came up and we developed two rolls of films. Had loads of fun laughing at our mistakes, one of which was attempting to develop the protective brown paper. Naturally anyone is able to conclude that it is our first experience, just as my trip to the Nemah was my first camping trip. Everything seems to be a "first" this summer, but anyway I will have learned lots.

Diary, Friday, July 31, 1914

After the mail came in I scrubbed the kitchen floor, cleaned the children and myself, then hitched Polly to the buggy. Arrived at Nahcotta

No. 3 Ansco

just in time but something was wrong with the train so didn't see Mama for a half hour. Willard looked darling, so stylish but pale. We were all very glad to see Mama and Willard. Of course Mother's stay in Portland was full every minute with dentist, doctor and visits to the relatives. She reports all well. Uncle Sid has a boy. Papa was in for dinner. I didn't go to bed till about ten as I was too busy reading. The children were all restless and noisy during the evening. Mama brought the girls Kewpie dolls, Edwin a canoe, Papa two shirts and me a book and green hose, etc.

Papa giving Medora and her friends a ride in the hay wagon at Ocean Park, 1914.

Farm Chores

Like farm children everywhere, the Espy youngsters were expected to help with chores, especially in summer when school was out. Even the smallest children stacked wood, pumped water, gathered eggs, chased stray cows, and weeded the garden.

Only the Espy boys, however, were required to milk. Mama felt that milking a cow caused enlarged knuckles and persuaded Papa that the girls shouldn't jeopardize their hands. If Papa didn't have a young boy working for him, he did the milking himself, until Edwin and Willard were old enough to do so. The girls, however, did belly under the barn looking for eggs—for this chore, Mama wrapped their long hair up in large dishtowels.

The least favorite job, even though it was the chore for which they were paid, was weeding the rows and rows of beets that grew in the lot next to the church. The beets were grown for the cattle, and the children were paid a penny a row for weeding. The rows were long—perhaps a hundred feet—and it might take most of a day to weed just one row to Papa's satisfaction. None enjoyed this chore, and their attempts to inveigle their friends to take over, à la Tom Sawyer, never had very positive results.

Pumping water, though harder work, was more to their liking. They took turns at the pump near the cattle trough down at the big barn, and also at the pump in the south garden. The latter was only an occasional chore, since on most days there was enough wind for the windmill pump to fill the rain barrels located on the house roof.

The children most enjoyed tramping hay. This involved riding on the hay wagon from the "big meadow"—where the hay was mowed—to the barn across from the ranch house, always with a full contingent of youngsters from the community. As Papa and his ranch hands pitched hay into the loft, the children commenced "tramping" to make room for the next load. It was a scratchy, dusty job, but done with gusto and lots of neighborly exuberance.

Occasionally, the boys would find a snake in the hay and, if Papa didn't notice, would harass the girls with it. Woe be unto those who Papa caught, however. He didn't cotton to tormenting either snakes or girls, and the culprit would be banished from tramping Espy hay for the remainder of the season.

Diary, Monday, August 3, 1914

We didn't wash this morning as Papa wanted to have us tramp hay. I did my kitchen work, then read a while. We put in five loads of hay. Marvin Bowen helped Sue and I tramp. The children (Ed, Willard and Mona) were just a nuisance. The whole Gilbert tribe came to help the last load. In between loads I read and wrote letters. After dinner I cleaned up and took my first German lesson. Mrs. Heinrick is a very good teacher I think.

Summer People

Since the earliest settlement of the inland valleys of Oregon and Washington, the cool breezes of the coast have been a sought-after respite from the summer heat of the interior. For years, the Columbia River provided the only transportation route to "the beach" for these inlanders. When vacationers arrived in Astoria, near the river's mouth, they either went south to the Oregon coastal beaches or north to the peninsula. Accordingly, the sandy shore in Washington was called "North Beach," and the name North Beach Peninsula became its official designation by the U.S. Board on Geographic Names.

With the completion of the Ilwaco Railroad in 1889, ready access to vacation properties along the 28 miles of beach gave the North Beach Peninsula an edge over the more isolated Oregon beaches. Tent cities blossomed along the railroad's route, and canny businessmen bought up wilderness acreage with an eye for future development. Summer residences and tourist resorts sprang up, and the peninsula became a popular destination, especially for Portland families. A number of Medora's Portland Academy friends were among those families that had summer "cottages"[1] in Seaview or Ocean Park, and Medora was now old enough to go off visiting on her own.

Diary, Thursday, August 6, 1914

...Everybody seems quite excited over the war. They predict the end of the world. I walked in my sleep. Mildred and Dottie Mac came over to invite us to their home for the evening. Foster McGuire dropped in about eight and talked war with me. Ruth and I arrived at Mac's about nine. Harry Clair, Donald Roberts, Lewis Koover, Ruth, Dottie, Mildred, Helen Dunne, Helen Hazeltine and I were there. We played Hearts and Animal—I was "Bowwow." They had the best fudge and Divinity. Harry Clair walked home with me.

Diary, Saturday, August 8, 1914

...German is coming along pretty well, though I just discovered that I don't need my credit as I thought and am disgusted that Papa is going to that expense.

Diary, Tuesday, August 11, 1914

Cousin Bob and Papa are working on the street for the county. I don't consider it a disgrace either because Papa needs the money. Am considering, rather studying, whether or not I had better put up a sign "Ponies and horses to rent Inquire within." I rented Coaly to Kistemaker today.

[Observations and Thoughts, August 1914]

No, Dorothy and I haven't quarreled, but I realize at last that she is not immoral but unmoral. I have half worshipped her all year but now, well, now I just don't. I still love her, but she is no longer my ideal. I want to be good—no strong, for I know we are in the world for some purpose. Why not make the best of my opportunities. Each individual counts; even I count. I am looking forward to a home and children. Therefore I must educate myself to the best of my ability. My education will be valuable to my posterity. A girl is not useless; I am glad I am a woman.

Dale, Edwin, and Willard, August 1914.

"The Great War"

In the summer of 1914, World War I broke out between the major European powers. The United States, however, would not enter the conflict until April 1917. An Armistice ended hostilities on November 11, 1918.

I don't want to be married till I am twenty-five but oh! I will certainly adopt two youngsters if I am an old maid. These poor little motherless tots and then hundreds of old maids worrying and fussing because they have been cheated out of so much. Absurd! I don't want to become famous, but I want to help my children to become honorable and useful citizens. So as they will inherit my traits, anything I don't want my posterity to think, do, or say, I must overcome first. It is wonderful that I have it in me to help the world, to make it a little better. If I had continued to do everything with what will Dorothy say always in mind, I should have become worldly. This next year I am planning to study. Mother and Father will be so pleased if I really work hard. I shall not give up all social duties, but some. I want to attend church regularly, for though I believe in being broad-minded, we must serve our God faithfully on the day that He put aside for that purpose. I think Holland Houston, Ruth Connell and Mama are the ones who are stimulating my present views…

Diary, Sunday, August 16, 1914

…Went over to Ruth C's for the night…Everybody is going to play tennis tomorrow except me. Darn it!

Diary, Monday, August 17, 1914

We all got up about seven on account of tennis. I felt blue and knew that I would feel worse if I watched them play so hitched up Danny and came home. I had a hard time to fight back the tears on my way home, but finally got myself under control. I am sure a fool over nothing. Jealousy is my worst trait or at least gives me the most trouble. After I got home I talked to Mother. I think I will have a house party on the 28th…Slept from two till four thirty. After sleeping I didn't feel nearly so blue. Then Mother and I talked about my German. Decided to drop it. So went down and broke the news to Mrs. Heinrick boldly. I am sort of sorry, still tickled to death.

Water, Water Everywhere…

From the time that the family moved to Oysterville, Papa saw to it that Mama had running water. It was only cold water, to be sure, and ran just to the kitchen sink and the upstairs bathtub, but this was far better than hauling water, bucket by bucket, from the pump in the south garden.[2]

Water was carried by pipe from five large barrels that Papa had affixed to the house roof. In Oysterville's wet and windy climate, the barrels were effortlessly filled eight or nine months out of the year. Papa had rigged up a connection to the south garden pump and windmill, and what the rain didn't supply, the well did. On occasional windless days in summer, however, the children took turns pumping—"one hundred strokes and then it's your turn!"

Hot water for daily needs came from a ten-gallon reservoir that was part of Mama's cast-iron, wood-fired, cook stove. She kept the reservoir filled by adding a kettle full now and then, and, as long as the fire was stoked, Mama had a constant source of hot water.

Bathing

Daily bathing involved, mostly, the washing of hands, face, and feet, using cold water poured from a bedside pitcher into its matching basin. Mama insisted on feet being clean before bedtime to save the sheets. On chilly mornings, faces were washed in the kitchen, where a ladle of hot water could be added to the cold.

On bath night, a wood stove in the bedroom adjacent to the upstairs "bathroom" heated up water. The "bathroom" was exactly that—a small, narrow room containing a large, claw-foot tub, a wash stand with basin and pitcher, and a small chest of drawers for storing towels and wash cloths.[3] Mama added hot water by the teakettle-full to the cold water running from the tub's tap. Several inches of tub water usually sufficed, and often the little children bathed together. In the summer, "bathing" was done in the bay. The sun-drenched seawater coming in on the tide flats often was as warm, if not warmer, than the bathwater at home.

Wash Day

Washing clothes for a large household of eight in the days before electrical appliances, color fast dyes, and quick drying fabrics was quite an undertaking. On washday, a 20-gallon copper boiler was placed on the kitchen stove and the water heated to the boiling point. Three large galvanized tubs also were put into service—two were filled by combining equal amounts of cold tap water and hot water from the stove's reservoir, and one was filled with just cold water.

Laundry was sorted by color and according to how soiled it was. Lightly soiled clothes were washed in warm soapy water in one of the galvanized tubs. The most heavily soiled clothing, however, was first soaked (perhaps overnight) and then placed with soap in the copper boiler and actually boiled on the stove. Dry clothing never was put directly into the boiler as hot water would set the stains. The hot, wet clothes were transferred from boiler to rinse water by lifting them with a broom handle.

Clothes were given two warm water rinses and a final cold water rinse, to which bluing was added for the white items to prevent yellowing. For selected garments, starch (prepared ahead of time) was added to a second rinse in water.

Colored clothes were sorted into light, medium, and dark, and washed in this sequence, since the natural dyes tended to fade and run. The colored socks and Papa's outdoor pants and overalls were washed last. The most delicate items, including lingerie and special linens with needlework, were set aside to be separately hand washed.

Mama had several clotheslines, all near the kitchen. Lines just outside the kitchen window were used whenever the weather permitted; those in the woodshed, when it was raining. If it was necessary for Mama to wash the lace tablecloths herself, rather than sending them out, she often waited to do them on a fine day, and spread them out on the lawn to dry in the sun.[4]

The Espy house in ca. 1925, showing Papa's five rain barrels on the roof and the windmill tower in the south garden. The view is looking northeast from Fourth Street. The south door under the porch (at center right) had become the "front door." An interior west door was accessed through the large roller door (at left) facing Fourth Street.

[Oysterville]
Monday, August 19, 1914

Dearest Mama,

Everything O.K. here. Papa returned last night alright. I washed the white clothes yesterday but have too much cleaning to do today to wash the colored. I don't know where on earth the huge washing appeared from. Two boilers full boiled.

I wrote letters yesterday afternoon while resting. The Fisher girls were here for dinner last night.

I hope everything is alright with you.

The children are good. I am cleaning and baking today for the girls tomorrow. It is sort of cloudy today. No news. There was a political meeting at Winslow's store last night. Democratic.

Cousin Bob wants you to please get him four pairs black cotton socks not to exceed 20c each. If they haven't any black for 20c get brown but he prefers black. The best for 20c.

Lots of love, Medora

Diary, Saturday, August 22, 1914

I certainly am sleeping lately. I had twelve hours sleep last night. Three weeks from today I start back and then it will be school again. I am anxious in a way.

Beach Driving and Approaches

Driving on the ocean beach frequently had the advantage over taking the rather poor roads on the peninsula, as the hard beach was "resurfaced" with a smooth layer of sand with every incoming tide. For that reason, the beach usually was the preferred route between Oysterville and "The Park," as Ocean Park was called.[5]

However, gaining access to or from the beach through soft sands at the upper tide line was another matter entirely. A number of public "approaches" gave vehicles access to the beach. Though these roadways were sometimes planked, sometimes graveled, they often were clogged with drifting sands and always unreliable.

Diary, Friday, August 28, 1914

Papa went to Astoria this a.m. so we got up early. It gave us such a nice start. Consequently we were already and waiting when the girls arrived about two—Mildred and Dottie Mac, Ruth Connell, Elizabeth Richardson, Marge Bronough and Helen Miller made the six. We went in swimming almost immediately after they got here. Sue and Elizabeth went up after Marge. I stayed in longer than anybody else because I went back out with Elizabeth. After dinner Ruth and Marge did the dishes while the rest of us went up to the ranch after some chickens. Edwin caught them. After we came back Ruth and Marge went for a walk while the rest of us just fooled around. About nine Don and Harry dropped by. Elizabeth and I danced. Had some cookies and cake about 10:15. Ruth and I walked up to the hill with Don and Harry. The boys left at 11:20 exactly. Harry is really awfully nice.

Diary, Sunday, August 29, 1914

We spent from 4:20 to 8:00 a.m. trying to get up…About four of the boys (Bob, Bruce, Harry and Don) arrived. We went down to the bay and went rowing. Ruth and I went out with Dora and Bob. When I came back discovered my green stockings on Harry. Poor kid had an awful cut on his finger so I ran barefooted to get a bandage. Had to rush after dinner to get a horse to take Don back. About nine started out on our hayrack ride. Harry and I got 10 cones of ice cream. We drove up the beach. Met Don, Rich and Marge by the Solano. Had an awful time getting up into the Park. The boys got off at Nahcotta. We got home about 2. Harry still has my socks. We were together all evening.

Diary, Monday, August 31, 1914

It seems to me everybody is leaving the beach tomorrow a.m. The McMasters, Clairs including Harry and my stockings, Elizabeth, Margaret, Helen and Bruce. I wonder if I will ever see Harry in Portland. O yes! Macs are going to ask Harry and I over to a dance on the 20th. Goody!!

Diary, Thursday, September 3, 1914

Why is it one has to pull between two fires all the time. When I am at school I so miss everybody here at home. Still the last few weeks I have been so impatient to get back to school.

Diary, Saturday, September 5, 1914

...After lunch I gathered up things to be packed such as books and clothes. A week from today I leave for Portland. I don't see how I can wait. I heard from Rosetta today and Dorothy is not going back to P.A. so I will. Mother doesn't approve of Dote at all...I taught Sue the little I knew about Five Hundred this afternoon. She is quite crazy about cards. She certainly will know lots more...when she goes away to school than I did. I hope she does too because it makes it a great deal easier than to be a molly coddle as I was and still am. But by next summer we will see!

Notes

1. Even substantial, two-story resort houses were referred to as "cottages" or "cabins" by their vacationing owners, perhaps as a way to distinguish them from their "real" homes elsewhere.
2. Mrs. Wirt, however, continued to do just that. She believed the Espy's well water was the best in town, and came across the lane every day to get a bucket for her family's drinking and cooking needs.
3. Added amenities—plumbing, toilet, and a real sink—didn't come until the house was supplied with electricity in the 1930s.
4. Usually, the towels and the bed and table linens were sent to commercial laundries in South Bend or Astoria.
5. Likewise, South Bend often was referred to as "the Bend."

"At the Oaks," from Medora's scrapbook—Medora, top row second from left; Sue, bottom center; the others are Medora's friends and an elderly gentleman escort. Sue, still a grade schooler, was visiting Portland at the time and joined Medora on the outing.

Alec you are so wonderfully fascinating to me…

Portland, 1914–1915

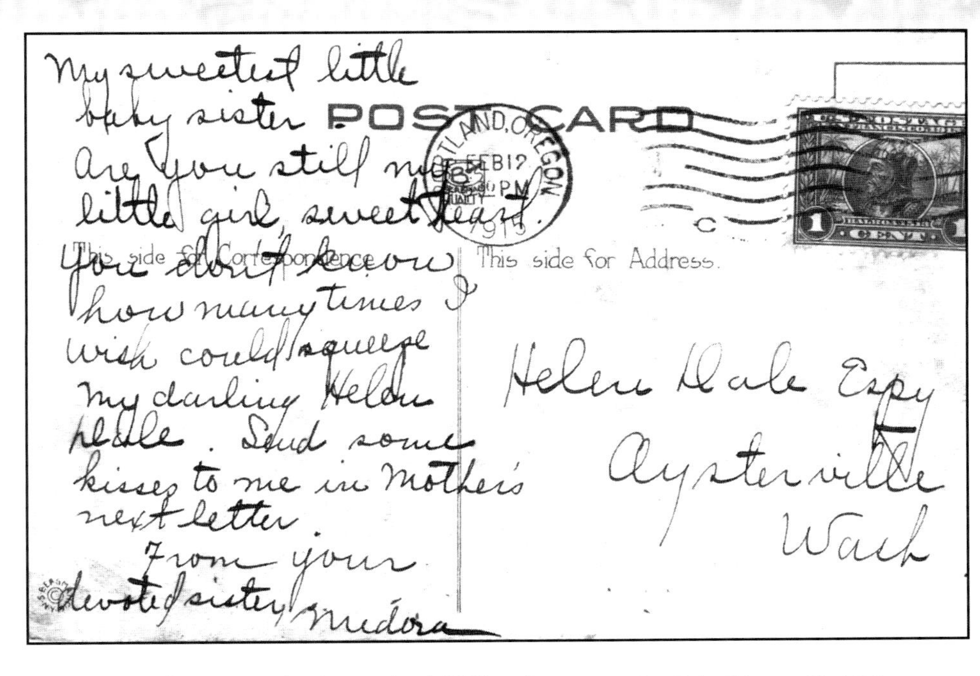
POST CARD

This side for Correspondence

My sweetest little
baby sister
Are you still my
little girl, sweetheart.
You don't know
how many times I
wish could squeeze
my darling Helen
Dale. Send some
kisses to me in Mother's
next letter.
From your
devoted sister, Medora

This side for Address.

Helen Dale Espy
Oysterville
Wash

Postcard to Dale, February 12, 1915.

Medora attended the academy during a time subsequently dubbed "Portland's Golden Age," which began with the hosting of the 1905 Lewis and Clark Exposition and lasted until America's entry into the Great War in 1917. Not only did Portland's stalwart citizens perceive of themselves as achieving the fundamental necessities for "the good life"—an adequate number of jobs, good housing, and a favorable urban climate for good health and security—but for many other refinements as well.

The city had an opera house, eight theaters, retail shops of every description, and numerous restaurants and cafes. The educational and cultural institutions included, among others, a library, art museum, Reed College, and the Portland Academy. A mild climate and close proximity to rivers, mountains, and the seacoast provided unlimited recreational opportunities. Mama and Papa were eager for Medora to enjoy all of Portland's advantages that their limited finances would allow, being ever mindful, however, of her most important obligation—schoolwork.

With other cultural pursuits in mind, the family also planned a summer trip to California. This somewhat daunting undertaking was the subject of considerable correspondence between Mama and Medora during the 1914–1915 school year. Between the exciting prospect of a summer adventure and an escalating interest in social activities—especially those involving boys—Medora was hard-pressed to find time to study.

[Portland]
Diary, Saturday, September 12, 1914

An awful trip up on the boat. I didn't speak a word to anyone. I felt miserable. Not a person to meet me and everyone had promised. Till suddenly Harry appeared. Gee! I was surprised. He took me up to the Hall…Miss C. is very sweet and has given Mary and I the front room and beds on the Porch. Also Rosetta.

[Oysterville]
Sunday, Sept. 13, 1914

My dear Girlie,

Everything is as usual here except for the missing of you.

School does not open tomorrow. Prof Jack would not give Mrs. Heinrick a permit. Now the date set is Oct. 5 when Mrs. H's sister is supposed to be here. Wouldn't it be a joke if they found she was not qualified either. This certainly is a nice mix up for the last minute.

Be careful what you say on postals as the post mistress reads everything.

Library clock.

Alarm clock.

It has been a stormy day, but a pleasant one for me as Papa has been home and we have had a chance to visit. Papa made the children a fine rocking horse. It is large and strong, and all five youngsters can ride at one time.

Sue has made several delicious pies lately and I have not helped her a bit. She is quite accomplished for so young a girl.

Papa had the big clock fixed and it seems so good to hear it strike.

Give my love to the girls.

As Always, Mama

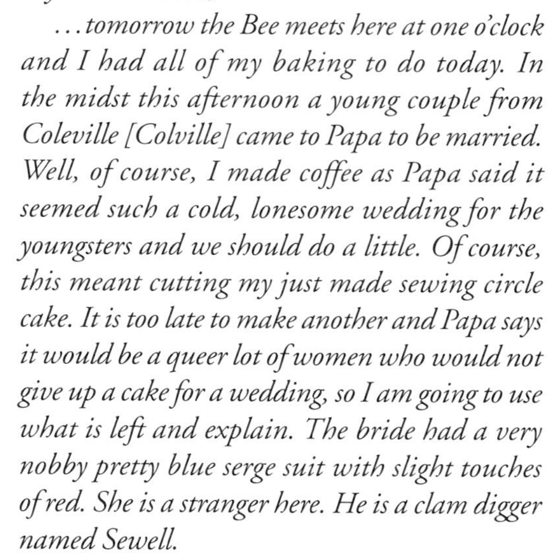

[Oysterville]
Wednesday, September 23, 1914

My dear Medora,

...tomorrow the Bee meets here at one o'clock and I had all of my baking to do today. In the midst this afternoon a young couple from Coleville [Colville] came to Papa to be married. Well, of course, I made coffee as Papa said it seemed such a cold, lonesome wedding for the youngsters and we should do a little. Of course, this meant cutting my just made sewing circle cake. It is too late to make another and Papa says it would be a queer lot of women who would not give up a cake for a wedding, so I am going to use what is left and explain. The bride had a very nobby pretty blue serge suit with slight touches of red. She is a stranger here. He is a clam digger named Sewell.

The men have been hauling oats and everyone is tired...

Dale was fussing today to have her rompers changed and I was too busy. Finally she said, "I do wish Doah would come home and keen me up..."

There are, or it seems to me there are, other things I want to say, but can't think what. I am glad you're having a good time, but study hard.

Devotedly, Mama

Diary, Wednesday, September 23, 1914

Rain and More Rain

After school I went swimming with Eliz Richardson and Eliz Bruere but didn't swim much as I fell and cracked my head which left me sort of silly. Mrs. Klocker was here to dinner and I am sure she thot I was a dunce but I simply felt awful from falling... I went right straight to bed after dinner. Miss Campbell tucked me in. She was so sweet to me.

[Oysterville]
Friday, September 25, 1914

My dear Girlie,

I have thought about your fall so much and hope your head is not troubling you. Go right to Dr. Nichols if you feel at all badly.

...don't make the mistake of worrying over the passing attentions of any boy. Be thankful that the attentions are just "passing" and have a good time with all alike. It is unfortunate and unbecoming for sixteen year olds to pair off.

You are just as intelligent, and have more good looks than many of the girls, but your trouble lies in being self-conscious. Forget your self and be your sweet natural self, and you need not worry. The best cure for self consciousness is to try and make others comfortable. In a crowd or any place the thoughtfulness for less fortunate girls soon makes one forget all about self and brings much inward content. I went through this same stage at your age, but goodness knows I had the best kind of a time after I stopped thinking about my imagined unattractiveness.

At fifteen I was quite certain I was doomed to be an old maid because I had not had a dozen "offers." Now I don't want my girl to be so silly. What a calamity it would be for a young girl of this age to be receiving marked attention. You have a strong character and a level head and I know you will make the best use of both.

"For life is the mirror of king and slave
Tis just what we are and do:
Then give to the world the best you have,
And the best will come back to you."

Well, dearie, I did not mean to lecture, but I do so want you to be sensible and kind and fair. "Judge not that ye be not judged."

Good night little girl and God bless you and lead you aright.

Lovingly, Mother

Please don't use that word "rotten." It is as vulgar and unladylike as gosh...

[Oysterville]
Friday, October 2, 1914

My dear Medora,

I will probably leave here a week from today arriving in Portland Saturday morning. I plan to stay at the Arthur and will probably take both Dale and Willard. Of course, these intentions are liable to change but will let you know definitely.

My suit skirt is at the Bend[1] *being cleaned so I pretty nearly have to stay in bed until it returns...*

Much love from your sleepy, Mama

[Oysterville]
Sunday 3 o'clock, October 4, 1914

Dear Medora,

We are having stuffed peppers this evening and I wish you were here.

It is a stormy day, but the town is agog because the school teacher arrived this morning. I presume school will start tomorrow.

I want to arrive in Portland Saturday as you can have those first two days I am there free.

Much love from all, Mama

Digging Clams for the Commercial Market

The North Beach Peninsula always has been a shellfish lover's paradise, and residents take seriously the adage "when the tide's out, the table's set." Oysters, clams, cockles, mussels, and crab thrive in the sandy shallows of the bay and ocean. In Medora's day, the seafood bounty was there for the taking, except for the oysters raised commercially on privately owned beds. "Limits" and "seasons" weren't regulated, and folks took what they needed when it suited them. Experienced gatherers, however, avoided taking shellfish during warm weather, giving their quarry a chance to spawn in hopes that next year's "crop" would be even better.

Several types of clams were in abundance. In the bay, New York clams, or "mud clams" as they were called locally, were readily available. Mama considered them "more buttery" and preferable for chowder. Along the gravelly shores of the bay's Long Island, Littleneck clams (sometimes called steamers) could be had by the bucketful and provided an incomparable taste treat when steamed. And for those who didn't mind a bit of hard work, geoducks up at the point, each weighing three to five pounds, promised a fulsome award for the industrious digger. But the most popular clam—if clams can be said to be popular—was the Razor clam found along the low-tide surf line on the ocean beach.

Almost everyone—locals and tourists, adults and children—liked Razor clams and as soon as there were canneries on the peninsula, there was money to be made by digging commercially. By the close of World War I, diggers stationed themselves up and down the sandy beach, filling boxes thrown out to them by "the cannery truck." A man who knew his business could fill eleven to fifteen boxes in a tide, with 22 to 28 dozen clams to the box. The natural "season" for Razor clams lasted about three months, and many a family eked out a living during the Great Depression by digging for the commercial market.

The Arthur
170 11th Avenue
Portland, Oregon

This small residential hotel located in northwest Portland was owned by Uncle Hine's father. Relatives often patronized "The Arthur" if in town, especially when it was inconvenient to stay with family or friends. Later, Uncle Hine and Ruth resided here for many years as building managers.

Digging clams in the good old days when diggers averaged 500 lbs. per tide.

[Oysterville]
Friday, 8:30 A.M. October 9, 1914

My dear Medora,

You don't know how disgusted and disappointed I am not to get off this morning. Everything is ready, even the suit case fully packed and clothes laid out to wear, but my skirt has not come. You know I have no substitute so here I am. Papa has urged my wearing a cotton housedress, but imagine landing in Portland thus. I can't say when to look for me, but I shall certainly go immediately when the skirt comes so presume it will be any day soon…

Do you enjoy Mary as a roommate? How does she come to be a senior? I can't understand how all the girls are doing this and you can't. It would mean so much to us financially…

Papa is digging clams but you don't need to tell the relatives. It was a case of have to and he digs on the bay. Not much in it—about 25c an hours work, often less and two or three hours on a tide, five days a week.

Everything O.K. here except everyone is cross about my skirt…

Devotedly, Mother

Mud Clams

It is said that mud clams were transported to the peninsula in the 1890s from the Atlantic Coast, not intentionally but as "accidentals." They apparently hitched a ride along with juvenile Eastern oysters that local growers imported, hoping to replace the depleted stock of Native oysters. The Eastern oysters didn't do well, but the clams thrived.

[Oysterville]
Sunday evening, October 11, 1914

I have heard from my skirt and now am planning to leave here Wednesday. I will leave on the boat at seven in the morning.

So far the teacher keeps fine order and the children stand in awe of her.

Willard and Dale are playing and one is God and the other Jesus. I have been trying to explain to them that they mustn't play like that, but they can not see "why." Here comes Edwin. He has been after the cows and is wet. He is such a help to Papa.

Lovingly, Mama

[Oysterville]
Tuesday A.M. Oct. 13, 1914

My dear Medora,

My skirt has not come yet tho they promised to have it here yesterday. The consequence is I will have to leave my coming this way—I shall still plan to leave tomorrow (Wednesday) arriving in Portland Thursday morning. However, do not meet me Thursday morning unless you have a telegram from me at Astoria tomorrow (Wednesday) saying I am on the way.

Those people certainly have kept me waiting for that skirt. Papa thinks they have ruined it some way so do not send.

Much love in haste, Mama

[Portland]
Thursday, October 15, 1914

Dearest Mother,

It was such a disappointment that you didn't come this A.M. I want to see you so very very much. Come the very first minute you can…

Mary K. is a dear, sweet girl and certainly an ideal room mate. She is just the opposite from Dorothy—more inclined to serve than be served. Our room is by far the most attractive in the house, also the neatest. Mary K.… is able to graduate this year as she had a private tutor all summer. Ruth Connell is graduating by taking five subjects and so are many others because they had first year Latin in the seventh grade. I would have to take six subjects to graduate and then would be unable to enter Berkeley as they require more credits. I would like to graduate too but it is impossible…

I hope to see you very very soon.

Lots of love, Medora

[Oysterville]
Friday, October 16, 1914

My dear Medora,

We were all ready to leave this morning, all dressed and horse harnessed. But the storm grew worse every minute until there was such a gale blowing that it was worse than foolish to start alone with the babies. One suit case is reposing at Nahcotta. I shall not set a day, but will leave at the first possible moment, telegraphing you from Astoria.

There is no news…

Mother

Diary, Sunday, October 18, 1914

Met mother at the boat at half past seven. Willard and Dale came with her. I certainly was glad to see them. We went straight to the Arthur in a taxi, cleaned up a little, then went out for breakfast. Ruth came down about noon. Also Bunch. It seemed so good to talk to mother again…

Diary, Monday, October 19, 1914

I left to meet mother about the same time as the girls went to school. First we had Willard's hair cut. Then we did a whole lot of shopping. I have my suit at last and like it real well. The coat is sort of Norfolk with a high military or flaring collar, the skirt has an over skirt on a yolk. I also bought an adorable yellow silk crepe waist, hand embroidered. Also some new shoes. I brought the youngsters up to Miss C's while mother was at the doctor's…

[Oysterville]
Monday, November 2, 1914

My Dear Medora,

There is nothing new except that the town is shingling the church, and Papa has traded old Coaly for the erection of a cow shed.

Edwin tacked up posters for prohibition today and feels very important.

I do hope you are not slicking up the sides of your hair. I know it will take the curl out. Ruth ought to be a continual object lesson to you as to how pretty hair can be ruined. You can leave it soft and curling around your face and still show your ears. In fact, when you take the frame of your hair from your face it is like plucking the petals off a daisy and leaving the bald pod. Some people's hair is not a necessity. Yours is—so is mine.

Please remember me to Miss Campbell.

How I do wish you were home! How long will your Thanksgiving vacation be?

Devotedly, Mama

[Oysterville]
Tuesday, November 3, 1914

Dear Daughter:

This has been election day and some way it has been strenuous. Papa, Mr. Stoner and Mr. Goulter have charge of the polls. Mrs. Stoner took the men up their noon meal and I sent dinner tonight. Our stove has been smoking to beat its record, and I had an awful time getting anything cooked. To top it off, your three year old brother went off with little Albert Andrews today and had an undress parade right down Fourth Street. I was so provoked. They were not together fifteen minutes. This happened while I was off voting. Willard has been threatened with dire results if he went ever since their last "undress

When sending Medora the following clipping from a women's magazine, Mama wrote at the top: "I thought this excellent, and you know that no body likes pretty dainty clothes better that I do!"

Correct Dressing for School

...

THE more simply one is attired for the business of school, be one pupil or teacher, the better one is equipped for the work at hand. Almost all of the arts and trades have adopted a sort of uniform, or distinctive form of garment, which has been found expedient for the special work. Leather aprons, linen coats and caps, bluejeans and overalls, mark both the artist and the artisan as ready for the day's labor; the housewife and homemaker goes about her business in suitable garments and in the business of school life it is not only expedient to be properly dressed, but it also marks an individual as possessing or lacking good taste, refinement and an understanding of "the fitness of things."

The business of school life is mental concentration. Therefore, any mode of dressing, extreme styles, bright colors, unusual or elaborate hairdressing, or any attire which calls attention to oneself is out of place in the schoolroom—as it tends to divide attention with the business of the day.

EXTREMES FROWNED UPON.

This has become so well understood in the older countries that to depart from the custom of simple and quiet styles makes one conspicuous and criticised. Large institutions of learning insist upon modest dressing, and many have adopted a sort of uniform, which the pupils are expected to wear. And because it has been proven that where the matter of dress is held in abeyance there is more time and energy and interest to give to teaching and learning.

There is a rigid custom among English people, which is being widely and wisely adopted all over America, that so long as a girl is attending school she wears her hair down her back. Young children wear it combed straight, older girls are permitted a ribbon or barrette, so long as it is black, but curls and gay ribbons are for gala occasions only. Sensible mothers see to it that their girls go to school suitably dressed, not so old-fashioned as to be noticeable, but certainly not in the exaggerated modes of today, nor gowned in their best, as though they had no other place to exhibit their finery.

THE IDEAL UNIFORM.

One can scarcely imagine anything more disturbing to the eye and mind when trying to concentrate upon a subject than the flutter of cubist designs and the weird garments fashioned from them.

Then there is another point of view from which one gets a moral: It is always illbred and vulgar to display one's possessions in the face of those less fortunate in this world's goods, and the girl who wears to school gowns and ornaments which are beyond the means of her classmates lays herself open to this charge.

The ideal uniform adopted by the majority of private schools and followed almost universally in large cities is the blue serge sailor suit, varied by the comfortable and tidy "middy." In the common fellowship of mental endeavor there is no place for the vagaries of Fashion.

parade" so I punished him this time and think he is duly impressed. It just goes to show that women belong at home and not at election polls.

Much love dearie. Take care of yourself, for remember nothing in the world could take the place of mother's first born.

Devotedly, Mama

[Portland]
Thursday, November 5, 1914

Papa, its your birthday. I wish I were home to give you a big bear hug. Tell Mama my head hasn't hurt me one bit and I feel fine. If I do begin to feel funny, I will go right to Dr. Nichols.

Love to each youngster and a great deal for yourself and Mama.

Medora

Andrews' store and post office.

Andrews' Store Credit

Typical were the Espy family's purchases in October 1915, totaling almost $15. The children's school needs and Christmas baking supplies added up much too fast for Papa's small dairying income to keep pace—

Oct. 6:
Tablet .10
Comp. Book .10
Pen Holder .05
Pens .05
Rubbers .01
Salmon .10

Oct. 7:
Envelopes .05
Hose .25
Garters .15

Oct. 9:
Pork 1.00
Axle Grease .25
Allspice .15
Nutmegs .10
Cloves .10
Tablet .15

Oct. 10:
Sausage .50
Eggs .35

Oct. 12:
Rubbers .50

Oct. 13:
Butter .80

Oct. 16:
Rubbers .75
Hair Pins .01

Oct. 17:
Tablet .05
Garters .20
Pillowcase Tubing .50

Oct. 20:
Chocolate .40
Coal Oil .20
Butter .40

Oct. 24:
Butter .80
Ribbon .50

Oct. 26:
Lard 1.75
Matches .10

Oct. 28:
Tablet .05
Coal Oil .20
Lamp Chimneys .20

Oct 29:
Butter .80
Child's Wagon 2.50
Coal Oil .20
Chili Con Carne .40

The Andrews' Store and Post Office

Like country mercantile establishments everywhere, Tom Andrews' store sold a little of this and a little of that—coal oil, writing tablets, horse liniment, sewing thread, flour, sugar—everyday items that the neighbors might need. For more extensive shopping, there was the Johnson and Henry Store in Nahcotta, there were catalogs, and there were trips to Portland.

Not only was Tom Andrews a storekeeper, he also served as Oysterville's postmaster from 1901 until 1913, and immediately following his tenure, his brother Sam took the position. The post office was situated at the back of the store, behind a counter where Tom and Sam "held court." From that vantage point, Sam passed out mail and sold stamps, while Tom weighed 10-penny nails and wrapped grocery purchases in brown paper and string. Tom was patient with neighbors needing credit, and generous in dispensing penny candies to children, who had been sent to get a much needed item, asking to "put it on our bill, please."

Villagers customarily went for the mail about 8:30 am, whether or not George Lehman's mail wagon had yet clattered into town. Usually, it was the men who went on this errand, since the women were otherwise occupied in getting youngsters off to school. If the mail wasn't "out" quite yet, they gathered around the pot bellied stove, visiting and swapping news. Those who didn't have to be anywhere at any particular time often stayed for awhile, engaging in friendly discussions about local politics and business concerns or just plain gossiping.

Increasingly, however, Mama depended on Medora to take care of many of the family's shopping needs. In Portland, Medora not only had access to department stores and specialty shops, but it seemed somewhat better to be billed at a distance, rather than to have one's neighbors as creditors. In spite of this, the Espy's bill at the Andrews' store would mount steadily.

[Oysterville]
Tuesday, November 10, 1914

My Dear Girlie:

Let me speak first of what is on my mind. Where on earth are our books? Do you know? Just now we searched everywhere and find The Shepherd of the Hills missing. There are a number gone. Please bring home with you all that you do not use, remembering especially the poems of Ella Wheeler Wilcox. Did we lend any that you remember this summer? It distresses us dreadfully to have the books disappear.

Your good long letter came today. It does us worlds of good to hear just what you are doing. Papa says do as Professor said and drop the Geometry. It is simply a mind trainer. It, in itself, is of no use to a woman in later life.

You are taking the classical course, Papa says. All your life you will find the literary and classical allusions taken from Cicero and Virgil a help to you. It gives an understanding to so much and in your library work will be essential.

Remember, I don't want you to wear your hair up. It does not matter who likes it up. Up in back makes you look like a Dutch waitress in a German bakery. On top is becoming, but too old. With little curls sticking out of a psyche, you would be a picture, but wait for awhile. I was in a rush to get mine on top, but am thankful my mother had me keep it down until graduation year.

About Rosetta's coming—Of course I would like to have you alone when the vacation is so short, but it will be all right. We can manage some way, but fear it will be dull. This seems an awful place to bring anyone in winter!

We have a nice wagon for Edwin's Christmas. Please go to M & F and look at wheelbarrows for Willard. Let me know as soon as possible how much a really useful, strong one would cost. Gussie has a nice one. I would want it as large as he could comfortably handle.

Papa wants you please to get immediately five of those brown chair bottoms to put in our dining room. Ours are disgraceful. Look at the "ten cent store" or furniture houses or department stores. Any place but please send immediately. Am rushing for the mail. Will enclose money for bottoms.

I wish you would plan to go out to Aunt Dora's soon. You could go out Saturday afternoon and come back Sunday. You must do this soon. Aunt Dora has always been nice to you.

Don't worry about Rosetta. It will be O.K.

There is no news here except that Tommy has a fine automobile truck.

A heartful of love, Mama

Diary, Monday, November 16, 1914

School this A.M. went pretty well. I may drop Geom.

Rosetta received a letter from Billie in Victoria. One enclosed from his chum for me. Thrilling. It really was crazy "My dearest Medorable," "ardent affection," etc.

[Oysterville]
Wednesday, November 18, 1914

My dear Medora,

Papa is getting out of patience about the chair bottoms.

I sent money and wanted seats immediately. Please mail at once. Those chairs are a disgrace.

Much love in haste, Mama

Chimneys and Flues

By 1915, three chimneys sprouted from the roof of the H.A. Espy home. Two were original to the house, and one was added in 1913. The latter served a large fireplace in the new living room, as well as the kitchen cook stove on the other side of the wall. The kitchen stovepipe tapped into the chimney at a convenient height for Mama to regulate the damper, but high enough so that the hot pipe didn't pose a threat to careless children.

One of the original chimneys served the library fireplace, as well as pot-bellied stoves in the nursery and in the bedroom just above. Since the nursery stove was in almost constant use, its chimney was the one that most often caught fire, probably due to creosote build-up.

The third chimney served the fireplaces in the parlor and the north bedroom directly overhead. As specified by the original house plans from England, these shallow fireplaces were intended to burn coal. In the early days, when oyster schooners from San Francisco carried every conceivable product as ballast on voyages north, coal was readily obtained and those fireplaces undoubtedly were used. Whether or not they were ever used by the Espy family is unclear—none of the children remembered that they were. Today, the fireplaces, with their lovely marble surrounds, remain intact, but the upper part of the chimney has been taken down and the hole shingled over—one less location for the unceasing winter rain to find its way indoors.

[Oysterville]
Sunday, November 22, 1914

My dear Medora,

Will you please bring two heads of celery and two of lettuce sure. I must have these for Thanksgiving dinner.

Those bottoms came, and no wonder you sent only three! They look a little better than the lids of the kettles which we have been using for some time, so probably we should be thankful.

The wind howls! Which reminds me that the chimney of the fireplace burned out this morning. The roar was enough to scare anyone. Papa was at South Bend so the neighbors came to my assistance. I would like to know what ails our old chimneys. Other people's chimneys are not forever catching fire.

Things are not in good shape here at home and I don't know what Rosetta will think.

The days will drag until you get here.

Devotedly, Mama

Enclosed find money order.

Parlor fireplace.

Library fireplace.

[Portland]
Sunday, November 22, 1914

Dearest Mother,

I am going out to Aunt Dora's on the 1:55 electric. I shall go right from S.S. I am going to wear my suit. I have so much studying to do that I hate to go.

I had a real good time Friday night. Carl came up for me about eight and we walked down to Helen Morgan's. We played 500; no prizes were rewarded. Mrs. Morgan is a charming hostess. Lemonade and candy were served during the evening and about half past ten we had ice cream and delicious cake. Carl brought me home about eleven. He is a real nice boy but so bright in school that he scares me. Imagine he is trying for the Rhodes scholarship and only about three people out of the whole state ever get that...

I went to Ruth Connell's informal tea. All the girls of the Black Cat Club were there. I saw a good deal of Pete, Marge's youngest sister. Her real name is Anna May. Harry Clair goes with her all the time since he came back from the beach. She is perfectly dear and I don't blame him.

I don't know how we are ever going to accomplish all I want to do Thanksgiving vacation but I think we will finish it all for Bunch won't need any entertaining. As long as she can eat cream and play with the babies she will be satisfied.

Miss C. is ready for church so I must hurry.

Lots of love, Medora

Diary, Wednesday, November 25, 1914

Tomorrow I will be home. Joy! Bliss!

[Thanksgiving vacation, Oysterville]
Diary, Friday, November 27, 1914

Got up late. Went for the mail about noon so Bunch could see the village folk gathered at the store. After lunch we donned slickers and rubber hats—Cousin Bob loaned them to us. We walked out to the beach and down the beach to the Solano in the pouring rain. Examined the familiar old H. D. + M. E. Poor old Herbie [Davis]. I wish I hadn't been so good. Of course we were awfully wet so had to change everything when we got home. Bunch, Edwin, Sue, Mona and I went.

[Portland]
Tuesday P.M. December 1, 1914

Dearest Mother.

Arrived safely this morning and were here at the hall in time for breakfast. I got home before anybody was up. It was pitch dark. We landed at the Taylor St. dock so I didn't have far to go.

Have dropped Geometry...

Love, Medora

[Oysterville]
Sunday Evening 10 P.M.—December 6, 1914

My dear,

...Be sure and send Aunt Kate a birthday card, even if you make a trip to mail it. Her birthday falls on Wednesday, 9th. Send one even if the chances are it will arrive a day late. Don't fail, as poor Aunt Kate is getting old. Telephone and ask Ruth to send one. Also Verona and Aunt Dora. It is a very little thing but would make her happy as a gold piece would you. Be sure to do this now. You can date the card the 7th.

Everything is as usual here. I have felt better today than for a week.

Lovingly, Mama

Diary, Monday, December 14, 1914

...After dinner played the piano and sang. It seems so funny to sing without being told to stop.

[Christmas vacation, Oysterville]
Diary, Saturday, December 19, 1914

It seemed so good to be home again. Mother hasn't been well since her trip to Portland in October...mother informs me that we are passing through a financial period that will end one of two ways so I certainly can't afford skates. I may have to teach school instead of going to college.

Diary, Sunday, December 20, 1914

Mama had a very severe headache last evening which we are inclined to think similar to a

The *Solano*

The four-masted schooner *Solano* ran aground on the ocean beach opposite Oysterville on February 5, 1907. The vessel was undamaged, and plans immediately began to re-float her. A salvage crew worked for ten months, readying for a re-launching on a high winter tide.

Arrangements were made for the Astoria tug *Daring* to tow the vessel safely to port, but the *Daring* never arrived. Incoming breakers finally drove the *Solano* back up the beach. There she remained, a land-locked curiosity gradually being swallowed by drifting sands—one of the more interesting sights for beach visitors. *The Solano* has been called a ghost ship because drifting sands bury her and then blow away leaving her visible again. The wreck was last seen in the 1950s.

stroke of apoplexy. It worries me but I think maybe she just needs a rest which I will try to give her during my vacation... I spent the next three or four hours tidying the bedroom from bureau drawers out. Papa began to read Cap'n Eri out loud while I worked... We laughed again and again. J. C. Lincoln certainly is clever to write such a humorous book without any apparent effort. Cousin Bob dropped in. He also cheers a person and Papa needs it certainly. He is so dear and has sacrificed so much for his family.

Diary, Monday, December 21, 1914

... The children are so dear. The little ones seem to have the keenest imagination in the family. They play all the time the queerest games. For instance Edwin pulled down cobwebs to-day playing each was a bear... I washed a few necessary rough clothes for the children. The poor youngsters are about destitute but we have to save every penny if we expect to go South next year. Lida sent Mother some of Frances' old clothes for Sue which are very good and useful.

I am too busy to be anything but happy to be home again and especially when I know that I am helping Mama. She is so lonely and has so much to do and not well. I think she is very brave.

The Christmas Program

The annual Christmas Program was Oysterville's biggest community event of the year. By the time the anticipated evening arrived, the town was in a high state of excitement. All fall, the school children made costumes, practiced singing holiday carols, and prepared their "pieces."

A few days before the scheduled event, the men brought in a big tree from the woods, and cut holly and other greenery for the women to place strategically throughout the hall. Everyone in town contributed to the exchange of gifts, ensuring that, no matter how meager their own family's celebration, each child would receive a present. The program was held in the Methodist Church, the most spacious accommodation in town, and everyone, young and old, attended.

One of Oysterville's school teachers, Alice Holm, reminisced about the Christmas program of 1917: "The Christmas tree with its uncertain wax candles twinkling might well have been considered the first number on the program. For days previously the children devoted his or her hand work to the making of paper chains and Christmas tree ornaments. These they added to the long fairy like strings of white popcorn and strings of rosy cranberries fresh from the nearby bogs. Bunches of holly from Mr. Stoner's trees and the smell of cedar made one further to know that Christmas had come.

"The audience arrived early, mothers, dads, grandparents, visitors and all others. They came, more or less, laden with babies and the next to the babies, too young for school. They also carried cakes and coffee donated for the social hour. The class known as Baby Sitters was as yet unthought of. Mothers shushed intermittently to nip in the bud any wail that might unexpectedly peal forth from their offspring to mar the program or make the mothers, themselves, conspicuous.

"An air of expectancy pervaded the place. It was a gala event but each sensed the responsibility of doing his bit and doing it well."

Diary, Wednesday, December 23, 1914

... Papa came home from the Bend with a useful present such as heavy shoes for each one. I wrapped Xmas presents while Mama strung corn for the church. Oysterville certainly is excited over this church Christmas affair—tree and program... We had wild goose for dinner. I do love Christmas.

Diary, Sunday, January 3, 1915

Sixteen years old to-day... A New Year and so many resolutions to live up to. Can I? I pray dear God that at the end of 1915 I may accomplish something.

From Medora's Diary, 1914—

Read Since Sept. 1st 1913

Cap'n Warren's Wards
Trail of the Lonesome Pine
Little Colonel's Christmas Vacation
Betty
Laddie
Lavender and Old Lace
Old Rose and Silver
Silas Marner
House of Seven Gables
Tom Sawyer
"Midsummer Night's Dream"
Molly Make-Believe
Pictures of Polly
My Lady of the North
My Lady of Doubt
Little Colonel's Maid of Honor
Little Colonel's Knight Comes Riding
Mary Ware
Mary Ware in Texas
Pandora's Box
Doughnuts and Diplomas
Rudder Grange
Nancy Stair
Princess Virginia
Lonesome Land
Mary Ware's Promised Land
Poppy
In the Bishop's Carriage
Call of the Wild
Birds & Bees
The Iron Woman
Doctor Ellen
The Maquet
Fighting Chance
Heart of the Hills
The Doctor
Chip of the Flying U.

New Years Resolutions

Make bed on time
On time to meals
Keep room tidy—never leave things in the girls rooms
Put away tooth brush
Do not yield to pranks of girls
Take back what I borrow
Smile, be nice to everybody—especially nice to Malvina
Do not say disagreeable things about anybody
Write Mother regularly
Keep account of money spent
Spend less money
Write diary only when I have something to relate
Omit humour in English
Pay attention in class (whispering, notes)
Pray
Don't carry my heart on my sleeve
Increase vocabulary
Better table manners
Study from 7 to 9:30
Keep things mended
Do not skip
Accomplish something in study hall
Modify voice and laugh
Attend church and view regularly
Cut down on slang—Fines
Talk less about myself in either a disparaging or a bragging manner

[Portland]
Thursday Afternoon, January 7, 1915

Dear Mama,

Doesn't it seem odd to write 1915? We have looked forward to this year since the Seattle Exposition in 1909. Just think!

...arrived here Tuesday morning after a very uneventful trip. I had a very good dinner in Astoria, tenderloin steak and french fried potatoes, costing the large sum of fifty cents...

Lovingly, Medora

[Oysterville]
Sunday, January 17, 1915

My dear Medora,

...Another disturbing thing is that Miss Friesen failed to qualify and school is closed until further notice. She "fell down" in Arithmetic and I don't know just what else. We are all sorry as she is a good teacher. It is an awful slap to her and she feels it keenly.

...We have eight new pigs and Sue had a sick one in the living room by the fire place nursing it. The poor pig died, however, but Sue felt worse about it than he did.

...Is your hair all right? We have learned that a sure and speedy cure for that oil in the hair is larkspur seed. Drench hair and scalp twice with cold infusion of larkspur tea made by steeping for an hour one ounce of the seed in six ounces of hot water. This is deadly poisonous and after twenty four hours a thorough shampoo must be taken with warm water. Keep these directions...

My eyes say quit.

Always devotedly, Mama

[Portland]
Monday afternoon, January 18, 1915

Dearest Mother,

...Hasn't the whole school been confused though this year? I am very sorry for Miss Friesen.

She seemed so competent. What is the school going to do? The youngsters are simply losing a year and Mona can't afford it.

I love all the little things about home that make up the term <u>news</u>...

Saturday evening I went to dancing school and did very well considering it was me...

Wednesday afternoon we (the Campbell house) are going to see "Hamlet" for Forbes Robertson is here on his farewell tour. We are going to be quite gay and spend 50 cents for a balcony seat. I really think "Hamlet" is worth more than 50 cents.

Lots and lots of love, Medora

Just think, <u>I</u> am on the <u>Honor</u> List!

[Oysterville]
Friday, January 29, 1915

Dear Medora,

Some news today, tho maybe you have heard that Nahcotta burned to the ground day before yesterday. Everything gone. It started in the old Petit Hotel, spread to Morehead's store, thence to other hotel across taking depot, post office and Duggans. Duggans stock insurance had run out on the 16th of this month. Isn't it too bad. I hope our laundry was not lost as it happened to contain some of the best clothes. It did not get off till Tuesday and I am wondering if it was still at the store to go next week. However, this loss would be small compared to what others lost...

Devotedly, Mama

The Portland theater scene.

[Portland]
Friday, January 29th, 1915

Dearest Mother:

Only one short letter this week...or has the fire in Nahcotta prevented any mail reaching you? What are the details of the conflagration? I haven't read the papers but have heard from different sources that there has been a fire.

Lovingly, Medora

[Oysterville]
Wednesday, February 3, 1915

Dearie,

We have been busier than usual and disturbed since the fire. Sunday afternoon Papa and I spent sorting clothes. He gave all of those men's clothes upstairs away. They were all wearable but out of date. He also sent a pair of trousers never worn but once. Another thing he gave three whole nearly new suits of underclothes out of that box. I was so glad we had the clothes and too am delighted to get them out of the way as you also will be. There were a few other things and a load of hay we sent as we have no money...

Lovingly, Mama

Fire

In the Pacific Northwest, where trees grow to monstrous size, it was a given that the bountiful supply of wood provided for most construction needs. Since towns were built of lumber, heated with wood, and surrounded by forests, fire was a constant threat. Weather played an important role in a fire's outcome. As often as winds might fan flames, a heavy rain might help control a fire. However, many buildings succumbed in conflagrations. Fortunately for Oysterville, a fire never swept through the entire town as in Nahcotta during the winter of 1915.

[Oysterville]
Sunday, February 14, 1915

My dear Medora,

This has been an unsatisfactory day. It seems as tho I took for ever getting dinner and we are just through. It is possible tho not certain that I will spend next Sunday with you.

I feel very much encouraged about our preparations. Sue is practically ready. I have brought her very pretty white drawers (3 pair) and plain (2) black bloomers. Those summer vests of hers are all re-bound and mended...Edwin, too, is nearly fixed. I must buy him good woolen suit and a best white while in Portland is all. He has four new wash suits and three new beach rompers besides the white suit of Herbert's.

That list we made is my guide. I certainly find it a blessing. I have three dresses ordered from the National for Mona—best they had—colored. I like your skirt pattern. It is pretty. I didn't think you needed any more waists. Dale, too, needs but little, just three rompers and some drawers.

Willard has new seersucker rompers but must have other clothes. I shall buy for him while in Portland. I will be so glad to get a chance to talk to you. I am on such a strain writing. I will let you know when I can tell definitely about our going.

I shan't buy for myself until I go up in May. Things will be cheaper. I may buy a house dress this time.

Maud sent pictures of their home which I will try to enclose. Such a good looking, lovely place.

Mr. W. is improving wonderfully. Could move his fingers yesterday. He walks with a cane now and Cousin Bob guides him.

Papa says to tell you he washed the bloomers with much love. He washed twice last week. Our laundry certainly is a problem. This I dread next summer [in California] as money will be scarce. Some places we can wash—Aunt Minette's, Mary's—but our wash would upset a place like Maud's.

Lovingly and longingly, Mama

[Oysterville]
Monday, March 1, 1915

My dear Medora,

Just a note to say we arrived home safely and found everything all right...

Please make that money last as long as possible as I have just $4 left in bank and Papa spent nearly all yesterday trying to borrow enough to meet overdraft on his account.

Always lovingly, Mama

Family Finances

Indebtedness was perennial for the H.A. Espys. In the years when the children were growing up, Papa seemed to spend half his time trying to borrow money, and the other half promising creditors that full payment would be made "without fail" as soon as he was able. The strain on Papa and Mama would take its toll in later years, even though, by then, finances wouldn't be as constrained.

Although Mama constantly admonished Medora about unnecessary spending, the younger children were blissfully unaware of the family's financial woes. Later, Willard would say that he always thought the family was rich, but "a special kind of rich people—the kind without any money."

[Oysterville]
Tuesday, March 2, 1915

My dear Medora,

Just a line to say not to charge a cent for anything at Meier F's. We have had two notices this week. Feb. bill came today and there is about $10.00 worth of stuff there that I knew nothing about. One item was $1.00 for a pair of hose—I never paid such a price for stockings in my life and take it for granted that you didn't. People in our circumstances are extravagant if wearing 50c hose. There was also voile and lace and velvet and various items...

By 1915, the Espys seemed to owe to everyone with whom they dealt. Most of the many bills sent by creditors were accompanied by personal pleas to settle accounts—

Feb. 16: David C. Cook Pub. Co., *Mother's Magazine*, Elgin, Ill.
Dear Madam, Evidently you don't believe in "The Golden Rule." We have sent you numerous statements and have received no reply...

Mar. 31: Andrews' Store, Oysterville—$19.75 (Jan. bal. $29.74; Feb bal. $22.74).
Please pay the above at your earliest convenience as I am badly in need of money and can't wait any longer...

May 21: Meier & Frank Co., Portland—$137.46.
...In April you wrote us you would give the matter attention very shortly, but to date no payment has been received...

June 30: Ilwaco Mill & Lumber Co.—$11.49.
Please settle. This is long past due.

July 22: Andreen's Shoe Headquarters, South Bend—$5.
Seven months old, and still unpaid—Kindly send me a check by return mail...

Aug. 1: Drissler & Albright Department Stores, South Bend—$22.48.
We'd like to close our Dry Goods Books and would deem it a favor if you will assist us in our effort to let us have the above amount to balance payment...

Aug. 12: Oak Bar, Siskiyou County, California—$65.
...I am much in need of the balance due can you please remit the amount by return mail, as this account has been a long time running and I understand you are about to make a sale of the property.

Oct. 30: Owen Delivery, Raymond.
I will have to meet some other heavy obligations within the next few days and am going to have to have some money to do so with. I hope it will not inconvenience you to send me the little due me

Nov. 26: Hanson-Bellows Co., Educational Publishers, Chicago—$8.
You will agree that we have treated you very fairly in carrying your balance...

It's time for dinner and anyway my eyes are on the rampage today so can't write much.

Much love as ever, Mama

[Portland]
Friday, March 5, 1915

Dearest Mother,

Your letter received yesterday and I am certainly very sorry about the M & F bill as I fear it is all my fault. Yes, I charged a pair of dollar silk hose the day of Carl Wilson's party because I was going to stay all night with Elizabeth Bruere and the girls here at the house laughed at my half dollar hose because they said one pair of dollar hose would last twice as long and they have.

The velvet was what I bought for that party dress. That dress cost less than five dollars and is very good looking, velvet $1.00, work $2.00, lace for sleeves (1½ yds) .75 and the susiune which I didn't use .25. All amounting to four dollars. The voile is that I bought for the waists, enough for two at 25c a yard. I am very sorry this has happened and will not charge anything else.

Lots of love, Medora

Sue and Pneumonia

Sue had several serious bouts with pneumonia and finally died of it on December 27, 1932, in Portland. Years later Mama would write:

"Suzita dashed into the world one bright July morning before I could even get my shoes off. There is not a definite incident that seems to mark the memory of her—just her glowing personality and gorgeous eyes that won the hearts of all men from the time she was two years old. She could achieve her own ends and dismiss obstacles like a magician. Brighter than average, she bluffed her way through school—was asked by a teacher in the third grade once what a dumb waiter was. 'Mama is a waiter,' she said, 'she waits on everyone, but she isn't dumb.' Suzita—staunch, loyal, loving, reckless Sue, my beautiful red rose."

[Oysterville]
Tuesday, March 9, 1915

Dear Little Sister,

Just a line to say Sue is getting along as well as can be expected. Dr. says we will see little change until after the crisis on seventh day. The poor child is in constant pain—and so patient.

I can't realize she is so sick when just a day or two ago she was so lively. That pneumonia is like a stroke of lightening. Dr. says she is strong and will come thru O.K.

Ruth gets here this A.M.

Much love, Mother

[Oysterville]
Thursday, March 11, 1915

Dear,

Sue is quite comfortable now. She spent a bad night and we were much depressed this morning, but a half hour ago she raised a great clot of blood and has been breathing easier and is clear headed since.

Dr. says we can look for no change before Sunday.

In haste, Mama

[Portland]
Friday afternoon, March 12, 1915

Dearest sweetest little mother,

Your short note arrived this morning and if it hadn't been for my good judgement I would have started for home tonight…So I certainly hope that you don't need me. I will come at once on receipt of any kind of message.

I am so sorry for poor little Sue. I think she is the best patient in the family which makes it easier for you.

Please take good care of yourself my dearest mother, because you are so precious to me. Ruth is well and strong and perfectly willing so please leave everything to her. Oh please Mother dear save yourself. Sue is going to pull through all right without you worrying yourself sick. Give Sue my very dearest love. I hope she is a great deal better…

Lots and lots of love, Medora

Diary, Monday, March 15, 1915

Another day of thoughts. Another day gone out of my allotted number. Death used to frighten me terribly but now I am much stronger and no longer fear the inevitable at least not as I did last summer.

Diary, Thursday, March 18, 1915

I have been wearing my hair up for two weeks and I don't like it at all but I want to impress people that I am <u>old</u>…

[Easter vacation, Oysterville]
Diary, Monday, March 29, 1915

I am really home and sitting on the edge of Willard's bed that has been everything from a boat to a forest full of bears, in the dear old shabby nursery. I love this old old fashioned house with all its nooks and corners that are so very hard to clean—I arrived safely in Nahcotta Saturday morning. It seemed so funny to see all the business buildings gone... I found Sue up and well though still thin and weak. She doesn't do anything about the house but amuses herself all day which is so different... scrubbed the kitchen and dining room thoroughly but that is all I really accomplished.

Mona.

Diary, Monday, April 5, 1915

April 4th Easter Sunday and no new Spring clothes but I didn't mind as I was in Oysterville... We had a gay time getting the children ready for Sunday, but they were finally dressed and all looked very well, especially Mona. She looked so dainty and dear. Mother wasn't feeling very well so I went alone to the program. It was splendid considering the amount of time the children had practised... We all got up early as Edwin started to school this morning. Mrs. Owens has eight little beginners. Papa is director for the coming year and has been kept quite busy all week with the district, fighting consolidation, compromising with two teachers. Mrs. Owens is to have the little ones in Winslow's old store which has been recently renovated. Sue isn't to start back to school this year although Miss Siler urges her. The darling babies how I do love them. I am so glad I have planned or rather decided to stay at home year after next. They all need me so much and I them. My poor frail, tired little Mother. I am really lost to know where I am the least lonesome at home with my beloved family or at school surrounded with amusements and pleasures beside the girls I love. I wish we could move to Portland but then I would want poor little old Oysterville.

... Harry Clair got on and was as cute and dear as ever. I had about five minutes talk with him but it seemed longer. I am sure if Harry liked me very much I would be very much in love with him. But it can not be. Harry likes me well enough, and I do him so that is all. I think my case on Alec has lessified during this vacation but I like him still. Why do I choose light, fair boys? Herbert, Harry, Alec.

I will never be in love but once, which perfect mate is to come. However, just now I am going through the thrills of cases which I can make into wholesome friendships if I wished. It was entirely unnecessary that affair about Alec but I enjoyed the sensation and wanted something exciting so exaggerated everything—that is all my love for him. I think I like him just as well if not better but hereafter, he is a friend in the true big sense of the word. I like boys and can have lots of fun with them but not silliness. So help your devoted author to be good, Diary...

[Oysterville]
Wednesday, April 7, 1915

Dearest Medora,

...They have formed a Parent-Teacher club here that is to meet every two weeks. I am president which does not please me in the least.

Edwin enjoys the school and Mona says he is at the head of his class...

Did I tell you that Aunt Minette sent a box of things—very acceptable too. I will tell you about them later—am hurrying for the mail now and haven't had breakfast. Yesterday morning and the day before I had breakfast for Papa at four o'clock. He was hauling clams for Wentworth.

Take care of your precious self for the sake of always your loving,

Mother

O, by the way, the babies each put a bag of shells in your box of clothes. Edwin's are for you and the other two sent theirs to "Medoah and Wozetta". I naturally slipped them out as they would have filled your clothes with sand and littered your room. Please thank the babies and don't give me away.

[Portland]
Tuesday, April 20, 1915

Dearest Mother,

I had the most wonderful time Sunday. All seven of us girls went in Irvings' Lozier with their chauffeur driving clear out on the Columbia boulevards to Oneonta Gorge—65 miles from town making 130 mile trip. We stopped at Ladderell [Latourell] Falls and Multnomah Falls eating our lunch at the Gorge where the Cascade Locks begin. The road was in terrible condition

Doctoring and Dentistry

Dr. Paul, the peninsula's only physician, considered Mama an excellent nurse and usually confined his consultations about any of Oysterville's citizens to a telephone discussion with "Mrs. Espy." Only on rare occasions did he ride his horse from Ilwaco to make a home visit. If in the Oysterville area, he stopped at the Espy household for a chat, generously sharing his knowledge and medical books, and often asking Mama's opinion in matters that puzzled him. For "serious" doctoring, the family traveled to Astoria, or to Portland, availing themselves of the services of specialists—in extreme cases, they went to St. Vincent's Hospital.

Dentistry was another matter. The nearest practitioner was in South Bend, and the children often were seen by him in assembly-line style. Although they all endured the horrors of the foot-driven drill, it was the dentist's surgical skills at removing tonsils that my mother Dale remembers most vividly:

"His office was right across from the Cassels' Hotel. Mama got a room and then took Edwin, Willard, and me over to the dentist. Edwin went first. He didn't make any noise but Willard and I were mighty scared when we saw the dentist carry him out and take him across the street to the hotel. Next was Willard. He screamed and when the dentist carried him out I thought he might be dead. I was the youngest so I was last. I don't remember much about the afterwards—we ate ice cream I think. It was the before that I could never forget!"

but the view made up for all that. We picked the most wonderful wild flowers. I am simply wild about the scenery and would love to go again soon. We girls all wore white skirts and shoes. Thank Goodness as the dust was frightful. I was never so sunburned in my life. I have a perfect V on my neck from my middy. Miss C furnished part of the lunch; the rest we bought…

Lots of love, Medora

[Oysterville]
Thursday, April 22, 1915

My dear Girlie,

I broke Tena's machine needle just now and am so sorry—especially as it may be very difficult to get more. I shall enclose a slip with description and want you to send me a couple by return mail if possible. Go to that Sharf and Duliver place on Morrison Street where they handle old machines. I am anxious to get that pongee fixed so I can wear it to the "Parent Teacher" meetings.

Grandpa is having another mental lapse. This time he is set on Cousin Bob and I starting off to the fair together. I told Bob that if Father would supply the money, we had better strike out while he was in the notion.

There is no news except that Aunt Minette is making Mona's summer hat. Aren't our relatives good to us! Aunt M. has room for ten guests so we can all visit her at once and can leave the girls longer.

Sue is going to school for her arithmetic class—no more. This is enough for her at present.

I am glad you had that nice trip. I thought the scenery along the river there near the Dalles the finest I had ever seen outside of Yosemite…

When is the boating party? Is the boat large enough to be safe? You know my horror of having you on the water in a small craft. Please don't sit on edges and railings.

Edwin's ringworm seems to be well again. Dr. Paul was in town last week and we called him in to see it. He sent me medical books to read saying he had never treated one of the scalp. Mrs. Owens has seen a great many in her school work and she says Edwin's is cured. I certainly hope so.

Give my love to the girls, Rosetta in particular.

Much much love dear from
always your devoted Mother

Diary, Friday, April 23, 1915

I went over to study hall, met Alec on the steps and the conversation was as follows:

A. "Oh ho Medora"

"Hello Alec" No blushes—Thank Goodness.

A. "Listen, are you going up there tonight?"

"Yes, I guess so"

A. "Would you go with me"

"Surely, I would love to"

A. "I am going to try and get a machine"

"Gee. That will be dandy."

A. "About what time do you want to go?"

"Well, Eliz wants us at eight."

A. "Alright about twenty to eight."

A very, very sensible sort of a conversation but oh! I do not see how I was able to keep so calm. I spent the afternoon preparing for the event. Kinks and I were ready at seven thirty. Alec and the Cadillac…arrived a little after eight. I sat in the front seat with Alec. I was too happy to think of anything tho' but the fact that I was with Alec. I can remember almost every word spoken all evening and I never never had such a good time. There were little pauses of silence which I didn't mind very much. I can smell his cigarette yet.

Diary, Friday, April 30, 1915

I forgot to tell about the excitement Wednesday night. Miss Campbell was cross as we were making too much noise so I rolled her old tin bucket down the stairs. My! She was mad. She nearly pulled me out of bed, trying to make me 'fess up. We all said we wouldn't tell. Her voice simply shook with anger. But she makes me tired. I will be so glad to get home to Mother.

[Portland]
Friday, May 7 1915

Dearest Mother,

I received the check Monday and thank you very much. It certainly seemed good to have some money in my possession once more. This financial end always takes the edge off the pleasure derived from each nickel. I will be so glad when I can spend one winter in Oysterville where money matters very little except for stamps. And supposing I am drawing in seventy-five dollars as teacher and boarding at home, won't I feel rich. I could wear all my old clothes as style surely doesn't matter for a schoolteacher, does it? I am getting quite enthusiastic over this idea…

Mr. Ewing announced in Chapel Monday that the directors had met and arranged that P.A. should continue in the future as in the past. This has been decided at last after two years of rumors and vague suspicions.

We also had a meeting of all the officers and committeemen of the Junior class Monday and decided to have the J.R. Kellog on Saturday night, May the 22nd. Papa knows the boat I guess. We are hoping to collect $150. The boat costs $60, and music, eats etc. will take up the rest.

[Oysterville]
Sunday, May 9, 1915

My dear Medora,

We enjoyed your last letter greatly and am glad you are having such a nice time…Don't forget those who have been kind to you. It is easy when one is having a good time to neglect those who made it pleasant when friends were not so many. And as Shakespeare says, no tooth bites so keen as "benefits forgot."

…I sent Tena's machine back. She must have thought I intended to keep it, and it certainly was lovely of her to lend it to me…

I hope you do take the teachers exams, tho I don't want anybody here to know a thing about it. I would not want you to jump in blindly or unprepared. Miss Friesen fell down on Washington State school law and Math. We have a school manual. By reading it thru a few times, I imagine you could hold enough to pass you through the law questions. I shall try to get an old set of teachers questions and send you. It would be an untold lift to Papa if you taught the year prior to entering University. It would nearly take you thro a year at school and in the meantime we will pray that Papa gets out of this awful money tangle. The education of the five who follow you must be thought of too.

It was a great relief to know something definite about P.A. It would have been a tragedy to close the school.

It was dear of the girls to think of me as Patroness of their picnic, and it would have delighted me, but there is no telling when I can get up to Portland, tho I hope to this month provided we can scrape up money for Meier & F…

Well, dearie, have good time but be cautious. You can't know how precious you are to us until a daughter of your own comes to you.

Love, Mama

[Portland]
Sunday, May 16, 1915

Dear Mama,

Last night we went to a dance held in the school gym. I had a dandy time. (Lately, I have cultivated the habit of always having a good time which helps a lot.) I never have had many boys about me, any competition I mean, but last night I was pestered to death. Five asked for the last dance, and in the tag two-step, a whole line. Oh! Lyman wants to take me to a ball game. I am going to the boating party with Lester White…

I must say, though, sometimes I feel plumb discouraged as after I do know a boy and they like me pretty well, I never can keep them—at least that's the way it was with Harry Clair. I would like to have a mutual case. First I wanted to just know boys and be able to act naturally with them. Now I want a congenial "beau". All the girls I know, that is practically all have had cases and boys since they were eleven. Sometimes I think I have been cheated, but other times I think it was much better, because all these good times of the past year are a novelty to me so I am very enthusiastic though not learned…

[Oysterville]
Tuesday, May 18, 1915

Medora,

I am glad you are having a nice time and hope your school work is getting along nicely. I am proud to have a daughter who has enough self respect to refuse the familiarities of boys. It pays now and always for the feeling of inward satisfaction, and outwardly it pays for the respect in which you are held. When the "king" comes, he does not want to find his heart's gold tarnished by the hands of other men, and happy the girl who realizes this in time…

Most lovingly, Mama

Diary, Friday, May 21, 1915

…The boy whom I adore, as truly as I could like any boy—Alec you are so wonderfully fascinating to me that it sort of scares me, as you are not

the boy that fulfills my ideal though you are very young and I think will become a strong man. That's what I want you to be Alec—strong, forcible, able to resist evil, not necessarily prominent but oh a man a real man and Alec you will never be my ideal until you can speak of your mother and father respectfully, reverently. I only wish I knew you and I would tell you. Anyway, Alec, I like you very much, almost too much I fear.

Diary, Saturday, May 22, 1915

I am going to the Prom with Harry Stevens. This was the conversation:

"Are you going to the Prom?"

Harry—"No I didn't get a bid."

"I will give you one."

Harry "Then may I take you?"

So I guess I have asked a boy after all. I heard from mother this morning and she said I couldn't have a new dress so I am not very crazy about going.

Dance Cards

As restrictions on dancing only with partners of equal social rank gave way to more democratic attitudes in the 19th century, dance cards became popular. A card was a way for a young lady to keep track of the gentlemen to whom she had promised a dance during the course of an evening. Afterwards, it served as a memento. Sometimes, gentlemen also were provided with dance cards. Generally, however, they were expected to remember who they'd promised to dance with. By Medora's day, young men and women scurried around in the minutes prior to the first dance, signing cards.

The cards generally were made of paper, but for special occasions they might have

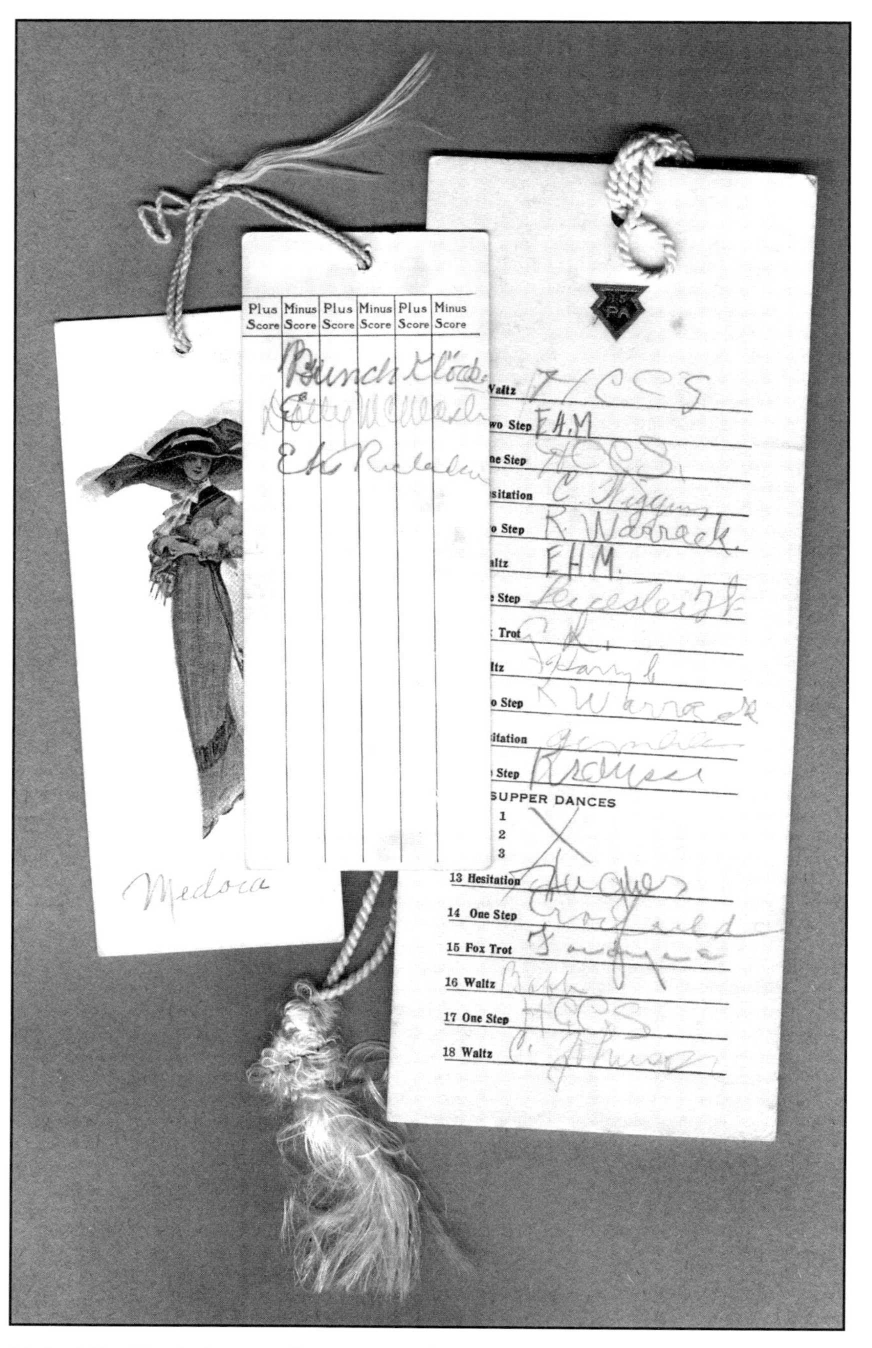

Medora's Five Hundred score card and prom dance card.

covers of bone, ivory, metal, or wood. They were small enough to be easily carried, and often had a small pencil attached by a cord, allowing the card to be suspended from a young lady's wrist or belt. The event, location, date, and sometimes even the price of a ticket might be inscribed on the cover.

A dance card usually included a list of the evening's dances, with spaces for the names of the partners who were promised a dance. Sometimes, dances were listed generically, such as "waltz," "polka," or "one-step." Other times, the name of a musical selection and composer were given; e.g., *"The Washington Post March*—Sousa."

[Portland]
Sunday, May 23, 1915

Dearest Mother,

I just got home from Eloise White's where I stayed all night. You know I went to the boating party with her brother. We left Portland about eight and docked at twelve. I had lots of fun—danced almost all evening. I am getting quite proud of my progress in the art. I am not afraid to accept any dance now, although I often get out of step but I am at least more confident. A boy I danced with quite a bit is going to take me to the Prom. I am sorry I can't have a new dress but understand the situation perfectly. I don't know whether I will wear the blue or the pink. I will have to have shoes and hose but I will borrow the gloves from Ruth. I really had a dandy time last night and am glad I went...

With lots of love, Medora

Diary, Monday, May 31, 1915

Mother arrived in town Friday and that night was the Prom. I had all my dances and had a dandy time. I spent Saturday with Mother. She left that night...

[Oysterville]
Tuesday, June 1, 1915

My dear Medora,

I arrived safely Sunday... Sue had gotten along fine and had a nice dinner ready—the most delicious dumplings I have ever eaten. She dressed the chicken herself. We also had nice salad and she made the dressing. For desert there was whipped cream cake and the table looked fine. She is a wonder! We don't half appreciate her.

This letter will probably reach you Thursday morning and I want you to please mail to me from P.O. or downtown somewhere that afternoon, Thursday, a 10c box of those Boston crackers—You know the round thick crackers that I split and toast for salad. They may have a different name these days but you can explain the kind. They are not so very hard as they split easily, so don't let them pawn any Pilot bread off on you. Another thing I want is two loaves of French bread. I want these mailed Thursday so I can toast the crackers on Friday.

I am anxious to know what the expense of my suit cleaning is. We have overdrawn at the bank and Papa is trying to find some place to borrow again. Poor dear man, I don't see how he can be so patient and sweet when he has so much to worry him…

I am so impatient for you to get home.

Please remember me to Miss Campbell. Tell Ruth C. she was the handsomest girl on the floor and tell Marge I hated to be so near and not have a chance to speak to her.

Much love, Mother

Harry Stevens & Hughes Martin
request the pleasure of Miss
Medora Espy at the Mallory
Hotel Saturday evening June
the fifth at 8 oclock.

707 Hoyt St.
Dancing. R.S.V.P.

Portland *Oregonian*, June 1914—

"Attired in the daintiest and most attractive summery frocks, dozens of pretty subdebutantes frolicked through the informal dance for which Master Harry Stevens and Master Hughes Martin were hosts last night at the Hotel Mallory. The ballroom and refreshment-room were artistically adorned with garden flowers, a charming combination of blue delphinium, canterbury bells and bright-eyed marguerites, intermingled with lovely vine maple, made a pleasing foil for the attractive young people in their smartest and prettiest party frocks. The future belles and beaux were received by Mrs. Charles H. Martin[2] and Mrs. E.T.C. Stevens, mothers of the two youthful hosts, and the ices were served by Mrs. James B. Kerr and Mrs. William T. Muir…" [The *Oregonian* article concluded by listing the names of the 61 young attendees, including "Medora Espy"].

Diary, Sunday, June 6, 1915

…Oh I had such a wonderful time last night. Why? Oh can't you guess? Two dances with Alec and he wanted to take me for a ride during the 5th and 6th dances. I certainly had the most wonderful evening. I am so glad I gave Harry Stevens a bid for the prom or I wouldn't have gone to this wonderful dance. I can hardly realize that I, an Oystervillian am considered by the newspapers a subdebutante.

All I do at present is worry about California. Even though I do love the children dearly and want to lift the burden off mother's shoulders, yet I don't want to be just nurse girl…Anyway the trip itself and the [San Francisco] Exposition will be very pleasant.

[Oysterville]
Monday, June 7, 1915

My dear Medora,

Saturday the teachers took lunch with me and everything went off nicely.

Yesterday all of us, even Papa, went with the Stoners clear around the Island and had a lovely time. It was a perfect day, so no one was sick.

You will find enclosed check. Papa went to grandpa's for the money.

Did you get the waist I sent and how about that suit of Willard's? Did Ruth give it to you and did she tell you about the underskirts that she was fixing for Mona. Mona has only those so surely bring them. I wish you would look again at M & F for a slip for Sue. She has to have something.

Much love, Mama

Diary, Tuesday, June 15, 1915

...[Last] Tuesday night Rosa woke Rosetta and I up saying that the Journal building was on fire at two o'clock and we didn't get back to sleep so had three hours sleep and I had two exams on Wednesday—English history and French. This is the first time in my life that I have cheated and I sure did this time; copied my kings and in French opened my book in my lap and copied it word for word. Next year I am only going to take three subjects and be virtuous... Thursday Bunch and I went to the parade with Dorothy and Jean. I don't care especially for the Rose Festival...

Papa met me Sunday morning. It seems mighty good to be home. The children are as dear as ever. Helen Dale's hair is curlier than I have ever seen it. Edwin is certainly doing well in school. After three months he has completed the primary work, reads from his primer, adds and writes his numbers. Willard, dear little fellow, can compose rhymes.

Notes

1. The local term for the town of South Bend.
2. The co-host "Master Hughes Martin," and his mother "Mrs. Charles H. Martin," were the son and wife of Charles H. Martin, a career U.S. Army officer with close personal and business connections to the Portland area. Charles Martin later served as Governor of Oregon, 1935–1939.

At last our dreams are realized...

CALIFORNIA, SUMMER 1915

For nearly a year, Mama made preparations for a summer trip "home," the first visit to California in more than eight years and the first ever with all six children. The Panama-Pacific International Exposition had opened in San Francisco in early 1915. Mama was determined to have the children attend "the fair," and, more importantly, to spend time with California relatives and her old dear friends in the Bay Area. Outfitting six youngsters for a 2½-month trip had been challenging, particularly with the family's constrained financial circumstances, but with help from Medora and the relatives, the undertaking was accomplished.

Their itinerary would begin in Berkeley, where the home of Mr. and Mrs. Bert Cross would be their "base of operations." Mrs. Cross—"Aunt Maud" to the children—had been one of Mama's closest girlhood friends and now was the wife of an up-and-coming San Francisco attorney, called "Uncle Bert" by the children. Aunt Maude had a spacious residence in which to house and entertain the Espy family. While there, they would have many opportunities to visit Mama's family, most of who lived in the East Bay.

They also planned to visit Papa's brother, Will, and his wife, Aunt Minette, who resided in the hills south of San Francisco, where Uncle Will worked on a Spring Valley Water Company project. And, the Espys were anticipating a trip south to Santa Cruz and Pacific Grove to visit more friends and relatives. Papa needed to remain in Oysterville for the first two months, but the plan was for him to join the family in the final weeks of summer. With Medora's able assistance, however, Mama knew she could manage very well indeed.

Medora and Portland friends, 1915.

On June 26, 1915, Mama and the children boarded the *Rose City* in Astoria. The journey to San Francisco took three days.

[3125 Claremont Ave. Berkeley, Calif.]
Diary, Wednesday, June 30, 1915

Do you realize Diary that I am in California, the land of our dreams? Those two weeks at home intervening between the eleventh and the

California Friends and Acquaintances

Arthur—Mama's first beau.

"Aunt Bess"—A girlhood friend of Mama's.

Marion Blankenship—A California acquaintance.

"Aunt Maud" Cross—Girlhood friend of Mama's living in Berkeley; married to **"Uncle Bert" Cross,** a San Francisco attorney; had a daughter, **Margaret.**

(The) Dingby girls—Sisters about Medora's age who gave a party in her honor in Berkeley.

"Aunt Mary" Hamlin—Mama's girlhood friend living in Santa Cruz, with husband and children **Edwin, Edith, Helen,** and **Laura.**

Clarence Hickock—Fellow youthful passenger on the *Rose City.*

Jenny—A friend of Mama's in California; helped Mama after Medora and Albert's births.

Emery Johnson—Inaugural Ball attendee at the Claremont Hotel.

Mr. Johnson—A member of Uncle Will's Calaveras Dam crew.

Mr. Larsen—Inaugural Ball attendee at the Claremont Hotel.

Mrs. Lindbloom—Inaugural Ball attendee at the Claremont Hotel.

Linden—A California acquaintance.

Edith and **Morton Margoyles**—Brother and sister; fellow passengers on the *Rose City.*

Edwin Markham—Inaugural Ball attendee at the Claremont Hotel.

"Aunt Leila" Reider—Lifelong friend of Mama's from East Oakland.

Henry Thomas—A California acquaintance.

"The *Rose City* is 336 feet in length, 43 feet in breadth and 22 feet in depth, having accommodations for 175 first-class and 230 second-class passengers. She was built especially for this service, is fitted with wireless telegraphy and everything necessary for the safety and comfort of passengers.

"The machinery...is of the latest improved type and oil is used as fuel. Hence there are no sparks or dust, as is the case where coal is used. The staterooms on these vessels are handsomely and comfortably fitted up, the general service is excellent and the table is not surpassed on any of the large trans-Pacific steamers. All conveniences are provided which will tend to add to the comfort and safety of the passengers."—San Francisco and Portland Steamship Company brochure, 1914.

twenty-sixth were very busy days. We packed, cleaned house, and did general overhauling... We left Saturday morning on the early train... arrived in Astoria about eleven; then followed a weary wait till three when the Rose City left. We had two large staterooms opening on deck. Only Sue was sick crossing the bar. Sunday morning was delightful, so calm and sunny. Just before lunch I got acquainted with... Clarence Hickock from Portland. We sat up on deck all afternoon and talked... Monday morning we arrived. Grandpa, Eva, Ruth, Buelah, Uncle Sid and Uncle Bert met us. Clarence asked to call. Ha ha! San Francisco is the thriving bustling metropolis of old; the bay, the fog and wind are all the same. But as we rode through Oakland I could see the difference. Out here in Berkeley are many beautiful homes. Aunt Maud's is very attractive, every little detail is so perfect, and the whole house is very artistic...

"Panama-Pacific Exposition," Feb. 20–Dec. 4, 1915

Also known as the San Francisco World's Fair, the Panama-Pacific International Exposition celebrated the completion of the Panama Canal, and also commemorated the 400th anniversary of Balboa's discovery of the Pacific Ocean. San Francisco had mounted an aggressive advertising campaign to host the event, successfully attaining the bid against rival cities, including New Orleans.

Although originally expected to be held in Golden Gate Park, it was decided instead to fill in mud flats at the northern end of the city, creating a new location later called The Marina. The fair encompassed 635 acres between Van Ness Avenue and the Presidio, and Chestnut Street and the Bay. Most of the palaces, courts, and state and foreign buildings consisted of temporary plaster-like construction,

OFFICIAL MINIATURE VIEW BOOK

of the

PANAMA-PACIFIC INTERNATIONAL EXPOSITION

Section of the Exposition Water Front

PUBLISHED BY ROBERT A. REID, OFFICIAL EXPOSITION VIEW BOOK PUBLISHER

150 Halleck Street, San Francisco

Copyright, 1915, by Panama-Pacific International Exposition Company

Medora's souvenir booklet.

Grandpa D.S. Richardson's widely published poem commemorating The Palace of Fine Arts—

Across the Lagoon

In Tribute to Maybeck's Palace of Fine Arts

If it be true that Beauty dwells
Apart from mortal eyes,
If, back of these transcendent forms,
More wondrous visions rise,
To him, star-eyed, who builded here
The blessed boon was given
To cross the golden bars and scale
The azure heights of heaven.

O happy eyes whose seeing led
My quickened eyes to see!
O happier hands whose cunning wrought
In shapes of wizardry!

'Tis meet that she should kneel whose form
To you chaste altar clings,
For lo, my ravished senses catch
The pulse of unseen wings.

intended to stand only for the duration of the fair. The Palace of Fine Arts, designed by noted architect Bernard Maybeck, however, was of more substantial materials and remains today as an elegant symbol of that bygone era.

The Exposition was of significant economic importance to San Francisco, still recovering from the 1906 earthquake and fire. The fair not only helped the city get back on its feet, but boosted the morale of residents throughout the Bay Area.

Earlier times in California, ca. 1895–1896, not long after members of the Richardson and Espy families became closely acquainted. From left to right: a "Mr. Hardy," Helen Richardson (before marriage to Harry), "Aunt Leila," Susie Espy, "Aunt Maud," and a "Mr. Tracy." Ruth Richardson, in front, is still a young girl.

Souvenir postcard from the "fair."

[Oakland]
Wednesday, June 30, 1915

Dearest Papa,

At last our dreams are realized and we really are here! Yesterday we...attempted to see a little corner of the Fair, but we only went through five buildings and did not see one thoroughly. It is immense compared to the northern expositions, a regular fairyland of beauty. During the entire day we only went through Canadian Pacific, Mines, Agriculture, Horticulture, Californian building, Liberal Arts and Transportation. Every minute I missed you, as I did so want to linger at different places where you would have been interested. Of course, yesterday we looked at everything with the children in view, forgetting the important educational value for grownups. However, we can get all this later if Mother's attentive friends don't demand any more time, though I would rather see her have a good time than any of us. Mother is keeping a date book, as every one demands her at once. Her friends are all so sweet, dear and cordial—very young and attractive too. They are very anxious to entertain her and kindly include me in nearly every invitation.

Lovingly, Medora

Front and back cover, Ford Motor Company brochure.

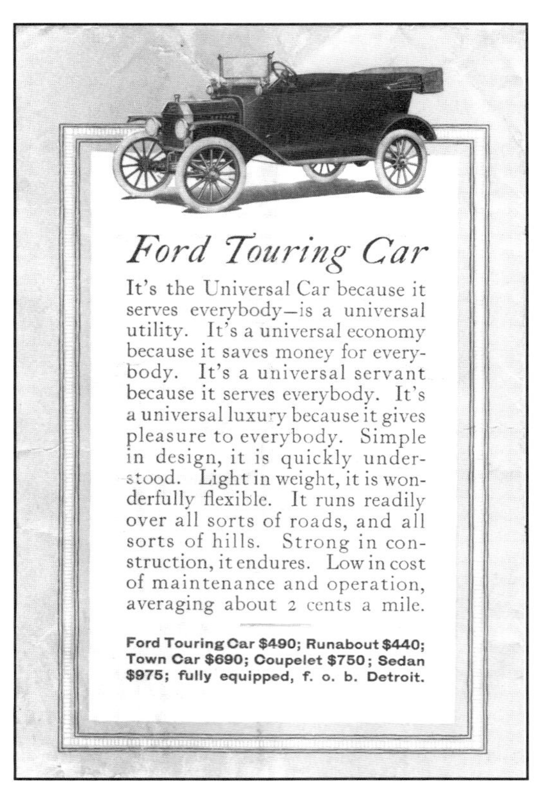

[Notebook on the Exposition]
My First Trip to the Exposition

...The Ford Motor Company has a very good place with literature on the subject, showing what sanitary conditions the employees live under. The two Fords are excellent men, very admirable characters. They turn out more automobiles than any other concern in the world. In Machinery Palace is a department where the machines arrive in hundreds of pieces and these parts are passed down a line of men, and the finished car passes out of the building every fifteen minutes. We walked down the avenue of

Eva—Grandpa Richardson's second wife. Their son Dan was born in 1909.

Palms, through the South gardens into the Horticulture Palace and ate lunch in the Hawaiian department...

Diary, Friday, July 2, 1915

...We spent the afternoon at Eva's. Dan is a pretty child but very badly behaved, so smart and impertinent. They have a pretty little home, very artistic because of all the little Japanese accessories. We ate watermelon in the summer house, which shows the different climatic conditions here. We don't have them in the north until the last part of August.

[Berkeley]
Monday, July 5, 1915

Dear Papa,

Mother will be very happy when she finds that your letter of the 2nd arrived this morning, as she has been very much worried, afraid you had fallen off the pier etc. We had a very pleasant day at Grandpa's yesterday, a sane fourth. Uncle Sid was there and was very much interested in cranberry land—wants you to be sure and come down as you may win a permanent settler of your brother-in-law in that way. I haven't seen any typical California weather yet—continual fog. Take good care of yourself.

Lovingly, Medora

Cranberries

Since earliest times, cranberries have thrived in the many natural bogs of the North Beach Peninsula. Local Indians tended and harvested wild cranberries, called *pil ollalies* in Chinook jargon. Smoke-dried and dipped in fish oils, the berries were healthful and considered delicious. They also were used to make poultices to draw poison from wounds, and to produce a rich, red dye. The *pil olallie* was an important trade item with other tribes, and later with white explorers, who were delighted to obtain the familiar fruit.

Early white settlers cultivated native cranberry vines in hand-prepared bogs. When commercial cultivation began in the 1880s, however, native berries were ignored. Not only were they smaller in size, but the vines grew closer to the ground, making them harder to pick.

Although both Papa and Grandpa Espy owned bog lands suitable for raising cranberries, they were more interested in oyster harvesting. Uncle Sid, however, found the possibilities intriguing, and in 1917 moved to Oysterville to try his hand at cranberry farming. He bought Mr. Holman's bog at the north end of town, reputedly the best producer in the area. After a few years, however, he moved to Medford, Oregon, finding that growing pears was more to his liking.

Diary, Tuesday, July 6, 1915

...We all went to lunch at Cousin Imogene's. Mother, Sue, Imo and I sat at a very daintily set table in the dining room while her three children and ours ate in a great big back yard. Sherwood age nine is a handsome child. Reed is a peppery red head age eight and Ethel age seven beautiful—auburn hair which is curly and great big brown eyes. Imo is very interesting. She told me a lot about Berkeley as she took a year of history there not long ago. She is expecting an addition to her family in the Fall. Isn't it wonderful to be a woman...

Diary, Wednesday, July 7, 1915

Aunt Maud took Mother and me to hear the oratorio "Elijah" at the huge new Oakland auditorium. It is an immense building...I enjoyed the affair very much but we sat too far away

The cranberry plant.

A low growing evergreen vine with runners from one- to six-feet long, cranberry grows in thick mats in cultivated bogs. Early American immigrants named the plant "crane-berry," because its pink blossom resembles a crane's head. Over time, the name was shortened to cranberry. The Great Blue Heron, a large wading bird referred to locally as a "crane," often is seen near the peninsula's cranberry bogs.

Uncle Sid Richardson, ca. 1920s.

from the stage. Three hundred and fifty voices hardly filled a house that had seating capacity for 9,000 and two thousand were there. It was in honor of the Baptists so we chose the most enjoyable affair for Grandpa Espy's sake. Clarence Hickock called up and I was simply dumbfounded... It was really awfully silly and how I managed to keep my head I don't know. It is the first time any boy has deliberately asked to call that I really liked. I have had them hint but that ended it. And Just think! I have only been with boys for one year...

Diary, Friday, July 9, 1915

...Clarence arrived sharply at one thirty... I discovered he was twenty six days younger than I and I was surely surprised though his figure is not developed at all, he is six feet tall, very slender, consequently round-shouldered, but I shouldn't criticize. Everybody remarks how very stooped I am...

Diary, Monday, July 12, 1915

...We took the 1:52 train for Milpitas. The trip was not very long, went along the edge of Alameda county to Niles then on to Milpitas in Santa Clara valley. There are so many fruit ranches in that district, mainly apricots... Milpitas is a thriving little market town... Aunt Minette lives nine and a half miles out of town up in the Calaveras hills which viewed from the valley seem almost impassable. Uncle Will is at the head of a big project there in the valley which is being carried out under the direction of the Spring Valley Water Company in order to furnish San Francisco with water. He has a hundred men under him, all a very transient class of laborers, tramps, and convicts...

Spring Valley Water Company

The successor to the Spring Valley Water Works, the company had supplied San Francisco with water for municipal and domestic purposes since 1865. (Before that time, small springs and streams within the city and county had provided water.) As an engineer for the company, Uncle Will was in charge of building the Calaveras Dam, located on Calaveras Creek in the Diablo Mountain Range. Here, a "hydraulic fill" dam was begun in 1913 and completed in 1925, which continues to be the largest of five local reservoirs maintained by the San Francisco Utilities Commission in the Bay Area. The family always was proud of Papa's younger brother, Will, and his highly responsible position with the water project.

Uncle Will Espy when he was attending Oregon State College, 1904.

Diary, Tuesday, July 13, 1915

I met a... Mr. Johnson who graduated from Berkeley this year. He is very dark, wore old English shoes. He is handsome with his hat on, and has very attractive manners... really very good looking... He has black hair, not curly but it stays in place and not too much of it either, long black lashes, black heavy eyebrows, a good nose, good strong mouth, an olive complexion, but he does not carry himself well, stoops, though he has a strong forcible face, he is about six feet when he stands erect.

Diary, Tuesday, July 20, 1915

We went to Palo Alto today, passing through Mountain View and visited Stanford University. It is very prettily arranged; the buildings are all of Mission architecture...

Diary, Wednesday, July 21, 1915

...No, I haven't any case as I simply couldn't be so silly about a man eleven years older than myself but the members of the opposite sex when attractive surely do stir up strange feelings in me. I guess I am sentimental... Well just because pants appear I am not at once upset, but if one wears good looking clothes, speaks correctly and is not a "sis," I can develop a queer sensational feeling at any time. No I am not too particular, though a pleasing manner and good eyes help a whole lot.

Diary, Thursday, July 22, 1915

Oh it has been hot all day. 100 in the shade! I have done an enormous washing and ironing. Occasionally during the forenoon I saw Mr.

Johnson pass, then about five I watched him ascend the hill to camp for the last time and something seemed to break. All of the good times I had had seemed years ago and I wanted to get out of the valley quickly. I went out to think it over in the hammock and to decide that I really had had more than indifferent regard for this man, in short I had developed a case but not a fierce one just a passing fancy, when his figure passed in front of the office tent. I lay watching him. He was dressed in his gray suit so I knew he was leaving and then Mother appeared. "Medora Espy come into your dinner. I am tired of this silly fasting." After dinner I went out again...How he knew I was there, I do not know. He asked to call me up and oh I laughed and am still laughing. I am very happy and so surprised! At six thirty we left in the Ford for Oakland after a funny day.

The Claremont Hotel

Begun in the early days of the California Gold Rush, the Claremont originally was a private home built to resemble an English castle. When it burned to the ground in 1901, only the livery stables, barn, and a few furnishings were left on the 13,000 acre site in the Berkeley Hills.

Eventually, Frank Havens won the property in a game of checkers. He dreamed of building a resort and in 1915 the sprawling Mediterranean-style hostelry was completed—just in time for the Panama-Pacific Exposition. Medora and Mama were in Berkeley at just the right time and with just the right people to be invited to the hotel's inaugural ball.

Diary, Saturday, July 24, 1915

...Mother, Aunt Maud and I went to the City...and shopped for a dress as I am going to the Claremont Hotel Inaugural Ball a week from tonight. And after looking at dresses at the Emporium, chose a pretty tho simple net dress. The neck is quite low, at least much more so than any other party dress I have ever had.

Picture postcard, 1915.

Ironing

"Various improved implements and machines have been perfected for ironing, but the old-fashioned flatiron heated on the range is still a well-nigh universal favorite...The patented flatiron which has a removable wooden handle is a great improvement over the old-fashioned iron which requires the use of cloth or asbestos holders...To do fine ironing it is necessary to have several kinds of irons. For shirt bosoms, collars, cuffs, a ribbed or other polishing iron is necessary. Ruffles will be improved by the use of a fluting iron. The puff iron for fine tucks, puffy sleeves, and other elaborate work is especially useful. This iron is attached to a standard and the cloth is passed through it. It may be heated at the ordinary range... Irons will heat more quickly and with less fuel and will keep hot longer if an iron or tin pan is turned over them while heating."—From Mama's copy of *Household Discoveries and Mrs. Curtis' Cookbook* (1909).

Diary, Monday, July 26, 1915

...Sue and Mona went to a movie; saw Charlie Chaplin for the first time. Even Charlie Chaplin dolls are being sold and he is so silly.

Diary, Wednesday, July 28, 1915

...I have been such a gay bird...a decided change from Oysterville, even during the summer when the beach crowd brighten the horizon. Here I am going all the time whether in a youthful or congenial crowd. I enjoy the sightseeing and the stage and show performances. However, when I do have a marvelous time it is always because there are attractive young people, and usually men or boys...I expected to be nurse girl and here: I have met Mr. Johnson and saw him for five evenings, Clarence and the wonderful moonlight hours with Morton Margoyles, that small dance where I met Henry Thomas and I would have seen more of him if he hadn't gone to the mountains, the dinner party and Linden (really a stupid affair), that luncheon the other day, the half hour with those sweet Dingby girls, and naturally I have enjoyed Mother's charming friends and the sightseeing, so I have certainly been more than nurse girl...During the afternoon Mr. Johnson called up. Gee! My second surprise. The first was when he asked to call up and the next was <u>doing it</u>...

Diary, Thursday, July 29, 1915

Mr. Johnson is really awful nice and I like him because he is so considerate of Mother and the children. He is going to call me up the first of next week. I can't decide whether I am sorry I told him not to come out tonight, or not. I guess I am confused. Now I am mad again. I don't understand myself at all. Why should I be so angry?

Diary, Friday, July 30, 1915

This morning I ironed for four hours steadily but it was worthwhile. Everything looked very nice. I am beginning to be quite confident in my ability as washerwoman. I washed, boiled, rinsed, blued, starched, dried, and ironed these clothes all by my lonesome and though they didn't look like laundry work they did appear well. I went over to Marion Blankenship's Afternoon given for me...They all asked me to come see them which is true California trick—hospitality in every form.

Diary, Saturday, July 31, 1915

We were all ready at six-thirty for the grand dinner and ball. I like my dress very much. Immediately after arriving we met part of our party and I sat down on the settee by Mr. Larsen, a very good looking Swede, who arranged my pillows for me at once. Another <u>man</u>. Am I not getting aged? There were twenty-two at our table—Mr. Larsen at my right and Emery Johnson, the leading man for the Liberty Film Company at my left. He was very handsome, tall, very tan and most wonderful eyes...Mrs. Lindbloom sat near me. She had a perfectly marvelous Irish crocheted dress with a long train—must have cost a thousand dollars at the very least...And the jewels! I have never seen anything like it even on the stage. Her stage name is Carrington and she plays for the Liberty Film Company, too...Had my first dance with Mr. Larsen...Then Uncle Bert and Mrs. Lindbloom led the grand march, followed by Edwin Markham and his suffragette friend. There were about ten dances and I had half...I enjoyed watching very much...There were lovely gowns and pretty dancing. I was fortunate enough to get the President of the Dancing Masters Association of America in the Paul Jones. He taught me a cunning two step right from Boston...

.. Menu ..

Toke Points on the Deep Shell

Clear Green Turtle Soup in Cup

Ripe Olives | Radishes | Salted Almonds

Striped Bass, au Gratin

Cucumber Salad

Roast Young Chicken with Dressing

French Peas | Potatoes Persilade

Hearts of Lettuce, Roquefort Dressing

Neapolitan Ice Cream

Bonbons | Small Cakes

Black Coffee

Hotel Claremont

July 31st, 1915

HOTEL CLAREMONT
JULY 31, 1915.
No. 98
First Prize by H. Morton & Co.
Second Prize by H. C. Capwell Co.
Third Prize by Taft & Pennoyer
Deposit either end in ballot box at door.

Menu and ticket stubs from the Claremont's Inaugural Ball.

Diary, Sunday, August 1, 1915

I have been terribly worried about this college business lately. Everybody gives me different opinions... I shall investigate thoroughly when Papa comes...

Diary, Tuesday, August 3, 1915

...There certainly must be lots of money in the Golden State. All over Oakland, Piedmont and Alameda are lovely homes. Everyone spends money for amusement, table, clothes, and keeps a machine. No one seems to realize the hard times which is so characteristic of the North. I am a true Westerner. I do not know which state to choose as mine. Washington is my home but still I know little of it except the small Peninsula, Olympia and Seattle and Tacoma slightly. I have passed down the coast line of Oregon many times and I do know Portland and the surrounding country pretty well. However, though it is my school state and I love Portland, I believe I shall be a true Native Daughter. I am much better acquainted with California and it is such a wonderful state. I wonder if I shall die feeling that I have not seen the territory I have passed over thoroughly. I have not done anything <u>thoroughly</u> along educational lines, disposition, and character development. I can hardly wait till Papa comes...

Diary, Wednesday, August 4, 1915

...We left on the one fifty for Santa Cruz, following the route to Milpitas until we reached San Jose where we changed cars for Watsonville. It was a very pretty forty-five minute ride among wooded hills intermingled with the bare hills. The cars were crowded so the Espy seven were distributed in the coach quite bountifully... Mr. Hamlin and Edwin met us at the station. Edwin is a boy fifteen years old who would have been handsome if it were not for a terrible case of harelip... Aunt Mary Hamlin has three girls younger than the boy... Mr. Hamlin is an artist. He paints and plays any instrument, making the violin his speciality, and composes. Aunt Mary

"Aunt" Mary Hamlin

Mary Hamlin (née Wallace) had been one of Mama's closest friends since girlhood. They had made paper dolls together, sent notes back and forth when sick, corresponded at length when parted, and shared all the secrets and dreams of their youth. As with all of Mama's good friends, the Espy children called her "Aunt" Mary, both out of respect and in acknowledgement of her closeness to the family. Mama and Mary exchanged frequent letters and infrequent visits throughout their lives. When Mary died in the late 1940s, her son Edwin wrote to Mama and recalled the long-ago visit of the Espys to the Hamlin home in Santa Cruz, confessing that he remembered having "quite a crush" on Medora.

Picture postcard.

"Medoyah"

Both Edwin and Willard had difficulty in pronouncing the medial "r" in Medora's name. Thus, "Medoyah" had become an affectionate nickname for Medora within the family.

has a wonderful mind. But they are certainly poverty stricken, certainly more so than we. An intellectual family but no culture. The house is even bare of necessities. Why! With the pictures, violins and books they could make an attractive front room. The parlor is very unimposing. It is just poor managing and lack of system…

Diary, Saturday, August 7, 1915

…Edwin asked me to go to the Unique and actually, I never have undergone such misery in my life. My first movie with a boy too. I hate to break boys in as it was Edwin's first girl. Deliver me from anything like it again. I had Alec's picture in my pocket which compelled me to behave decently. Therefore, I talked my head off except during the show which was rotten.

[Santa Cruz]
Sunday, August 8, 1915

Dearest Papa,

A long, long neglected letter but a very happy one as we are all so glad you are coming down. It has made the trip seem less like a needless expense to mother, delighted all your friends and especially your small daughter. It will be such a vacation for you, the money-making member of the family, just as it has been an education to me. However, I have not become fully able to bear the title of learned and need your assistance and incidentally brains, decidedly.

I have been to the Fair four times and for the lack of suitable guide, have not seen anything thoroughly. We could study it together, rather you could teach me during the days of that week which is filled with dinner engagements…

It has been a wonderful trip from beginning to end and such a treat to us all, tho' I shall not be satisfied until you are here and we have gone over the ground together—not only the Exposition but the university. I am very confused about the latter as everyone has given me different ideas, some of which worry me and I want to see if my fears are unfounded or not.

As for what I have seen, it would take hours to relate and we will be able to talk so soon.

We all send love and best wishes for a speedy voyage.

Very affectionately, Medoyah

Diary, Monday, August 9, 1915

…we made our 8:15 train… This time we rode between sand dunes and bare hills finally reaching Pacific Grove at 12:10. [Cousin] Aubrey met us. We drove to the Pryor home in a Hupmobile. I am so sorry [Cousin] Frances isn't here, but the family are expecting me to spend the summer here next year but I don't think I shall. In the evening we went to the Masquerade… and I had a dandy time tho' I was not masked. All my dances full except two—pretty good for a total stranger. Aubrey gave me a compliment—said I was a good dancer. Will wonders ever cease! Though I know I dance better every time I put my feet on the floor. I can feel it. Mother says so too. At last!…

Diary, Wednesday, August 11, 1915

Aubrey and I spent the morning in the yard taking pictures… He has the best looking ring. He had me try it on and I am mighty glad it was small. I would not want to wear my cousin's ring even if he is a third. I don't want to wear any boy's jewelry. I do not like it unless one is engaged. Still, I would love to wear a frat pin for fun. If Aubrey were as attractive as the ring, I might have worn it providing he was not a relative.

Diary, Monday, August 23, 1915

Papa arrived on the noon train... Elizabeth Ayer called up early this morning. I can hardly believe that I am going to really see her after two years separation. Mother, Dad and I had to go down to the 16th Street Station to meet Frances Pryor... I met Jack Stubbs, a life long friend of the Pryors... We had a nice long walk out under the stars and he asked to call me up. Oh! the sweet thing!!! I will never see him, I know as he just loves to kid girls along I know. And for the fifth time this summer, I was taken for twenty-two. Aren't men the limit? They have absolutely no idea of ages.

Diary, Wednesday, August 25, 1915

...About ten thirty Mrs. and Elizabeth Ayer arrived... Elizah Jane has not changed a bit since the old days at O.H.S.—the same open hearted girl with multitudes of freckles... went down to the Pig'N Whistle and got an awfully good lunch—chicken salad, stuffed peppers, clam broth and French pastry.

Diary, Saturday, August 28, 1915

I went down to Cousin Imogene's... She is dear as are all of Mother's friends and relatives, a charming group. I certainly hope that my friends stand the test of time as Mother's have...

My great great Aunt Ellen was there, deaf as a post, poor old soul, has been neglected and she was so grateful for my attentions. Then Aunt Shae a great aunt and she is the most amusing and clever relative I have. And Mary Bamford, a second or third cousin finished the relatives. She is the queerest thing... I enjoyed the aunts very much though my throat is raw from yelling.

Willard's Heart

In later years, Willard claimed he had only the vaguest memories of the 1915 trip to California. My mother, Dale, however, even though 11 months his junior, had one vivid remembrance of the time the family spent at the Exposition—she had to walk, while Willard rode in a perambulator.

"The folks thought that Willard had a rheumatic heart and so he wasn't to get too tired," she'd say in a tone of amused disgust, "so I had to walk!"

Six or seven years later, when Willard and Dale were a little older, Mama and Papa again felt that Willard needed special attention due to his heart trouble and frail condition. A doctor recommended that Willard spend the summer outside as much as possible, rather than staying indoors to read, write, or draw, which were his usual preferences. So the folks devised a scheme.

Two meadows were located south of Oysterville on the east side of the road. In the smaller one—"the little meadow"—Papa raised hay for cattle, whereas the adjacent "big meadow" was where the cows grazed. The folks decided that the fence between the two meadows would be taken down, and Willard and Dale would ride the erstwhile fence line to keep cattle out of the hayfield.

Willard, spying an abandoned bateau at the high tide line at the lower end of the meadow, went about fixing up an area under its deck with books and a flashlight. Bribing Dale by letting her ride his horse ("a better one than my old plug," she remembers), Willard convinced her to do all the patrolling, while he sequestered himself in his dark, dank hideaway. Mama and Papa soon became aware of the deception. After the fence was re-built, the children were put to work pulling weeds in the beet patch near the house.

These days, a solitary stone bench sits in "the little meadow." On it is a signed inscription in Willard's hand: "I can watch the slow breathing of the bay, six hours in and six hours

"Elizah Jane"

Elizabeth Ayer, of Medora's Olympia High School days, would be one of the first women to graduate in architecture from the University of Washington and the first woman licensed to practice in the state. Concentrating on residential design, she was known for her "traditional" houses in Cape Cod, New England, French Colonial, and English-country styles. Most were expensive and some became well-known landmarks in the Seattle area. In addition to Seattle neighborhoods, her homes can be found in Tacoma, Olympia, Aberdeen, Everett, and other Pacific Northwest communities. Elizabeth never married. In 1974, she wrote to Dale from Panorama City near Olympia:

"After 50 years as an Architect in Seattle I am back near my birthplace and, by sheer chance, Marie Strock settled in across the street. She has held very responsible positions with the state thru the years." From the Olympia High School days, Marie was a friend of both "Elizah Jane" and Medora.

out." The quotation is from the Afterword in his book, *Oysterville*.

Diary, Thursday, September 2, 1915

...I read all afternoon and tried to calm the youngsters down. They all are in need of a ten acre lot and a sound spanking...

Diary, Tuesday, September 7, 1915

We sailed! Uncle Bert went over to the city with us where Grandpa met us with a chauffeur and went down to Pier 40. Uncle Sid came down with us...so we had quite a delegation to see us off...

Souvenir postcard.

Diary, Wednesday, September 8, 1915

This trip has certainly done Papa good. He is so jolly and at least 5 years younger and to think that we are nearing home and everybody has certainly enjoyed the summer. At least I have!

Diary, Thursday, September 9, 1915

We arrived in Astoria at five thirty this morning and it was a typical Oregon day, cold and rainy. We had breakfast at the Imperial, then crossed the bay on the Potter. Took the train at Megler and all the way down the beach. I didn't see a soul I knew...Oysterville is just the same and so very uninteresting. We had dinner at Mrs. Kistemaker's, then went to Grandpa's to see Aunt Dora, Verona, the cousins Mary and Julia.

Diary, Friday, September 10, 1915

The house seems so shabby and dirty after all the beautiful homes we have been accustomed to this summer. I have two days to get things fairly presentable and there is so much to do. This day I cleaned the bed rooms and Papa swept it thoroughly, so it really looked very well by the end of the day...Oh! I am so glad it is nearing the 13th. I can hardly wait and oh! thrills! Alec.

Diary, Saturday, September 11, 1915

Papa was ill all the day. It is the first time I can ever remember of seeing him in bed. Just a stomach attack but rather uncomfortable.

Diary, Sunday, September 12, 1915

...It was a beautiful fall day and I certainly enjoyed the view from the bedroom. The blue blue bay with a few white sails in the foreground, then the lovely purple hills, at the feet of which the brown cliffs appeared mere specks to my eyes. The sky a clear blue with white fleecy clouds enhancing the lovely color. Aunt Dora and the rest of the guests went up with Papa and me to Portland...

I am still young, only sixteen but I think big thoughts...

Portland, Autumn 1915–January 1916

In mid-July 1915, the First International Bank of South Bend voluntarily closed its doors, insisting it was not insolvent, but that recent heavy withdrawals from accounts had caused a shortage of ready cash. The situation, they maintained, could be dealt with easily. By mid-September, it was clear that the bank, in fact, was insolvent, and depositors need not count on recouping more than pennies on their dollars. Papa had $11 in the bank at its closing.

For the H.A. Espy family, far worse than losing their small savings was the fact that many folks with whom Papa had business dealings lost their money as well. Gone was the possibility of collecting on several rather significant notes. The situation was further compounded by two additional Pacific County bank failures that summer and fall—the Raymond Trust Company, and the Fisher Bros. and Steiner Bank in Lebam. The ripple effect throughout the county caused the Espys' already precarious financial situation to reach desperate proportions.

Added to their financial woes was Mama's frail health. Her doctor in Astoria strongly recommended "female surgery" as soon as possible. As the tension mounted in Oysterville, it seemed providential that Medora soon would graduate from the academy. Increasingly, the family looked forward to Medora's return to Oysterville as a time when some measure of relief would be at hand.

Medora, 1915.

Diary, Friday, September 17, 1915

School again and I am beginning to like it though I haven't had a lesson yet this week. Alec was in my English class again. I was quite surprised to see him as I thot he was merely visiting

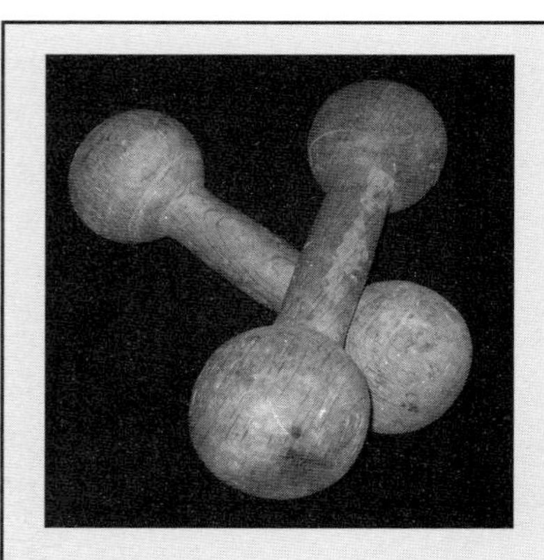

Indian Clubs and Dumbbells

As the name implies, Indian clubs originated in India, eventually making their way via England and Germany to the United States. Generally made of wood and shaped like bowling pins, they were swung in complicated circular patterns in order to expand the chest and exercise the upper body muscles. In Medora's day, they were used in most school physical education programs, and were said to help correct a tendency to stoop. Medora's Indian clubs no longer survive, but her wooden dumbbells (also used in her gym class) do. They are stored in an upstairs closet, along with several well used wooden baseball bats and a pair of old-fashioned ice skates.

yesterday but at last I have his program clear in my head.

Me	*Alec*
U.S. History	*German*
English	*English*
Study Hall	*Cicero*
lunch	*lunch*
Eng. History	*Chemistry*
Geometry	*Geometry*
Study Hall	*Study Hall*

It is awfully silly of me to worry about his program but I find myself quite a fool as far as Alec is concerned.

[Oysterville]
Sunday, September 19, 1915

Medora:

Is there any place you could get a suit not to exceed twenty-five dollars and charge it? We cannot pay more than this, and want you to get it as much cheaper as possible. Do be careful. Don't buy one the scale that you got your shoes. Six dollars was dreadful. This would get two or even three pair for the rest of the family. There is a saying that nothing is so bad but what it can be worse, but I verily believe the worst stage has reached us financially. We don't know from day to day how things may turn. However, I know there will come a time when we can make up to you for this skimping.

Papa says he wants you to make better marks during this your senior year. Send for your application blank right away to enter Stanford.

Hastily, Mama

[Portland]
Sunday, September 19, 1915

Dearest Mother and Papa,

Everything looks the same around here. Miss C. has had the floors all done over and that's about the only change. I found my French and Caesar books all right... also my Indian clubs.

If this letter is not coherent, please don't blame me because I am watching the football boys practice in between words and I am surely excited. Oh! How I adore the game.

Please don't work too hard, either one of you, for when I am a successful librarian I want a young father and mother to exhibit, who didn't lose their youth though they did make many sacrifices.

Lots of love, Medora

Diary, Wednesday, September 22, 1915

...Nobody is like Alec to me. I wonder why it is. It can not be that subtle something that draws men and women together. I am not in love, I know, tho it seems as if he were the only man and

Portland Academy football team, 1914. Alec is in the center of the middle row.

I am not the only woman to him. It reads like a tragedy. I think I am over sentimental and young in my ideas. I dwell on him too much…Met RuthieD at four and shopped with her till five fifteen. I was certainly glad to see her. All my aunts are dears.

[Oysterville]
Sunday, October 10, 1915

My dear Medora:

There is so much to do and so little time and strength to do with. I get so discouraged and disgusted that it seems useless to try. The girls might almost as well be away in boarding school. They do the night's dishes and absolutely nothing else. If I were only able I would much prefer doing everything than listening to their wrangling. Stay by your resolution to perfect your library work. If I had any sort of a profession to turn to, I would certainly hire my housework done and get rid of this nagging strain. Nothing has seemed right lately. Failure is all I can see for myself. It sometimes seems as though things would run just as well if I were out of the way. I don't mean to imbue my letter with the doldrums, but do feel "blue." Burn this. I don't want anyone to see it and conclude that your mother is a grouch. I am going to take some liver pills tonight and my disposition may be improved thereby.

Much love from, Mother

[Portland]
Wednesday, October 13, 1915

My dearest Mother:

Please don't get so discouraged, Mama. It doesn't pay. Mama, you know how much you mean to me and to all of us, so it is silly to think that you have failed. What would I have been without you—boy crazy and ambitionless. I firmly believe we are put in the world for some purpose and you have been faithful to yours and I shall live mine in single blessedness while I am making you and Papa comfortable.

Lots of love, Medora

P.S. I heard from Stanford that I can't possibly enter before 1917 even though I put my blank in now. Two whole years, Mama!

Friday, October 15, 1915

My dear Sister,

Where shall we begin? Things have been moving rather rapidly since last I wrote. Day before yesterday our chimney caught fire and created quite a bit of excitement in Oysterville. It was not quite so bad as that first fire we had, but plenty bad enough. Papa was fortunately in town and I was relieved of the responsibility. Poor little Edwin was frightened nearly into a spasm. He went screaming down to grandpa's to get Papa, arousing the whole town as he went. Both he and Mona were home from school sick that morning or I would not have had anyone to send after Papa.

I have been so uncomfortable lately that I decided to run over to Dr. Estes in Astoria and get his opinion and some treatment for today, Friday, planning to take Mona and have her eyes tested. She suffers continually with headaches.

Well, yesterday, just as I was about to wash Mona's head, Edwin came in crying which of course frightened me, and I finally found that his right arm was broken. You may imagine! Papa tried to get the doctor and the phone wouldn't work so he sent for Bert Andrews to run them right up to Mr. Lehman's—he has had considerable experience and said it would not hurt to wait until morning and take him to Ilwaco.

I couldn't well break my engagement with Dr. Estes, as we are in no position to pay for unkept appointments, so Papa decided we would all start out together and he would take Edwin to

Mama's Condition

Mama had suffered considerable discomfort following Medora's birth in 1899. Upon examination, a doctor informed her that she had a severely lacerated cervix and recommended "treatments." She described the treatments as "severe," but continued them on and off for years with several physicians, depending on where the family was living. Although the condition seemed to improve with each series of treatments, the trouble had cropped up again with the arrival of each new baby. Presumably, a hysterectomy was finally recommended and considered.

Dr. Paul while I went on to Astoria with Mona. I hated terribly to think of not being at home with Edwin tonight, but know he will be all right with Papa. I won't know the extent of his injury or anything about it until tomorrow. He was wonderfully gritty and cheerful—seldom murmured unless his arm was touched. He put in a restless, miserable night last night but did not cry.

He was standing up in his wagon and Lloyd was pushing. The latter stopped suddenly and Edwin lost his balance pitching out on to his dear little arm. I am so grateful that it was not his back or neck. A broken right arm is sufficient. The injury seems to be just below his elbow, I think, but Papa thought it in the elbow.

I had an exhausting treatment this afternoon and suffered horribly but feel that the examination was thorough. He says I must have an operation. The trouble is higher up than we thought. I can explain better when we are together. What a blessing it is to have a dear girl I can talk everything over with.

If you are out of school next year I shall have the operation then, early in the Fall as Dr. Estes says it will take about a year for me to regain my normal strength, though I will only be in bed a couple of weeks.

Expense seems inevitable, doesn't it dear?

You mustn't get blue and moody, Medora. Make the best of your young girlhood. Don't let Alec cast any shadows into your days, dear. Try to be bigger than this infatuation. I know just how it is, but some day you will realize that this is but an awakening of your woman's nature, a forerunner to all the great absorbing life light that will come later.

You are not the girl to have a new fancy every week—like your mother these things strike you hard. But try to look it squarely in the face and not think of it as serious or final. I know from my own painful experience that my feeling for Arthur [former California beau] as compared with my love for your father was "as moonlight unto sunlight, or as water unto wine."

Do you want to stay out a year in order to enter Stanford in 1917? I would love to have you home a year and it would be such a comfort to have you with us again. Of course, we will have to see how things work out...

Devotedly, Mama

[Portland]
Thursday, October 28, 1915

Dearest Mother,

I wish I were home and could talk to you. I can't stand Ardis Fischer, the other girl at the hall, and simply can't get away from her. I am controlling my dislikes as best I can. The reason that she is so uncongenial is because she is ruining the reputation of the hall by doing terribly rash things such as talking to a half a dozen boys who she has never seen on the phone until 11:30. Mother, just think! She let the boys think that it was I who asked her to call them up...one of the nicest boys at the Academy is going with her just to make a fool of her, either that or his morals are rapidly degenerating. I can't do a thing but keep myself above such actions. Still all those boys know me and what will they think...

I want to come home.

Medora

[Oysterville]
Tuesday, November 2, 1915

My dear little girl,

Troubles never come singly, do they? I was so sorry to learn of your discomfort at the Hall... The boys know your conduct with them and I do not believe associate you at all with Ardis' boldness. Those who would believe a stranger, and one of her type, are not worth worrying over. The sooner their friendship is lost, the better. One thing you have not lived long enough to realize (and tho it is so, I never will know why) is that all masculine gender old and young will play with a frivolous girl. Often a fine lad will associate madly with a girl, who if his sister chummed with, would make him indignant. But this is always a superficial attraction. In their hearts they do not respect these women. Often a physical infatuation exists, but rarely a fine man either loves or marries his butterfly toys. The boys know your habits of the past two years so don't worry about their associating you with the indiscretions of other girls.

If I were in your place, I would take some one of the boys into my confidence. Tell him of what Ardis is doing and how it embarrasses you. A plain talk has been my solution to uncertain situations. I always found the boys in particular so open and companionable that it was not mortifying to talk freely. If Alec is influenced by this kind of girl, consider yourself as having had a lucky escape…

I fear you would not be very happy at home just now. We are on such a tension that one can feel it in the air. The strain is terrible. No one can see the end. Still, as I say to Papa, if we can keep our health and one another, the greatest in life is still ours. The Ilwaco bank has called in its note and three mortgages have come due at once, all in addition to the South Bend bank failure. I can not see any thing but bankruptcy, tho there may be some way out that is hidden now. Yet, worry never helped anything. By the time this is over, we will have worried ourselves unfit to cope with whatever comes. Worry is mental cancer—it kills. I am trying to find a silver lining and "suppose" things will be all right—

"'Suppose that this here vessel,' says the skipper with a groan,
"'Should lose 'er bearin's, run away, and jump upon a stone,
"'Suppose she'd shiver and go down, when save ourselves we couldn't,
"The mate replies
"'Oh blow me eyes,
"'Suppose again she shouldn't."

So dearie, "we should worry!" Forget the boys and cling to the sweet girls who know you. They understand and are the ones to tie to after all. The boys probably will drift out of your life anyway, but the girl friends will be yours twenty years from now…

I have a feeling that you will soon find your troubles a thing of the past as I went through similar difficulties in my own school experience.

Always your loving and sympathizing,
Mother

[Portland]
Study Hall Last Hour
Thursday, November 4, 1915

That wonderful long letter arrived this morning and was surely welcome… Yes, as you predicted I am in a much more cheerful mood than when I last wrote… I will be with you all three weeks from today and we can have some good long talks… If an opportunity arises, I will tell some one of the boys the whole story.

I am disgusted with the way lots of the girls act with boys. Perhaps I am too rigid in my views. I think it is the girl's place to be entertaining and ready to participate in a boy's sports or pleasures but this sentimental bosh "gets" me. Thank Goodness you have taught me to behave myself and I am quite sure I will never disgrace the family…

Willard, Edwin, and Dale, 1916.

Medora at The Hall.

How is dear little Edwin and give Papa a great many wishes for a happy birthday and a happier one each year. It is all coming out alright I know.

Lots and lots of love, Medora

[At Astoria]
Sunday, November 6, 1915

My dear Medora,

This morning I took the seven o'clock train for Astoria and am now on the boat about ready to start back.

I had my treatment and as usual am feeling pretty miserable as a result for his treatments are very severe. I had him examine my ear, and he says that there is a bulge in the inner ear cased by a secretion from somewhere. He does not want to handle it and told me to go to a specialist. More expense. Am going home to talk it over with Papa. Isn't this interesting!

I am counting the days until you return.

There is no news. Edwin's arm is doing beautifully. It is straight but stiff. I think this will gradually wear away.

I have that squirrel fur on and maybe you think I don't feel awful. It is shedding in chunks. My eyes, ears and nose are full and, as it is stormy, I have your black coat and really it looks like a sick animal simply covered with loose hair. Moths must be in the fur. I can't imagine what else ails it. It is a good thing I haven't sent it to you. Lew is on the train and the moulting condition I am in makes me feel so foolish that I'm avoiding seeing him.

Later—Well, Lew saw me and we talked. He is as nice as ever.

Lovingly, Mama

I hope you burn my letters up. They certainly would be beautiful looking things to hand down to posterity.

[Oysterville]
Monday, November 22, 1915

Yes, I think you had better plan to be home next year, as I must have my operation as it may add a good many years to my life, in fact must be done, and the doctor says I will be a year regaining normal strength. It would be impossible to pay for help and keep you in school. You are young, and I really do not think will lose much by the lapse of time.

Now be a good girl and be happy. Make sure you are perfectly well. Remember it would be no kindness to us who lean on you so strongly to allow yourself to go uncared for. It is your sacred duty to be well—or see to it that you get well if ailing.

Only a few days now before you are home. We must make the best of things as they are this Christmas and enjoy the spirit of the day, overlooking the lack of material things.

Good night dear.

From Mama

[Portland]
Sunday, November 28, 1915

My dearest Mother,

Last night was another stormy siege and I had dreadful dreams about you all. Not having heard since the special delivery addressed to the Arthur, I am rather disturbed, fearing that you have all been swept into the bay as the ill fated Bay View hotel was into the ocean. Aren't the storms terrible. I wish I were home as you must be terribly depressed by this weather.

I am still at Mrs. Klocker's and undecided whether to return to the Hall tonight or not. It has been a very pleasant vacation if it had not been that I thought of you continually. Thursday evening Helen's father brought Helen and me over here in the electric [automobile]. I wonder what Mrs. Wirt would think to see me driving about Portland in an electric.

Friday Mrs. Klocker took Rosetta, Helen and me to the Priscilla Tea Room at Meier and Frank's for lunch. It is a lovely place and is well patronized by society. Splendid service and expensive food. We then went to a movie and it was the spookiest thing I have ever seen. Came home and dressed for the party. I really had a dandy time though three dances were not taken—not so bad out of twenty five or six numbers. Russell Sewall was my escort and he is very nice. He asked me just a day or two after the bids were out and James Gamble says Alec was sore because he had intended to ask me.

Do you remember long ago when you said I might have a house party from my graduating class? About the second week in July I want Jean and Carl, Marge and two other boys down, perhaps one will be Alec.

I am going over to see Ruth some time next week, though I must read a lot. I have Mallory's "Morte d' Arthur" and "Cloister and the Hearth" to finish before Christmas.

If you only knew how I long to see you, the dear babies, my ever patient and noble father, and the growing sisters, I am sure you would be surprised as my letters are inclined to be troubled, gay or money seeking. The more I think of next year, the more I wish for the time to come when I can be home with my family.

Lots and lots of love to all my wonderful family and especially my sweet, patient, and ever indulgent Mother,

Medora

Diary, Friday, December 3, 1915

I wish I could follow and be my ideal girl for she is briefly: A happy good natured girl bubbling over with good spirits and enthusiasm, a cheery smile for everyone, especially thoughtful of older people, always kind, never making a mean or sarcastic remark. And she is serious when the occasion demands it, earnest and reverent, a bright well-informed girl, one who takes advantage of every opportunity. A faithful friend and a wholesome companion to all boys, ready to participate easily into all their sports and pleasures. Then, too, she is neat in personal appearance, careful of her health and pure minded. Above all ready to give to her prince and husband, perfect (as God could wish) womanhood. So may I be. I am still young, only sixteen but I think big thoughts.

Medora sleeping.

[Portland]
Sunday. December 12, 1915

I received your letter yesterday and will do as you say. Can you send my check early as my poor washwoman is getting impatient for her money. I haven't paid her for two months and my laundry usually averages fifty cents a week. Will we ever be away from this burden of money? I am perpetually owing somebody, never get paid up entirely and still I never seem to spend much. I hate money and debts. I don't think I will ever go to college if I have to be encumbered with the thought of debts. How can you and Papa be so cheerful? I would like to rob a bank.

[Oysterville]
Tuesday, December 14, 1915

My dear Medora,

This letter is a last resort. We simply can not get money and I must have something for Leila and Grandpa [for Christmas]. I have not gotten one thing at M & F but you must try to get me Riley's Poems of Friendship for Leila and get something in prose, the latest or near latest of Ella Wheeler Wilcox for Daddy. I must have something and don't want you to fail me. Didn't Ella Wheeler Wilcox write some book on "New Thought" that you were speaking of? Bring these with you but try not to get expensive ones. I will get check for your ticket to you some way.

Papa says don't bring trunk—save fifty cents and borrow Ruth's suitcase. Bring your white petticoat. Sue has to wear long dress in entertainment. If you have time, get at the 10c store a spray of some sort of pink flowers. She is "June" in the Program and has to have flowers. I don't want to spend more than 25c.

Please learn what Ruth wants. Has she a sandwich tray? We will have to get for her in Astoria unless you do at M & F's. This may be best, only not to exceed $1.50—can get silver plated perforated sandwich plates at M & F's for $1.50 and $2.00. She does not want books and I am at sea. Find out and get (but remember our means.)

Dale has no special desire for a "baby doll." Any cute doll will do. I don't think celluloid heads much more durable than bisque. There are endless varieties of 50c dolls. Edwin wants "Jack straws" and these cost only 15c. Books are fine but too expensive.

Did I ask you to get McNally's salad oil?

Those books I asked you to get for grandpa and Leila will cost more at Gills.

About wearing your good suit and hat home, I hardly know what to say. If you do, hang onto your umbrella as we can't get another outfit soon, if you have to go naked. I would like to have you look presentable in Astoria, but not at the expense of your best clothes. Use your own judgement.

I will meet you Saturday morning at 9:45 at dock—or if it is too wet, wait in Dr. Edmund's waiting room. Tell him who you are. I don't want you getting wet. Wear rubbers.

About Papa and me—we would really rather you didn't use the money on us with money as it is now.

Be careful of your health. You must not neglect Grippe and develop pneumonia.

Only a few days now before you are home.

Lovingly, Mother

Enclosed find check for $10. Bring back what change you can as we will need every cent in Astoria. This will be our last chance for last minute purchases.

[At Astoria]
Diary, Saturday, December 18, 1915

I have three quarters of an hour before Mother arrives so I shall take advantage of the time.

Diary, this waiting room is an awful place to write and I can't think but the one thought, Alec. I am such a fool. Our friendship can never come about. We both pull the wrong way. I am so shy and foolish when he is around and he blushes all the time. Oh! Diary, I am glad I am going home where I will be away from all these disturbing elements for a few weeks. I am so glad I am going home and see my dear family and tell Mother of Alec.

Diary, Saturday, January 1, 1916

The first day of the New Year—May 1916 accomplish more than 1915 did in building my character! Though I feel far better satisfied with the past year than the one before, and thus may the years continue, each one more perfect than the last until I find everlasting peace. A complication of affairs is keeping me at home this next week from school and in those extra seven days I want to help my dear family as much as possible. There is so much to do in a household of eight which my little frail mother can not manage.

Diary, Monday, January 3, 1916

My seventeenth birthday. Why I am really becoming a young lady! I shall live this year cheerfully without any sentimental attachment awaiting my prince, and preparing for him. If in all the long years he never comes, I have lots to do for others.

[Portland]
Tuesday, Jan. 11, 1916

Dearest Mama—

Just a hasty line to let you know I am perfectly safe. It seems good to be back in a way tho' I wish you were all here. The snow is several inches deep and it is bitterly cold, far more so than at the beach. I wish I had a winter coat.

Exams are near and I have enough to keep me awake nights but last night I retired at seven sleeping twelve hours straight. Why do I need so much sleep?

[Oysterville]
Friday, Jan 15, 1916

My dear Medora:

We had not had any <u>*weather*</u> *before you left, compared with this week—It has been fierce!*

Papa and I have been worried about your health and comfort. We were quite relieved to hear that Ruth had let you have scarf and sweater. Papa was disgusted to find your rubbers. We certainly hope you are keeping dry feet and taking care of yourself. The "town" has been coasting every night and of course Sue has gone. We will be glad when this unusual spell has passed, tho it shows no signs of leaving yet. In fact, snow is falling at intervals today and the wind howls.

I have a pair of papa's underdrawers over mine today. Papa insisted and I am glad he did, for I feel warmer.

We certainly miss you. It was such a comfort having you home.

Don't do any risky things dear. Remember what you mean to us and take no chances with your precious self.

Always with love, Mama

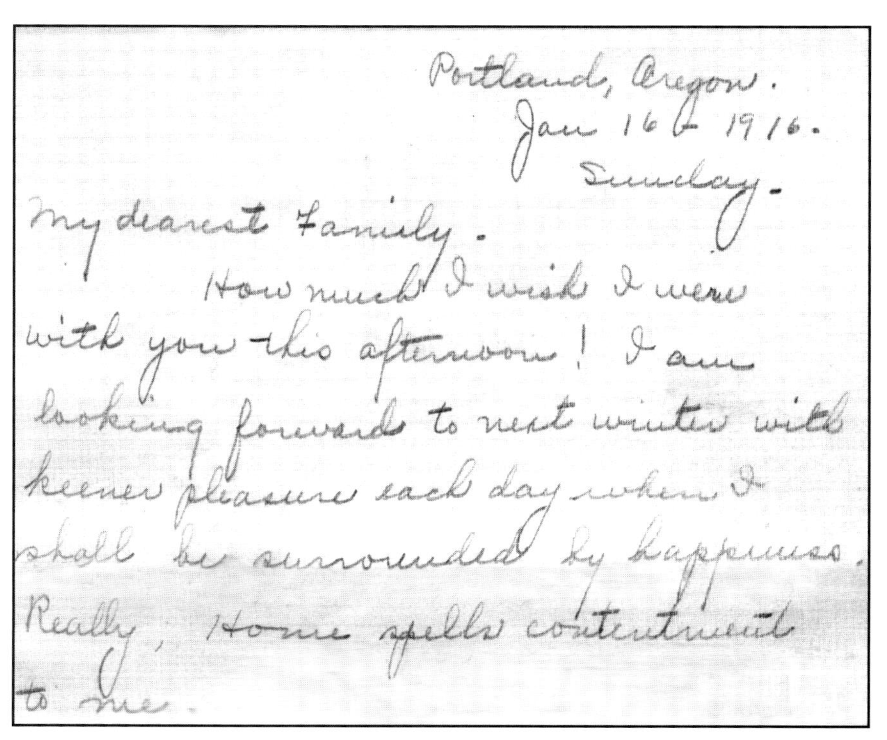

Portland, Oregon.
Jan 16 – 1916.
Sunday.
My dearest Family.
How much I wish I were with you this afternoon! I am looking forward to next winter with keener pleasure each day when I shall be surrounded by happiness. Really, Home spells contentment to me.

First part of Medora's final letter—found unsent, on her desk at "The Hall."

South Bend Journal
Friday, January 21, 1916

Senator Espy's Oldest Child Dies in Portland

Cerebral Hemorrhage Causes Death of Oysterville Girl

Miss Medora Espy, the 17 year-old daughter of Mr. and Mrs. Harry Espy, of Oysterville, died suddenly on Tuesday, January 18, in Portland, Oregon. She had retired in apparently the best of health the night before, but could not be aroused from what appeared to be a deep sleep the following morning. A physician was summoned, but despite all medical aid, she died before noon without having regained consciousness. The cause of death as diagnosed by physicians was cerebral hemorrhage. Her parents were immediately notified of her illness and rushed to Portland, but unbeknown to them, on account of the delicate condition of the mother, who for the past few years has been practically an invalid, their errand was only for the purpose of burying their first-born.

The funeral was held in Portland Wednesday, January 19. As token of respect, the Portland Academy, of which Miss Espy was a pupil, was dismissed and eight of her most intimate girl classmates acted as honorary pall-bearers, while six boys acted as active pall-bearers.

Medora Espy was born in East Oakland, Calif. Jan 3, 1899 to Harry A. and Helen Richardson Espy, moved to Oysterville in 1902 with her baby brother who died Jan. 1905. She received her grammar school work at Oysterville and at even this early period of her childhood she studied and enjoyed deep books, taking interest in many works in her father's library. Great responsibilities seemed to rest on her shoulders. She comprehended the seriousness of life, always toiling for some one's comfort, always thoughtful of the mother, always thinking of others and respecting their wishes when for their happiness, like her good grandmother who was known in this county as an unerring example to motherhood and an inspiration for her associates.

Medora took her first year high school work in Olympia, then entered Portland Academy from which school she was to graduate next June. Naturally, she stood at the top in her class work and was loved by her classmates and respected by her professors.

Next winter was looked forward [to] by the entire family with a great deal of happiness and satisfaction as a time when Medora would spend a year at home before entering college. During the holidays this winter, she spent three weeks at home and the mother and father were beginning to realize the comforts of raising such a daughter who enjoyed everything that they enjoyed and sympathized with everything that they sympathized with.

Besides the father and mother, three sisters, Suzita, Mona, and Dale and two brothers, Edwin and Willard, survive.

From Mama's Scrapbook—

Medora

Dear helping hands that led,
Down life's thorn strewn way.
Dear loving hands that fed,
The wants of every day.

Now in my greater need
And loneliness for thee
Dear gentle hands O, heed
The anguish of my plea.

Lean a bit across the strand
And lead me where you are
A beckon of your guiding hand
Will prove the gates ajar.

Edwin, Dale, and Willard in 1917.

Let the memory of Medora be that of a happy dream...

AFTERWORD

My mother Dale was just two months beyond her 4th birthday when Medora died, yet parts of the time that followed are still etched in her memory. "Mama stayed in her bedroom for days. No one could go in except Papa and I remember that she would only eat steak, blood rare. Papa would dash through the house with her plate so that he could deliver it piping hot, in the hopes that she would eat at least a bite or two. It seemed like she was 'gone' for a very long time."

Indeed, Mama struggled mightily to revive. On February 24, 1916, more than a month after she had taken to bed, her father wrote from San Francisco:

My dear daughter Helen:

Your pathetic note of the 21st has just been placed on my desk and I drop everthing else to tell you how happy it makes me to receive something directly from your hand. It proves to me how bravely you are trying to get back to earth. Do not fear, my dear girl; everything will come out right. There is nothing which we can say or do for each other in times like this. Philosophy, and even religion itself, must take back seats for awhile until we have out our cry. But there is a philosophy waiting to be recognized and sooner or later all tired souls may fall back upon it if they will. I believe you are headed that way and that the light will break upon you soon. I see it in your recognition of dear Harry's patient kindness and unfailing tenderness. You will read it in Ruth's sisterly devotion and the mute efforts of the little ones to do what they can to help. Do you know that wonderful story in Arnold's "Light of Asia" about the poor mother whose baby had been kissed by the snake? The Master, to whom she appealed for help, sent her on a long quest from which she returned not quite so unhappy as when she set out, for she had learned that her lot was the common lot of all. That, I believe is the only helpful philosophy. You must get to thinking of others. When you think you can't stand it, let your mind wander for an instant to desolated Europe where death and disaster have invaded nearly every household. You have a thousand things to live for. You are rich compared with millions of your sisters in all parts of the world.

Let the memory of Medora be that of a happy dream. When you remember how short life is, why should we give up in despair because a loved one crosses the bar a few days in advance. I know nothing of the hereafter—nor does anybody else—but I do have an abiding faith that all is well. It is not fair to ourselves—it is not fair to those who love us—to perpetuate grief...

My love to all the dear babies and everyone else. Try to write to me again as soon as you can and keep up your courage. Do not lose faith in anything that has ever brought comfort because of this affliction. Your religion is just as good as it ever was. You would not understand life's mysteries any better when she lived than you can now. It is all a part of that "far off divine intent" towards which the whole creation moves. By accepting it we conquer; by rejecting it we are lost.

Lovingly, Daddy

Eventually, of course, Mama did return to family and household duties. The "operation" that she anticipated with such anxiety during Medora's last year never occurred, and although she remained somewhat fragile throughout her life, she spent the next 38 years devoting herself to Papa and the children and grandchildren. Her father's difficult advice of

Mama, ca. 1917.

Mama, ca. 1918.

Papa, ca. 1920.

letting "the memory of Medora be that of a happy dream" apparently was accepted. By the time I came along, her references to Medora were joyful ones, with just a touch of that melancholy her own children remembered.

Perhaps with Medora's death, Mama began to realize that Oysterville, after all, had become the place where she would live out her life. Certainly, when Grandpa died just two years later, there was no talk of moving back to East Oakland—nor in 1925, when Aunt Kate died. By then, Mama realized their lives were forever entwined with Oysterville and the Pacific Northwest. Though she might long for friends and family in California, returning no longer was a possibility.

The family's money troubles continued for another two decades following Medora's death, and Papa labored mightily to keep the household afloat. The effort and worry cost him dearly, and, by the time the youngest three children were in high school, Papa's health finally broke. For most of 1924 and 1925, Papa was bedridden with severe, chronic asthma.

In 1926, Mama and Papa decided to go south to Redlands, California, where Edwin and Willard would enter the freshman class at the University of Redlands, a Baptist school. It was thought that the southern California climate would do Papa good. The family stayed there for the next six school years, until Dale also graduated from Redlands in 1932.

Sometime during this period, Papa, having exhausted all traditional medical advice and methods prescribed by doctors up and down the coast, sought out a medical man living in the Mojave Desert, even though he was reputed to be "a quack." Papa was advised to confine his diet to greens and meat fat, and, within weeks, he was much improved. Gradually, he included other foods in his diet, but until he died in 1958 at age 82, greens and fat were a part of every meal that he ate, even breakfast.

Mama and Papa's finances improved in the late 1930s, when experiments with Japanese oyster seed in Willapa Bay proved successful. Suddenly, the "worthless" tidelands that Papa had so tenaciously hung on to over the years became valuable. Mama and Papa's waning years were comfortable and worry free, thanks to the "lease money" Papa received from the oyster companies that grew oysters on his bay property.

As for Medora's beloved brothers and sisters, all remembered their childhood in Oysterville with great fondness. As East Oakland always remained "home" to Mama, Oysterville remained "home" to each Espy child. Though their lives took them to far-flung places and to lifestyles that could not have been imagined by Medora, each would return home often and several moved back to Oysterville permanently in later life.

Suzita (Sue)

Although none of the remaining children stepped into Medora's role as Mama's "strong right arm," efficient, capable Sue certainly did her part for the family during her remaining years at home. But hers was a different personality—vibrant, charismatic, and by the 1920s, the quintessential flapper. My own mother, eight years younger, thought that when she became old enough, the boys would flock around her as they did Sue, and wryly claimed disappointment that it didn't turn out that way. (Although, according to Dale's contemporaries, she had her fair share of admirers when her turn came!)

Sue, too, attended Portland Academy and then was sent off to Lasell Female Seminary in Boston, a finishing school for girls, perhaps with the hope that she would be protected from the colorful life she seemed to prefer. In 1922, she married handsome, adventurous Wallace Pearson, who spent the early years of prohibition making big money as a rum runner. In 1932, they settled in Portland, Oregon. Sue died there of pneumonia on December 27 of that year, at age 29.

To their everlasting regret, Mama and Papa weren't in good enough circumstances—health wise or financially—to take in Sue's two young sons. But even though Wallace Jr. (age 8) and Charles (age 4) went to Minnesota to live with the Pearson relatives, Espy family contacts with "Sue's boys" remained a priority.

Ruth Muriel (Mona)

Mona always thought of herself as the "ugly duckling," not because of her looks, but because she considered herself the least intellectual and accomplished student in a family that valued education above all else. She was petite, scarcely five feet tall, with luxurious auburn hair, envied by every girl in the Espy family. Following high school, she studied nursing at Washington State College (Pullman), and then worked as a practical nurse on and off throughout her life.

Mona spent most of her adult years in Southern California, was married and divorced twice, and had no children. She became interested in politics, and, like Papa, was a devoted Republican. One of her prized possessions was a letter signed by President Dwight D. Eisenhower, thanking her for working as a committee chairman during his 1952 presidential campaign.

After Mama's death in 1954, Mona moved to Oysterville to care for Papa. She spoke of herself as "Papa's girl," and certainly took after him in many respects. She was loquacious and gregarious, readily relating to folks from every background, every walk of life. The attendance at her funeral in 1972 was the largest in Oysterville's history.

Sue, 1922.

Robert Hamilton Edwin (Ed)

Edwin, as the eldest boy, took on the role of Papa's "right hand man" from an early age. Though small in stature (5 feet 5 inches), Edwin was robust, enjoyed physical activity, and proved a great help on the ranch.

At the University of Redlands, he was active in student affairs and achieved, among other honors, membership on a prize-winning debate team, presidency of his class, and the student body presidency. He received a Bachelor of Arts from Redlands in 1930, and a Bachelor of Divinity from the Union Theological Seminary (NYC) in 1933. Ed spent most of

Ed horse seining on the Columbia, ca. 1924.

the next six years in Europe where he studied for his doctorate at Tübingen and Bonn. He interrupted his studies to take charge of preparations for the First World Conference of Christian Youth, which was held in Amsterdam a few days before the outbreak of World War II in 1939. Ed then returned to New York, continuing to work with Christian youth organizations, eventually becoming Student Secretary of the YMCA. In 1944 he received his Doctor of Divinity degree from the University of Redlands and, also that year, married Cleo Mitchell of Raleigh, North Carolina (they had no children). In 1950, he received a Ph.D. from Yale University.

Edwin devoted his life to religious administration and the world ecumenical movement. For ten years before his retirement in 1973, he was General Secretary of the National Council of Churches of Christ, and often referred to as "the Protestant Pope." Although Edwin inherited the finer facial features and smaller stature of the Richardsons, he had the outgoing, charismatic personality of his father. It was Ed who kept the family in touch with the many Espy and Richardson cousins and their offspring. He died in Doylestown, Pennsylvania, in 1993.

Willard, ca. 1940.

Willard Richardson (Wede)

Willard started school in the fall of 1916, not yet 6 years old. By the end of the first year, he had completed the primary work and soon caught up with Ed, who was two years older and already had "skipped a grade" himself. The two advanced in the same grades for the remainder of their school years, both going through the tenth grade in Oysterville. By then, Ed was driving and they could get to school by using the family car. They went on to graduate in 1925 from Ilwaco High School—Ed was 16; Wede, 14.

Mama and Papa felt that the boys were too young to begin college, so they continued on at Ilwaco for another year taking a business course. Later, Wede often remarked that the typing class he took that year was the single most important part of his schooling, as typing would be an every day activity for him for the next seven decades.

Like his siblings, Wede was kind and personable, but unlike the others, he was more introspective—a dreamer who preferred writing, reading, or drawing to more active pursuits. Many are the stories of Willard, sprawled on his stomach reading a favorite book, oblivious to the goings-on around him. He read voraciously from an early age, and had read the Bible twice by the time he was 8. Mama said in later years that she once suggested to him that he skip Genesis. He replied, "But how will I know who is who if I don't read all the begats?" From then on, she said, she avoided Willard when he was reading the Bible for fear he would ask her questions she couldn't answer.

Willard graduated from Redlands in 1930, and then spent a year in France studying at the University of Grenoble, and the Sorbonne in Paris. Upon his return to the States, he worked for several small newspapers and magazines until 1941, when he joined the *Reader's Digest* staff as Promotion and Public Relations Manager. His book writing career began that year, too, with a political treatise, *Bold New Program*. Of the sixteen books he wrote afterward, all were celebrations of the lighter side of language use, with one notable exception, *Oysterville: Roads to Grandpa's Village*.

Willard married three times—in 1933 to Ann Hathaway, with whom he had one son (Ian); in 1940 to Hilda Stanley Cole, with whom he had four daughters and one son (Mona, Freddy, Joanna Page, Cassin, and Jefferson); and in 1962 to Louise Mannheim. He died in 1999 in New York City and is survived by Louise, as well as his eldest son, his daughters, and numerous grandchildren and several great-grandchildren.

Dale, 1928.

Helen-Dale (Dale)

Dale remembers her childhood in Oysterville as the happiest, most idyllic years of her life.

During those times, there were thirteen boys about her age living in or near town—including, of course, her brothers Edwin and Willard—but no girls. Consequently, in her own words, she "became the tag along." It is hard for me to picture my very feminine, always-dressed-to-the-nines mother as a tomboy, but a tomboy she was—riding, running, swimming, taking dares, and getting into her share of mischief!

She attended the first seven years of grammar school at Oysterville, the eighth grade in Nahcotta, and her high school freshman year at Ilwaco. In 1929, she finished high school in Redlands, California, and in 1933 received a B.A. degree in religious education from the University of Redlands.

While at the university, Dale met William "Bill" Woodworth Little from Boston, and they married in that city in 1934. In 1939, the Little family (which now included me, born in 1936, and destined to be an only child) moved to Portland, Oregon, and in 1941 to Alameda, California. My father was employed by Montgomery Ward & Company, and after the United States entered World War II in December 1941, my mother went to work as a pipe fitter's helper at the General Engineering shipyards. During her time there, she was voted "Miss Safety-Queen of the Shipyards," and sent to Hollywood as a goodwill ambassador for the war effort.

After the war, we moved to San Rafael, California, and my parents began an import business, specializing in gift items from India. In 1957, Mom opened her own business, the Little Lamp and Shade Shop, designing, making, and selling custom lamps and shades. In 1972, she and Dad retired to her childhood home in Oysterville. They became active in local affairs, especially historic preservation efforts, and were instrumental in Oysterville's placement on the National Register of Historic Places.

Dale's sparkling personality, devotion to family, and loyalty to friends have been hallmarks throughout her life. She now is the last of the H.A. Espy siblings, and the last of the eighteen grandchildren of Grandpa and Grandma Espy. However, even in her nineties, she still is the "dear little Dale," who Medora often longed to give a squeeze.

Dale sits in a P-38 fighter at the Lockheed aircraft plant, March 1944. She was on a public relations tour as "Miss Safety-Queen," representing General Engineering and Dry Dock Company of Alameda, California.

Oysterville

As for the village itself, the changes that have occurred no doubt would amaze Medora and Mama. There are fewer buildings now—only about two dozen in the town proper, and half of these are "new." Since 1976, when the village was designated a National Historic Dis-

Hilda Cole Espy painted this portrait for the H.A. Espys' 50th wedding anniversary in 1947. It hangs in the nursery where Mama and Papa spent many happy hours of their "golden years" near the warmth of the nursery stove, corresponding with family members and reminiscing about bygone times.

trict, it has become a tourist destination and a fashionable place to have a vacation home. It no longer is a working man's town, nor are there any young families with children in residence. We are an aging population, and growing fewer in number all too quickly.

Each year upwards of 20,000 visitors wander along the lanes and sign the guest book in the church across the street from Mama and Papa's house. There now are only fourteen full-time residents in Oysterville, and perhaps three times that number who own property and come for an occasional weekend stay or vacation. The village has taken on a gentrified air—new residents from large urban centers bring an unaccustomed sophistication to the weathered old oyster town.

The blackberries and salal that grew in profusion along the roadside have given way to ornamental fruit trees and stands of daffodils. The windmills and outhouses are gone, and the last barn fell in years ago. The church hasn't held regular services since the 1930s and is used mainly for weddings, summer vesper services, and an occasional funeral. The schoolhouse, now a community center, closed its doors a half-century ago, when there were too few children to continue holding classes in Oysterville. A cannery building at the north end of town is the only structure remaining that gives testimony to the settlement's original reason for being. These days, however, only its owner resides in town; employees need to be "imported" from other nearby communities.

Still, a few of the "old" families hang on—lamenting some changes, marveling at others, and often reminiscing about the way things "used to be." The store-post office continues as the morning meeting place and central exchange for news and gossip. And, when neighbors gather round cozy wintertime fires, the old stories are told and retold. In Oysterville, the "Forgotten Years" are still remembered.

In the late 1960s or early 1970s, Dale, Ed, and Willard removed Medora's and Albert's graves from Portland to the family cemetery plot in Oysterville.

INDEX

(Illustrations indicated by *italic*)

D

E

F

G

H

P

R

S

T

SALESMAN WITH AN AK 47

Alan Barry

ORIGINAL WRITING

The names of some of the characters in this book have been changed
to protect their identity.

ISBNS
Parent : 978-1-78237-838-9
epub: 978-1-78237-839-6
mobi: 978-1-78237-840-2
PDF: 978-1-78237-841-9

A CIP catalogue for this book is available from the National Library.

Published by Original Writing Ltd., Dublin, 2015.
Printed by Clondalkin Group, Glasnevin, Dublin 11

Dedications

MY FATHER WILLIAM JOSEPH BARRY 1936 - 2009

"When I was a boy of 14, my father was so ignorant I could hardly stand to have the old man around. But when I got to be 21, I was astonished at how much the old man had learned in seven years."

Mark Twain

NIGEL STUART CLARIDGE – 1966-2006

A fine Grenadier, Father, Son, Brother and Friend

Stand down Guardsman, your duty is done. May you rest in peace.

Acknowledgements

Thank you to my wonderful children, Nathan, Catherine and Connor for making me a very proud and lucky father. Without your love and support the world would be a lesser place.

Thank you to Violet, for giving me the greatest gift I have received, our three wonderful children.

Thank you to my wonderful Mother Ethna. I could not have wished for more love and caring throughout my life.

To my brother Colin and my sister Yvonne for their support and love throughout my life.

My best friend Mark Weir for dragging me back from the abyss in 2010.

Thomas Bartlett for his help and advice in writing this book, I could have never achieved this without him.

Last but not least, thanks to my loyal friend Paul Stokes whose support and assistance on this project has been invaluable.

Contents

Chapter 1

I HAVE NEVER FORGOTTEN THE THINGS THAT SAVED MY LIFE

May 2006 Kabul, Afghanistan

The dirt kicked up high as the Hummer sped through – aliens on an Afghan moon. The wrong people, in the wrong land, at the wrong time. The story of my life. But then it was not my life: I was sitting a couple of miles up the road in my office inside our secure building in Kabul.

The Hummer collided with the taxi, panicked, drove over the occupants and fired a 50cal machine gun into the crowd killing between 2 and 12 people, depending on who you asked. There were a lot of viewpoints, and even more blame. The crowd began to buck and seethe. Writhing in the Kabul trap, caught between the Taliban, the Americans, the Afghan Army and Police, poverty, history and the surrounding mountains; ancient pressures pushing and re-forming them. I was sitting at my desk oblivious when the crowd turned violent. So many reasons: the bodies on the ground; the bodies in front of them; and the Hummer, a beacon of America and a natural target for Afghan aggression.

The Afghan mob, crowd, or insurgents had decided they were going to storm Afghan Wireless's office building. I was inside minding my own business, rolling out the telecommunications network and working on benign sales targets, team building and staff training. The word came in, the crowd, the mob, the locals were gathered outside. There was an AK47 propped against the wall beside me, beside me is where I kept it. I also had a Glock side arm on my hip, or maybe it was in my drawer as I was in the office. A long time ago I'd learned the hard way not to sit around with a loaded weapon.

The three thousand strong mob were intent on storming the compound in righteous anger, directed at us and every other building that screamed establishment at them. I'd made the decision that I would not be taken alive a long time ago in a different place. This was not my first mob, nor my first riot. Old training kicked in, before the sales training and telecommunications, back into the mists of things I don't talk about. But I have never forgotten the things that have saved my life.

Looking out across the ancient bullet ridden skyline, I thought to myself that I could probably make it across the roof tops outside, at least I wouldn't be penned in and I'd have the chance to escape. The mountains looked on watching everything, unmoved.

Thankfully the doors and gates to our building held. Everything outside the compound, every vehicle or sign was destroyed, the security hut burnt to a cinder. I knew how the mob felt. Afghanistan; that's how they felt.

Afghanistan

Afghanistan, more than anywhere else I've ever been on earth exists in a perpetual state of flux – destruction and creation, the mountains, the crumbling walls, fragile allegiances – construction to destruction. The mountains, the representation of the earth's fissures and man's conflicts.

I had been holding it together a little bit myself of late. Was this the inciting moment? Yeah, that and twenty years of success and failure, maybe throw in some Northern Ireland, some love and loathing. All the little pieces that went together to make me. Pieces now falling away as I found myself once more in the breach. Pretty much where I liked to be. I never would have said I enjoyed the danger, but looking back I have always courted it. Often ran straight towards it.

The mob moved on and destroyed an aid organisation and some more ISAF[1] platitudes about improving security and moving forward. The Taliban were back; making every alarm, every incident more heightened. I went back to my desk, sat down and tried to remember where I was and what the hell I was doing there.

---

1 ISAF International Security Assistance Force. Nato led security force in Afghanistan.

Chapter 2

Losing our innocence

1964 Dublin

I was born in Holles Street Hospital, Dublin, without a problem in the world. My Dad was a fitter, repairing machinery in Bachelors, my Mother a house wife, both from Cabra. Both intent on getting out of Dublin as soon as possible to rear their family. I'm the eldest of three. It wasn't much longer before we rocked up on the concrete shores of Birmingham in 1966 and Dad secured a job in Cadbury Schweppes, trebling his salary. My parents were trying to move up, like most immigrants they wanted to change their lives and those of their children. That is the way it went in those days in Ireland, stay poor or leave.

I've vague memories of our first stop in Birmingham, Slade Road, Erdington, near the site of today's spaghetti junction. It was much like living in any working class community in Dublin. After a year my parents sent me back to Ireland to live with my grandmother. As a child it didn't make much difference to me. I was used to it before I knew not to be. I lived with my grandparents for a year and every couple of months either my Nan would take me over to visit my parents or they would come back to Dublin for a few days. My parents where Irish immigrants and like many before chose to work as many hours as they could in order to save up enough money to purchase a house in a more upmarket area. My parents achieved this in a nice residential area of Birmingham called Sutton Coldfield. We were on the up. England had allowed us to change our lives.

My parents were practicing, but not strict Catholics. We would go to mass some Sundays but not all. Our primary school was a different matter: St Peter and St Paul's. It was so Catholic it could have been in Ireland. The only thing they taught you there was how to pray, how to pray and how to take a beating. The headmaster Mr Minister was a sadist. It was a brutal regime. Everyday some boy would get a hiding, and I mean a clobbering. I was no different and regularly found myself on the wrong end of the headmasters' fists or his hand. In the wrong place at the wrong time, perhaps it was the beginning of a theme? Mr Minister was a strict Catholic. Whatever about that, he used to commit acts of savagery on children I've seldom seen since.

Mr Minister never caned us; he punched us, punched the living daylights out of us. We boys had to wear short trousers all year round, so we'd feel the sting of his slaps on our legs until we got older and graduated to his punching. He picked on all the boys, never the girls. Once during communion, I failed to find the way back to my pew quickly enough. In between the punches he memorably told me I'd been "chewing the host like chewing gum". After another infringement, when I'd apparently been using my fork incorrectly, he pushed my face into my dinner and held it there.

I remember when I first started in St Peter and St Paul's, I did get bullied by this one boy, Martin Pitt. Mum still recalls the story and tells it admitting she was terrified herself. I was walking home one day, my mum saw me getting hassled and she came over and asked me:

"Why are you letting him pick on you like that? Look at you, you get two strong meals a day."

It felt like a mixture of permission and instruction. So he did it again and I gave him what he was looking for, the six year old version anyway. And that was the end of that. I was never a bully. I didn't like bullies and even to this day I don't like them. I never went looking for trouble, but if someone came looking for it, I certainly wouldn't have walked away. From then on my mum never worried about me, she knew I could take care of myself.

I was very lucky with my mum. In many ways she was the best mum a man could ever want. She was very loving, generous, always there for us. My Dad was like a lot of Irish men in those days: often taciturn and somewhat withdrawn. There were two sides to him, the good Billy and the bad Billy, and when he'd had a drink the bad Billy would come out.

We weren't very well disciplined as children. None of us were. My parents worked full time, so my brother, my sister and I were brought up by my grandmother. Your granny, as most can attest to, will always cut you a little bit more slack. When my Nan died years later, I was completely devastated. It was like losing a parent we were so close. I was twenty eight when she died. She was a wonderfully wise woman and a Scorpio, so she was a handful.

My parents worked hard to ensure we grew up in a pleasant suburb of Birmingham. We lived directly opposite Pype Hayes Park. It functioned as our whole world in those days. We'd disappear in the morning, spend the day in the park, make a den in a tree, or build a raft with a pallet and float on it across the lake. Carefree days, like Brummie Huckleberry Finns. Some of the things I got up to I'd be horrified to hear my own children had been doing the same, but all us parents grow up to be a little hypocritical.

At the age of fourteen I started coming to Ireland every summer. My cousin John lived in Artane in Dublin. The two of us were great mates. I simply became a member of John's family while I was staying with them. Mostly John and I listened to heavy metal and went to the famous Grove disco in Clontarf. I've remained close with my father's sister Bridie and her husband Sean since and they are still a part of my life today. A truly wonderful couple and a great advertisement for marriage.

Whenever I was back in Ireland I'd also spend time with my uncle Mark who owned a plant hire shop. Mark served as a role model of sorts for me as a teenage lad. A great all round guy and truly fantastic salesman. Even in Ireland, the home of great talkers, he was considered a brilliant salesman. I'd like to think I learned a thing or two about sales working with him. Those summers, while most adults were still treating me as a child, Mark would bring me out boozing to nightclubs and set me up with girls. Naturally I slightly idolised him.

Bishop Walsh Catholic, my Secondary School in Sutton Coldfield, was a lovely place, situated in a beautiful part of the city, alongside fabulous fields and generally a really green natural environment. I continued my Boy's Own childhood there, excelling in sport. I was quite bright but I never really applied myself to learning or study. I could run the 100 metres in 11.4 seconds at the age of fifteen. As a member of Lozells Harriers Athletic Club, I competed regularly at athletics events. Our parents had made it clear they wanted us to get a job after we left school so grades were never that important. As kids, despite the fact we were left to our own devices, we were always aware of a loving safety net around us.

I've had a lifelong interest in the military and I was a member of the air force cadets in school and the scouts. I grew up loving war movies and adventure, spending any free time off with mates having war games in the woods, Swallows and Amazons, well our version anyway.

I suppose I was born a bit reckless. Summer 1973 booting along on my Chopper bicycle a good friend of mine on the back, we had a desperate accident. I fractured my femur. I'll always remember me sobbing, my Dad

carrying me to his car, a Hillman Imp, driving to the hospital. I was in agony. Very few injuries feel like a broken femur in the back of a Hillman Imp. The phenomenal number of bumps shuddered the pain and agony through my bones right into my soul – or so the ten year old me thought.

In the Birmingham Accident Hospital they put me in traction for two months. Being only ten, when I heard the loud explosion I didn't really understand what it was. I didn't hear the second one, or maybe I only heard the second one, they were only ten minutes apart. I'll remember the night of sirens forever though. Later the bombs became known as the Birmingham Pub Bombings. 21 predominantly young people died in those two explosions, with 182 people injured. For Birmingham it was one of the worst nights in its history. The city felt betrayed by the Irish community and grieved for their young dead.

Savagery

Doctor Henry Proctor had operated on my femur. In the days and hours after the bombings, he operated on many of those brought in. Dr Proctor was also interviewed on the television after the bombings particularly on the extent of the injuries. Unforgettably the wood from the pubs' furniture made the surgeons' jobs infinitely more difficult because wood was not detectable by X-ray. This small grim detail still makes me shudder with its lethal implications.

Doctor Proctor spoke about the horror on TV news and what he said has echoed through the city ever since; everyone in Birmingham remembers their own awful souvenir alongside the deaths. For me I'll remember forever him talking about:

"one man with a chair leg right up his thigh, entering at the knee and going right up to the groin."

Birmingham Accident Hospital was a world leading major injuries unit at the time but they couldn't save everyone. No one could.

It was a horrifying ordeal for Birmingham. The British, and the people of Birmingham were understandably angry. We can say what we like about the British, but they normally didn't hold the IRA against us. The bombings in Birmingham were different. My Dad, a real Paddy, and universally liked, was told to stay home from work. My sister was kept home from school because it was known as an Irish Catholic school. There was so much animosity towards the Irish in the city. The windows in the Irish Centre were smashed in and many people were almost ashamed to be Irish or associated with Ireland for a period after the bombings.

But the British and the locals in Birmingham let us go back to our daily lives. My sister and I returned to school, my Dad to work.

There were two other bombings that the British took very personally: Warrington, when the IRA killed a child on the high street; Guildford, when they targeted a couple of soldier's bars, I used to drink in them myself in the years after. But to plant two bombs in Birmingham, in two bars frequented solely by young people, there was no justification for that. Shooting a soldier in Northern Ireland, we were considered a legitimate target, I could get my head around that, but the Birmingham Pub Bombings scarred a city for life. It robbed children of their futures and parents of their lives' sanity.

The IRA lost their way killing innocent civilians. They blew away their supposed legitimacy. A legitimate target is a person you consider the enemy, not just because they are a national of that country. You certainly don't kill women and children. The old IRA never did that. They killed G-men, British soldiers, Irish Constabulary, spies, whatever. They didn't go around killing women and kids.

The Birmingham Pub Bombings are something I remember from my childhood, but they did not have any profound influence on me at the time because of the simple fact that I was too young.

Years later I met Lord Chief Justice Denning at a drinks reception in London whilst I was a serving Guardsman at the Palace. I'd been invited to the evening by my then girlfriend, who lived in Lincoln's Inn Fields in the apartment below Lord Denning. I got chatting to him, and when he found out I was a serving soldier from Birmingham, he was not afraid to speak openly. What he didn't know was that my parents were both Irish Catholics. How would he?

The first thing he mentioned was the Birmingham Six. The campaign to have them released meant they were very much in the news at the time. Lord Denning simply stated that in his opinion, despite the Birmingham Six being guilty, due to overzealous police work the case was going to collapse. He talked about how if Britain had capital punishment we would not have these problems, as the Six would be dead. A not uncommon view at the time particularly in the midst of the British Establishment.

Denning, along with many others at the time, was convinced the Six were guilty. The investigation in to the Birmingham Pub Bombings was an incompetent police operation, marred by brutality and witness coercion. The police botched it and wasted lives and time convicting six innocent people rather than finding the true culprits. Lord Denning famously remarked when asked whether the Six should be allowed to appeal, that the repercussions for the English legal establishment if they were found innocent would be worse than six innocent people serving life in prison.

"This is such an appalling vista that every sensible person in the land would say that it cannot be right that these actions should go any further."

When I was growing up I considered myself British, despite my parents being Irish. I went to school in England, I had a British education, learnt British history. I was British as far as I was concerned. It wasn't until I served in Northern Ireland that I started to wonder.

Chapter 3

The elite of the British Army

79 Battle honours.

I left school in 1982, just after Maggie got in. Unemployment was rife, and the waiting list for the RAF was over a year. Instead I applied for the RAF regiment – the soldiers that guard the airfields. There was a recession and Maggie was sorting out the mess. Other than the army, the infamous Youth Training Scheme was the only thing you could do around that time. Most employers used the YTS as an excuse for free labour. Infuriatingly, even after I passed the RAF entrance exam, I was still looking at a six month waiting list. I was getting fed up tapping my foot and kicking my heels with part time work; I was anxious for some action.

Walking home past the Army Careers Office one fateful day, something inside caught my eye, a picture of the trooping of the colour and all those magnificent red tunics and bear skins outside Buckingham Palace. I walked in as seriously as I could, and spoke to the recruiter,

"I'd like to join the Irish Guards."

He looked me up and down before replying,

"The Guards no way, you're not tall enough lad. Actually hold on. Maybe you would just about scrape in. Come over here and I'll measure you."

Five foot eight and a half was the regulation, and luckily:

"Five foot eight and a half, you just scraped it. Come back tomorrow and do the entrance exam."

I passed and within two weeks I was at recruit selection in front of an officer. The officer gave me some great advice:

"You scored 85% in the entrance exam, you shouldn't be going into the Guards or any infantry regiment. You should get a trade, join the Royal Electrical Mechanical Engineers, or the Air Corps."

But I was not to be dissuaded by good advice. I was adamant.

"I want to be a Guardsman",

"Why do you want to be a Guardsman?" looking right into my eyes.

"I don't know, I just do."

"It's not the uniform is it?" he asked peering right into my mind.

"No, no it's not. It's because they are the elite of the British Army." I said dead earnest sticking my chest out.

I was telling the truth, that's really what it was, well that and the uniform. I admit it, when I looked at that uniform I was star struck. All I could think about was how dignified I'd look. But much more than that I'd always wanted to be the best, to be top of the tree. It's been the same my whole life. And for me the Guards were the best, the elite of the British Army and they still are today.

My great grandfather had been a Scots Guard. I had no affinity for the Scots Guards as I was not Scottish, but I'd been hearing about the Guards all my life. The Irish Guards were not looking for recruits that day and the Grenadiers had two battalions to maintain, so I ended up joining the Grenadiers. The Grenadiers are known as the First Regiment of Foot Guards, because they are the only regiment to have stayed loyal to the British Crown throughout their history. The Grenadiers are the most senior regiment of infantry in the British Army. They wanted the best and trained us to be the best.

After King Charles was executed, the Grenadiers were formed as a Royalist regiment in exile in 1656. Due to problems after the death of Cromwell, the British decided they did actually want a monarchy and Charles's son Charles II came back in 1660. Grenadiers are called the First Regiment of Foot as part of the Household Division. When I saw the bear skins the Grenadiers wore, I knew that was what I wanted. After the regiment had defeated Napoleon at the Battle of Waterloo, they were given the bear skin as a battle honour as well as their name. It was the headdress of the French Imperial Guards. I wanted some of that.

My mum saw me to the train at New Street Station in Birmingham the day I left for basic training. She cried, I am pretty sure it was the first time I'd ever seen my mother cry. On the train from Waterloo to Brookwood Surrey it was obvious who was going down to Guards' training. We'd been instructed to wear a suit when we left the barracks, this included the journey down and each of us looked as gawky and awkward as the other. I looked around and thought to myself, I won't be hanging around with some of these lads. I didn't like the look of half of them.

As soon as we disembarked we were met by a six feet tall sergeant shouting and roaring at us to get on the buses. One recruit took one look, turned right around and got straight back on the train. We were brought to Pirbright, the Guards' Depot. There were five regiments of foot: Grenadier, Scots, Irish, Welsh and Coldstream Guards and two regiments of Cavalry; Blues and Royals, and the Lifeguards. We were all trained together. Everyone's training was six months long and pretty much identical.

I joined up at the height of the miners' strike. A lot of the recruits had been miners. Many of them had worked in the Derbyshire and Macclesfield Collieries. Unsurprisingly, one skill all the ex-miners possessed was the ability to dig trenches like demons, which in the infantry comes in really handy. The Northerners seemed to be from a different planet. Their planet liked gravy on their chips instead of salt and vinegar and seemed to speak a different language. I hadn't a clue what they were saying half the time. There were a lot of working class accents, 80% of Number 10 platoon was made up of boys from Manchester. The army wasted no time in training us in drill and regimentation, how to be Guardsmen.

The first day most recruits could not march, so we were walked down to the barbers, then given all the kit we'd need as soldiers, except our rifles, which were kept in the armoury. The first day slid by in a blur of administration. The regimentation was already afoot.

For the next six months there was a sergeant standing around screaming at us at all times.

"Mark time. Left right left right." The marching and the shouting was endless.

Lance Sergeant Wilson was a Coldstream Guard and Platoon Sergeant Morgan was a Welsh Guard. They trained us. Together they had a warped sense of humour, often making us laugh even when we were in pain – both great army characters. I remember all of us outside for sports day exhaling plumes of steamy air when Sergeant Morgan bounded up and asked who fancied playing football, rugby and so on. Before we started to peel off to our chosen sport, Sergeant Morgan added generously,

"I have a special on today. Darts? Anybody, game of darts?" What could be better?

The two unfittest guys in the platoon put their hands up, with visions of themselves throwing darts down the Naffi[2]. With a glint in his eye, Sergeant Morgan looked at them and said,

"Great. You two can go for a dart round the cross country course."

We all laughed as the two wheezed their way around the course. Any chance to laugh was taken. That's army humour for you, always slightly functional. We attended classes all day, learning about combat, weapons' instruction, drill instruction, fitness, first aid, and so on. Every platoon was broken down into four man sections called bricks, the same as when we joined our battalion. In the evenings as we polished our boots the NCOs quizzed us on regimental history, ensuring we understood we were to be part of a long line of Guardsmen, and how important the Grenadier's history was.

We were recruits until we passed out. I never met any other Irish while I was there. The army knew about my Irish birth. Not sure if anyone else knew. If they did they never mentioned it. If you'd asked me I would have said I was British. I didn't accept that I was Irish at the time.

Army training in those days was all about breaking you – much more so than it is now apparently. However, it was not the nightmare often portrayed in the movies, well not for me

2 Navy Army Airforce a type of social club were we used to play darts.

anyway. Yeah, we were beaten physically if we fell on the ground, and if the Non Com Officers (NCOs) thought we were faking it, they would kick us until we stood back up. When one recruit was perceived to have a hygiene problem, we were told to give him a bath. Some of the other recruits put him in a bath with Vim, the scouring agent, and all his equipment. The screams were awful. I balked at this type of thing. I just thought it was cruel. The NCOs used the recruits whom they knew would comply. The Guards did not suffer fools gladly; they wanted tough soldiers that would not break.

The Commandant's 'March and Shoot' half way through training was seen as an ideal way to get rid of weak recruits. We had to run ten miles in full kit; thirty six pounds of equipment, our rifle, our helmet, all as a squad. Next we had to do an assault course. At the end of the assault course we had to carry another recruit in all his kit in a fireman's lift for one hundred metres. Finally, we had marksmanship on the live firing range where we had to score at least 75%. If we failed at any stage, we would be back-squaded. Back-squaded meant being taken out of the platoon and sent back, normally a month, which meant doing the 'March and Shoot' all over again.

The overarching feeling during basic training was anxiety: anxiety that we'd get back squaded or worse, fail training altogether. This was my memory of it anyway. Many failed. I think out of seventy four of us in number 10-11 platoon, only twenty six made it through. I really wanted to be a Guardsman.

Sometimes we'd be given passes to the local town, Guildford. Saturday night was squaddie night out. We'd march hopefully down to the Guard Room in our shirt and tie, stand to attention. The Sergeant would inspect us, anyone not deemed smart enough was not allowed out. Guildford is down the road from Aldershot, hence the paratroopers would be out as well wearing their normal civilian dress; desert boots, jeans and a bomber jacket. There is massive rivalry and competition amongst all regiments but especially between the Guards Division and the Parachute Regiment; both consider themselves the best. The discipline insured there were never any fights. All of us were hammering the pints down, but we were mega fit, we could just throw it off us. Drinking ten pints was no problem, we'd swim home and be up fast and strong the next day.

Sandhill was a hill made of sand designed to sap every ounce of energy out of you by the time you reached the top, echoes of the Sean Connery movie *The Hill* from 1965. It was so gruelling that it was often used as a punishment alongside the regular climbs that were an integral part of our training. My own squad had to do it once in our number one dress when we were adjudged to be insufficiently turned out for one of the Adjutant's inspections. Our Platoon Sergeant marched us to Sandhill and beasted us up and down it again and again. That in itself was awful, but worse was trying to get our number one dress clean for a week afterwards. The Four Sisters was another famous Guards' training landmark: four hills that we all got to know very well over the six months as we climbed up and down them day and night in full kit; all 36 pounds of it.

The Bayonet Assault Course remains one of the most singular experiences of my life, never mind something difficult that stands out from the Guards' training. We all knew it was coming, the day began with a good old fashioned beasting , a three mile run in full kit, stopping for press ups and sit ups. A couple of trips up Sandhill. Pushing us to our limits, and winding us up and up as tight as they could. This was nothing new, but that day there was an extra edge to everything, that day we knew we were going to do the Bayonet Assault Course.

Every infantry soldiers needs to know how to use a bayonet.

The assault course consisted of pits of mud to wade through, burning tyres to jump over, thunder flash grenades, real grenades without shrapnel being lobbed at us, GPMGs[3] being fired over our heads with blank rounds: basically mayhem. The army wanted to replicate a battle, to induce the near psychosis needed to mount a bayonet assault at an armed enemy.

Amidst the chaos at the starting line, a lone Scots Guard stood playing 'The Crags of Tumbledown Mountain' on his bag

3 General Purpose Machine Gun

pipes. The tune was composed in the Falklands War by a Scots Guard in the aftermath of the battle. It is a tribute to the Scots Guards' heroic bayonet assault on the summit of Tumbledown Mountain. With ammunition running low, the command was given to fix bayonets. The first person into the enemy position was Major Kiszely, who was awarded a military cross for his bravery. The charge was one of the last bayonet charges by the British Army.

We lined up individually to attempt the course, each with our blood boiling over. We all knew what the bag pipes signified and together with the sounds of war coming from the assault course and our previous three hours exertions we were amped up higher than we'd ever been.

"Fix bayonets" the NCO roared at us, a command that sends ferocious shivers juddering up the spine of every British soldier.

This was followed by the NCO shouting brutal descriptions of what the enemy had done to our families.

"They killed your family.

They raped your sister and your mother,

Then they murdered all of them."

Louder and louder. Screaming at us by this stage.

"What is a bayonet for?" they yelled.

And we screamed in answer, each like a raging animal,

"To kill."

"What are you going to do with it?"

"Kill."

We roared our raging reply fully believing it. We went screaming as we tore along. One by one we charged, sprinting, going full pace over each obstacle, only pausing to plunge our bayonets into the uniformed enemy dummies. The training and the adrenalin pulsing up our veins delivering us to the next enemy attacker. The army had filled every dummy with pig guts to ensure we got our kills and our blood. Every obstacle was overlooked by another officer shouting. We tore the enemy apart with our bayonets then charged to the next with another savage thrust, splattering ourselves with the blood and guts, as lost in the fog of war as it is possible to be in an exercise. By the time we finished we were unsure if we'd imagined it, a near psychosis.

In the aftermath as my head cleared I thought briefly of those Scots Guards in the Falklands, charging up the freezing mountain into the machine gun nests, and what the real thing must be like.

I wondered if I would ever get to experience anything like it again, and how I would react if it was the real thing.

Guard's training culminated in a two week long simulated battle camp. We lived in the field in dug in trenches. Lots of live firing exercises; river crossings with full equipment, our gear wrapped in our ponchos; night time raids on our camp – this all took place in Thetford in Norfolk, near enough to where they filmed the TV series *Dad's Army*. But we were no "Dad's Army"; we were the younger deadlier version.

Over the two weeks in the trenches the NCOs were constantly trying to catch us out with weapons inspections in the middle of the night, or gas attacks while we were eating our first meal for 24 hours. After it was all over the NCOs sat everyone down in a big group and went off in a huddle to decide our fates. The sword of Damocles hung over each and every one of us.

I squeezed through, I will never forget the feeling:

"Jeez I've done it, I'm a Guardsman."

That final day after the battle camp I was filling in a trench when Sergeant Wilson called me from a truck window. To us he was known as Mad Dog Wilson. I was eighteen, he was in his early thirties at the time. He was my platoon sergeant, the man who trained me and I looked up to him. Yes he was very hard but he was fair; a combination I have always responded well to. Ultimately I could owe my life to him and my training. Out of all the instructors I had, he was the one whose memory stayed with me.

"Barry" he roared. I sprinted over, "Well son you've done it. I'm proud of you."

It was a proud, proud moment in my life. He finished with,

"Love me or hate me, you'll never forget me." And he was right. Thirty two years later I've not forgotten him and I never will.

After the battle camp those of us who remained smiled secretly while we worked on parade preparation. We knew we were soon to be Guardsmen.

The last day of being a recruit, we wore our number one dress and had our passing out parade at the Guards Depot. My family turned up to see me become Guardsman Alan Barry. It was a simple good feeling, and I stood to attention in front of my family with great pride.

Chapter 4

Guarding the Queen

Guardsman Alan Barry was posted to the 2nd Battalion Grenadier Guards stationed in Chelsea Barracks, London. As soon as I arrived at Chelsea, I was immediately posted to the athletics team and I didn't really put on a uniform, well at least not a dress uniform, for my first three months as a Guardsman. When I eventually joined up with Number 2 Company, there were a fair few remarks about my absence. I was billeted to a room with three other guys. They'd all been in the battalion a while and they looked after me.

Barrack room lawyers are soldiers who take it upon themselves to make sure new recruits know their place. In Chelsea Barracks they taught us our place through violence. Thankfully the first evening they came looking for me I was out of barracks. Later on when I got back my roommates warned me I was being hunted. Luckily that night the fourth bed in our room was empty, that Guardsman had a girlfriend and spent most nights out of barracks. I snuck into his bed and covered my head, when they came back asking where I was, my roommates repeated that nobody had seen me.

The following time I wasn't so lucky, they dragged me up to the ablutions as we called them. They gave me a few decent digs. The third time was a couple of days later. Four of them beat the daylights out of me. I got back to my bed and I thought, I'm not having this and, having identified their leader, I went into his room while he was asleep and I smashed a broom stick over his back. He sprung up and hit me and I hit him back. He sneered at me,

"You're dead sprog." Sprog was the nickname given to all the new guys.

I nodded my agreement with him,

"You'll need to kill me, because if you come for me again and don't kill me, I'll definitely be back, so you best sleep with one eye open. I know you're the ring leader and I'm not taking this shit again."

This violent altercation seemed to satisfy something in him as his eyes glinted, and neither he nor his cohorts ever came for me again. Others were not so lucky. One chap was called "football head", due to him continually getting his head kicked in. Other new recruits were nailed into boxes overnight, some hung outside the windows in mattress covers. I never took part in any of this, it sickened me. I'm not sure why, but beating up on the underdog was not something I needed or wanted to be a part of. The sergeants only ever did something about it when it got so bad that they could no longer ignore it.

In Chelsea Barracks there were four weekly guard duties: Tower of London, Windsor Castle, Buckingham Palace, and St James' Palace with Clarence House, where the Queen Mother lived. Clarence House was the easiest. Tower of London was a doddle, or it was viewed as a pleasant guard duty anyway. On guard duty we did two hours on stag, as we called it, four hours off and 24 hour shifts. For the four hours off we mostly spent them in the barrack room; we'd sleep or watch TV. We fought the boredom with the latest video releases, books or eating in the canteen. We never needed to fight anything else, the job was mostly ceremonial.

I recall vividly the first time I mounted guard at Buckingham Palace, marching out of Wellington Barracks with the regimental colours in front and the band playing The British Grenadiers, the sergeant telling us:

"Now lads, chins up, this is your regimental march."

Tourists looked on admiringly taking our photos. I was just nineteen and I was still only 5'8", but nevertheless I felt ten feet tall.

While on Windsor Castle Guard Duty one beautiful morning, Her Majesty the Queen was out strolling whilst having a chat with a member of her staff, very close to number six post behind her private residence. Her Majesty looked straight at me and made eye contact as I presented arms. This was one of the proudest moments of my life. After all, the Grenadiers are her personal Household Troops, their allegiance sworn to protect the monarch and her family.

Once on the Old Guard at Buckingham Palace, I found myself in some discomfort with my newly issued, very tight bearskin. Warrant Officer 1(WO1) Barry Inglis was in charge of drill on the other guard, New Guard. Everyone called him Julio behind his back because of the famous singer Julio Iglesias at the time. We, the Old Guard, had finished our duty and were set to march out. I was always on the left flank, front rank. My bearskin was excruciatingly tight and I was in a lot of pain. I'd just come off sentry duty, so I had been wearing it for over two hours, and it was killing me. I quickly flicked my head to alleviate the pressure for a millisecond. WO1 Ingles marched from the New Guard across the square up behind me and whispered in my ear.

"What's your name?"

I told him "Guardsman Barry Sir"

He marched over to my sergeant of the guard and spoke to him. When we arrived back in barracks I was informed I'd been seen flinching, and put on report for moving on Royal Guard. I was marched in front of the Regimental Sergeant Major, the RSM, who roared at me and there was nothing I could say. I was jailed for 24 hours and put on restriction of privileges for seven days. The next time I was back on guard at Buckingham Palace, WO1 Barry "Julio" Inglis marched up to me and in one of those strange confusing questions so beloved of people in authority asked,

"Guardsman Barry, my favourite Guardsman, why do I like you so much?"

I genuinely hadn't a clue. "I don't know sir." I replied.

"What's my first name?" he asked.

I replied again slightly bewildered, "I don't know Sir." At that stage I had no idea who he was.

"When we dismount guard, you'll tell me my first name, and then you'll know why I like you so much."

In the guardroom later I asked Guardsman Nigel Claridge who'd been in for a while,

"What the hell's he talking about? What's his first name?"

"Barry Ingles, that's what Julio is going on about Barry."

And he laughed. I got to know Nigel Claridge's sense of humour well as we became good mates in the battalion. That first time though I didn't laugh, but I had an idea I thought might get me a bit of respect. After we dismounted guard WO1 Ingles came up to me and asked again,

"What's my first name?"

I stood to attention and in a very loud voice I said "Julio Sir"

That was it, jailed again. Another week of no privileges, even the RSM while he was screaming at me later was trying hard to stifle a smile. I've not been to many regimental reunions since, but I went to one about fifteen years ago. The non-coms remembered the incident and were still laughing about it.

Another Warrant Officer dubbed Slimy Young was completely mad. One evening as I was minding my own business walking back to my billet, Slimy approached me and ordered me to name ten battle honours from the regimental colour. I couldn't, so he punched me quite beautifully into the stomach and jailed me; he was drunk and had just come from the Sergeant's mess. Funny moments looking back, postcards compared to what was to come.

The stark contrast in the Grenadiers was one minute being ceremonial Guardsmen and then suddenly being thrust into action. There were a couple of unusual duties. When Rajiv Ghandi came to London, we were deployed to Heathrow on patrol to provide security and help the police. In those days the police were not armed. The powers that be were rightly worried the poor man would be assassinated, and he was years later back in India.

I am not sure people realise how close we were to being deployed when the 1985 Brixton riots were taking place. We'd just finished our Northern Ireland training consisting mostly of riot tactics, thus we were considered the best placed to go in. We were called back to the barracks on that Saturday night during the worst of the rioting and put on standby; we were going in if the police lost further control.

At the time if they'd sent the Grenadier Guards to Brixton, there would have been serious trouble. Back in the day, black guys were not permitted in the regiment. They simply were not allowed in. If you were a black person you could not join the Guards. How they got away with it for so long, I don't know. If you had a sun tan you could not join the Guards. It was exceptionally racist at the time. Now you even have a soldier in the Scots Guard wearing a turban, as it should be. The Grenadiers were able to get away with it because of tradition and history, the usual sticks to enforce unwritten rules. It was not until the mid-80s when Prince Charles was reviewing the trooping of the colour and famously decried the lack of coloured Guardsmen that the regiment was opened up, although it still took years.

Our officers were recruited from the elite of society. Even young men whose fathers had done well in business and been fortunate to afford a good private school, they could still not join the Guards as officers. They would have needed a double barrelled surname and a private income outside of the army salary. There was not much difference between that system and purchasing your commission back in the day. Hence our officers came almost exclusively from Eton and Harrow. There was one officer who was brilliant. He was an ex-Selous scout from the Rhodesian Army. Probably the best officer I ever had, he was incredible and I was fortunate to have him as my platoon commander in Northern Ireland. They were not bad guys, the double barrels. Most of them were really in it for the prestige before going into the City of London. That was the impression we had anyway. The young ones scared us as they never seemed to quite grasp the gravity of military leadership. The career officers were excellent. We had very experienced NCO's and the smarter officers used them. This is normally the way, it's a well known fact that throughout the history of the British army that a smart officer will realise he has a platoon sergeant with possible ten years plus experience and potentially a couple of active service tours under his belt. A smart NCO will guide his Officer into making a decision and that is the way it should be so as the chain of command is never compromised

Chapter 5

LIMITED LINES OF SIGHT

Northern Ireland, January 1986

Towards the end of 1985, 2nd Battalion was informed that we were being deployed to Northern Ireland. The Troubles were in full tumult, with soldiers regularly being killed in action. Before we went, we did the specially designed Northern Ireland Training. It mainly consisted of riot tactics with some classes on urban patrol. The training area was a replica Derry City, murals on the walls, burnt out cars, tight alleys and limited lines of site. In preparation we drilled street patrols and checkpoints in hostile terrain. Everything was done to mimic Northern Ireland, to get us used to what we would face over there. We were put into a security base at the side of replica Derry, living there just like we would be when we got over to Northern Ireland.

During riot training, the army, with its customary sense of humour, used actors and fake rioters from a regiment that didn't like us. In the Grenadiers' case it was the Parachute Regiment. Our arch rivals, dressed in civvies threw petrol bombs and stones at us, and generally simulated a riot. While they were causing a commotion, we worked on riot tactics. Our standard formation was a slow moving Saracen[4] or Green Giant in the middle, Guardsmen either side with the long riot shields, and behind the formation were Guardsmen with fire extinguishers and rifles covering us. It was like a modern day Roman legion cohort[5]. The simulations were pretty lifelike up to, but not including, firing rubber bullets into the rioters. I was known to be pretty quick, a fast runner, and I was put in the snatch squad which peeled off the main group, or went from behind the main body of the riot, to grab the leaders or the most troublesome. When we eventually arrived in Northern Ireland

4 The FV603 Saracen is a six-wheeled armoured personnel carrier built by Alvis and used by the British Army

5 Definition

we were in a couple of riots. One particular riot in Portadown involved Protestants incensed with the recently signed Anglo Irish Agreement.

The following year in the middle of a particularly dirty riot, petrol bombs raining down on us, a fellow Guardsman turned to me squinting his eyes and through smoke and sticky air said,

"They never told us about this in the brochures, all I saw was wind surfing and rock climbing." So we had a laugh. Smoke everywhere, screaming and yelling, rubber bullets going off. The brochure couldn't have captured the glamour as there was none; Northern Ireland felt like going to war in the roughest part of the UK, and like going to war in a parallel universe. Zero glamour.

January 1986 the Grenadier Guards 2nd Battalion was stationed to Ballykelly, Limavady, County Tyrone. Northern Ireland was a bemusing experience for me. I am not sure what I expected but it was not what I got. I thought of myself as British but with a lot of time for the Irish, I reckoned I would be feted by both sides, or something like that, not exactly carried aloft up the Falls and down the Shankhill, but recognised as someone with a balanced outlook. I was, I realise now, delusional.

The first day we were patrolling through the Head of the Town in Strabane. At the time Strabane was dubbed the most bombed town in Northern Ireland, a badge of sorts. I was crouched down in a front garden behind a small typical Northern Ireland red brick wall. The owner opened the front door and I greeted him politely. I think I said "Good morning." In my slightly Brummie accent,

"Fuck of ye Brit bastard", was his reply, which made me laugh. That day I was most definitely English. Similarly the day I got off a school bus, after I'd just finished searching it up and down for a suspect. My ears were ringing with "fuck off ye Brit Bastard", and unbeknownst to me, my back was covered in fifty school boys' phlegm and spit, yeah I was British that day as well.

Whilst we were stationed in Strabane, there was a Catholic secondary school in the town. Often when we sped past, the boys – some of them not that much younger than us – would miraculously appear with stones and bricks and hurl them at us. Tyrone was not exactly a barrel of laughs; we felt surrounded. It was a generally oppressive atmosphere so any chance at some levity was grasped, and when I suggested to the rest of my brick that we have a wee bit of a laugh, everyone was up for it.

We pulled an Irish national flag, a tricolour, from a lamppost in a Nationalist estate and attached it to a broom stick. Already laughing ourselves half sick, we drove our Land Rover to the school and stopped outside. We waved the big garish green, white and gold flag from the open roof hatch. The boys came running out ready to stone us and froze, I can still see them rooted to the spot, mouths agape, all trying to figure out what they were looking at. For as long as I live I will remember their astonished faces as the thoughts fled across them,

"Is it the Irish Army?"

"Is it an invasion?"

"Did the IRA nick it?"

Then just as the spell was wearing off, we opened up the hatches and started laughing and shouting at them and giving them the one finger salute. The young lads roared back, chased to the gate to pelt us with the ever-present stones.

Both sides went back to their positions in the trenches. The battle was rejoined.

Chapter 6

Rhyme or reason?

Northern Ireland makes you choose every day – choose where you're from, if you're Catholic or Protestant. Dealing with the Ulster Defence Regiment (UDR) was very uncomfortable for me. I regarded them as thugs in uniform. They were outright sectarian in their behaviour and this rankled with me. I saw myself as a British soldier and there to do a job. This is what soldiers tend to say and feel about their circumstances the world over. Our focus on our job and our duty, as well as adherence to the training, gets us through. It also prevents situations from descending into complete chaos. When soldiers are involved in the politics, you are going to have worse problems – the UDR being a case in point.

It was a thick summer's night during the 1986 World Cup and Northern Ireland had been playing. We were on a checkpoint in Country Tyrone, between the towns of Six Mile Cross and Five Mile Town. We were with some UDR and two Royal Ulster Constabulary (RUC) Officers. They were breathalysing drivers as they came through the checkpoint. The RUC had pulled over two drivers who'd failed the breathalyser. Soon after, another quite clearly inebriated man pulled up. The UDR and RUC laughed and joked with him and waved him on.

I asked "Why'd you wave him on?"

"Well he's on our side."

"What do you mean?"

"He's a Protestant."

"Well what about those two over there?" I asked.

"They're Fenians[6]", was the response. I thought to myself: they've all taken the risk drinking and driving, they've all broken the law.

"That's not right." Was my reply.

---

6 Catholic Nationalists

"What do you mean that's not right? They're Fenians." He replied incredulously.

"You can't do that. Just because someone is a Protestant doesn't give you a reason to let them off. My father is an Irish Catholic and he could be one of those two guys just as easy." was my response.

"That's different." He said.

"No, not having it, you either bag everybody or nobody, but you can't just arrest someone depending on whether they're a Catholic or a Protestant."

"Well that's the way it is here." He retorted, upping the bullying ante. I hate bullies.

"Listen lads that's not going to work, either you take them all in or you let those two go, we are all here risking our necks and we are not here to support blatant sectarianism."

"Really, is that right?" Was his reply.

I stood my ground, the three guys in my brick all backed me. The UDR let the two Catholics go. Kind of sums up something that was wrong with Northern Ireland, why not arrest all of them? They were all way over the limit.

A complaint was handed in and I was spoken to the next day by my Platoon Commander,

"You know your problem Barry, you think too much. We are here to do a job, we are not here to get involved in local politics." There is never any point in answering back to an officer in the Guards.

Northern Ireland kept asking me the same question: "Where are you from?" Each time I answered I was a little bit more certain.

Another lovely summer's evening at a border checkpoint on the way through Aughnacloy to Omagh, a route used by a lot of Southern cars as a short cut to Donegal. I was in the centre sanger[7] with an RUC officer and my job was to check

7 A sanger is a protected sentry post, normally located around the perimeter of a base. Its main function is to provide early warning of enemy/terrorist activity/attack in order to protect forces both within the base and those deployed within sight of the Sanger.

documents. The soldier in the front sanger covered the border with a machine gun and would sound a buzzer to tell us when there was a car approaching from the Republic. The front sanger radioed the plates to Central Intelligence to run through the system. If a car had been registered to a known player or involved in an incident, we would pull them over. Each soldier had Aide Memoires, like the American deck of cards in the Iraq Wars with a list of known players. Aide Memoires were a list of men and women connected with known terrorist organisations. Much like a Filofax, giving details of their history, a picture, names and aliases.

A Ford Granada estate, big family car with a mother, father and two children, pulled up with the old Southern Irish red number plates. As my eyes scanned the massive pink driving license, I noticed that the father was from Artane in Dublin.

"O you're from Artane are you?"

The man took a second or two to react, did a double take, and then answered,

"Yeah I am." He replied still looking puzzled.

"Do you know the Grove disco?"

"Course I do."

"I used to go to the Grove disco there in Clontarf when I was a teenager."

We had a bit of a chat about going to the Grove as youngsters. I stood there with my Grenadier's beret and a sidearm, chatting to him about Artane and the famous alternative North Dublin music club. The whole situation was pretty alternative alright. The father got over the shock and chatted amiably for a few minutes. I let him on his way, with a word of caution not to stop in Omagh; Omagh was not advisable for anyone with a Southern reg.

When I returned to the centre sanger the RUC officer in his fly green uniform said nothing at first, but couldn't hold it in. With his two thumbs pinned under his shoulders, looking at me like a peacock he asked,

"So are you Irish then?"

"Yeah I'm Irish." I am not sure I had ever really said it before, I was certainly never sure of it before.

"What's your surname?"

"Barry." A very important question in Northern Ireland, as it indicates which religious background you have.

"So you're a Catholic?" The crux.

"Yeah what's that got to do with anything?" I asked ever so slightly tensing.

"I just find it strange that you are in the British Army?"

I was taken aback by this.

"What's that supposed to mean? I grew up in Britain and I wanted to be a soldier, so I joined the best regiment in the British Army."

"What's more," I insisted, "down South nobody ever asks: are you a Catholic or a Protestant? Both live in harmony."

I couldn't stop myself then, I was only young, I gave him my whole speech.

"In Phoenix Park in Dublin there's a memorial to 375,000 Irish soldiers who fought in the British Army and the 50,000 who died fighting in the First World War. Out of a population of three million people, that is a significant number of men. And most of those were Catholics."

I thought I was on a roll so I kept going,

"If you were ever to set one foot out of Northern Ireland into England, you would be treated as well or as badly as any other Paddy. No one's bothered that you're a loyal Protestant who loves the Queen. If there's a bombing and you're rounded up, I promise you'll be treated as a Paddy or a Mick, don't doubt it. To the average Brummie or Cockney, you're just a Mick."

He didn't say much else after that.

My brick used a starburst formation whenever we left our barracks on patrol, each of us sprinting out and running in different directions. Exiting the base is when you're the most vulnerable, or at least it is the one thing the enemy knows you have to do. One day leaving Sion Mills Barracks in Tyrone on patrol, I saw a young man I'd previously noticed earlier that week. He was standing at the exact same corner. I was suspicious, reckoned we were being dicked by the IRA.[8]

We made our way down the road in standard two by two formation; two men one side and two on the other, with the final Guardsman responsible for guarding the rear. While I was approaching the suspect, my radio sounded and startled him. He sprinted away, we gave pursuit. The suspect ran into a hair dressing salon where we cut him off and caught him. Unbeknownst to either of us, Violet, the woman I would later marry, was the manager of that salon.

I interviewed the suspect in the salon; he had difficulty speaking due to his shy disposition. I questioned him, taking down his details. It turned out he was a no one, not what we called a player, just a local unemployed lad with nothing to do, wiling away his time. The manager of the salon, Violet, vouched for the young man.

In March 1986 two friends of mine died in very tragic circumstances. I'd joined up with Paul "Ronald" McDonald from Manchester; he'd been back squaded for something or other in basic training but he'd caught back up and joined the 2nd Battalion. Then there was Brian "Virgil" Hughes from Chester, a particularly good mate of mine. They were in the QRF on that fateful evening, the Quick Reaction Force, a group within the regiment tasked with reacting to any immediate danger. That awful day a warning came in, intruders had been spotted inside our base and the QRF was dispatched. Virgil and Ronald were in the back of the Land Rover that sped to the location.

The main coastal Belfast to Derry rail line ran through the bottom of our base. The QRF Land Rover mounted the railway tracks in pursuit, the intruders escaped and the QRF Land Rover got jammed and stuck on the tracks. My description

8 Dicked was when the IRA had someone watching us, spying on us, trying to identify patterns in our behaviour. Once identified, the IRA would then use a sniper or an IED or a car bomb to ambush and try to kill us. Being dicked was what we called their reconnaissance gathering missions.

separates a sequence of events that all happened virtually simultaneously. Mangled into a blur, the driver, the impending train, the charging heavy metal, the train engulfing the Land Rover then catapulting it into mid-air. Those Land Rovers had no back doors to allow for an easy exit in an emergency.

The ferocity of the train's impact hurled Guardsman Hughes and Guardsman McDonald out the back of the Land Rover. The barrel of McDonald's SLR[9] went straight through Virgil, right through his abdomen. McDonald was killed instantly. Virgil had massive internal injuries and he died a few days later. The surgeon told our platoon commander that the only reason Virgil had survived for so long was his physical fitness. I was badly affected by this. They were so young, like I was. Just kids. Virgil was blond and had blue eyes, with an amazing complexion so we nicknamed him Virgil after Thunderbirds. I still remember them both. I understood their lives but I found it hard to make sense of their deaths. In a murderous land, accidents seem even more out of place. Fruitless looking for rhyme or reason.

We were on patrol right on the border beside Strabane not far from Clady. We'd been doing a route clearance down a road somewhere in the midst of County Tyrone and we'd stopped to have tea. The British Army runs on tea. There we were having a cup of tea at the side of a culvert at the bottom of a little bank, when behind us the dirt exploded followed by a roar; simultaneous to this we dropped into our positions, and instantaneously began a section attack on the farm building at the top of the ridge where we'd been fired upon from. I remember knowing to do this immediately without thinking.

"Move" we shouted.

Two moved up, the other two giving covering fire. Then they ascended while the front two provided covering fire. At all times fire was being laid down on the enemy position. We used a magazine each sprinting up the ridge. When we reached the

---

9 SLR Self-Loading Rifle has a magazine of 20 rounds of 7.62 mm, and was the standard British Army Infantry Assault Rifle.

top there was no one there. We'd been fired on by an M-60[10], an American heavy machine gun, we found some shell cartridges in the grass on top of the ridge.

After all the adrenalin and commotion had died down, the first thing that came to mind was the Bayonet Assault Course. I'd wondered since that day in basic training what it would feel like to be involved in combat. I'd asked myself almost every day, what would I do? How would I react? That day I got my answer. I did what I'd been trained to do, we all did. We didn't need to think, training told us what to do, focused us on the job.

The lingering thought was of my instructors making us go through that Godforsaken Bayonet Course.

They really did know what they were doing.

---

10 M-60 GPMG was the American General Purpose Machine Gun 7.62 Calibre. Rate of fire 675 rounds per minute.

Chapter 7

HARD HAT AND SOFT HAT

I found it difficult to tolerate the apartheid regime in Northern Ireland, turning a blind eye to the Ulster Defence Regiment (UDR). For myself, the most difficult aspect of the initial period in Northern Ireland was getting used to working alongside the Unionist security forces who dominated the country. I sometimes found it awkward guarding Orangemen as my realisation of my Irishness grew. I say all these things in hindsight, but in truth my Irish identity did not matter to the job at hand and I was given more and varied responsibilities as time went on. I was a British Soldier, there to fight terrorists and keep peace in Northern Ireland, which is what I told myself and what I believed most days. Perhaps in moments of doubt, I think back and wonder was the reality the opposite. Had I just been there like all British Soldiers to maintain an acceptable level of violence?

Wherever the British Army see active service, they try and adopt a hard hat and a soft hat status. When the conflict is over they put on their berets in an attempt to further deflate the conflict, and with it the levels of tension and confrontation with the locals. The British Army arrived in Northern Ireland with the berets and the process worked in reverse. As far as I am concerned, there were two real antagonists in Northern Ireland: the IRA and the Unionists. The violence of the IRA arose out of the blatant sectarianism of the Protestant Unionist agenda. When I went there as a professional soldier, I went there for a reason: because it was my duty. I certainly did not go there because I believed the six counties should be part of the United Kingdom, but I accept there is not much we can do about it anymore. It's a catch 22 situation and in my view only time and healing can bring peace.

Some of the Protestants I met in Northern Ireland were bigots. They were closed minded and bunkered into their own little community. Nowadays they still blatantly antagonise the Catholic population with their marching. The Orange Order is basically the Ku Klux Klan of the North. As a British soldier I did not want to believe that I was there in any capacity to protect any type of bigotry.

I admit to not really knowing a great deal about the North before I arrived; the only thing my father had said to me was,

"Son they are not like us, don't mix them up with the people you've met in Dublin."

It was being there that opened up my eyes to it. I could not believe the rampant sectarian antagonism. It awakened in me an awareness of my Irish identity that has remained with me. While some of us Guardsmen didn't much like it, to many of the others it was just a job. The average British soldier did not want to be there and could not understand why we were there. The soldier was stuck in the middle with a target on his back. Unlike my fellow Guardsmen, who'd pretty much spent their whole lives in Britain, I'd been to Ireland and my parents were Irish. I didn't like what I was seeing. I didn't like seeing Catholics being treated as second class citizens, very much as they'd been treated for hundreds of years.

It is important to remember that the British Army went in there to protect the Catholic population from the Special Bs; a quasi-military reserve force of thugs in uniform. When the Special Bs were disbanded most of them moved into the Ulster Defence Regiment. The UDR was rumoured to be riddled with members of the UVF and other sectarian right wing Protestant groups. I did meet very decent Protestants, but they were few and far between in my military dealings there.

Forgive me for being baffled recently by the tributes that poured in at the death of Ian Paisley. That man caused nothing but havoc in Northern Ireland. This is the man that interrupted Pope John Paul II's speech to the European Parliament in 1988 with an anti-papist diatribe, shouting and holding up posters calling the Pope an antichrist: not exactly the actions of a man of peace.

I continued to grapple with my nationality and person. I could understand more and more why the Catholics had risen up against the oppressive regime, but I still believed in what

I was doing. Growing up in Birmingham I remembered well the IRA's Birmingham Pub Bombings, I'll certainly never forget them.

In Northern Ireland it was apparent the Catholics were educating themselves. As an ex-British soldier I've respect for Martin McGuinness, I would like to shake his hand if I ever met him, and I hope he would shake mine. McGuinness has proven to be a true statesman. I say this as someone who would not have hesitated in giving him the *Good News* back in the 80s and would have expected the same treatment from him. Thankfully the war is over and it's down to leaders like McGuinness and the late David Irvine – men who took up arms for what they believed in and then turned to the path of peace and reconciliation. They deserve respect.

My feelings on being Irish and being in the British Army have always been difficult. Somehow the contradictory nature of the two feelings embodies who I am. Like many Irish in Ireland maybe I am partly West Brit. Who knows? My dual loyalty was confirmed on the Queen's 2011 historic visit to Dublin: a very proud day for Ireland and Britain, and long overdue.

I am asked every year or two, normally when someone finds out a little bit about my past,

"How could you, being Irish, go to Northern Ireland and serve as a British Soldier?"

My answer changes or evolves each time but I tend to reply,

"Well, if you are asking me do I believe that Northern Ireland is British, I would say no, I don't. I would love to see a united Ireland one day, but I didn't go there to defend Northern Ireland as a British territory, I went to fight terrorism and protect the people, including the Nationalists."

It was my job.

I spent a year based in Limavady, but saying that I could be in Strabane, Castle Derg or Aughnacloy. They moved us where they needed us. I was put into the intelligence unit that formed part of Headquarters Company in the battalion. We moved about the North in a variety of civilian disguises. It was gulp gulp but I liked it, I think we all did. My job was to drive and surveil. The battalion had a shortage of drivers so this suited me as the job was far more interesting than being in a rifle platoon. The Intelligence Cell performed a wide variety of duties: some mundane like escorting army wives out shopping, ensuring they were safe; some more serious like keeping an eye on undercover lorries filled with British soldiers.

The following week we could be back inside the barracks in uniform, but once we joined the Int Cell we no longer went out on standard foot patrol. No further foot patrol was to ensure we were sufficiently demilitarised when we were out and about undercover, that we didn't come across as soldiers; we had to loosen up our bones, watch how we held ourselves, our gait.

In my new company, being able to drive, I was given a job driving unmarked cars and transit vans. Normally in these unmarked vehicles there would be two of us tooled up, each armed with a Browning pistol and maybe a sub machine gun, driving around the Province carrying out surveillance and ferrying dignitaries.

A patrol might radio with a grid reference, we'd take the transit vans with civilian plates into bandit country, this could be anywhere and we'd extract the patrol units, particularly when the dark gloomy Northern Irish weather had come down and the helicopters could not fly. Doing that job I was always on edge. This was around the time of the horrific incident when the two corporals, David Howes and Derek Wood, found themselves trapped by a funeral procession. The two corporals were dragged out of their car and murdered in Belfast, their bodies found dumped in a waste land. None of us will ever forget those images. I knew it was a risky post, and I knew what could happen to me. I just got on with it like everybody else. I remember one dark winter's night coming back from the airport, taking a short cut along the Glenshane Pass, near Coleraine and seeing a torch being flashed up ahead. For a split second I thought,

"Fuck, an IRA checkpoint."

The IRA frequently set up their own checkpoints in remote areas as a show of force.

I cocked my weapon. I was not going down without a fight. We all knew what happened if the IRA caught us: tortured to death, our bodies dumped and never found. Turned out to be a man whose car had broken down, bizarre normality. My heart was in my mouth, but I swallowed it and I lived another day hand on weapon.

Chapter 8

Monsters in the Night

Everyone knew everything and everybody in the North. We all knew that "yer man" was a part time RUC officer, as well as a cattle farmer in Tyrone. The man in the street knew that "yer man" didn't always carry his weapon, that he was an obvious target walking around his farm. Everybody in Northern Ireland always knew who'd killed whom. It was in the air and the longer you were there the easier it became to decipher. Didn't make the place any less dangerous – the opposite in fact.

As well as driving, the new job meant a good deal of surveillance. It was not beyond the realms of possibility we could be nestled in a lovely comfortable Ulster bush for two days, in the thick, damp, cold air, watching said part time RUC officer's farm house. There could have been four of us, three asleep one on stag, working off an Army Intelligence tip. We could have been fully armed waiting to see a van pulling up, to see armed known players getting out and then taking them out if needed.

That would have been bad enough, but there were worse things out there. One afternoon on a lurk[11] somewhere in deepest darkest County Tyrone, we were observing a farm house belonging to another part time RUC officer. There was a whole platoon surveilling from various hidden positions.

My brick were inside a small coppice, a wooded area. One of us on stag, three asleep. Whilst I was asleep in my sleeping bag, head resting against my Bergen[12], I was disturbed by a rustling somewhere under my head sufficient to wake me up. There was something moving inside my Bergen. I thought to myself, "Jesus Christ what is that?" I knew fine well what it was, but I didn't want to know, and I certainly didn't want to have to look at it. But I had no choice, I opened the Bergen and looking right into

11 A lurk was our version of a stake out, a surveillance operation.

12 A rucksack.

my eyes was a gigantic farm rat, a thing was the size of a cat, just staring at me and eating my rations. An East Tyrone rat.

If I'd jumped up as I wanted to that would have compromised the mission, nobody knew we were there. So I got a hold of myself and tipped the Bergen upside down. The rat ran off. It had eaten its way into my Bergen to get at my rations. We were there for 48 hours and when you are in a situation like that you don't ever move outside your location. You urinate in bags and so on. Ever since then I have an absolute phobia of rats.

In 1986 I was on an escort duty when we arrived into a barracks to grab something to eat. As always before we entered the mess, we unloaded our weapon and cleared the action. I bumped into a corporal and a sergeant I knew from guard duty at Buckingham Palace, they sat opposite and chatted while my fellow Recce Platoon member and I ate in silence.

My Browning was in my shoulder holster.

The two NCOs were deep in conversation about the Browning. The Sergeant I knew asked me could he borrow my weapon. When an NCO asks you for something you give it to them, end of. They were discussing the pros and cons of half cocking a Browning and the speed advantage this gives you. The disadvantage being the Browning is the easiest weapon to have a negligent discharge with, an ND. I only know all this in hindsight I was not really paying attention to them at the time. I handed the weapon over and continued eating.

While the corporal was talking he actually half-cocked the weapon and unbeknownst to me put a round in the chamber. The sergeant, not knowing this either, handed the weapon back to me, I foolishly saw the hammer was back and fired the weapon; there was an almighty bang, the bullet penetrated the table and went through my colleague's groin, luckily clean through. I'd shot him at point blank range. For micro seconds I thought I'd killed him. It was my weapon, I was responsible for it, irrespective of who loaded it. Thankfully it was a 9ml round and it went straight through at close range. Because the pistol was pointing down nobody was severely hurt, although it'd missed his testicles by inches.

I was in deep shit. I was charged with all sorts and the incident was investigated by the military police to find out whether anybody had had a psychotic episode. In the end I thought I was lucky. I was charged with having a negligent discharge and fined a month's salary, my colleague was back on duty in a couple of months and kept his testicles.

I was back on duty within a few weeks armed with my Browning. When you are carrying around loaded weapons accidents do happen. I wasn't the only soldier to have an ND that year, and as a good friend from the battalion said to me only recently, I wasn't the last.

A few years later in another land far far away from the alleys and hedgerows of Northern Ireland, I was caught in the middle of something more serious and I had to take someone down. But that is another story for another day and another book.

Years later those incidents would come back to haunt me. The truth is they never left me. What really throws me to this day, is the PTSD inside me lying latent. Or partially latent, it infused everything I did one way or another for the next twenty years and dictated my behaviour, despite me being unaware of it and appearing, on the surface at least, perfectly healthy.

I was fearless in those days. Nothing bothered me. Why? Well I was to find out later why. Suffice to say that it should have been a cause for concern, but in truth it never even occurred to me.

I'd like to ask my old self, is it normal at 24 to shoot a man?

Is it normal to see your friends killed in front of you?

But I can't.

Chapter 9

The forgotten wars

My grandfather John Barry, my Dad's father, was in the old IRA, the IRB[13]. A tailor by profession, he's buried in Glasnevin. He died the same year I was born, so unfortunately I have no memories of him. Grandfather Barry was on crutches his whole life as he suffered from Polio and thus had very weak legs. Grandfather Barry worked for the IRB in the 1916 uprising when he was very young. They had him running messages around Dublin because he didn't look like a threat. He looked like an inoffensive character and he was able to move about Dublin City relatively un-harassed. Messengers like my grandfather had to memorise and then destroy the messages. Unfortunately this meant that if they were caught they would be tortured to get the information. Sean MacDiarmada, one of the executed leaders of the Rising, also suffered from polio. Neither man allowed the polio to get in the way of his bravery. For years after the Rising, people in the neighbourhood, who were unaware of the Polio, told tales of how Grandfather Barry had been shot in the leg in the "Rising", after each telling the story got better and better like all classic Irish tales. My Dad would always tell me,

"That was the old IRA back then son."

My mum's grandfather Patrick Nolan was a Scots Guardsman who fought in the Boer War. He was involved in two campaigns: Cape Colony and Orange Free State. He was awarded the Queen's South Africa medal in 1902 and discharged in 1906. When he returned from South Africa Patrick Nolan met my great grandmother, an O'Toole from County Wicklow, and they married. They lived their years off Dorset Street, at 61 Lower Wellington Street, Dublin. Although he'd already been a professional soldier

13 Irish Republican Brotherhood 1858-1924

he re-enlisted for the First World War in the Middlesex Regiment in 1914. One can only imagine what he witnessed but whatever he saw and felt he never recovered. When he returned he was not the same. Before he went he had been a very loving caring man, a well-disciplined man. After his return he suffered from extreme bouts of anger and whatever happiness he'd carried inside of him had been extinguished on Belgian fields. He never spoke about it and, like many First World War vets, he took to the bottle.

One normal day when he came home with a few drinks on him the rage seized him. He snatched his First World War medals off the fireplace and hurled them into the fire. They were never recovered. I have no idea how he handled the homecoming many Irish had, coming back to an island riven and ready to revolt. Dublin was not as welcoming to a British soldier as when he left it. Although he was never good with people he worked as a hand craft tailor in Arnotts the department store in Dublin until 1946 when he passed away.

My great grandmother Julia was a business woman and ran the family shop. She kept guns under the floorboards for the IRA during the 1920s. The Black and Tans would come into the shop in Dublin, see the picture of her husband in the British Army uniform on the wall and maybe go a little bit easier on her. She was never caught.

Having a grandfather in the IRA and a great grandfather serving in the British Army is part of who I am. These are the myriad thoughts that linger and confuse when one side or the other accuse me of being on the wrong side.

My grandmother loved Michael Collins. We were brought up listening to tales of his daring exploits when we'd come in from school. She grew up with a father who wore the poppy so she and her sisters would always wear lilies just to rile him a little. The lilies are a symbol of remembrance for those who fell in the Easter Rising. Prior to my passing out of the Guards, I was having a look around the regimental gift shop and I found my grandmother a little Scots Guard

Piper to remind her of her father. She broke down when I handed it to her. She also brought a tear to my eye when she said to me,

"He would have been so proud to know his great grandson became a Guardsman."

My nickname within the rugby brotherhood is The Tan and I don't have a problem with this as I guess, in some kind of way, that's what I was except it also helped me to come to terms with my Irish identity. Everyone despised the Black and Tans. Everyone talks about the atrocities they committed. Who were they? They were professional soldiers that survived the First World War. Nowadays historians would explain if anyone asked that the Tans were not all British that some of them were Irish. In fact approximately 20% of the Black and Tans were Irish.

The Black and Tans were not prisoners that had been let out on day release on the proviso they went out and killed Irish people. They weren't lunatics that had been released from the asylum and all the other myths that Irish folklore has come up with. The Black and Tans, like the Auxiliaries, were men that had survived the trenches in the First World War. But of course that in itself would have been enough to kill a man inside. If you shot at them they would shoot back, if you didn't shoot at them they would shoot back. One mad day, in an alleged reprisal for a previous attack on British troops, the Black and Tans burnt Cork City to the ground after going on a crazed rampage throughout the city. They were named after a combination of the uniform that they wore, kaki top with black trousers, and a pack of wild dogs, hunting hounds that formed part of a fox hunt. They came to Ireland from the war and they never stopped fighting. They probably all had PTSD one hundred times worse than anything I could ever imagine.

When I served in the North in what we now call the Forgotten War, the RUC put all the Catholics in one guilty melting pot as IRA or IRA sympathisers. To them, every Catholic was a Republican. I split the two, as far as I was concerned the IRA were distinct and over here; the rest of the Catholic community were over there. Those children that spat all over my back, they were only doing what had been bred into them. Most of them would have gone on to have respectable family lives.

NORTHERN IRELAND
Portrush
Coleraine
Ballykelly
Londonderry
LONDONDERRY
ANTRIM
Ballymena
Strabane
Clady
Sion Mills
Draperstown
Castlederg
Newtownstewart
TYRONE
Cookstown
Bangor
Belfast
Omagh
Sixmilecross
Dromore
Dungannon
Lisburn
Fintona
Aughnacloy
Lurgan
DOWN
Fivemiletown
Portadown
FERMANAGH
Enniskillen
ARMAGH
Newry
REPUBLIC OF IRELAND

Chapter 10

Mirroring the past

My new surveillance job in Northern Ireland allowed me a little bit of leeway with my overall physical appearance. I had slightly longer hair, a more dishevelled, scruffy appearance and a fake student ID. Together they got me into Trax Nightclub in Portrush the fateful night I spoke to Violet for the second time – a chance meeting that would impact my life forever. I didn't look like a soldier as I was in my civvies. Soldiers weren't supposed to be in the club and the doormen wouldn't have let me in if they'd known. I was dressed as a student, chatting to her sister when she walked up, I recognised her from our previous encounter when we'd chased the suspect into the hair salon. We got to talking and we were together for the next twenty two years.

Northern Ireland's next twist; Violet was from a staunch Loyalist household. Her father had died many years before in a tragic car accident, but her mother maintained a strong Loyalist ethos in the house. Since it was Northern Ireland, we began seeing each other covertly. While the relationship was not exactly army permitted, the secrecy was definitely more to keep it from her mother. New Year's Eve eight months later, when I invited my new girlfriend Violet over to meet my family in Birmingham, things came to a head and my life changed forever. Violet's mum was appalled her daughter had taken up with a Fenian. A Catholic, Irish Fenian, the worst sort.

"Once a Fenian always a Fenian." Was her comment apparently. So much for my guarding and fighting for Queen and country.

When Violet's mother found out I'd invited her to meet my family she gave her daughter an ultimatum. She told her that if she went to Birmingham she'd never be allowed back into her home. Violet went anyway. She enjoyed the convivial kitchen table atmosphere in my family home with my Nan, my mother, brother and sister. She loved that she was immediately accepted. Meanwhile her mother called the barracks to report that her daughter had been kidnapped by a British Fenian Soldier. We've not had any contact with her since. That was the final decision from her mother, but that's not my story to tell.

Violet's aunt and uncle were wonderful people over the years we were married and always made our family feel welcome. More than anything, they have given our children a link with their Northern Irish roots. I am not sure after all these years I can fully grasp the depth of resolve it requires to maintain the impasse her mother has. Even after all the hurt between Violet and I, I still feel for her as I know what she gave up when she decided we should build a future together.

Northern Ireland is confusing, like being stuck in a room of cracked mirrors, looking over your shoulder at distortions, trying to figure out if the reflections you see are really you. I went back to my regiment, but after that things were different. Violet's mother had phoned the barracks in 1987 and I was transferred. She knew everything about me and my commanding officer felt I had been compromised as a result.

A century old story playing itself out again. Tell young people they cannot be together and they grow closer. More than anything else her mother drove us together, and for that I am grateful as I have three wonderful children and a lot of great memories of the 22 years we spent as a couple.

There I was a serving British soldier in Northern Ireland going out with a local girl. My great grandfather from Maguire's Bridge in Northern Ireland had been a serving Scots Guard when he met my great grandmother: an O'Toole from Wicklow. They fell in love despite her family being staunch Irish Republicans. She wanted to marry him. So they asked her father for his permission.

Her father replied,

"If you marry him, you are disowned from this family."

She chose to get married anyway and her parents never spoke to her again. My great grandmother's dying wish was to be buried in the O'Toole family plot in Kilranelagh Graveyard. Coincidentally the same cemetery as Sam McAllister, the United Irishman leader in the 1798 rebellion, is buried. In the end my great grandmother's brother gave up his place in the family plot to allow his sister to be buried there.

Violet and I were following ghosts, dancing those same steps, except in reverse. My own grandmother couldn't believe the similarities, and yet I think they pleased her somehow, made her happy.

I spent a few more years in the army and I was given an exemplary discharge in 1991.

When I left the army I was a time bomb just waiting to go off.

I'd been out about a year or so, working and selling advertising in a local newspaper in Birmingham, when I bought my first expensive suit. It was a Hugo Boss; all the rage at the time. I'd put it on and felt like a million dollars. Perhaps due to my military training, I've always felt it's important to dress really smartly. Looking smart gives an ever lasting impression – I've constantly wanted to be the best, so looking the best has always been part of that. Maybe I've relaxed a bit now, but I still like to look the part.

When I left the army I was a coiled spring.

A year or so into my time as a civilian, I was out with the sales team. My eldest son had just been born. I was feeling great, wearing my new suit, hitting my targets and believing I'd made it. After a few drinks I left the bar on Broad Street in Birmingham. As I was looking for a taxi, this man came towards me at speed, and another unseen man grabbed me from behind putting his arms around my neck. The front attacker reached to get my wallet from the inside suit jacket pocket. I pulled the attacker in front towards me and smashed my forehead onto his nose with tremendous force. The noise and violence of the impact were horrific. He fell to the ground, blood everywhere; the other mugger tore off as I wrestled with him. The screams of my attacker as he writhed in agony on the ground added to the sense of terror. I was drenched in blood, but all I was bothered about was my Hugo Boss jacket. I thought he'd ripped open my suit pocket. The unfortunate attacker on the ground, his nose obliterated, screaming and screaming.

A crowd gathered and a doorman appeared, he took a quick look around and suggested I make myself scarce.

When I left the military I was a fully trained fighting machine.

I got home that night covered in blood. I hand washed my lovely blue shirt, everything came out physically but I was shaken by what I'd done. There had been no decision just reaction. People would look into my eyes when I was younger and they would know. I was never aggressive outwardly, but inside I was intense. I held myself very confidently. If someone tried to mug me now, I would put up my hands and let them take whatever they wanted. Now I'd be thinking about the knife sliding into my back. Back in those days it just didn't occur to me, I never took a step back. I charged through the whole of the nineties.

It was madness. Or perhaps I was the madness.

I'd had a few drinks that night. But I reacted like my training taught me.

When I left the army I was back to square one.

Troubled

What did you do in the army Daddy?
Did you fight a war?
I've only seen a few old photos Daddy,
Please, tell me some more.,

I wore a scarlet tunic son,
A bearskin with a plume of white.,
I guarded the Queen in London son,
To make sure she slept safe at night

But did I fight a war son?
Politicians will tell you no.,
But let me tell the facts son,
The truth ,as it was, just so.

I went to a beautiful country son,
That is known as the Emerald Isle.
To the North of the South we young men went,
To a place chocked with hate and bile.

I walked the streets with a rifle son,
The enemy hiding from view,
Behind the hedgerows & in vans they hid,
Their mission, our lives to undo.

They wouldn't come out in the light lad,
They'd only fire from the dark.
Too timid to stand toe to toe son,
A yellow streak was their flags mark.

But how do you define a war son?
Is it bullets bombs and death?
Friends dying from enemy ambushes son?
If it is then my answer is yes.

Yes I fought a war my boy,
Though the government denies it all.
They said we just had some troubles son,
Behind a cracked Irish wall.

But didn't they give you a medal Daddy?
The one with the face of the Queen?
All shiny and Silver, your name on it
A ribbon of purple and green?

They did and it brings back that world son,
When I fought alongside real men.
It recalls those honest true friendships son,
The likes that I will never find again.

So yes I fought a war son
No matter what the politicians say
I would love those same politicians to pick up a rifle my lad
And be troubled for just one day.

Chapter 11

THE NINETIES CAROUSEL

For years I was an exceptionally confident individual and I never stressed about anything. I was oblivious to hubris or karma or anything else that might have given me even a slight pause for contemplation. After leaving the military I knew I didn't want to be poor. It was the only thing I was certain of. With no formal qualifications all I was actually qualified to do was manual labour. Not going to college had caught up with me, as had the advice of the recruiting officer. He had been 100% correct – I had eventually become bored with my life in the military and I'd never learnt a marketable skill. Not much call for a weapon's expert or a trained soldier back in 1991.

Violet and I moved into a very basic apartment, a little bed sit near the centre of Birmingham. I would never call those early years fun. We were probably forced together by circumstance more than anything. The reality is if Northern Ireland and her mother hadn't disowned her we may have never stayed together. I've always had a strong sense of responsibility so I felt practically wedded to Violet from then on. My first job was as a lorry driver, although I had no intention of driving for a living.

While making a pick up one day I saw a well-dressed man get out of a swanky car. Intrigued, I asked what he did, apparently he was in our sales department. Sales: the best job anyone could get without a formal education. That week I handed in my notice. I remember going back to Violet, to our tiny flat, her working as a hairdresser at the time. I told her what I'd done. She couldn't believe it. Not best pleased.

The following Monday morning I walked around every recruitment agency I could find in the centre of Birmingham. I was offered a job in one agency by an ex-military man who had served in the Royal Signals. I was behind a desk, cold calling people, placing candidates in jobs. It was a great start. I enjoyed the recruitment job, however I was eager to move up.

Next up on the nineties carousel I swung into the world of advertising. I had a company car, and initially everything was great. Travelling all over the UK selling but still driving. I did that for about a year and then moved on to another job with a larger UK based advertising firm, Morgan Crampion. I was an area sales manager, an increased salary, a better car and my own office: in short, a higher profile role. Violet and I got married and bought our first little house. My father paid for our wedding. I was that guy. I was on success autopilot, trajectory unknown.

Then the Black Monday bombshell, the recession came with a very loud bang. Norman Lamont withdrew Sterling from the European Exchange Rate Mechanism, suddenly nobody was advertising. Well that's not completely true: mobile phone companies seemed to be going great guns, car phones were all the rage. One of my clients, a mobile phone company, wanted me to come and work for them. I jumped at the chance.

The first month selling mobile phones, I made four times as much as my previous monthly salary. Violet and I were really on our way to the rest of our lives. A friend worked for Martin Dawes, an aggressive expanding organisation based in the North of England. I knew I could make good money there so I joined them. Going to work for Martin Dawes was one of the best decisions I ever made in my life. They were a well-run organisation and I thoroughly enjoyed working there. I became national account manager. If you were good at what you did you were given a licence to go ahead and do your own deals. I met my best friend, Mark, there. We worked together in a sales team of 130 people. Mark and I consistently shared first and second place in the sales league. We were dealing with big ticket sales, in 1996 I was awarded the largest mobile phone contract ever in the UK with British Gas. I did very well that month, very well indeed. I stayed with Martin Dawes up until 1998, through a total of about four years.

I'd first met Mark when he came up to the West Midlands office for a client meeting. There was an element of competitiveness at first and I am not sure we took to each other in the beginning.

Eventually, we developed a friendship of sorts based on mutual respect more than any closeness. Mark was very good at the office politics. He seemed to have the management wrapped around his little finger. I knew I was already very good at selling and was never overly fond of the political side of the job, preferring to let my record speak for itself.

When Mark left the company he started Anglo Communications. Once his company started to do well, he needed someone he could trust as sales director to push the team, particularly a person who would watch his back. The two of us agreed a deal and I went to work with Mark as the sales director of Anglo Communications. From then on our friendship grew. Anglo Communications was a service provider with 30,000 business to business (B2B) subscribers and we had a licence to sell Vodafone and Cellnet (which later became O2). B2B customers spend far more than private customers. Our largest client was McNicholas Construction, they had 750 phones with us. Our head office was in Hampshire. We had a five person sales team and Mark as MD. We were small and very nimble. I spent the next five years selling, making pots of cash and enjoying life. I was earning £20k a month by the end. I was always number one and developed into the stereotype of the nineties sales man: good, brash and very arrogant.

As the nineties ticked on living in England began to bring us down. Despite us living in an upmarket area, our family home was burgled three times in a relatively short space of time. The second time, when Violet came home the burglars were still in the house. The third time they stole my alloy wheels and tyres off my BMW. The car was discovered early one morning at the front of the house on bricks, by a neighbour walking his dog.

We knew we needed to change, but go where?

Chapter 12

The Dalkey dream

Around the time of the burglaries Violet and I were over at the Rose of Tralee on a jolly and missed our ferry home. We took a drive through Dalkey and ended up staying the night there; both of us smiling and musing on how lovely it would be to live in Dalkey. We fell in love with Ireland all over again. Ireland always made us feel like we were home, and we were very enamoured with our stay. Violet and I were both Irish and we could feel the allure of Ireland. Everything back in England seemed more impersonal, harsher and disparate. All the signs were telling us to go home. Ireland seemed easier, rosier and of course smaller. We were less likely to get lost. And most of all we wanted our children to grow up in Ireland.

So we moved to Ireland.

Arriving in Ireland in 1997, I would love to tell you we did everything right, but that would be a lie. For my children, for all of us it was beautiful – great schools and fantastic quality of life. We had pots of cash and life in South Dublin is always easier with pots of cash. I am ashamed to say we got caught up in those heady days somewhat, although we never quite developed the kamikaze approach to property portfolios that many other Irish did. For Violet and I, it was hard to get our head around how a normal everyday Joe could end up owing anybody 23 million. The very thought of paying those exorbitant amounts for property terrified us. We put our children into Castle Park School in Dalkey, which at the time was an olde worlde West Brit type school: a throwback to an imaginary idyllic past.

A perfect example of Castle Park's unique charm was John Hurt giving a reading at the Christmas carol service that had everyone feeling they'd witnessed greatness. Every Christmas, on the last Friday before school broke up, the school put on a Christmas carol service. Although the school was predominantly Church of Ireland, they would invite the local Catholic priest for the service in St Patrick's Church, Dalkey. One special year John Hurt, whose son was in my daughter's class, read a passage from the Bible and it was quite thrilling for everyone. He probably could have read the whole Bible to us and everyone would have enjoyed it. Violet and I had come from a hard lonely British city existence to the soft connected suburban Dublin life. We met people through the local Church of Ireland or the school and we kept ourselves to ourselves. Family life was as good as it gets.

I was still working in the UK to maintain our lifestyle, travelling the length and breadth of the country. I'd fly or drive over on a Monday or a Tuesday and then back on a Friday while Violet got on with things in Ireland. I spent the weekends with my family while during the week I was living it up with the big job in the city. Mark and I would be out every night, up to all manner of activities my wife would not have approved of. These activities stopped short of adultery, but I was still doing far too much carousing.

Violet and I bought a house on an acre of land in Wicklow on the basis that we could afford it. Property prices around Dalkey were insane. Two examples: an ex-corporation terraced house in Dalkey was bought for 15k in the 1990s then sold in 2004 for 600k; a friend purchased a house in Blackrock – postage stamp garden, overlooking the shopping centre – paid €1.9 million. People from outside of Ireland were looking at us, thinking the Irish had lost their minds. Property was being bought with borrowed money and thus everybody forgot the true value of everything.

Buying multiple properties was one thing, but Violet and I had no such qualms when it came to spending our money. We had it to spend. With our children in the best local schools, we got involved in equestrian sports. I had never ridden before, but when Violet suggested it I jumped at the chance. Money was no object after all, so I kept telling myself.

The other riding club members thought we were *arriviste* millionaires and saw me as being overly flash. I was a little naive, but there is no lack of smugness in any riding club. The members watched with barely concealed glee as we hastily bought our first horse without any real idea of what we were doing. Instead of helping us make the right choice, they wanted to see us fail. Perhaps to a certain extent we deserved their scorn.

We got rid of that first horse very quickly, it was an ill thought out venture from the beginning. We waited, learnt more and bided our time until the right horse came along. This time Violet knew what she wanted and she bought a really good horse named Fido. Violet was much more talented than I was in the sport. She had Fido for ten years, a super horse, good at dressage, cross country and jumping; everything really.

Professionally, I had lofty ideas of transferring my UK success over to Ireland, with a view to eventually working in Ireland full time and spending more time at home with my family. Unfortunately, I have never quite come to terms with the Irish way of speaking and doing business out of both sides of their mouth. I recall my Dad telling me that the average Irish man would live in one ear and rent out the other at the same time.

Despite that, I believed I would be able to do some business in Ireland, especially when my UK client Tesco bought a large Irish supermarket chain . I was given an introduction to the manager in charge of mobiles. The manager in question assured me repeatedly,

"Yes we are definitely going to do business."

This was my introduction to paddy-whackery and codology.

Of course we never did any business. The long and the short of it, and there was far more long than short, was that this manager had no intention of switching mobile operator, our various business lunches were to serve some other purpose I was insufficiently Irish to grasp, lunch probably. In England I'd have been told "no the business is not up for grabs" and I would have moved on. The Irish way of doing business is completely different to anything I had ever experienced in the UK, it is much more between the jigs and the reels.

I also came across an infamous deal maker, well known in Ireland, who absorbed everything I knew about mobiles all the while dangling some business in front of me. It was a brain drain, my brain being drained into his; Paddy style. I should have learnt something about Ireland and its ways after I had wasted so much of my time messing around.

The whole experience brought to mind the rest of what my Dad told me prior to moving to Ireland.

"The Irish are not fools. Remember it pays to act the fool. That is the mistake the English have made for years. While the English are laughing at the thick Mick, the Irish are running rings around them."

In the end I gave up and decided to do all my business in the UK. Much as I loved living in Ireland and I truly did and do, I had no interest in doing business in Ireland. I could not handle the side mouth double speak way of doing business. I didn't really know what to make of it, so I happily went over and back to the UK every week, pretending I was not way over extended on my own accounts, living our idyllic family life in Brigadoon, followed by my salesman life, then followed by my rock and roll life.

What could possibly go wrong?

Chapter 13

Living it large

And so it went; I spent the week in London, nightclubs and strip clubs, the nineties salesman living large. I never did drugs, which is probably how I was able to sustain it for so long. Instead, I would quite regularly blow £1,000 a night in London on Champagne and strippers, which is equally as ridiculous. I suppose I could blame the decade, blame the nineties customer's demand for lap dancing and largesse, but I could have said no at any time and I didn't, I was content to lead my triple life.

At least I had Mark by my side. They really broke the mould when they made Mark Weir. One story gives a flavour of the type of shenanigans we were up to. Vodafone invited us to see Manchester United play Anderlecht in the Champions League in Belgium. We flew out on the team plane and got the coach to the hotel with the coaching staff and team. I sat next to Dwight Yorke and got a shirt signed by the whole team. We arrived into the team hotel and immediately Mark and I absconded around the town drinking. We came back in the early evening, fairly on it. I spent the first part of the evening chatting with some of the Man United coaching staff before I realised Mark was no longer with me, apparently he had absconded with a hooker.

I started chatting to a group of female American students who were travelling around Europe in style, staying in 5 star hotels. There were five girls amongst the group and I knew that Mark would not want to miss out. I hurried upstairs and got a hotel employee to let me into his room. He was lying on his bed stark naked and comatose, very *Pulp Fiction*. I shook him a couple of times to no avail, dead to the world. I whispered into his ear that there was a group of wealthy American students in their mid-twenties downstairs. Like Lazarus he leapt from the bed and within minutes he'd showered and we were back at the bar regaling the girls with our stories.

Coming up to midnight Mark and I announced we were going to a strip club, one of the American girls revealed she was bisexual and wanted to join us. Apparently she had never been to a strip club. So off we went. As soon as we got there I found myself alone ordering the Champagne, I was very wary of allowing the club to take my credit card to charge bottles of champagne to it. I knew the way these things went. When I went to pay for the second bottle I discovered we were being charged €500 a bottle. What a total rip off. Going off in search of Mark I finally found him getting a big kiss from a lap dancer while the American girl was giving the stripper a big kiss from below. Acrobats all of them.

"Mark, Mark we're being ripped off" I said, somewhat inconsiderately.

When he finally turned his face around to look at me through the sweaty fog of pleasure, I repeated myself.

"We are being ripped off."

Mark looked at me as if I had just told him the shipping forecast and replied slowly,

"Do I look like I care?"

To be fair, he didn't.

My weekends were on the exact opposite end of the spectrum, spent with the children, show jumping King my new horse and taking it easy. A far cry from the manic night-days in London. Violet and I were doing a lot of equestrian, perhaps too much. I was pretending to be a normal guy at the weekend. My marriage suffered as I was so worn out from the week that I was beginning to let things slip. There was no way I was putting in the work any marriage needs.

Then one day Anglo Communications was bought by Recall plc. Bingo, a big payday. Needless to say I blew it on cars and holidays. When Recall purchased Anglo Communications in March 2001 we had 5,000 subscribers and turnover was £225k per month. As of March 2002 Anglo was billing £1.1 million per month with 25k subscribers and the business was growing at a tremendous rate of 500%. Anglo were the fastest growing service provider in the UK Marketplace with the lowest churn[14]. We successfully developed business partnerships with Devon County Council, Rothschild's, Tibbett & Britten, Norbert Dentressangle, Clancy Construction, Mc Nicholas Construction, and BA.

Despite our business model being great we were heading for trouble. We were locked into a share purchase agreement. Recall had a deal with BAE Systems that sadly collapsed about 12 months after they bought us. Overnight our shares were worthless and we could not off load them. Suddenly we were sitting ducks, with a board of well-paid City directors and the company listed on the Alternative Investment Market.

Every month we were fighting to stay alive, we'd enough in invoices but we were not getting paid on time and it was killing us slowly. In one year everything Mark had built from scratch was destroyed on the back of one poor decision. We should never have sold to Recall but one of our investors had forced our hand and we were slightly blinded by the thought of a big payday. What if, what if, what if?

During this tumultuous period, Mark had been diagnosed with sleep apnoea; connected to stress. I began to suspect that the illness and the stress were clouding his judgement. He ultimately lost his way. I would like to think I was there for him as he would be for me later on. However it is mostly up to the person to find their way back and Mark would not be back for quite a while.

Mark and I relied on each other much more than we understood at the time; with Mark's illness our dynamic was diluted and rather than argue with him on some key decisions I may have acquiesced too easily. We were different people but we'd always complemented each other very well. I'd always been the more aggressive one, and whichever extreme either of us had veered to, the other would encourage them back to sense. This was no longer happening. The relationship and the business were unbalanced.

14 Customers changing to other providers

Anglo Communications went under because we were taken to the cleaners by two of our creditors. They played us like fools. One creditor in particular, 'John'; we met him in the Institute of Directors and he assured us he'd pay the £300k he owed Anglo. John and another creditor Dave, more of a common crook, realised we had liquidity issues. They used their knowledge of our predicament and the industry to manipulate the situation to their liking and our demise. John and Dave simply anticipated what we were going to do. They knew we were on borrowed time with a drum tight cash flow. Our solution to keep the business afloat was to factor the debt. We found a factoring company more than willing and they came in and financed us. They invoiced on our behalf and took a commission.

The £300k John owed us would have gone a long way towards steadying the ship. I wanted to shut him down but Mark wanted to give him the benefit of the doubt. We'd always seen the world differently and until then that had contributed to our success. John looked us in the eye and promised us he was going to pay and didn't. We lost the business. We discovered in the period in question that John and Dave had been re-invoicing and getting all their customers to pay them directly.

August 2002 the receiver arrived early one morning and announced himself. By coincidence, neither Mark nor I were there to meet him. And so ended Anglo Communications, the company faded away into oblivion.

From then on everything became a bit of a struggle for me. My life changed, I began to fall to earth, slowly at first. I was suddenly unemployed, with monthly outgoings of €10k. Mark had a break down and went AWOL. He met and married a Brazilian lap dancer and spent the next two years rediscovering himself and getting a lot of free lap dances. His life was never the same. Nor was mine. I still think a lot about those years, as I spent the next decade trying to get things back on track. Today I understand that my particular "track" was always leading me over the cliff. But I wasn't to learn that for a while yet.

Now looking back at that time, while I didn't have any affairs, I was not leading a healthy lifestyle for someone married and in their thirties. I'd blown a lot of money, and when Mark and I lost the business, I cursed myself for not having had the foresight to have put something away.

I was right in the middle of my own debt disaster movie but I thought it was only a blip, a once off. Of course I thought the next thing was a once off as well, and after that it was a series of once offs. I'd spent the better part of five years living the Dalkey dream. It was now time to pay the consequences for my years in Brigadoon. The legend of Brigadoon is the story of a mythical village that emerges from the mist for one day every 100 years. This enchanted day is spent in joy and celebration. Those who happen up Brigadoon may remain in this beguiling place, only if they love another enough to leave the world outside. Dalkey was my Brigadoon.

Chapter 14

Destroying the illusion

Saying all that, I was not doubting my immortality yet. I was still manoeuvring around obstacles with a swagger. Surely, I thought to myself, all was not lost. I'd built up plenty of contacts over the years and I was confident I could get back in the game. I put myself out there once more, got a consultancy job in London and was hanging on to the vestiges of my equestrian set lifestyle. I jumped my horse King in the RDS in 2002. So while there was gloom around the corner, I did not recognise it yet. I presumed it was merely the shadows of my largesse.

In November of that year, I ill-advisedly went horse riding in Wicklow with a lot on my mind. King and I were following an inexperienced rider over a jump when her horse refused the jump, and turned sideways in front of the fence. I tried my best to pull King up, but the ground was very muddy and he lost his footing, stumbled and the two of us hit the ground. I ended up with a badly fractured femur – not an injury I would wish on anyone. Not to mention this was my second time breaking that same bone, albeit it on the other side. That day King knew I was in trouble , he stood over me as I lay on the ground with my very badly fractured leg. King knew an ill wind when he felt it. Who says horses are dumb animals? I can tell you King was not.

After being rushed into hospital and operated on the next day, I was incapacitated. The surgeon told me my nailed and pinned leg meant I'd be out for six months. I didn't have it in me to laugh but six months was a pipe dream, I had two weeks. I couldn't afford the luxury of lying in bed. I had to carry on. Once I could make it out of bed on crutches I went back to travelling back and forth to London. Driving was easier than flying – flying with the leg was an excruciating nightmare. Every time I squeezed into the micro space of economy class with my eyes closed, the head shaking regret coupled with life questioning pain made me swear never again. No fun.

Driving seemed the lesser of two evils, until winter January 2003, when I slipped on ice and broke the pin in my leg. Momentarily as I lay on my back after falling, as the pain shuddered into my psyche, withering me, I remember a warning briefly flashing through my mind. I ignored it. The fall set my recovery back a year.

How many signs did I continue to ignore? The fall had been my fault, nobody else had asked me to go out on that horse. I started to rely more and more on my mantras.

I have to take responsibility.

I have to keep the ship afloat.

I have to keep the show on the road.

I have to keep on limping forward.

My precious mantras, glib as they were, kept me going. Although my sense of responsibility has been a boon and a burden throughout my life, in those years it was often all I had as motivation. This slightly lunatic and intensely bizarre scenario carried on for a year.

Ireland had become very much home. But the commute was murder on my fractured aching bones and my disintegrating ego. I convinced Violet to move the family to the New Forest in Hampshire, England, close to where my offices were. By this stage I think we both understood things had gone amiss in our marriage, but it was one thing to understand it, quite another to do anything about it.

The children were not very happy about the move, but we all gave it a go. At this stage Ireland had been our home for 7 years but I believed there was opportunity in the UK for me, it was what I knew. I hoped there was a chance things would improve both in my professional and my personal life. I believed our closer proximity would help cure the separateness and the drift in our marriage, both had begun to take further toll. I knew I needed to spend more time at home, to stop being away all the time. Violet and I hoped moving to England would help repair the damage to our marriage. We were wrong. Our distance apart had allowed us to harbour the illusion that we still had a chance. Closer proximity was to destroy that illusion.

In the New Forest we replicated our Dublin lifestyle, put the horses in livery and continued competing in show jumping. I have never shaken the idea that our equestrian adventures had a lot to answer for: giving us both the opportunity to avoid each other whenever the other was free; giving us both a five year alibi to avoid the subject; and costing us an absolute fortune, 2k a month in livery fees alone.

We were in one of the most beautiful parts of England, wild ponies galloping around the New Forest. The people we met were extremely polite, nonetheless Fording Bridge did not feel like home. I missed the quirkiness of Ireland and my friends. Worst of all, my children were not happy. In August Violet and I came back to attend the Dublin Horse Show, and we both knew. But we had become experts in avoiding what was right in front of us.

The final straw came on a very low key New Year's Eve. Violet had gone to bed early and I looked around at the children and thought "this is not good." We all missed Ireland so much.

"Let's go home. Ireland is home." I said to myself as much as anyone else, but the whole house heard me and started packing immediately.

As for the marriage, Violet pretty much thought it was over. Maybe I did as well and didn't have the guts to say so, like a lot of men. I think my family might have resented me dragging them over to the UK. They probably did, but that is what families are for right? I'd felt that I could make it in the UK work wise, and I didn't. Ultimately the telecommunications industry had changed and I'd quickly become a dinosaur. There was not the same money to be made anymore. The trip had turned out to be a somewhat of a financial disaster and it left some deep scars on all of us. Despite everything, I feel it was an exercise worth doing because I learnt once and for all that Ireland was our home. Thankfully the children were happy to be back and that was great to see.

Violet and I continued to fade out of each other's lives. More than anything the respect had gone, from both quarters. We still loved each other, when you've loved someone that long it's almost impossible to ever fully lose the love, but we definitely needed our space. I went to live with a friend of mine, then got an apartment. After 4 months we decided to give it another go, to admit defeat was beyond either of us. This was the wrong decision and ultimately ruined the future for both of us. One of us should have had the courage to call it a day.

Coming back from the UK meant that I was back commuting.

I got involved in trading mobile minutes. I'd identified an opportunity and I was back trying to climb my way back to the top. Mobile minutes are traded on an exchange much like shares. This led me into more international circles and it was from there that I was to be given a chance to alter my self-inflicted circumstances and return us to the lifestyle we'd grown accustomed to. Whatever that meant and wherever the hell that was.

Chapter 15

Afghanistan, back on top of the world

I began trading minutes full time. As you would expect trading in minutes is primarily trying to find reliable value internationally. When the carrier business deregulated about twenty years ago, minute trading really expanded and there was a lot of money to be made in it. I was working in the UK selling international termination globally. Trading minutes is the stock exchange with minutes instead of shares; watching a screen, knowing the price, knowing what you can sell it for, what you can buy it for and of course making a margin. I was always pretty good at it.

My attention was repeatedly drawn to Afghanistan. After the US war with the Taliban, the market there was growing rapidly. I identified an opportunity and made contact with a company called Afghan Wireless. I met with the head of the carrier side of their business in London. He agreed that they might be interested in doing some business and invited me over to the US to meet with the CFO of Afghan Wireless's parent, Telephone Systems International. We got into a lengthy conversation on the GSM mobile business. Due to my background in the industry, I was able to give him some good advice on issues he was facing with Afghan Wireless.

"That's interesting. These things have been causing us problems for a long time." he told me.

No more was said. That night I went back to my hotel. The CFO emailed me and asked would I be able to meet again. I agreed. Now I was interested.

"Look you strike me as the type of guy that we could use. If you are interested we have a requirement in Afghanistan. We need someone to head up the sales department. Sales are not doing as well as they should be."

He offered me a job in Afghanistan.

In mulling over my decision, I thought about my disappearing marriage and the major financial pressure I was under. I desperately wanted my family to be able to continue to live the way they'd always done. The very idea of not being able to meet my requirements to my family struck real panic into me.

Afghanistan in the abstract represented, not an adventure or some danger lust fulfilment, but money. I rang Violet who might as well have been working for Afghan Wireless herself, she was so keen on the idea. She'd grown up in Northern Ireland and didn't see it as the risk others might have. She assured me with my military background I could look after myself. Initially I didn't bat an eyelid either, probably because of what I'd gone through in the army. It just didn't worry me. I don't mean to sound arrogant but that is the plain truth. And, deep down, the risk and the unusualness of it attracted me.

"This could get me back to where I need to be."

Another one of my mantras. My eternal search to get back to where I needed to be. Perhaps if I'd been more self-aware I might have realised this quest for the nirvana of where I needed to be was coming at a huge personal cost. But I wasn't. After being out injured I was back sprinting. Sprinting towards my new problems and away from my old, away from my merely personal issues towards some brand new altogether more serious type issues.

I believed I could make a difference, that I could be a success in Afghanistan. Although nothing I knew had prepared me for what I encountered; how could it? There was a natural apprehension, but I wasn't afraid. I had been close to drowning in debt since the business had gone under. I yearned to be away from worrying every minute of every day where the next chunk of cash was coming from. I knew I could take the burden and the pressure off Violet and my family. I also thought deep down that this might also help cure our marriage. It turned out I was right on some fronts and delusional on others.

In late 2005, Afghan Wireless made me an offer I couldn't refuse, so I duly accepted it.

I was to be based full time in Afghanistan. January 2006 I flew to Dubai and stayed there overnight. It was only then, floating on my back in a roof-top infinity pool with the Gulf filling the horizon, that I began to feel creeping tinges of anxiety.

"Shit! Tomorrow I am going to be in Afghanistan," occurred to me.

Momentarily as I floated I struggled to understand where I was or what I was doing. I gazed right back through my life, angry I'd made so many bad financial decisions, angry I was not sitting at home in Dublin living off a property portfolio. But there was no way back at that stage and the fear of my family losing everything far outweighed the fear I had of Afghanistan.

Nonetheless for the first time in my life, I felt truly scared.

Too late.

The next day I flew out of the old Terminal 2 in Dubai. Terminal 2 was used by airlines that could not afford to fly into Terminal 1. All the destinations on the board were straight from the headlines; places like Kabul, Kandahar, and Islamabad. I got on board the ramshackle Ariana Airlines, the Afghan carrier. It was falling apart literally. The plane was from the 1970s and a nervous traveller's worst nightmare. The plane filled unsurprisingly with Afghans and foreigners going to do business. The man beside me on the flight, going there to repair Humvees, asked me what I was doing going to Afghanistan. I told him about Afghan Wireless. He said that reminded him he needed to get a mobile sim when he arrived. My salesman mind immediately kicked in and I was already putting in place a deal to sell on flights.

Why don't we hand the sim cards out on the planes?

We had a lot of success doing our version of this in later months. We bribed the right people, always key, and sold the arriving passengers sim cards while they picked up their luggage in the Kabul terminal.

Kabul Airport was a shock. The war may have been over three years, but it looked like it was finishing the following week: burnt out planes at the side of the runway, craters everywhere you looked. The airport didn't have a baggage belt, it was total bedlam. Everywhere you looked there were bags strewn all over the floor. As soon as our bags were dumped, Afghans started running towards us shouting "baksheesh, baksheesh". I'd come from corporate England's tassels and loafers and the thought immediately occurred to me that I was not going to last five minutes in Kabul.

Eventually someone took my bag and ushered me out. I was not all there, I think I was vaguely in shock, vaguely in awe. When we got out the man carrying my bag was knocked out of the way by Wahid Khan an old Pakistani from HR holding a sign with my name on it. Wahid told me not to give the Afghan any baksheesh whatsoever. I gave him something anyway, what else was I supposed to do? Wahid shrugged and escorted me into a waiting car with three guards armed with automatic weapons inside. As well the guards in the car, there was a pick up in front with armed guards. I never went anywhere without this escort, you couldn't risk it.

Every guard had an AK47. Every building or structure, everything we passed was riddled with bullets, blood and dust. There was no left or right hand side to the road I could discern. Why would there be? Everybody had far more important things to be worried about, staying alive mainly. Traffic consisted of cars mingling, motor bikes weaving, donkeys moseying, and limbless beggars begging. It was the middle of winter in Kabul, meaning sub-zero temperatures. Any time we stopped, children would crowd around the window begging. One girl in particular reminded me of my youngest child, sitting that same day in a private school across the world. She was up begging at the window in her bare feet on her dirty tip toes. I handed her $10 despite Wahid urging me not to. He was probably right. Within a minute there were thirty more around the car, children only in their bodies, their dull adult eyes spoke of short perilous lives. I was startled and effected by this at first, but I soon got used to it, which says something melancholy and wise about me and Kabul I suppose.

We drove in our own little armed convoy to my accommodation on the outskirts of the town. The company owned accommodations called guest houses, with security guards on the door, barbed wire ringing the property. I met all the staff and the owner of the house, Mr Mana – a man I would come to know and respect: a friend whom I would never forget. Mr Mana ran the guest house. He was a very devout Muslim, an astonishing cook, as well as being probably the nicest person I've ever known. We used to call him Papa Smurf, because he was completely tiny and had a long goatee beard. Everyone who worked in Mr Mana's guest house was charming and I felt renewed hope.

Next I was brought to the office: a heavily fortified and guarded building. In the boardroom I was introduced to the CAO[15], Bassir Bayat, and my direct boss JMG, or Jean Michel. Jean Michel was an entitled Frenchman from central casting – arrogant, treated the locals like his servants, and displayed outright disdain for those around him. Jean Michel had an appalling way of dealing with people. I've been around plenty, but none as bad as him. Little did I or he know at the time, but the powers that be had already made up their minds; Jean Michel had to go. But I didn't know any of this at the time and I was pretty concerned at my poor welcome.

Jean Michel's hackles were up due to my arrival, they'd never been down his whole life. It was obvious from the outset he didn't want me there. He was right not to. However, I was still worried that they'd brought me all that way to work in a department headed by a guy who clearly wanted rid of me before I'd even unpacked. The other two in the office were Indian, Kaaliya and Tanish. I hadn't had much cause to work with Indians up until then. I was soon to learn that Indians from the north, and in Tanish's case Delhi, often held themselves aloof, they were the top of the caste ladder and they acted like it. Kaaliya could have been from anywhere, suffice to say he would have sold his own grandmother to anyone, an international sleazebag.

I'd been thrust into an environment with three people who wanted nothing to do with me. I would either sink or swim, or maybe die. It was an inauspicious start, but I really had nothing to lose. The first thing I noticed was Jean Michel never left the

15 Chief Administrative Officer

office, the consummate desk pilot. The two Indians definitely had no intention of ever leaving the office either; they said it was too dangerous. I was given the title of regional sales manager. I suspect Jean Michel *et al* regarded this as a poisoned Afghan chalice. I intended to do my job and go to the regions far away from them. I hoped my being out and about all over the country would bring into sharper focus Jean Michel's cowardly reluctance to leave the office.

At the end of my first day, I got back to the guest house and rang my family, and they all quizzed me on what it was like. I told Violet,

"You would not believe it. An Islamic Mad Max."

"Well you've got to do it, you've got to do it." The support I deserved.

Violet was worried I was going to come home. I'd never even told my mother where I was going. My time in Northern Ireland had taught me, where my mother was concerned, she presumed every death was automatically me until she had proof of life, or a phone call. I hadn't told my Dad either, owing in no small way to the lingering embarrassment at needing to do something so dangerous because of my own mistakes. It was difficult to hide or admit it when I spoke to my Old Man.

I spent a week in the office trying to work with Jean Michel, Kaaliya and Tanish. This mainly consisted of them stonewalling me on every request, constantly trying to make my life uncomfortable, their very own unsubtle version of constructive dismissal. I knew they were trying to get me to quit. I don't quit.

Chapter 16

The outer regions

I knew for certain I had to get away from the office and visit the regions, my regions. The six regional offices were Kandahar, Kunduz, Jalalabad, Mazar-e-Sharif, Herat and Khost. I went to meet Amin Ramin, head of security, a fearsome looking Afghan who glared at me, probably silently wondering what another bloody expat was doing in front of him. He would soon become a very good MD of the company, but to me he will always be Winston the Wolf from *Pulp Fiction*, the man who could fix anything. He was mister connected. His brother was the Minister for Agriculture and he knew everyone in Afghanistan. He was a ferocious looking, lethal individual, an ex-Mujahidin fighter who'd fought the Russians. He had a terrifying charisma. I liked him.

He spoke first before I had a chance to say anything,

"Great, another expat, here you come promising everything. But never delivering anything. Those three clowns downstairs, Jean Michel, Kaaliya and Tanish, they haven't delivered anything. What are you going to do different? What are you going to promise to deliver?"

Although I was slightly taken aback, I stood my ground.

"I don't know, I have to have a look around first."

Making clear he had heard it all before, he asked me,

"Yeah OK OK what do you need to do your job?" Presumably he was expecting to hear the usual drivel.

"I need two reliable guards and a suitable vehicle to go out and have a look at the situation in the regions."

I knew I needed to prove myself to management as quickly as possible. I'd surprised him I think.

"OK anything else?" he was still glaring but his demeanour had shifted a touch.

"I need my own weapon."

"No way you get a weapon. Are you crazy? What would you do with it?" Ideas of me driving the narrow and wide streets of Kabul drunk, taking pot-shots at imaginary foes no doubt. I explained to him I was ex-military that I'd been a weapons instructor as well as a trained soldier. He confided in me he was ex Mujahidin. I tried to be as blunt as I dared, and I explained politely but assertively,

"I am not driving round Afghanistan unarmed, end of story. I'm prepared to go out and do what needs to be done, but if I need to look after myself I'll feel a lot more comfortable with a weapon."

He thought about it for a minute looking at me, and agreed. I got a Glock as a sidearm and an AK47 for the regional travel, along with the necessary licence.

The following day, my new driver Rafiola, two guards and I left the office and began our tour of all the regional offices. I brought Engineer Abrar, who was to prove a great ally and wonderful friend. At all times we had pickups with armed guards escorting us. The only places we didn't go to by road over the next few months was Kandahar or Khost, simply because you couldn't, it was bandit country up by the Pakistan border. East Tyrone all over again, but less green and far more dangerous.

First we drove north to Mazar-e-Sharif: the fourth largest city in Afghanistan with a population of over 300k. It's the main city of its region and is known for its iconic blue mosques. In all the regional offices everybody was Afghan and most importantly from that particular region. In Afghanistan local knowledge is the only knowledge, it'll make you money and keep you alive.

When I arrived to the Mazar-e-Sharif office, I was not surprised to learn that nobody really knew what they were supposed to be doing. Sales personnel were making sales in a purely reactive way. They were merely order takers. The local Afghans wanted phones, so there was plenty of demand. Most of the staff in our offices had their job because of their relatives and friends. This is the way it is in Afghanistan. Over 80% of the population are Sunni with the remaining almost completely Shi'a. Irrespective, tribal loyalty and family loyalty rule the day generally.

In Mazar-e-Sharif, I met the regional manager and straight away he told me that no one had ever worked with him, no sales manager had ever visited from head office. Sales staff used to just sit there and do the best they could, mostly made up as they went along. All those highly paid expats sitting back in the fortified compound never going anywhere. Obviously, King Tut himself, Jean Michel, had never visited even once.

After Mazar-e-Sharif, I went to Kunduz – the fifth city of Afghanistan, the regional capital of the Kunduz province, and the main agricultural centre in the country. Kunduz is where they took the famous photograph of the ancient Kala-i-Jangi fortress crammed full of Taliban after they had surrendered to the Americans. The Americans were using it as a prison, and it was there that the CIA found John Walker, dubbed the American Taliban.

Incredibly, the regional manager of the Kunduz office was even more incapable than the first guy I'd met. It wasn't fair to judge them really. No one had ever trained them. Although all the regional manager ever did was come into his office, sit there and smoke cigarettes. I memorably met his cousin the marketing manager, who proudly said to me,

"Let me show you my marketing cupboard."

Whereupon he sauntered over to the marketing cupboard with me in tow and opened the door. I looked inside. It was full of absolutely everything: mugs, calendars, posters, and banners; all the marketing collateral going back years. Not one single item had ever been used. In his defence he thought he was doing a great job, he thought he was saving money.

I explained to him that all of it needed to be distributed and displayed. He looked distraught as he imagined his Aladdin's Cave being emptied. I asked him,

"What is the point of having ten thousand pens hidden away? They all need to be handed out to the schools and anywhere else that'll use them. Cups and mugs need to be handed out to all the coffee shops, the banners need to be up on the streets."

He was taken aback but he was listening, I continued,

"You're the best kept secret in Kunduz, nobody even knows you are here."

I spent a week working with the marketing manager talking him through the fundamentals. Of course I emptied his marketing cupboard, but he forgave me and was genuinely pleased in the end when he saw the difference the materials made. We had a good time working together. Overall I ended up spending a month in Kunduz. Together we took their monthly business from $200k to nearly $600k.

Head office noticed, and the Kunduz regional manager was named regional manager of the month. Within four weeks, he'd gone from being the least successful regional manager, to the most successful in Afghan Wireless. I educated the sales team, emphasising that instead of sitting in the office waiting for people to come to them, they needed to get out there and sell to the customers. We took every vehicle in our compound, packed them with staff and marketing material, and went out to surrounding villages and towns. The mobile phone is a vital part of the fabric of even the most rural Afghan village. They needed them and they wanted them. Mobile phones brought relatives and friends back into their lives that otherwise they may never have seen again, and also allowed the communication needed for trade.

We looked at towers and sites not generating any revenue and sold to the people in those areas. Straight away more people started connecting to our network. We gave the local traffic police fluorescent jackets with Afghan Wireless on them – free advertising for the company, increased brand awareness.

While I was in Kunduz, besides a bar and a German restaurant, there was nothing much else to do except work, so we worked. What sales angle did we have? Well truthfully we didn't really need one. Afghans wanted mobiles and often they'd never been actively sold to before. So they were delighted. Many tended to be illiterate. We used the local dealers, who had a better handle on the sales landscape. The sales team had never been shown how to go out there and sell. I demonstrated to them that I was prepared to leave the office to go out and sell.

And like anywhere on earth, leading by example remains the most effective management technique.

I have always endeavoured to avoid being the aloof expat expert that lived to order the locals around. Besides the fact that I got on with the Afghans easily, I've never believed I've some God given right to be respected. I believe respect needs to be earned. It's not something you should expect, it's something the person should give freely. This would range from eating my food with my colleagues and sharing bread with them, to working alongside the team. I proved I was prepared to be proactive and get out there, to work and sell. I never asked anyone to do anything I was not willing to do myself. I was another part of the team. We travelled around all the villages together, anywhere they went I went, unless I thought it was too dangerous and then nobody went. Straight away the sales teams saw I meant business and responded well. If he's doing it, why shouldn't we.

When I returned to Kabul my arch enemy Jean Michel tried to orchestrate my ousting. He stormed into my office, convulsed with some trumped up charge, determined to antagonise and provoke me into leaving.

He told me,

"You're completely disruptive, you're not a team player." And then absurdly,

"I only told you to go and visit the regions for a week, and you stayed for four weeks."

I responded,

"You never told me anything whatsoever, you never told me to go anywhere as you wouldn't speak to me. I'm not sure you said a single word to me in the whole week before I went."

A scene that perfectly encapsulates the overly macho world of expat intimidation and posturing.

Jean Michel then resorted to abusive mails, I warned him that abuse and rudeness would not be responded to either. I felt more self-assured after I had proven myself, therefore I was prepared to make a stand. Physically he could not intimidate me, which made him angry, and in his anger his treatment of everyone around him deteriorated further. Rather than dwell on his outrageous behaviour, I will say that he was the one who got ousted. However, I was in the dark about this when I was summoned to America. They flew me to the States, over to our parent company, I was nervous. Immediately I was told,

"Those three guys don't want you there."

Outwardly I remained calm.

"OK"

"We are going to get rid of them." I exhaled with relief.

"Really, we couldn't let you go. Unlike a lot of guys we've come across, you actually do what is written on the tin, you talk big but you deliver big as well. So we'd like to make you sales and marketing director. I suggest you keep Tanish, what you do with Kaaliya is your choice, but Jean Michel is gone."

The word 'payback' loomed large in my mind crossing the globe back to Afghanistan. Jean Michel had always treated everyone around him appallingly, but in particular his driver seemed to suffer his whims. Jean Michel made the man stay in his car all day in the freezing cold for no reason. Worse while out in the freezing Afghan nights, he'd insist the driver waited in the car while he spent three, sometimes four hours in a restaurant, again for no discernible reason other than power lust.

I was allocated Jean Michel's vehicle, but I kept Rafiola and relocated his driver. I also refused him the use of it as a form of petty revenge. Very unlike me, I am not a spiteful person, but I wanted him to get a taste of his own medicine, not really for my benefit but for the benefit of the employees. I made sure that for his final trip out of Kabul, Jean Michel got Farid's car: the worst car in the fleet.

Farid drove a battered old Toyota Corolla, it was in appalling condition and was used to transport crap, much like Jean Michel. It did not even have the right security passes to enter the airport. This meant he had to walk the last mile to the airport all on his own with his bags, scuffing along tail between his legs, and without his bonus. The transport manager who'd suffered Jean Michel's wrath more than most, had the pleasure of telling Jean Michel he would be traveling in Farid's Corolla. The servants, his staff and I were all delighted to see the guy go.

One story in particular encapsulates Jean Michel's approach to the people around him. After one of his shirts was ruined in the laundry, he made a big song and dance about it. Eventually he bullied one of the men working in the guest house into admitting it was his fault. Jean Michel made him pay $50 to replace the shirt. The man would have been on $200 a month or less, but to Jean Michel it was always about his ego and his desire for dominance.

Nobody whatsoever bid him farewell.

Not a single person in all of Afghanistan was sorry to see him go.

So ended my first day as head of sales for Afghan Wireless.

My Parents 1963

Christmas 1967 with my Father

Dublin 1980 in my Grove disco days

Grandfather John Barry

Great Grandfather Patrick Nolan

South Tyrone 1980s front row kneeling

South Tyrone 1980s

In my ceremonial dress uniform

Windsor Castle Guard 1985

Charging down the Bayonet assault course as a recruit

Typical 1980s riot scene
Photographer Sean Hillen

Sales man of the nineties

Cavan Equestrian Centre 2002 with King in a jump off final

With my dear friend engineer Abra

If looks could kill, Afghanistan 2006

Chapter 17

Local politics

I slotted into the sales and marketing job, determined to make the most of it. I continued to travel around the country meeting all the regional managers, assessing the situation and helping; I was determined to be a success.

Kabul was full of ex-military mainly working for security companies and NGOs. The security at the embassies was primarily outsourced to ex UK, US and South African military. I got on OK with the security people, being ex-military myself.

Afghanistan adheres to the Arabic weekend, Friday and Saturday. I tended to work the Friday anyway but I liked to have Saturday off. I would visit a souk or one of the shopping malls. There were certainly bars to go to, but the best places in Kabul were Chinese brothel-restaurants. Everywhere you looked there were Chinese restaurants doubling as brothels. The waitresses served food and also worked as prostitutes on the side, or maybe it was the other way around? You could get a very nice meal of an extremely high standard, then entertain yourself with a waitress. When I went there I never involved myself with the ladies, but I did enjoy the singular atmosphere. Curiously, living in a semi war zone can often be a dull affair, and we all needed to unwind from the relentless tension.

Our favourite was called the Happy Hour Café. The Mama San, Wen Wen, was a tough cookie who supported her whole family back in China. She played the worst music I've ever heard, bar none. It was frightening. She allowed me on occasion to play my iPod for a little aural relief, but in general it was a tortured cacophony of various countries' greatest hits. You could get hashish in the Happy Hour Cafe, put it on the shisha, and get off your head. There was gambling, hookers, drugs and booze, a spicy Kabul melange.

The Happy Hour Café bar was like the bar from Star Wars, a monsters' ball of security contractors, soldiers, expat wannabees and various other nationalities and ethnicities from all over the solar system. It's a wonder there was not more trouble there, as it was Afghanistan and in Afghanistan everyone is armed. The only time I was ever involved in any type of physical altercation, was when one of a group of ex Indian Army Ghurkhas, working as private contractors, started slapping around a Chinese waitresses. I was having a drink with a six foot four American friend at the time and I leaned over and said to the ex-Ghurkha,

"Very easy to slap a woman around. Not so easy to slap a man around. Why don't you have a go at me?" I am not really sure what I was thinking speaking to a Ghurkha like that. But I said it with the help of about 8 large glasses of Johnny Walker Black Label.

The Ghurkha came at me, threw a punch, I threw a punch. Briefly it kicked off as everyone got involved in the melee. It was a soldier's fight, no weapons. A mass brawl in the middle of a Chinese brothel. Although there were guns everywhere, not one shot was fired and not one gun was drawn. It was broken up by the arrival of the ex-Ghurkhas' commander. The officer walked up to the original offending Ghurkha and crowned him with a lead lined baton. After being reprimanded by his officer, he came over to me to apologise. While he was apologising a different Chinese waitress smashed a bottle over his head from behind, he did not flinch.

The vivid red blood trickled down his face as he finished apologising. Expressionless he turned to her, looked straight through her, turned back to me, wiped the blood off his forehead, shook my hand and left.

That was a rare occurrence. The x-factor involved, of never quite knowing who you were getting involved with, the smoking, the danger all around, meant that places like the Happy Hour Café were relative oases in the midst of the encroaching danger.

In Afghanistan family is everything, there was no point in us fighting a national culture that has existed for millennia. When it comes to giving out jobs, Afghans give them to their families, without exception. My job was then to cajole, train, explain and in very extreme examples transfer our Afghan employees. I enjoyed this aspect of the job immensely.

Of the two Indians in my department, I kept Tanish who, despite being a pompous ass, was an excellent marketer. He simply had that Delhi way about him, for want of a better description. But he knew his stuff, he understood the need for a coherent marketing strategy and was good at coming up with campaigns. I was learning on the job. I'd never done any marketing, I learnt a good deal from him. We ended up developing a good working relationship once Jean Michel had been eliminated. Tanish eventually left us to work in Africa.

Kaaliya was a different matter. I couldn't decide if I wanted to keep him or let him go. I told him that he was on a three month trial, and that he would have to change how he operated if he wanted to stay. He had this subservient cap doffing routine, constantly offering to carry my briefcase, opening doors for me, it used to drive me up the walls. Subservient bullshit. Jean Michel had obviously loved all this, but it went against what I wanted to instil. I was forming a results driven team. Kaaliya was an unusual man, but I still wanted to keep him on. I really hated admitting defeat and firing people. However it was all brought to a head one day when he damaged his own laptop, was seen doing it, then blamed it on someone else because he wanted to get them fired. Luckily some of the house servants witnessed the incident and I fired Kaaliya on the spot.

I hired a Pakistani, Awais, from Karachi as my new sales manager. In general, I found Pakistanis very good to work with. All very honourable, stuck to their word. Awais went out and travelled the country meeting people and putting together sales campaigns. The team responded well to him and he was generally successful.

The Afghan Wireless business structure was such that each city had an exact replica of the head office. We always hired the regional manager from the area, they were able to navigate local politics, and had the contacts needed to make things happen. There was absolutely no point in putting an expat of whatever ilk in charge at a local level, zero. Our ability to train our employees was at the heart of the success we enjoyed. Dealing with individuals you realised what was needed. So what if the marketing manager was a cousin not a marketer, no matter, we worked with them and trained them as marketers and sure enough almost always we'd have success.

In 12 months we increased AWCC's turnover from $4 million to $10 million.

We were increasing revenue and sales month on month. Central to this was an exclusive deal I'd secured with Ashraf from Peshawar. Ashraf's family had been traders for centuries, they had continued trading during the Taliban times, were part of the intricate tapestry of the country, and gave us access to markets we'd never have known about. Ashraf traded all over Afghanistan.

He'd often come sit in my office and we'd talk about family and friends, share our varied stories: chew the fat. Our primary business consisted of selling top up cards and Ashraf treated them as a commodity, much like the Nestle milk powder he also traded in. This proved to be a very lucrative sales channel and ensured that everywhere Ashraf traded sold our sim cards and our top up cards. We gave him an 8% discount for bulk orders, and he would keep 3% and pass on the other five to the outlets. Ashraf was dealing in millions of $USD, so 3% was a nice margin to have.

Sadly Ashraf was assassinated in November 2008. He was sitting in his car on a normal lethal Afghan afternoon, shot dead and no money was taken. I was very saddened to hear it, as I'd always liked him. People suggested it was something to do with a financial dispute, although knowing him as I did, it was over someone owing him money rather than the other way around. No one really knows why, but it stopped me in my tracks when I heard about it. All I could picture was his face and the expression he'd always use when he wanted something from me,

"What to do Mr Alan, what to do?"

Another person I'll never see again. On earth anyway.

My relationship with Amin Ramin had improved, and with him as the MD we turned the company around. I ran everything past him first, always made sure I had his support before I embarked on any new plans. This was essential, I needed his opinions and insights into the complexities of the political and business landscape of Afghanistan before implementing any strategies.

Anywhere I have worked before or since I have always sought the loyalty of the local staff. In Afghanistan my staff had my back and I had theirs, they kept me informed of what was going on around me and I made sure to be in their corner if they needed me. I ran my department along loose military lines. Everyone understood that we worked as a team and we did things for each other.

When you look at Islam, a subject never out of the news, like most anything there is a good side and a bad side to it. All we ever see in the West is the bad side: Jihad, suicide bombers, people flying planes into buildings, blowing up buses, ISIS killing people simply because they are not of the same faith or not the right type of Muslim. But my own experience of Islam when I lived in Afghanistan and Iraq was quite different. The people I encountered there were some of the most decent human beings I've ever met. An Afghan who earned $200 a month would not hesitate to give you the shirt off his back. If you walk into a room in Kabul and there are two Afghans sitting eating Afghan bread and that is the only food they have in the world, they offer you a third of their bread every time. I have met so many decent Muslims that it has made me ashamed at how our Western media portray them.

Every now and again, we would have a barbeque out the back of the guest house. We could just about see the minarets of the mosque next door. There were some Germans in the house along with me and we could get as much pork as we wanted from the UN shop. For the most part, Mr Mana would insist on barbequing for us. But we never asked him to cook pork. I asked him once what would they do next door in the Mosque if they ever smelt the pork. He didn't seem overly worried. He told me that most Afghans have no idea what pork smells like so it was not an issue, we both laughed. During Ramadan we would be happy to respect our hosts by not cooking pork, as a mark of respect for the Muslim's holy month.

Mr Mana could make soup better than any chef I've ever come across. I was always on at him to open up his own line to sell in Harrods. As a bit of fun, I asked the graphics guy in marketing to design a label, "Mr Mana's Soups of Kabul". We all had a laugh and he really enjoyed the compliment. By the time I left, he was doing soup for all the surrounding guest houses. Whenever we both had a free evening we'd wile it away happy and melancholy in the garden, talking slowly and quickly about our lives and our families, sipping Afghan Cha. Two humans.

The mosque next door had three different mullahs performing the five daily calls to prayer, one castrated, one cranky, one harmonious. Crazy Ed with a PhD in rocket science had been living with us in the guesthouse for a couple of months. He was an American. While socially inept Crazy Ed had some problems fitting in with us Europeans, he really couldn't fathom the Afghans. In particular he seemed to have a little Jihad of his own going against Islam. Each month he became more and more disturbed, each month he would spend more and more time in his room rocking back and forth on his rocker until he pretty much fell off it. It came to a head during a final call to prayer of the day. I heard him at his window screaming at the top of his lungs at the voice coming from the minaret on the mosque,

"Shut up, shut up."

"Shut up, shut up."

Head stretched out, neck craning at the sky, wailing at the Islamic prayers he so hated.

"Shut up, shut up."

"Shut up, shut up."

This was not the first time he'd been disrespectful with the locals, but it was the worst. I ran into his room and grabbed him back inside, much to his dismay. We had him transferred home before he got himself and us all killed.

Poor Crazy Ed, ranting about his beloved bacon, and shouting at the real and imaginary voices in his head. He was a staunch Republican who apparently had an IQ off the Richter Scale. He thought he knew everything, although he'd only been in telecoms for a couple of years. Ed kept telling us about his blessed PhD in rocket science. He was highly intelligent but socially apart, and there was a real sense of relief around the guesthouse when he went home.

My remit had evolved during my time in Kabul and I found myself travelling all over the region, particularly India, recruiting and interviewing staff. It was there that I met my first Anglo Indian. An Anglo Indian is a white-skinned, blue-eyed Indian. This man was called Kevin O'Keefe. My guide brought him over as he looked like an Irish guy but sure enough he was Indian. I was charmed by his name and easy manner. Kevin worked in an Indian restaurant in a place called Nasik in the middle of nowhere, very far off the beaten track. His Irish great grandfather had come to India to build the railways and stayed on. Later my guide explained that for Kevin being white meant he was often discriminated against inside their strange caste system. Yet another experience I would never have had if I had not taken up the expat lifestyle.

I've always tried to help the locals when I could, wherever I was and whoever they were. In Afghanistan when I was asked I'd help out with various unexpected expenses. This tended to be in the form of some cash for family matters. In the beginning I helped people I knew, Afghans who worked in the guest house and Rafiola. Eventually as word got around I had to ask Mr Mana to have a word with those who didn't work in the guesthouse, tell them to stay away. Unfortunately it had gotten out of hand. I would get home after work to a few Afghans waiting in the hall for a private consultation. It was like a doctor's surgery. My multinational colleagues were complaining, telling me I was considered a soft touch and that as a result they were being pestered as well.

Afghanistan is no place for the faint hearted, but I have to say I wanted to help, soft touch or not. This was not about loaning a fiver to a friend in the boozer, the people asking were not squirrelling money away, they truly needed it. The Afghan custom is to ask those more fortunate for help in times of trouble. OK maybe I never learnt my lesson, but perhaps it was a lesson I was reluctant to learn.

My expat colleagues always arrived at work en masse at eight o clock every morning. I was wired up about IEDs[16] and ambushes from the moment I arrived in Kabul. I hadn't forgotten the dangers of creating a pattern that could be turned into intel, intel that attackers could then use.

On one particular day, I'd arrived early into the empty parking lot and was walking across the road to the office when I spotted a woman sitting with a child, no more than three years of age. The child's arm had been severed at the wrist, the arm so badly burned I could barely stand to look at it, the woman was in tears. I couldn't walk past her, nor believe the anguish in her eyes. It was a horrific sight that appalled me. I'd been told numerous times not to give money to the Afghan beggars. I handed her a $100 bill and was about to tell Rafiola to bring her to the hospital when all the guards game running over. One grabbed her, another grabbed the child's charred severed limb and yanked it, I recoiled horrified. Above the woman's protestations the guard showed me an animal's limb, definitely not a child's, the bone had been stuffed up the child's sleeve. The child seemed drugged and supine.

I asked Rafiola,

"What the hell is going on here?"

"She's a professional beggar, you shouldn't have given her any money, look look." Rafiola said, as the guard continued to wave the bone, the fake child's arm. They took the money off the woman and gave it back to me. I didn't really know what to think, I was not happy. What kind of life was this woman and her poor kid living, a type of grotesque begging show, it was awful. The guards and Rafiola looked at me like I was a mug. For a while that incident gave me the harsh callous shell necessary to prevent me from acknowledging any of the grief stricken stories I witnessed every day.

16 IED Improvised Explosive Device.

Yes, it hardened me for a while, until we were in Jalalabad a few months later. Engineer Mohammed, Abrar and myself were visiting dealers, weaving in and out of the market stalls. I spotted a very young, horribly disfigured crippled child using two pieces of wood to propel himself along in the dust, well maybe more dragging himself along the filthy dirty ground, no more than ten years of age. I have to say, despite everything I'd already seen, I was shocked. I had to do something about it.

I have no idea why I thought I always had to be the expat saviour, but I am a glutton for punishment. I spoke to Engineer Mohammed and asked him whether we could get the boy a wheelchair. I was to be in Jalalabad for a week. I told the child to be at our office that afternoon. The wheelchair cost me $200 and when the child turned up at the office, I gave him the wheel chair and a hundred dollars and wished him the best, I felt good knowing the boy would not be crawling around in the dirt anymore and I walked around a little lighter the next couple of days.

Two or three days later, we were back in the market and of course the child was back dragging himself through the dirt begging.

"Where's the wheelchair" I asked in exasperation to no one in particular.

Engineer Mohammed answered me, "His father sold the wheelchair because it would affect his begging."

That's when you get a wakeup call. You can do these good deeds and you can try to help. But you really need to be channeled in how you do it. Unfortunately the harshness of the land is more easily changed through slow seismic shifts. Did I learn my lesson that day? I have no real idea what the lesson was supposed to be. Don't give beggars money? Do give them money? To this day I don't really have a firm grip on what I was supposed to have done and I don't begrudge any of them what they got. Professional beggars or not, I wouldn't do it, and they are welcome to whatever they can get. It's a godawful tough life they lead.

Chapter 18

Three flights closer

The first dusty year in Afghanistan went by very quickly, I was back in Ireland every three months for at least a week. I also had quite a few meetings in Dubai, so I was in and out of Kabul and the UAE quite often. Each time was an emotional roller coaster. Four flights stand out as I got closer and closer to death.

Dubai Kabul Ariana Airlines.

A few minutes after we took off from the Dubai tarmac, all the passengers were still trying to sense whether the plane had enough oomph to get up. The plane levelled off and started to fly in tight banked circles over the Arabian Gulf. The captain came on the loudspeaker and said something in Pashtun. Suddenly the cabin crew looked very worried. When I asked what was going on, the ashen faced crew replied that we were dumping fuel. Ariana Air was a bankrupt airline, so it had to be something serious for the plane to be dumping fuel. We eventually turned back and landed in Dubai. By this stage everyone was borderline petrified. When the plane came back in to land, it landed like a MiG screeching to a halt. We were all quickly evacuated. It turned out the hydraulics had been leaking.

When I finally got back to Kabul my friend played me the TV news clip of my plane landing in Dubai with smoke coming out the back of it. Afterwards they had to close the runway for other flights while they towed our plane off. Funny thinking of that heap of junk blocking all those shiny new Emirates aircraft from landing. It was a lucky escape but no big deal.

Dubai Kabul CamAir

A Finnish friend and I were flying over Afghanistan towards Kabul, when the pilot came on the loudspeaker and in an American accent announced that we were going to have an in-flight quiz. We were all given paper and pen to write down our answers. The American pilot started asking random quiz questions.

Next thing,

"For those of you who have not seen Kandahar it is to the right of the plane",

He proceeded to tip the plane to the right to afford us a better view. By this stage, what with the tipping and the quizzing, everyone was beginning to wonder whether the pilot was doing enough piloting.

Kabul is 4,000 feet above sea level, surrounded by some of the highest mountains in the world, both of these factors give it an extremely unique flight path in and out from any direction. On our approach to Kabul Airport, our quiz master decided to bring us in his own way. Immediately it felt all wrong and I became extremely anxious. Next thing the engines roared as he abandoned his landing and we were flying right between the mountains. Out the window we could see bewildered villagers looking up at us in terror from no more than thirty or forty feet away. I thought, "Right, we're dead." This was not long after another plane from the same airline had flown into the same mountain in identical circumstances. Everyone on the plane started praying and crying, myself included.

That particular flight was probably the most frightened I had ever been in my life. Until my next flight.

The final flight Kabul Delhi Air India.

Immediately after we took off from Kabul, we started banking severely. There was a loud thud and the plane levelled off at around two thousand feet – nowhere near high enough to get over the surrounding mountains. This pilot was a genius as he guided us in and out between peaks. Unable to fly the plane above them, he had no other choice. We could see the mountains vividly from no more than twenty feet. All the passengers were too scared to even breathe, everybody concentrating on not disturbing the pilot. The only time I have ever experienced a flight like that was in the cinema. He got us down. When we disembarked the aircraft, on the left hand side we saw the engine had picked up debris on take-off and this had caused it to explode. I laughed. What else was I going to do? Cry?

Chapter 19

WHO WANTS TO BE AN AFGHAN MILLIONAIRE?

After two years with the company, I became chief commercial officer, with a sales director and a marketing director both reporting into me. With my knowledge of the industry I was given a lot of responsibility. I had a very good working relationship with my boss in the States, Dan. He worked for Telephone Systems International (TSI), our parent company.

We were approached by Abdullah who claimed to have the Afghanistan rights for the highly successful TV show *Who Wants to be a Millionaire*. We were very interested and I entered into negotiations with him but nothing was happening: echoes of my Irish adventures. I got the impression after three months or so that he was talking rubbish, he was spoofing. I did a bit of research, and found out that the rights for *Who Wants to be a Millionaire* were owned by Sony Media. I contacted the actual person in charge, who said,

"Yes I am aware of the gentleman in Afghanistan, Abdullah, but he has not paid the required deposit."

I wasn't sure what he meant, I asked him,

"What do you mean by deposit?"

"Well for us to enter into exclusivity you would need to pay us ten thousand dollars. And then we'll give you the exclusive rights to *Who Wants to be a Millionaire* in Afghanistan. We have asked Abdullah on several occasion but he hasn't paid the money."

It was becoming obvious to me that unfortunately my friend Abdullah was at best a chancer, a wannabe deal maker with no capital behind him. Why did I need Abdullah in the first place? From then on I dealt directly with Sony Media. We signed the non-disclosure with them, and entered into an agreement granting us exclusive rights to the programme in Afghanistan. This was the all clear to go ahead and produce the programme in partnership with Ariana TV; our sister company. We devised a programme schedule, we paid for the set, which was flown in already built and ready to put together. Initially we had been thinking about filming in India as opposed to Kabul, because it was thought that Kabul wouldn't have the facilities. But common sense prevailed and we found the studio space we needed.

We hired famous Afghan TV presenters and made sure to have an all Afghan studio audience. It was a very good way of generating revenue, all the communications were exclusively through the Afghan Wireless network. If you wanted to appear on the programme, you had to send a text message using Afghan Wireless. The entrance questions were generated through Afghan Wireless, answering the questions correctly was the only way to qualify as a contestant on the show. It was a real coup for Ariana TV, for Afghan Wireless and for me personally. The broadcasts were reported around the world as a sign of Afghanistan opening up again. Internationally, female contestants in particular were seen to be a positive development for the country.

Jokingly one day I suggested to Bassir, the owner's brother, that he might be interested in doing an Afghan version of *The Apprentice*. Bassir was always firing people; his day was not complete unless he had ruined someone else's. I mentioned it to him,

"Why don't we do an Afghan *Apprentice*? You already fire people every day in work, this would be another way to make that pay. Every week we could have you telling someone "you're fired" live on national TV."

The joke was short lived as Bassir, never known for being the wit of the group, thought I was being serious and had already begun to envision what he was going to wear. I had to tell him I'd only been joking. He did not take too kindly to it; so that was the end of that.

Naturally as a result of being away all the time, what was left of my marriage fell further asunder. And while financially we were back on top, whenever I came home I felt Violet regarded me as an inconvenience. She had her life and my coming home for a couple of weeks did not fit into that life. As soon as I arrived she was waiting for me to leave. But my children were in Ireland and I loved to spend time with them.

When back in Dublin, I slept in the spare bedroom. But at least I was unarmed. That was something.

AFGHANISTAN
UZBEKISTAN
TAJIKISTAN
TURKMENISTAN
Shir Khan
Kunduz
Mazar-e
Sharif
Baghlan
Toraghundi
Jalalabad
Herat
KABUL
Ghanzi
Shindand
PAKISTAN
Kandahar
Zaranj
IRAN
INDIA

Chapter 20

The return of the never gone away Taliban

By 2008 I had a department of 200 people with six managers reporting directly to me. However, I no longer felt secure in the guest house, the security was slipping. More and more I'd come home to find the guard asleep with his weapon out of reach: an easy target for any attackers. The guards were almost pointless anyway. It began to prey on my mind. Especially the idea of a kidnapping, I felt uncomfortable relying on other people for my security. My bedroom balcony offered a means of escape and I spent some time working through what I would do if they came for us. No point in planning your exit while they are kicking in your door, preparation is always best. I was not going to wait in my room if I heard a commotion downstairs. I was going to get out of there. I slept in a locked room with a chair under the door handle, a Glock on the bedside table. Kabul had become an extremely dangerous place all over again and I was worried.

When I first arrived in Kabul, it was relatively safe and I tended not to even carry my side arm most of the time. As the years went by, in contrast, Kabul began to tighten, the air crackled and once more no one and everyone was everywhere. There was an increase in the number of suicide bombings and people were talking about how the Taliban were back and had infiltrated the Afghan Police and the Afghan Army. I flew the Irish flag from our back garden, I was not sure it would do any good but it might give someone pause and it made me feel slightly more secure.

Many of the bars closed down and all the Chinese brothel restaurants went in a mass clean up by the Afghan Police. There were even more suicide bombings.

An American truck, five or ten ton crashed into five cars because its brakes failed. Or as others claimed the Americans' SOP, their standard operating procedure, was to drive as fast as possible through the cities. After, when the crowd got angry, the

Americans or the Afghan National Police or whomever opened fire into the crowd with a 50 calibre machine gun, killing more people. The crazed convoy then drove over another car on their way out.

There was a criminal element to the outraged crowd, as criminals realised the rampage was an opportunity to loot. The mob ended up outside our office trying to smash the door down. We could see them surrounding the building on the CCTV. I grabbed my AK47 and went around the back. We were on the third floor, and the only way into the building was up the large central staircase. I knew I'd be able to get out through the boardroom on to the roof. I thought if I see anyone come in the doors I'll give them the good news. I was not prepared to be captured. No way was I being taken hostage.

Thankfully it died down later that day. The doors held and although every single vehicle in the transport department was burnt out and the security hut was destroyed, we were all OK. They also tried to get into the Aryana TV building and that ended up like the siege of the Alamo. At one stage, the Ariana presenters were appealing live on TV to the Interior Minister to rescue them. In the end the rioters found a new target. They destroyed the offices of an aid company. The wisdom of mobs.

It was highly unlikely that we were going to be taken hostage, as I suspect it was not insurgent led. But we would surely have been killed, as the mob's anger was raw and fuelled by more than the one incident. It was a wonder there were not more crazed mobs. Worst of all, they also burned down a pizzeria in that well known mob fervour, visible worldwide, of destroying anything that symbolises difference or foreignness. There was a curfew that day.

I missed those pizzas.

Everybody in Kabul knew the Taliban were back and had infiltrated the Afghan security forces: the police and the army. After their initial defeat, the Taliban had retreated back into the mountains and into Pakistan. As the years passed they trickled back. One day in Kabul there were two suicide bombings that acquired their intended targets. I stupidly asked the head of security was it safe to leave the building and he looked at me as if I was a lunatic and said,

"You tell me. Nowhere is safe today." He shook his head.

That day I left the building with my Glock and sat in the front seat, put the guard in the back making sure he understood my own SOP: that if anyone remotely resembled someone who might detonate a suicide bomb they were to be shot between the eyes. I got home without incident.

Another murderous Kabul afternoon, Rafiola and I were driving up to our Jalalabad Road office. The road was known as Dodgeville due to the number of military compounds up there; it also was an extremely wide road, so all in all it was lethal. Firstly we heard an almighty explosion, in the distance I saw debris flying in the air. It was a UN convoy caught by an IED bomb blast. The explosion went on for an eternity within those split seconds, we turned around and decided not to visit the office that day. It could wait. Another daily stark reminder of where we were. The real value was that it served as a clear example for Rafiola as to why we should never follow convoys too closely, something I had been at pains to explain to him. I wanted him to understand that IEDs don't care, they kill everyone and foreign convoys were the most prized targets out there.

Kandahar, the second largest city in Afghanistan is very hot, very dusty, rammed full of Taliban and the feeling that it could kick off at any moment. A most worrying place. As tensions built country-wide, I was in Kandahar when the Taliban attacked the prison, killing nine police officers and eight prisoners: a devastating attack resulting in all the other prisoners escaping. The attack consisted of a suicide truck bomb at the front gate, a suicide bomber at the back gate and rockets fired by Taliban riding motor cycles. 600 prisoners escaped in total. No messing. These type of incidents were daily occurrences and we just got used to them. That was the way of life in Afghanistan.

In 2008, an Italian consultant and I had to go to Jalalabad near the border with Pakistan by helicopter. The head of security walked up to me as we were getting on board and handed me an extra magazine for my AK47 and another clip for the Glock. The Italian looked aghast and asked,

"What do you need that for? We're going by helicopter?"

I replied,

"Well almost all of the territory we are flying over is under Taliban control. Granted it is highly unlikely we would survive if we got shot down so there is probably nothing to worry about. But if we have to make a forced landing and we survive, we'll need some protection while we wait for help. And this is our protection. Two magazines, 60 rounds of 7.62 mil and the Glock's two 15 rounds of 9 mil. If we have to use the 9 mil then they are very close and we are in deep shit. So I will save the last two for you and me."

I laughed, he didn't. He looked a touch green, as well he might. I was not mocking him. I was deadly serious. That part of the world had laid waste to larger forces than my Italian colleague and I. 160 years before on the road to Jalalabad, the Afghans had wiped out a retreating British garrison.

The beginning of the end came on 6th January 1842, when the garrison left Kabul and fled towards Jalalabad to return to the comparative safety of India. The garrison contained British and Indian soldiers, 4,500 soldiers, including 690 Europeans and British civilians, 12,000 wives, children and civilian servants.

The journey was hell. From the moment they left Kabul they came under sustained attack. This was despite having left British officers and their families along with most of their guns as hostage to ensure safe passage. Every night saw civilians and soldiers dying from exposure as they were forced to make camp without putting up their tents. The soldiers had to endure being picked off by snipers, constant ambushes and their officers being tricked and fooled by local tribesmen, who'd not forgotten past battles. Eventually the decimated garrison had no other choice but to make a last stand; this is known as the Battle of Gandamack. They did not stand a chance and were all killed. The Afghans let one man live, Surgeon William Brydon, telling him "go back and tell them this is what happens." The newspaper reported of Brydon's entry into the city of Jalalabad,

He seemed more dead than alive but, when asked 'Where is the Army?', Assistant Surgeon William Brydon managed to reply: 'I am the Army.' [17]

In Jalalabad the past has not gone anywhere. The first time I went to Jalalabad had been by four wheel drive, and we'd driven over the Silk Road – basically a dirt track with a thousand foot drop off to the side -- weaving in and out of Afghans with millennia old eyes staring at us wondering what fresh hell we were bringing. Why was I doing these things? Well I suppose I was the one they asked. I just did what was expected. I went where I needed to go.

When we were doing a major development, expanding the network down in Kandahar, the local village elders wanted to meet a senior executive from the company. Who were the local elders? Well supposedly it was not the Taliban, but it was really. Local representatives representing the Taliban. Around half the villages were back under Taliban control at this stage. I met with the village elders and we negotiated our tower locations. They allowed us to build our towers when we suggested that we would hire our security guards locally. A cell site was a mobile phone tower with two generators, a mast and a BTS[18] on top of it. The site provided mobile phone coverage for the surrounding areas. The management came up with the clever idea, instead of hiring outside security to guard the towers, we'd employ locals. Typically we would employ six or seven guards from that village – generally relatives of the village elders. Everyone was happy. As I was an Irish citizen, it was viewed that I should help with those delicate negotiations rather than the Americans or British. After all, how could they know I once guarded the Queen?

---

17 Kyle, T., 2013. Incredible Story of the British soldier who was the only survivor of a 19th century conquest - and the warnings for today's military missions.. *The Daily Mail,* 25 March.

18 Base transceiver station, a giant dish.

However, in 2007 the Americans took out a Taliban commander with a cruise missile; they tracked him and located him using his satellite phone. The cruise missile landed in his living room, killing him and a few members of his family. As a result of this the Taliban contacted all the operators and told us we had to close down all our towers in the evenings. We couldn't do that as it would have resulted in a massive loss of revenue, evening is the busiest time for phone calls. In that region the other mobile operators employed foreign security firms to guard their towers. Many of their towers were attacked and destroyed, our towers were left alone. The mobile sites were a serious source of revenue for those villages and they protected them as such.

Some villages were Taliban and some were under the protection of a local warlord. The only recourse we had to navigate these relationships was to employ the local guards. The Taliban did try once to attack one of our towers, but the villagers confronted them and told them to leave the tower alone. The Taliban refused so every villager came out, told the Taliban that this was an income for the whole village, warned the Taliban if they did anything the villagers would tell ISAF exactly where their secret crossings into Pakistan were. Our towers carried on functioning, it was a great victory for them and for us as we were able to continue operating. But by me saying *villagers,* don't ever get the impression these people were shrinking violets. This was Afghanistan. Everyone is armed and the whole country was designed by their God as a death trap.

Most Afghans just want to survive their impossibly difficult lives. Unfortunately various and numerous parties, including the Western powers, seem to like "interfering". The Afghans could be forgiven for thinking they have seen it all before. Mainly because they have.

Afghans have been invaded by Alexander the Great; Genghis Khan; the Persians, numerous times; the British Empire a few times over the last couple of hundred years; The Soviet Union; and, of course, now NATO, the Americans and ISAF. So maybe we should cut the Afghans some slack in their distrust of us foreign devils.

Chapter 21

Dialling it in

My driver and friend Rafiola had been with me from the start, I called him the Transporter after the Jason Stratham character from the movie, which he liked. We all had Toyota Prados with government number plates and a siren. The Kabul traffic was mustard, medieval vehicles and modern attitudes. The Transporter would call for me every day, sticking his head over the balcony announcing himself with a "Top of the morning to you Sir, *céad míle fáilte*." I used to teach him these and other Irish phrases on our long drives up country. I'd laugh, he always wore a Guinness cap and the car would sparkle. I'd already given him a couple of army tips about driving around the city. Rafi would often turn on the siren when we got stuck in traffic As things in Kabul got worse I had to ask him to stop, explaining that drawing attention to ourselves could get us killed. I outlined how important it was to always leave at least a car's length in front to enable evasive manoeuvres to avoid kidnapping and attack. And most importantly not to follow convoys of American military vehicles as they were primary targets, following them could result in being caught in the melee, despite it being an effective way to cut through traffic.

Over the years when we had time and were out in the countryside, I taught Rafiola everything I'd learned in the military. Later on when things got heated in Kabul again, much to his chagrin, I asked him to stop washing the Prado and to remove the siren completely. He protested he'd get in trouble with the transport manager, but I squared that up. A clean vehicle with a white face in it was a lightning rod for trouble. Blending in and being inconspicuous was the name of the game from then on. Rafi was a good friend by the time I left. At least I left him a seriously good driver and with a deadly nickname.

Once the Taliban found out our rural employees worked for an American owned company, some quit, but the majority simply never went home. They didn't get to see their families for years: a serious hardship for an Afghan. The Afghans I worked with or knew did not want the Taliban to come back, but on the other hand they were not keen on what was happening at the time either. The West had come in, corruption was rife, a small coterie of wealthy Afghans were making a fortune but the average Afghan's life hadn't changed. The only thing that had changed was that there was more freedom, especially for women – girls could go to school. Although Afghans were not comfortable with the way things had gone, they certainly did not want to see things go back to the way they were. They also did not hold with foreigners in general being involved in the running of their country.

The man who ran the Herat office near the Iranian border was called Engineer Sali. If you had a degree in Afghanistan your title was "Engineer" plus your name. Engineer Sali worked right through the Taliban reign. When we were travelling around Herat Province, he would regale me with outlandish yet serious stories.

"You know they used to have the check point here."

"What check point?" I replied.

"The beard check point, coming out of town the Taliban would stop you and check your beard length, they would measure it and examine it for signs of trimming. If they suspected anything they would make you get out of your car and a Talib would comb the beard holding a white handkerchief underneath and if any hair fell out that meant you had trimmed your beard. Once you were found guilty they would beat you with sticks, shave your head, throw you in the back of a donkey cart and put you in jail for two weeks."

"Then they had other checkpoints," Engineer Sali continued.

"What were they checking?" I admit I found it morbidly fascinating,

"Well they could stop you and order you to pray, make you get out of the car and recite the Koran. If you failed to do this you would be beaten with sticks, head shaved, thrown into a donkey cart then jailed."

Engineer Sali had lived through those times and he used to laugh about it, despite there being a more deadly side. The reason the checkpoints came up, was we were at Islam Qala on our way from Herat to the Iranian border when we suddenly came across this amazing Mosque in the middle of nowhere. They used to have the checkpoints outside the Mosque. We did a lot of business on the Iranian border; there was only one mobile operator in Iran and calls were very expensive. Iranians would cross over and buy our sim cards. We made good money in the border region.

Satellite phones are vital in a country with a topography and geography such as Afghanistan. Large swathes of Afghanistan are not within distance of a tower and have zero GSM coverage. We had NGOs, American Military, ISAF and embassies as customers who wanted to be able to use the standard Afghan Wireless mobile network and to have their phones automatically switch to a satellite signal if they moved out of GSM coverage. The handset would have duel sims enabling an easy switch. The service provider was a UAE company known as Thuraya, owned by telecommunications giant Etisalat. The now infamous New Ansari was the sole licensed provider for Thuraya phones in Afghanistan at the time.

Telephone Systems International had obtained a satellite licence in the US in its own name before I arrived. TSI was our New Jersey based parent company. Not foreseeing a problem, we shipped about five hundred satellite handsets to Afghanistan, with a value of $1m. But we couldn't get them out of the airport, because Afghan Wireless itself had not acquired the satellite licence for Afghanistan. Despite TSI being our parent, the Afghan authorities insisted we did not have a licence to sell satellite phones in Afghanistan. So the satellite phones were stuck in customs, even baksheesh couldn't get them out, which was a first. This should have been our first warning that more important players than us were lurking in the background.

Why was this such a problem? At the time in question the company that held the Thuraya licence for Afghanistan was called New Ansari Ltd. New Ansari was the sole distributor of

Thuraya satellite phones in Afghanistan. Kirk Meyer, former director of the Afghan Threat Finance Cell, states that New Ansari in its various guises "*was born from the narcotics trade, was heavily involved in the laundering of drug proceeds, had links to the Taliban, and supported numerous corrupt government officials.*"[19] These facts had not been established yet, however this was Afghanistan and everybody suspected. In January 2010, US treasury officials raided the offices of New Ansari and in February 2011 they placed it on a blacklist, forbidding any US citizen or company to have any dealings with it. Hence a number of our customers were reluctant to buy satellite phones from New Ansari, as the company's offices had already been raided.

The NGOs, the embassies, the Americans and ISAF all knew what the dogs in the street knew, so they wouldn't buy the Thuraya handsets from New Ansari. The rumours were, and in Afghanistan there is never any reason not to believe rumours, that the satellite phone top up cards were being used to wash drug money out of the country. I never saw any proof of this but it later transpired to be true. Moreover, it was only a minor aspect of the New Ansari operation. Bottom line, Afghan Wireless's customers were not about to buy phones off a drug money laundering operation if they could help it. We needed to find a solution.

Then there was Akram – an Iraqi who'd left Iraq for Canada years previous and now was back cutting deals and doing business in Dubai. He was a real wheeler dealer, who wore a dish dash all the time. He loved the whole Emirati look. We met with him numerous times, expressing our concern that we still didn't have a satellite licence in Afghanistan. He assured us that he could get us a deal. I travelled over to Akram in Dubai to fix the problem.

---

19 Freeman, M. F. & Kator-Mubarez , A., 2014. *KIRK MEYER, FORMER DIRECTOR OF THE AFGHAN THREAT FINANCE CELL.* [Online] Available at: https://globalecco.org/kirk-meyer-former-director-of-the-afghan-threat-finance-cell [Accessed 29 April 2015].

Akram and I met with the Thuraya management team in Abu Dhabi. We had the meeting, and I was given a verbal agreement from them that they would give us our own licence. I came out of the meeting believing that we had a deal. For Akram this was also good news as we were going to buy all of our top up cards from him.

On our two hour drive back through the desert, as we were basking in the minor glory, Akram told me,

"I have often heard of the white man who could sell sand to the Arabs, now I can say that I have truly met him." We laughed.

He confided in me that he liked a drink and "I also like something else too." My mind boggled with a plethora of sexual scenarios,

"O yeah?

"I like pork." Then we were both laughing.

"Do you?" I said between the tears.

"Very very tasty." He confirmed.

When we arrived back to Akram's office, Thuraya had sent me an email informing me we would not be given the licence after all. I rang, but whatever chance we had was gone. They were in no mood to change their minds.

"Are you mad? You are losing so much business." I tried everything. But they wouldn't budge.

In the end we had to off load the handsets. Thuraya stuck with New Ansari who it seems was keeping everyone very happy.

The deal disappeared like sand through my fingers. The joke on me.

Chapter 22

Kabul Bank and a busted flush

Among the countless tales of corruption in Afghanistan, Kabul Bank stands out as being a true representation of the extent to which the Afghan people have been robbed by their own leaders.

The first time I encountered the flamboyant banker Sherkhan Farnood was when I bumped into Kamal, our CFO, in Kabul Bank. Afghan Wireless employees, along with most of the country, were paid through Kabul Bank. I was brought upstairs with Kamal and into a room three or four times larger than any office I've ever seen in my life. The walls were lined with chairs according to the Afghan custom. The room was so large that perspective was difficult. In the middle of the room was a desk. Wow, you could have landed a helicopter on it with ease. A beautiful large leather chair, trying to swallow the desk was on the other side. The man sitting somewhere in the chair was Sherkhan Farnood; former professional poker player, winner of the World Series of Poker Europe in 2008 and founder of Kabul Bank and Shaheen Exchange.

Sherkhan had worked for the communists in Afghanistan then fled when they were overthrown. When he was in Moscow in the eighties and nineties he operated Hawalas, the ancient Islamic money transfer system that transfers money without actually moving it. These Hawalas were used to funnel opium and heroin money in and out of Afghanistan and the Soviet Union. Sherkhan Farnood was one of the licensed owners of Shaheen Exchange Hawala, which operated out of Dubai. New Ansari Corporation operated a branch out of Kabul Bank. New Ansari had two branches in Dubai, several others in Asia and Europe and one in California.

The CEO of Kabul Bank was called Khalil Ferozi, a man on paper with no banking experience who'd been involved in playing both sides in the Afghan Civil War, after which he curiously became CEO of the most important bank in

Afghanistan. Khalil Ferozi's past is even murkier than Farnood's. Both Farnood and Ferozi together owned more than half Kabul Bank and were also shareholders in Pamir Airways. A synergy Anglo Irish Bank would have been proud of. According to the Washington Post, "The roots of Kabul Bank stretch back to the Soviet Union. Both Fruzi (sic) and Farnood got their education and their start in business there after Moscow invaded Afghanistan in 1979."[20]

I was introduced to Farnood by Kamal and we chatted amiably. When we left Kamal confided in me that Sherkhan regularly flew to Vegas and blew a million dollars. In retrospect this should have been a red flag, maybe a million red flags.

Sometime later, all Afghan Wireless employees were given the option to use a new airline called Pamir Airways for company flights. It later transpired that the food trays on the airline were filled with hundred dollar bills and the pilots were on a bonus package. Normally on flights out of Afghanistan, I would not partake of the inflight meal, I may have been mistaken when flying Pamir Airways. Another positive was that planes were relatively new and not 30 year old death traps.

In 2010, rumours began to circulate that Kabul Bank was under investigation for corruption and fraud – using bank deposits to purchase property overseas, much of which was in Dubai. Having been recently assured of the banks strength by President Karzai, his brother and many others in the crooked administration Afghans had deposited their life savings in the bank. In August 2010, fearing the bank was going to collapse, thousands of worried Afghans rushed Kabul Bank to try and salvage whatever was left of their savings. $300m was withdrawn, said to be a third of the bank's assets. It was only the Afghan Army and the seizure of the Kabul Bank by Da Afghanistan Bank (DAB) that saved the bank from total collapse.[21] Farnood and Ferozi were also removed from their

20 Masterova, A., Partlow, J. & Higgins, A., 2010. In Afghanistan, signs of crony capitalism. *Washington Post*, 22 February.

21 Ellis, E., 2010. Why Farnood was Flushed Out of Kabul Bank. *Euromoney*, 1 November.

positions. Sherkhan Farnood is quoted in an interview, in response to being asked about the Dubai purchases, "What I'm doing is not proper, not exactly what I should do. But this is Afghanistan."

The Afghan elite had bought property all over the world with loans and dubious transfers from Kabul Bank, probably using New Ansari hawalas. The figure bandied about by the Afghan Threat Finance Cell working out of the US Embassy was nine hundred million dollars in cash missing from the bank since the invasion. Most of it suspected to have left the country in the planes or using the Hawalas. Not to mention being well sprinkled around among politicians, to ensure that nobody noticed and that everybody got paid.[22] The world's biggest bank heist was an inside job.

In March 2013 Farnood and Ferozi were sent to prison after being found guilty of theft. According to the BBC "*In addition to the jail sentence, Farnood has been fined $288m (£190m) and Ferozi $530m (£350m) by the Kabul Bank Special Tribunal – the value of the assets they are deemed to have stolen from the bank.*" As of today the money they stole has still not been found. It is suspected that what did not leave the country went to the country's small elite. The real figures are lost in the clouds but sure as shooting they are higher than the mooted one billion. According to US officials, the real figure might be higher than $4bn[23]. The sky is the limit with Afghan corruption.[24]

22 Filkins, D., 2011. The Afghan Bank Heist. *The New Yorker*, 14 February.
23 Black, B., 2010. Kabul Bank: Where They Don't Fear The Regulators Enough To Even Hide The Abuses. *Business Insider(US)*, 7 September .
24 Quentin Sommerville, *BBC*, 2013. Kabul Bank fraud: Sherkhan Farnood and Khalilullah Ferozi jailed.

Chapter 23

Deal or no deal

Late 2007 while at a conference in Dubai, I was approached by two men representing Vtel Holdings, a Middle Eastern investment company interested in buying Afghan Wireless. They were on the acquisition trail. I picked up the phone to my boss in the States. He confirmed that we were interested. We had an initial meeting with the Jordanian based firm, a multi-million dollar business with varied interests ranging from pharmaceuticals to farms in Saudi. This was not the last time I was to come across this extremely successful business family. Initially they seemed keen on buying AWCC. We proceeded to a period of exclusivity of purchase while they conducted due diligence. We met with them again three months later in New York. They put an offer on the table, but the offer wasn't anywhere near the value we placed on the business.

Nothing more happened with Vtel but AWCC had the taste for it now. We went out to the market to have a look around. I was credited with the idea, thus I was given a contract stating that if the company was sold I was to get 2 million dollars. This 2 million was going to put me back where I needed to be.

Wherever that was.

Vimplecom, a large Russian global telco operator stepped into the fold. They moved very rapidly sending a team to do the due diligence almost immediately. A figure of €500m was being bandied about. This would have made all of us very comfortable.

I had returned to Ireland for a week, dreaming of the big payoff, when I received a call out of nowhere from my mother, telling me my Dad had been in a car accident. I'd hardly seen either of my parents for four years. Something that had not really been on my radar was now front and centre and it left me reeling.

The doctors were not happy and they wanted my Dad to go in for more tests. They were worried that he had a lesion or a tumour of some description on his brain and they needed to operate on him, to have a proper look in order to confirm or allay their suspicions. The tests and procedures were set to take place in July of that year, which was a disaster for me as that was the month the Russians were to perform the due diligence. I was one of five who actually knew the business was up for sale. I was also the commercial head of AWCC so I was expected to be in Kabul with the Russians. I spoke to my Dad offering to come home.

"No it is your job, I have Yvonne and Colin with me. You need to focus on your job son."

The surgeon was going to operate to see what was going on and to decide what could be done. I couldn't leave Kabul as I was orchestrating the deal that was going to put me back on top. I was grief stricken, and I was barely able to deal with it. But I had to focus. Despite speaking to him, the night before the operation I was very upset. Mr Mana saw how upset I was and asked me what was wrong. I explained. As I was watching TV later on, that kind hearted man told me he had organised for the imam to mention my father in the final call to prayer of the day. He promised to give me the heads up in time so I could ring my Dad. Later on,

"He is now praying for your father Mr Alan."

I rang Dad as the prayers were being broadcast from the minaret from the next door mosque,

"What's that?"

"Dad that is a mullah/ imam praying for you here in Kabul."

"Is it?"

"Yeah not many people in Birmingham have had a mullah praying for them in Kabul today have they? And certainly not many Catholics."

"That is true son." I could tell he was upset, I was crying and so was he.

He seemed pleased but like anything else with my Dad he did not actually say so. He was a man of very few words when it came to emotions. I found out afterwards from my sister, that he'd spent the rest of the evening telling anyone in the ward that he thought was a Muslim,

"My son has just called me from Kabul, he has his own bodyguards and he just had a mullah praying for me in Kabul. I bet you never had a mullah praying for you in Kabul." The Muslims he met laughed and agreed that yes that was really good, that he had a good son on the other side of the world pulling Allah onside in his battle.

My sister had mentioned that Dad's driving had become a bit erratic, sure enough it was my old man's driving that had given him away. Through one of life's simple ironies it was a minor car accident that revealed the tumour. They performed the operation and did what they could. Afterwards the doctor told him that they had removed as much of the growth as possible, but the operation was only a partial success. He was given two years to live.

This man who loved swimming and golf and the independence that driving gave him, was suddenly told he would not be able to do any of those things. He was a very fit man and loved activity in any form. Dad had stopped drinking when he turned sixty, he had never been much use at drinking anyway. Unfortunately he was one of those people that changed totally after a couple of drinks, very much in the Jekyll and Hyde mould. He devoted his later years to his grandchildren and golf. Or perhaps it was his golf and grandchildren. He was an amazing grandfather who was affectionately known as Granddad Golf.

When Dad heard what the surgeon had to say, he just gave up. He began waiting to die. He sat in the chair asking,

"What's the point?" It was so sad to see it transpire right in front of our eyes.

I thought at the time he would get through it, that he would fight through it. But he didn't really. I saw him as much as I could, but I didn't see enough of him.

I didn't make enough of an effort as I was focused on one thing: the $2million bonus from the sale of AWCC. At that stage certain other things had started to happen in my life as well. In January 2008 I split up with my wife. We knew the marriage was over in 2007, all we did was row constantly, no more trust between us. The love had dissipated as well. A last holiday with the children in Florida made it apparent the situation was getting worse. Florida was our traditional family holiday, we'd been there six times. But we were barely a functioning couple. I didn't have the courage to separate, even though I knew I needed to leave home, I knew the rows were unhealthy for Violet, for me and especially unhealthy for the children.

We muddled our way through one last Christmas and in January I finally moved out. I rented a beautiful seafront cottage in Dalkey and embraced the life of the bachelor. I tended to travel two weeks a month. I was able to do a lot from home. Much of my work was involved with the due diligence, interspersed with regular trips to the USA, Dubai and the UK. Between January and June, all I did was work on the sale. I had a few girlfriends. Meeting women socially was not difficult. Working in Afghanistan meant I was slightly different to a lot of the men women would meet. It gave me something interesting to talk about. I had a great job, plenty of spare cash and a flash pad.

In the early days of single life I went out on dates. When I told women what I did for a living they would be intrigued. There would be the immediate attraction, but I was very immature. I'd rapidly lose interest and I'd then try and put them off me. A classic male tactic, I've since been told. I couldn't see myself settling down with these women. Unlike a lot of guys, I cannot fake feelings I don't have. I was always at fault, I was in essence a 23 year old in a 44 year old's body. I had met my wife at 21, married her at 23, and spent 22 years in that relationship. I was a fish out of water. I was all over the shop emotionally, already beginning a slow downward spiral. The circles were still too big for me to notice but they were there.

Apart from what was happening with my father, I was still hopeful for the future; I continued working on the due diligence. I look back upon it now and I wonder why I was not more aware of how serious my Dad's condition was. I had no handle on his mortality. I knew about the tumour and I understood it, but I guess I believed he would pull through.

I did not want to accept he was so ill.

Chapter 24

Reunion of old foes

Late summer, early autumn 2008, I was ready to get my life changing bonus. We had everything ready, the share purchase agreements had been drawn up and the due diligence had taken place. For Vimplecom, Afghan Wireless fitted into their global map. Ehsan Bayat owned 78% of the company and the Afghan government the remaining 22%. The whole thing seemed to be a firm reality. Vimplecom had signed a letter of intent. The due diligence had shown up some theft but nothing particularly unexpected. In an environment such as Afghanistan you always had to manage it. You kind of did your best.

The irony was rife, we were in a post-Taliban Afghanistan. The Russians had invaded in 1980. When they went home they left Naji Buller in charge to run a semi-communist government. A fifteen year civil war followed that even for war hardened Afghans destroyed their souls and their faith in anything other than autocracy, stability and order. The Taliban filled that vacuum. After the Taliban took control they marched into the UN compound where Naji Buller had been given protection and took him. Naji Buller was executed, hung from a police sign post in Kabul. But that was then. The Russians were back and we were selling them Afghan Wireless and nobody batted an eyelid. The Taliban were back as well. It was a reunion of old foes.

This irony was brought into sharper focus one day during the due diligence when I brought Vimplecom's technical team up to the Salang Pass. The Salang Pass is a road with a 14km long tunnel built by the Russians to protect their convoys. Back in the seventies and the eighties when the Russians occupied the country they would send in convoy after convoy along the Salang Pass and they would be picked off by the Mujahidin fighters. There are famous ITN news clips of Russian tanks, trucks and soldiers being blown off the road by the Mujahidin. To prevent such losses, they built the Salang Pass tunnel to go through the mountains rather than over them.

The Russian head of security from Vimplecom was standing on top of the Salang Pass, musing over how he could not believe he was back there after all these years. He'd been down in the Salang Pass as a young soldier and now he had returned. The area around there is a dusty metal graveyard of tanks and aircraft from whichever war you care to mention. Gunships and Hind Ds from Charlie Wilson's war, T72 tanks left by the Russians.

Afghanistan could be forgiven for not believing a word that any invader, pacifier or rescuer tells it. The Afghans had painted over Russian vehicles with Islamic symbols to ensure their message was loud and clear. The painted vehicles were testimony to lots of things. The Afghans had seen and heard it all before. The odd forgotten Hammer and Sickles on otherwise stripped mechanical carcasses, proof that neither communism nor capitalism could really understand or defeat the Afghans. A country designed by their god for guerrilla warfare and a people who are in no rush. The Afghans know, like Ho Chi Minh, that you can't stay forever. Whoever you are.

One of the guys who worked with me, a truly wonderful man, was a Hazara by the name of Engineer Abrar. Hazaris have a very distinct look about them and they are the descendants of the Mongol Genghis Khan. In the Afghan hierarchy, despite their lineage, Hazaris rarely rise to senior positions as they are considered very much a downtrodden people. The Pashtun would always regard themselves as above the Hazaris.

Engineer Abrar had become a great friend of mine and was a lovely man. He had lived through the full gamut of recent Afghan history. When the Russians and Naji Bullah were in power, he'd joined the communist party. When Kabul fell to the Taliban, he had to flee. He went to live in Moscow for a few years as a refugee and spoke fluent Russian.

I thought he was great. When I'd tried to promote him in 2006 I was informed that was not possible as he was Hasari. At the time I'd only been in Kabul a short time and I was not aware of the tribal cultural hierarchies yet. I got around it by giving him extra responsibility. Engineer Abrar started going to the regions and running sales. One day he was involved in a horrific car accident. His driver was killed instantly. Their vehicle overturned and Abrar fractured his right leg. He was taken to a hospital in Kabul. Abrar was a diabetic and the hospital didn't monitor his blood sugar levels properly, which resulted in some kind of blood poisoning setting in. Tragically this meant they had to amputate his good leg, his left leg. He was left with a very badly fractured right leg after his left leg was amputated above the knee.

I felt dreadful, almost responsible, and I knew that in the ultra-violent world of Afghanistan, Engineer Abrar was barely even a number in that hospital. I put a call into my CEO that probably saved his life, otherwise he would have fallen through the cracks of a broken system. Together with the CEO stateside, we were able to get him a lot of support. We had him transferred to a better hospital, this was no small thing in the scheme of things and we also had his salary delivered to his home.

The tragedy was compounded by his wife already being an invalid, paralysed down one side due to a mortar falling on her, close to her family home during the Afghan Civil war. Once Engineer Abrar felt strong enough we sent him to India to get a good prosthetic leg, paid for by AWCC, followed by a desk job. This was not a one way street. In many ways he'd been my right hand man, had always kept an eye on me making sure I never got myself in too much trouble. I did my best for him as he had my back. I relied on him especially in the early days when I was pitted against the Frenchman.

Vimplecom believed that Afghan Wireless fitted into their portfolio and more importantly their global strategic map perfectly. They owned mobile phone operators all over Russia, Georgia, Uzbekistan, and Kazakhstan. Afghanistan was another piece in their regional jigsaw.

I returned to Ireland to finalise my divorce from the woman I had been with half my life, only to discover that Violet had a new man. I was 43 and we'd been together 22 years. We have three beautiful children. This discovery brought me down and despite the naked hypocrisy of the whole situation, I still could not bear to think of someone else being with her. I did not deal with it very well. I understood how ridiculous I was being, but I could not handle thinking about it for months. The main reason, apart from anything else, was my own dysfunctional relationships, which sullied how I saw anyone else's. I got over it eventually. I realised I was still in love with Violet deep down but that was an utterly pointless and self-defeating notion.

I was beginning to disconnect.

My brother Colin, and my sister Yvonne and I should have realised the severity of our Dad's brain tumour, but we were in a form of denial. None of us could reconcile the fit and healthy man our father had been with the idea of him only having two years to live.

My Dad was trying to cope with his illness, he tried his best to fight it. He still couldn't play golf or drive. None of us know what being in that situation feels like, how we would react, what we would do. But he was trying his best and showing some fighting spirit.

Chapter 25

WHAT COULD GO WRONG?

Friday the 5th of September. 2008

I bought myself a top of the range four wheel drive and a new horse on the basis that I was about to get a big bonus. I had two horses in livery, the three children in private schools; I was supporting one home, and living in another. Everything was wonderful. My ex-wife was happy, I was happy. Life was great. I was debt free.

As far as I was concerned, life was trundling along just fine. I am sure there were signs but I cannot for the life of me remember what they were. I woke up on my 44th birthday, September 2008, to a wonderful feeling of excitement, that life was back on track . Everything felt great, what could go wrong? But six months down the line the answer turned out to be: every single thing. I remember that feeling of everything moving in the right direction. Even my Dad's illness, I felt he was dealing with it; although maybe I was in denial.

I wasn't to have those feelings of positivity and progress again until 2011.

In October 2008, I was sitting in the CEO's office in the States. He was discussing what he was going to do with his bonus after the sale went through. How much he was going to donate to his church was uppermost in his mind. Earlier that week, Lehman Brothers had collapsed and suddenly things were looking bleak. I asked the CEO if he was worried about this. He replied,

"Why would I be worried, this will not have any effect on us," he assured me.

"But they are talking about this global recession. Back in Ireland everybody is talking about the economy falling apart." I persisted.

"Yeah OK things are not good, but these guys are Russians. Their economy is booming."

I suppose I was somewhat placated but really deep down I knew. I began to recognise what I could sense, but not yet see: the cold shadows in the distance.

We had been due to seal the deal at the end of October, but there was no word. Early November, Vimplecom pulled out saying they didn't want to borrow the money with the world in so much tumult. At first they didn't pull out entirely, they merely said the deal was on hold and that they were understandably worried. But eventually just before Christmas Vimplecom fully withdrew and made their mergers and acquisitions team redundant. The dream was over. It was on the face of it a reasonable decision. Vimplecom were going to have to borrow a lot of money and were worried that with the global economy collapsing their borrowing capabilities would be restricted. That this would affect the funding of their current business.

For me it felt as if they had taken my future plans and burnt them in front of me.

We got together in the office in New Jersey and everyone was stunned. There was consensus that we had come this far and needed to carry on. I was tasked with finding another buyer, all of us satisfied in the notion we had a very valuable asset and that there was someone out there to buy it. I made several approaches. I was looking for the right prospective buyer. I knew that Zain, a major Middle East operator based in Kuwait, had money to spend and that Afghan Wireless fitted into their footprint.

The weekend I got the phone call from my sister, I had just spent the night at a fancy dress party at Castle Leslie, Glaslough, Co Monaghan. On that truly amazing night I met Sir Jack Leslie and his niece Samantha. Sir Jack Leslie has led a truly remarkable life: captured at Dunkirk, prisoner of war for five years, never married, famous for going to rave parties while he was in his nineties. He is 98!

Castle Leslie itself was a magical place. I went dressed as a Talib. I remember telling Sir Jack Leslie that I had been stationed in the North of Ireland, that I'd protected Lord Caledon. The

Caledon estate is directly next to Castle Leslie. Of course Sir Jack knew Lord Caledon very well and it all added together to one of those wonderful nights, when the past, the present and the future seem one and everything we say seems important. We got a tour of Castle Leslie and Sir Jack himself told us all the ghost stories of the place. The fantastic band only added to what was one of the best Halloweens I've ever had.

I received a phone call from my sister telling me Dad had been admitted into hospital. I flew over. It was around the third or fourth of November. They were still running tests but the surgeon told him that he had six months to live. The surgeon elaborated telling him that when they had a further look the cancer had spread.

My Dad sat there and just said, "Thanks for telling me."

He didn't shed a tear.

Dad only looked at me and said,

"Well that's it isn't it? I'm bollixed", a classic Dublin saying.

"Come on Dad, you can fight this."

"No son, that's it, lights out. I just got to accept it."

We'd always had a strained relationship ever since I was a child. I'd never been that close to him. He was much closer to my sister and very close to my younger brother. I was closer to my mother and my grandmother. Dad was an unusual man, although for his time he was the same as a lot of Irish fathers. He had never been a loving man. No matter what I had done in life, at school, winning gold medals, whatever I had achieved, he'd never once told me he was proud of me. I always kind of resented that. To have heard those words from him would have meant the world to me.

I asked to speak privately with the nurse and we found a quiet corner. I urged him to tell me straight,

"What are we dealing with here? I need to know because I need to tell my brother and sister."

He told me and I'll always remember his vivid description,

"It will be like a computer shutting down. His body will eventually start to shut down piece by piece. He will lose the use of his limbs, and he will end up in a vegetative state and eventually his organs will shut down. He'll live for about six months. He could live a bit longer but not much."

"Thanks for being so honest." I could barely see through the torrid image imprinted on my mind and the tears. I had to compose myself before I went back into Dad.

I told my brother and sister but not my old man. And that was it. They discharged him. All they could offer him was palliative care. They promised to make him as comfortable as possible so that he wouldn't be in any pain. I flew back to Dublin and I felt completely and utterly gutted. I had to carry on. Keep the ship afloat. I was still whistling that same tune, although more and more off key.

In December in Dubai, I met the head of mergers and acquisitions (M&A) for Zain. They were very positive and for them cash was no problem. I introduced the head of M&A to my CEO. We signed an agreement. They received the due diligence pack and came back in January saying they were very interested.

We got to January and my Dad was losing the use of his legs. Things were not good. I didn't want to travel. The Americans said they could not pay me if I was not in Kabul. We compromised and I accepted a reduced salary to spend more time with my father. Financially I was not worried as I knew I had the big payday coming. I'd begun to realise that I'd come to the end of my time in Afghanistan. My personal issues coupled with the increased danger over there, in addition to the relentless near misses in the planes, which had fatigued me and had caught up with me. After five years, I was tired of Kabul and ready to make a break. I had so many other things going on I could not even think about Afghanistan and its spectrum of dangers and mistrusts.

My Dad was in a hospice at this stage. He was so very ill and it was felt the hospice was the best place for him. My mom had started to look after my Dad despite them having separated more than twenty years before. My parents had split up when I was seventeen. When my Dad was in the hospice I'd see them together and it was like they'd never been apart. While they weren't exactly laughing and joking, they were still to my eyes a couple, still Mum and Dad.

One day I was watching my mum mopping his brow.

I said to her, "Mum, you know he never stopped loving you."

She started crying.

"Why did he never tell me that?" she replied.

I've always believed Dad had never fully recovered from the break-up of their marriage, that he'd always loved my mother. When she was caring for him towards the end, you could see that there was still a love of sorts between them. It was one of the saddest things I've ever had to witness. But also beautiful at the same time.

Chapter 26

THE END OF ALL ROADS

The Zain deal looked all set to go through by the end of the month. It was the second week of February and I was in the UK visiting my Dad. He was exceptionally ill by this stage. His body was closing down.

I got a phone call from the head of M&A in Zain. He simply said,

"We are pulling out."

"What?"

He confirmed,

"Yes we are pulling out. We have been made aware of a pending legal action and have decided to withdraw from the process."

Boom.

I picked the phone up immediately and in complete shock, phoned my CEO in the States. He said,

"I haven't got a clue what they are talking about."

I replied somewhat taken aback and very miffed.

"Well they've obviously found something."

"Leave it with me." He replied.

That was it. Irrespective of whatever my boss unearthed, Zain had pulled out. While Zain pulling out would have huge repercussions for me, I was completely focused on my Dad. My old man was my only real concern.

Unbeknownst to us, two British men, Stewart Bentham and Lord Michael Cecil, who had been involved with setting up AWCC had heard of the potential sale. Bentham and Cecil had discovered through their contacts that Afghan Wireless was to be sold. They were about to take a case in the English High Court in April 2009, which they would lose in a July 2011 Court of Appeal ruling[25]. The mere insinuation of an ownership issue

25 Hastings, P., 2011. Telephone Systems International and Ehsanollah Bayat Defeat US$400 Million Claim Brought by Lord Michael Cecil, Stuart Bentham and Alexander Grinling Bringing 9 Years of Litigation to a Close, *London: PR Newswire.*

raised a lot of red flags for Zain and they decided to pull out. All this came out over that February and March. The details of the case did not matter to me or to Zain, the only thing that mattered was that they were out.

Nonetheless, I could think of nothing else except that my father only had weeks to live. I was full of remorse that I'd seen him so little the last four years. While I had been away in Afghanistan I'd been focused on my job. I was in a constant state of anxiety about the imminent death of my father. Despite the huge impact the acquisition falling through was about to have on my life, I only cared about my old man.

Friday night March 9th 2009, my father passed away peacefully in his sleep. I was home in Dublin with my youngest son when I got the call. My Dad had passed away with my brother, my sister and my mother at his bedside. I'd made a mistake I have been unable to shake to this day. I was supposed to go over that weekend but had changed my mind because my son was playing in the school orchestra on the Saturday. I'd wanted to be a part of that. My sister and I'd both believed he would survive another week or two, which was the advice we had received from the medical team, but he didn't.

I phoned my Violet. I wanted us to get together as a family. But the marriage was over and it was not realistic. I phoned my girlfriend, but she couldn't make it. I felt dreadfully alone. Through timing and life, neither of the women in my life were able to give me much solace. I was at an incredibly low ebb and no one was there for me. There in my house with my ten year old son, I sat there watching TV completely miserable – the most alone I have ever been. Violet picked up Connor the next day and I flew to Birmingham. I dealt with it myself.

That was it. My father William Joseph Barry was dead.

When someone dies in the UK, as opposed to in Ireland, it takes a long time to bury them. And so it proved we had to wait nine days before we were allowed to give him the send-off he deserved.

We buried him on the 18th of March 2009.

I brought Nathan, Catherine and Connor over for the funeral in St Gerard's Church, followed by reception in the Irish Club, or as we knew it, The Paddy's. We celebrated his life with a proper traditional Irish funeral. When my father was young in Dublin, he used to sing professionally in the ballrooms. He sang all the old Frank Ifield and Slim Whitman songs. According to family lore, this was how he'd met my mum. The man who did the Karaoke in the Irish Centre approached me and said he'd always really liked my Dad and would like to look after the music on the day free of charge; we happily accepted this. It was a lovely touch that added something further to the day. My sister, my brother,myself and all his grandchildren, nieces and nephews got up and sang songs to celebrate his life.

Everybody gave him such an incredible send off, very near to where I grew up as a child. I have many happy childhood memories of St Gerard's over the years. I smiled through the tears thinking back to the time I was on leave from the Guards Depot in my Grenadier Guards' uniform and I'd walked into The Paddy's.

Me wearing my peak cap and smart number 2 dress caused a row between my Dad and an armchair Provo. During their row, I'd been drinking at the bar with my friends but I could see Dad involved in a heated altercation with someone he knew. Afterwards I'd asked my old man what was said. Apparently the man had been an acquaintance of my Dad's, he'd told Father ,

"It is disgraceful and inappropriate that your son's walked in here with a British Army uniform on. Disgraceful."

My Dad had turned round and asked him straight out,

"Where are we? Yes that's right we're in Birmingham. Aren't we?" and the guy had said,

"Yeah, so?"

"If my son wants to walk in here in his army uniform let him. You are over here taking your Queen's shilling same as the rest of us. You've made Birmingham your home. If you really feel that way, then move to Belfast and live up there. Don't be bringing that type of shit over to Birmingham."

The argument had ended on that nonviolent impasse.

Dad had looked me up and down, shook his head and asked,
"Did you really have to come in here in your uniform?"
I'd laughed,
"You're an awful little bollix at times." he'd said laughing.
He was right, I was a little bollix.

My Dad's sisters had come over from Ireland for the funeral and in total over a hundred people attended. I know that he would have liked it. Surrounded by family, friends and music in Birmingham, that English city he had carved out a bit of Ireland in, that had embraced him as one of its own. We all came to say goodbye to William Joseph Barry.

Goodbye Billy. Goodbye Dad. Goodbye Granddad.

Chapter 27

A NEW REALITY

The emptiness from the loss of my Dad began to envelop me. I headed back to Ireland where I went off to see the *Quiet Man* cottage in the West of Ireland. He'd always loved the movie and I thought it was a fitting tribute. I stayed in Ashford Castle. I thought about my father a lot when I was there. I kept thinking about the pub scene in the film when John Wayne starts singing "The Wild Colonial Boy", my Dad's favourite song. That trip was a tribute of sorts to him. I love my rugby, and that weekend Ireland won the Six Nations Grand Slam, March 2009. That amazing Irish performance would have made my old man's day. The culmination of many things made it an emotional weekend. But the culminating was not finished yet.

I came back to Dublin, back to a new reality. My old man was gone and there was no way of getting around that.

My mind was in no place to make any types of decisions. This heralded the real beginning of my problems although I was still relatively oblivious to them. My body and my mind, through the catalyst of events, had begun its own shutdown. All of me needed a break. The sale of the company had fallen through. Violet had filed for divorce proceedings. Financially, I was beginning to find myself under pressure, due to the reduced salary and the amount of time I had taken off work.

Afghan Wireless got in touch and said they needed me back in Kabul immediately. "We are going to see if we can find another suitor, but you need to get back to your day job."

I agreed and I packed my bags. I was to fly back to Afghanistan, despite the deal having been called off and everything being in turmoil. I was flying out on the Sunday and I was shopping on the Saturday with my two sons. On my way home I got a text from Violet.

"I'm away this weekend. You need to be here to look after Conor."

Conor was ten.

I replied, "Well I have to fly out tomorrow."

"Well it's not my problem." She was away for the weekend in Rome.

Reality was I could have done something about it, I had two older children more than responsible enough to look after my son. I sent an email to the company telling them I could not fly Sunday. Told them what had happened, I was in no mood for Afghanistan.

Afghan Wireless were not happy but they said, "OK, fly next week". The Thursday of the flight came round. I could not face it. I said to myself, I am not going. I was beginning to realise the truth, I was never going back Afghanistan. How the hell could I?

I sent an email and resigned from my job. It had started with an excuse, which eventually turned into my resignation. I was divorced, fatherless and unemployed. I am not sure what I was thinking. I did not have much money in the bank. I had massive commitments from all elements of my life, family finances and personal finances; I had debts, financial and emotional, that were all coming due. I had no way of paying any of them.

What followed was a year of my life when I went completely and utterly off the rails. I did nothing but drink, party and play sport; I paid barely any bills. I lived on my wits despite the fact that I was completely witless. Every now and again, Afghan Wireless gave me some consultancy but I was nowhere near paying my way.

So everything that happened was my fault and I take full responsibility.

Chapter 28

Sports therapy

I first started show jumping with Violet in the local riding club after we moved to Ireland. I'd never been on a horse in my life prior to that. Both of us immersed ourselves in equestrian sport for the next ten years. Over time instead of it bringing us together it drove us further apart. My desire and need to keep proving myself annoyed my wife more and more. Instead of it becoming an enjoyable couple's pastime, a sanctuary from the outside world, it became the manifestation of my unremitting desire to win. And of course in the long term I only really lost.

If I could relive the past I would stop myself from ever getting on a horse. I know it's a folly to ever regret the past and I don't, except for my equestrian hobby stroke obsession. I can think of very few people I met during those ten years from the so called horsey set that I would keep in my life, besides our four horses that is. In my experience, the show-jumping set are the greatest bunch of back-stabbing poisonous oddities one could ever meet. The animals tend to be lovely and the humans the complete opposite. They are truly a bizarre bunch of closed minded, weird and curious individuals best left to themselves.

From the outset the show-jumping set loathed me. They regarded me as new money. – as someone who had no talent. But what really infuriated them was that I actually won rosettes. In the beginning I hadn't a clue what I was doing and I was very fortunate to have found a horse as good as the King. He was a fabulous horse. The King was my school master, he taught me and enabled me to compete way above my level. This infuriated them because they wanted to keep me beneath them. That was where they believed my level was.

When I was not winning, they said it was because I was a useless rider. When I eventually started winning, they said it was because I had a great horse. When I kept winning, they said I was destroying the horse. I couldn't win with them really. I am not sure now why I ever tried or cared. My competitive nature never sat very well with any of them. Every time I jumped everyone wanted me to fall off and fail. After I fractured my femur in 2002, I was back on a horse within 6 months. It was complete madness, absolutely crazy to get back on a horse so quickly, my leg was so weak I couldn't even grip properly. If I had fallen off the horse again I could have ended up in a wheel chair. What was I trying to prove and to whom?

This is my favourite joke, and one that goes a long way towards explaining the Irish culture of begrudgery that I encountered in the Irish horse riding set:

An American comes to Dublin and arrives to stay in Dalkey. He strolls contentedly down to Bullock Harbour. The fishing boats are coming in and they are pulling all these very large lobsters out of the boat. There are big crates full of these lobsters lined up all along the harbour. The American eyes them and says

"Wow they sure are fabulous lobsters." In his long American drawl.

The fisherman replies, "Thanks aye, they are the finest Irish lobsters, fresh from the Irish sea, the best lobsters in the world."

The American noticeably enthralled says, "Wow they really are amazing. You have a full crate of them there, watch, that one on top is about to crawl out."

The fisherman looks at him confused with his eyebrows raised and tells him seriously, "Didn't I just tell you they were Irish lobsters."

"Well what difference does that make?" the American asks slightly bewildered,

"Well, when one gets on top the rest drag him back down."

This is so true of the Irish and of everyone in the show-jumping world here or abroad. They are all Irish lobsters.

Late 2008, a few months before my Dad died, King was around fourteen and he couldn't jump anymore. Another horse came on the market called Fred and I bought him . By this stage my leg had completely healed. After many lessons and thousands of Euro invested, my riding had come on. I took it seriously and I knew what I was doing.

A few months after my old man had passed away I was competing in a show jumping event. I could see a small group of the riding clique watching and willing me to come off. Was this all in my mind? Sadly not. I wondered to myself, why am I doing this? Why am I spending all this money on a sport with people that I don't even like or want to be around? Fred refused the fence twice, then ploughed through it on the third attempt and off I came, first time since 2002. The poor horse had picked up the negative vibes from me, the way I was and the way my head was, nature mirroring the misfortune of man. I went back, put Fred in the horse box, drove him back to the yard, put him in the field and have never ridden since. The livery contacted me and told me I owed them three months fees.

"Sell the horse, sell the tack, and let me know what's left."

That was it, just like that I was finished with a ten year passion. I haven't been horse riding since and don't have any desire to ride ever again.

I was never suited to the sport. I hadn't been involved in it for long enough before I started competing and I didn't respect it enough. I took it for granted that I would be good at it, when in actual fact I was competing against people who'd been riding since they were children. They used to take one look at me and think,

"Look at that fucking idiot. That English man with all that money. He's a gobshite."

In that miserable year I had after leaving Afghan Wireless and losing my Dad I couldn't face any responsibility. I couldn't deal with anything that involved concentrating. All I wanted to do was feel sorry for myself and drink, I never became an alcoholic thankfully there was still something in me that prevented me from that fresh hell. Instead I threw myself into sport, cycling at first, cycling all day from Dublin to Wexford or Carlow, whichever I reckoned would keep me moving and away from my life the longest. But the cycling was not enough, it was too solitary. It gave me opportunity for reflection, which was an anathema to me then.

I was watching the Dubai Sevens on TV when I decided that I wanted to start playing rugby. I had never played rugby in my life, but I couldn't shake the idea. My local club in Kilternan was called De La Salle Palmerstown. It is known as DLSP. I phoned up the rugby club and simply asked them,

"I'd love to start playing rugby, but I have never played the game before in my life, in school I was more into football. What can I do?"

Gerry, who runs the clubhouse said, "The J4s train on a Tuesday night. If you come down I will introduce you."

I was in a very dark place emotionally, and things were falling apart. But I went up anyway. I dropped the ball more than I caught it, but nonetheless I was welcomed in with open arms: especially in the crunching tackles. I was on the fringe of the subs' bench and that was OK. The players were a mish mash of electricians, guards, lawyers – people from every walk of life. In many ways the club saved me, I found the lads just when I needed them. For the whole of 2009 the club was my life, it was my only real social outlet. Mentally I was numb at best, but the group of guys in the club helped me, mainly by treating me as they would anyone else. They knew nothing about me. They didn't care, which was refreshing and a sanctuary away from the Greek chorus of hate I had begun to hear from other quarters.

Initially, after hearing I had worked in Afghanistan, the rugby team started calling me McNab. That soon changed to The Tan after the Black and Tans. The club has remained an integral part of my life. It has served to be a useful way to spend quality time with my youngest son who also plays for the club. But unlike his father he has talent and good hands. I am very grateful to the club and the friends I have made there.

Next up was boxing, as I continued my bid to exercise away my demons, literally and figuratively. The boxing was great for getting rid of anger and frustration and of course a fantastic way to keep fit. All I wanted to do was keep my mind distracted, and the only way for me to keep it distracted was with sport. I couldn't work, my brain couldn't focus on anything important.

When the rugby season finished, I was invited up to the local boxing club to train and somehow allowed myself to be talked into competing in a white collar tournament. Even more extraordinarily, my planned opponent, a man roughly my own age and ability, pulled out late on and was replaced by a 25 year old lad with a bit about him. I was 45, hanging on by a thread with nothing much about me.

The match was supposed to be an exhibition bout, one of twelve on the night, but I was not in that type of humour. I hadn't been for quite some time. I decided, despite the age and ability gap, to give it every single thing I had. I vowed I would leave it all out there. The first round I charged in like a wild bull, the second round I was somewhat more circumspect, and the third I was punch drunk, I could hardly catch my breath. When the bell rang my opponent came over and congratulated me on a great fight. I have to admit I felt at once like I had been hit by a truck and, despite having lost, that I had won the world championship belt. The following day was a slightly different story as my body screamed at me that perhaps my days of fighting young lads were over.

Sport was all that I could manage and it masked my deteriorating health.

Chapter 29

The descent

I would like to be able to tell you that I got my act together not long after that, but I didn't, I remained a wreck. I found it very difficult to care about anything and I found little solace except in physically pushing myself. Sports were simply distractions, as more and more little pieces fell off inside and I could not put them back. I came to the realisation after a while, even through the worsening fog, that there was something wrong with me. I went to see my family doctor first who told me he thought I'd had a breakdown.

I was not ready to hear that so on I went.

I was up to my eyeballs in debt, although not as bad as some. From April onwards, I just coasted through life in this dream world I inhabited. I was a completely different person, pretty much the opposite of the person I had been. For want of a better word, I became a real asshole. I didn't take responsibility for anything. I felt detached from everything. I couldn't even read a newspaper. My mind was a blur, it would not let me focus on the print. I knew something was wrong and so did those close to me.

Finally I plucked up the courage and I sat down with a psychiatrist; I had a number of different sessions and for the first time in my life I told someone my life story. Start to finish. She focussed in on the two shooting incidents. This was like opening up Pandora's Box. I broke down. I was at the end of my tether, I simply couldn't control my emotions. I cried uncontrollably. I had been pushing and twisting the memories down into myself for the last twenty three years and never dealing with them. She said to me "Alan you've been suffering from post-traumatic stress disorder, PTSD since the age of 24."

I was not quite sure what she was talking about. "What?"

"Alan you have been dealing with this issue, since you were 24 years of age. And you have lived with it. If we go back over your life and look at your behaviour, we see that you exhibited an unusual lack of fear, a lack of fear that has allowed you to do the work you have done. Particularly in Afghanistan, visiting places like Kandahar, Jalalabad, contemplating killing others to save yourself. Not normal, not how normal people live. You have dealt with it like it was a normal way of life. You have seen things in your military service which people will never see."

"So I was not me, I have just been acting as me?" I only saw negativity.

"I am telling you now from 24 years of age you have had PTSD. This has manifested itself throughout your life in you being a risk taker. Why? Because your body and your mind have never dealt with what happened back then. Since those incidents you have lived on the edge. You have been successful in business, successful in sales. But you have done it because of your tenaciousness. What has come to pass is because of all these things: the death of your father, the loss of your home, the break-up of your marriage after 22 years, the break-up of your relationship, the failure of the sale of the company, the loss of your job. Your body and mind has told you it can't cope with it anymore. In essence you have had a complete and utter breakdown"

The counsellor explained and reiterated that I had been suffering from PTSD and that my life up until then had been overtly affected by it. Now my body and mind were telling me no, no more, they could no longer handle it. As I reflected on this I came to the conclusion that my life had been a lie. Everything I had achieved through me being me, had really not been me. It was all someone else and maybe this fucked up failure is who I really was.

November of 2009. I was:

Emotionally wrecked;

Financially broke;

Psychologically unwell;

Smack bang in the middle of a catastrophic breakdown. I could no more pay a bill than I could go back to work. I was fucked. I was in the wrong place again.

Chapter 30

CRASH LANDING

I opened my eyes and I found myself on top of Killiney Hill in Dublin, an idyllic place that previously had been the scene of some of my happiest moments. I sat slumped on a bench listening to the water and my life stream slowly into the sea. I wanted to dissolve. I tried to find meaning in the stunning view. It was 6am and I was wearing my pyjama bottoms, a t-shirt and trainers. I couldn't sleep and was trying to find peace and tranquillity. I am not sure what drew me to this location. The moon was still out even though it was the break of dawn. I thought to myself, my life is over, this is it. A car would wander past behind me on the Vico Road, the tyres on the fresh morning road giving me something to attach my disintegrating thoughts to. I couldn't imagine how I was going to dig myself out of the unholy mess I had gotten into. My focus was shot to shit. I couldn't face dealing with my problems. I had no fight left inside. I was empty.

If I didn't have children, I think if someone had given me a Glock I would have blown my brains out. In fact I can think of one or two people who would have bought tickets to watch. But the love I have for my children saved me. I couldn't do it to them. The only thing I had remained through my hell was a fully committed and loving father. I knew if I'd done it, I would be at peace, I would be away from all these problems I'd created for myself through my bad judgement, especially that I would be free of the mental torture I was going through at the time. The allure of the peace was strong; how relaxing it would be.

I rang my poor mum. She could hear I was at my wits' end. I broke down and she broke down. She is an old lady and I shouldn't have laid it on her but I was alone. I am not the last man to turn to his mother at his darkest hour. She couldn't handle it either. The transformation from what I had been professionally and personally was a terrible thing for her to witness. The shining light had changed into this blubbering wreck. She was in England and there was nothing she could do for me, but hearing her voice did help. My mother has never judged me and has always been there for me 100%. I got back in the car.

A few hours later, I rang my best friend Mark. He could hear the pain in my voice.

"Where are you buddy?" he asked.

"I'm in Dublin."

"Stay there I am coming over."

That afternoon he phoned me, he was in Dublin. He'd come to find me and, I suppose, to save me.

"Alan you're coming back to the UK with me."

"No I'm not. I have to stay here," For what I had no idea, to watch myself swirl down the drain?

"You are, you're coming back with me. You can't stay here. Come with me, we have to get you right again."

That was it, I went with Mark to England for six to seven months working in his business, putting my life back together piece by poxy piece. Each month I improved. I started flying back to Dublin at weekends to see my children, while getting myself back to normal.

Debt, illness and grief had brought me to Killiney Hill that December morning, unable to face going forward. The culmination of all three had done what the IRA or the Taliban had failed to do, they had taken me down.

Although I was abroad, I could still hear the negative vibes from the mess I had left behind me, I was clearly not far enough away. Stories would work their way back, how my friends had been confronted at parties about their friend Alan, who owed millions. These ridiculous rumours about me were now being spread by people I'd never even met. Classic Irish tales of €10,000 debt growing to €100,000 every time it was told.

Ok, I had spent my days drinking in Bono's local bar until closing, going to house parties, drinking 'til early morning, wiling away the afternoon drinking coffee in cafes; never doing any real work, feeling sorry for myself – yeah I had become that guy. In fact, I was worse, because I was that guy and I was not paying my bills. I'd not been faking it though, I'd been lost. For eighteen months I'd been a broken and very unwell person.

I went to see the local priest. I will never forget the words he told me:

"Life is like a long river, smooth currents and calm waters followed by rough currents and then rapids. You, my son, are in the rapids. Believe me calm waters will come again."

I just had to ride it out.

During my eighteen months of madness, I was determined to shield my children from the issues I was facing. It was my responsibility to tackle my demons alone.

I am still coping with the financial and emotional fallout of that 18 months of madness, of my 50 years on this planet. But now I am dealing with it.

Thankfully the very bottom waned further and further away. Like most fortunate people who survive after hitting rock bottom, I worked my way out of it through the love and support of my family and through working with an old friend. Working with Mark helped me begin to regain my self-esteem and self-worth. The counselling for PTSD also helped immensely. No one can do it on their own.

Let him who is without sin cast the first stone.

Judge ye not lest ye be judged would be my advice to the ghouls out there who tried to have me exiled from my own country and my own life.

My old regimental motto is *Honi Soit qui May y Pense.*

It is Latin for *shame be to he who thinks evil.*

I leave that verse to those who hear it.

Chapter 31

FROM HELL TO PARADISE

I had begun to see light at the end of the tunnel, to use that tired old adage. Tired and true. Through the work and getting paid, I was regaining some element of my self-esteem. I had dealt with all the hell but I was still emotionally scarred.

Back up on LinkedIn, I was approached by a head-hunter called Duncan from RP International, Singapore. He was looking for someone with my background to go to Papua New Guinea and sort out some problems for his client. He wanted a strong marketer to manage a mobile operator that was in a bit of a mess. My remit was also to include a week per month building their sister business in the Solomon Islands.

It was a very well-paid job and gave me my own opportunity to continue rebuilding my life after the kick-start I had from Mark. I completed three successful interviews and was offered the role of Chief Commercial Officer for Bemobile in Papua New Guinea. I would need to move to the other side of the world. Just where I needed to be. There was only one drawback; I would be 24 hours away from my children. But I had no choice. I owed it to them and myself to seize the opportunity and rebuild my life, as they relied on me and I had responsibilities.

I left Dublin in July 2011 and travelled to Port Moresby, the capital of PNG. The first thing I'd been told was the country was rife with random violence, military coups, cannibalism, and car-jackings. But I liked it. After the previous 18 months I was ready for anything. Sure you had to keep your wits about you, but that was always something I had trained into me. OK there were certain parts of PNG that you wouldn't go near, you would probably be shot in the street. Yeah we all lived in a secure compound. White women could not go round on their own. Theft was rife. There was still something about the place that sat well with me. And obviously compared with Afghanistan it was a walk in the park – Afghanistan was back being the most dangerous place on earth after a brief respite. I was glad to have survived my time there. More than anything I could no longer sense the negative vibes from the ghouls that I had brought into my life in Dublin. A negative frame of mind can attract negative people and sadly I was no different to anyone else. It was time to put distance between the ghouls and myself. Even they could not be felt in PNG. My head was thawing out. A new clarity had replaced how I used to feel before I had my breakdown.

I like to think I'd become a better person by then, gone the brashness and a lot of the arrogance of someone who'd always expected everyone else to succeed like they had. My first real experience of having no money had also been a very humbling one. I hope that since my illness I have shown compassion to those who have suffered similar fates. I'd lost respect for myself and I'd lost respect for everything in my life. I realised in PNG that I had self-worth. PNG allowed me to understand and believe I was not a complete failure.

I had always tried my best with my staff and with locals in general. But the breakdown had made me humble; something nobody had ever accused me of before. I was now walking away from those things into a better future. I hoped as the wounds healed that I'd be left with scars to serve as reminders of the virtue of kindness and understanding.

It's true that although it nearly killed me, in the end it made me stronger. Each one of the things I'd had to deal with would have brought a person down, brought them to a breakdown. Never mind all of them at the same time, all at once they were almost cataclysmic.

Time, distance and healing was PNG's first attraction.

To get to PNG, you travel for a full day. Dublin to Singapore takes in total around sixteen hours – then another flight for eight hours.

The capital Port Moresby was not that heavily populated, but it was a very interesting place: a South Pacific island and a serious culture shock. If you are going anywhere serious in PNG, you fly. The islands are full of history and very different tribes. I learnt that people from the Highlands were incredibly aggressive and that was something I'd just have to get used to. There were two main islands

– New Britain and New Ireland. The Sepik people who lived mostly along the coast were different to the Highlanders, much easier to get along with. I took to the place quickly.

We used to fly into the Volcano city Rabaul, the capital of New Britain, in over the Bismarck Sea, so called because PNG had been colonised by the Germans up until the First World War. Rabaul had been destroyed by a volcano in the 1970s and the city moved further along the coast. We flew in through the smoke wafting out of the volcano, which, along with the acrid smell of sulphur, was overpowering. They served to remind me that I was a long way from home, and I was into it.

The Northern Islands were still mostly Lutheran and home to many German graveyards from when they colonised the islands. In 1919 at the Treaty of Versailles, Germany lost all its colonial possessions. After the First World War PNG become an Australian protectorate. During the Second World War, in January 1942, while the bulk of the Australian Army was fighting in North Africa, four thousand Australian reservists and the Papuan Infantry Brigade (PIB) found themselves in a two year siege with the Japanese. The Bomana cemetery outside Port Moresby is full of too old or too young Australian soldiers who'd stood firm against the Japanese attacks, despite taking huge casualties.

The Japanese had invaded the city of Rabaul and New Ireland. The only soldiers the Aussies had left were territorials, mostly reservists, the wrong ages to fight apparently. Along the famous Kokoda trail the Japanese came within sight of Port Moresby, but were beaten back by the supposedly inferior Australian troops and the PIB. The eclectic group of part time and professional soldiers refused to give in and fought to their death. Eventually Australia was able to get regular soldiers there to relieve the worn out depleted force and the Japanese never took Port Moresby.

Independence for PNG came in 1974, and like most new countries it's had its problems. When I arrived the long-time ruler, Sir Michael Sumare, had just been ousted while on medical hiatus in Singapore. He was ousted by a government led by Peter O'Neill. Samare came back putting PNG in the unusual and awkward position of having two governments, two foreign ministers, two everything. Despite some calls for delaying the scheduled election it went ahead and Peter O'Neill is the current prime minister of Papua New Guinea after a failed military coup.

None of these things perturbed me too much, I fell back on the old soldier's adage of being there to do a job. I was up against an Irish owned firm called Digicel , who were and are the market leader and definitely the top dogs. Everybody was in awe of them. Well not everyone, I was happy to have my shot at their title.

Bougainville is the largest Island in the Solomon archipelago and became part of an independent Papua New Guinea in 1975. Bougainville is home to the world famous Panguna Mine. Right from the opening of the Panguna Mine in the sixties there were tensions, violence and conflicts of interest. The mining company Bougainville Copper Limited (BCL); the PNG Government, the landowners on the islands, both in favour and against the mine; the Australian and New Zealand Governments were all involved. The civil war took place from 1988 to 1998 and involved the PNG Army and the Bougainville Revolutionary Army; it is considered the largest conflict in the South Seas since the Second World War, with between 15,000 and 20,000 dead. The dispute over pollution, land ownership and independence all centred around the Panguna mine, which at one stage accounted for 45% of PNGs exports.

A peace deal was signed in 1998 and the ceasefire has largely held. As of the April 2015 the mine has not reopened yet. However, some on the island are calling for the reopening of the mine to help fuel the Bougainville economy. Elections are due to be held later in 2015. There remains some dispute as to whom owns the geological rights on Bougainville. The regional government of the autonomous region Bougainville, and the PNG Government of Peter O'Neill in Port Moresby both claim the rights as their own. [26]

26 Carl, A. & Garasu, L., 2002. Weaving consensus: The Papua New Guinea - Bougainville peace process. *Accord,* Issue 12.

My own business, Bemobile, was in worse shape than the government. It was an expat feeding trough, with inflated bonus structures leading to falsified numbers, up and down the profit and loss account. They had many over paid consultants as well as a convoluted, murky shareholding.

I also had responsibility for the Solomon Islands, a group of Islands that have very little to do with PNG other than Port Moresby being 874 miles away from Honiara, the capital. The Solomon Islands lie to the south east of PNG.

The Solomons have had their own problems, but to look at them, they were a paradise on earth. I was based in Honiara a city on Guadalcanal, the main island. Not so long previously it was the scene of ethnic unrest that ended up with the Solomon government requesting foreign help to resolve the issue. Guadalcanal is an island known for a very famous battle in the Second World War. Following Pearl Harbour, the first battle of the South Pacific between the Americans and the Japanese was fought on the Solomon Islands. The main bay outside of Honiara is called Iron Bottom Sound, because so many ships sank there, and remain there. When we were building our telecoms network across the Solomon Islands, we would come across live ordinance from the Second World War that would have to be dealt with by local specialists.

As well being a historical gem, the Solomon Islands are also a tropical paradise. The water is crystal clear, the tropical fish swim around you. It is a vivid, colourful reminder of the earth's splendour. On the darker side the island is poverty stricken as there are no natural resources there, or more accurately they have not accessed their natural resources. The Solomon Islands are said to have a lot of mineral wealth, oil, gold, gas, but they are all untapped. It has no real economy of its own besides tourism.

When I arrived in PNG, the company was in complete disarray. Bemobile had been the original national telecoms provider before it was privatised.

The primary issue we had in Bemobile, was that three years previously, after privatisation, they'd brought in grossly overpaid expat consultants to set up and run the new firm. These consultants had made a complete dog's dinner of the company. In my professional career I have never come across a mess of such magnitude as I encountered there. I had been recommended to the job by the CFO Andy, an ex-colleague from Afghanistan. Presumably he thought I would be up for the challenge.

I encountered a major contradiction in numbers, which was almost impossible to get my head around at first. However, time would soon give me a clear understanding of exactly what was going. The bonus structure was based on the growth of the company from a subscriber, or an active customer point of view, this is not a good idea any day of the week. All bonuses should be based on revenue and profit. The previous management had indulged themselves in all sorts of shenanigans to achieve perpetual growth in the reported numbers of new users. The real revenue figures and the reported revenue figures were two vastly different numbers; they were strangers that had never met.

The company was owned by the PNG government through a company called the Independent Public Business Corporation (IPBC); the investment arm of the government. IPBC had a representative on the board and a share of the business. The second shareholder was a company called Steamships; a very profitable PNG based property business. The remaining shareholder was Hong Kong Investment Company. A number of people were robbing the business on a monthly, weekly and daily basis. The PNG government via IPBC were becoming more and more disenchanted with what was going on. They had absolutely zero faith in the expat employees or in the management, but they were somewhat hamstrung as the government did not want to give the impression of meddling in private enterprise.[27] (Morauta, 2011)

---

27 Morauta, T. R. H. M., 2011. The theft and waste of public money in Papua New Guinea's Public Enterprises, Port Moresby: *The Ministry for Public Enterprises*.

Chapter 32

Walking disasters

The first Bemobile CEO I worked with was a man called Patrick, an Irish guy earning $35k a month, spending approximately three days a week in PNG. The rest of the time he would laze around his palatial pad in Cairns Australia. Tuesday morning to Thursday night was his typical working week, doing as little as possible besides informing people how he was only waiting for his bonus. He didn't engage with the staff. I worked with him for approximately four months. In that period of time I had very little interaction with the man, other than listening to him tell me he was only waiting for his bonus and that he was going to leave as soon as he got it.

Any time I went to him with any issues he didn't want to know. The problems would have affected his bonus so he had no interest in addressing them. Whatever about him, he only stayed four more months (he didn't get his bonus but he did get the boot), there was another Irish guy, Brian the COO, doing exactly the same thing; they were a double act. The other fella lived in Brisbane and he was on about $30k a month, so he only did two days a week, flying in Tuesday night and leaving Thursday night.

In the middle of this I was trying to do my job, dealing with massive churn. Why? For nearly a year Bemobile had been falsifying subscriber numbers. What we were reporting as our active customer base, and our actual active customer base were two altogether different figures. We had a really big churn issue, whereby we were losing hundreds and hundreds of customers every month. But we actually weren't; they had never been customers or even people in the first place. Under instruction from the CEO Patrick, the sales department had been sending phones out to retail outlets with the sim cards already connected as if they had been sold to someone already. To add to this, top up cards were not configured properly on the Online Charging System (OCS), the billing platform. Essentially, customers' phone credit sometimes never expired. Finally the OCS billing system was not fully integrated, which resulted in our not being able to bill our customers correctly.

Another problem we had was that in order to show these Monopoly figures the Irish duo had been doing three for one promotions every week for the guts of a year. If you bought ten units you got thirty. This was across the board, one hundred bought you three hundred. So we had a revenue of 3 million Kina[28] a month sitting on our billing platform, which was not real revenue. This revenue did not represent real money, nobody had actually ever spent it, it was no better than Monopoly money.

I uncovered all of the figures. Actually all I did was choose to notice them, everyone else had chosen to ignore them. They were right in front of everyone. I was paralysed with shock and I didn't really know what to do with the problems they were so vast, far reaching and entrenched. After the CEO had told me to mind my own business, I went to see Andy the CFO about this. Luckily at the time the Andy had the ear of the board. The board and the Irish CEO agreed to part company as a result of this.

The Irish CEO and his side kick were removed and Andy was given the CEO job on an interim basis. Andy had a great approach to business and we set about correcting the balance sheet. Despite everything I have said, I wouldn't like to give you the impression that I didn't enjoy my job in PNG. Job satisfaction wise, on a scale of one to ten, it was ten. It was simply brilliant fun and exactly what I needed. We spent our days firefighting and they flew by. Every time we looked at some issue or another it would reveal another mess. I'd never experienced anything like it. Afghan Wireless was an extremely well-run company and had been nothing like Bemobile.

I got a lot of experience going forward. I was suddenly involved in operational issues. Previously I had only been involved in the commercial side: developing customer bases.

28 Currency of PNG.

PNG continued to enchant me. Never mind what you hear on the news, it is a wonderful place with beautiful people. I worked a Monday to Friday standard working week. I lived in Port Moresby. We were twelve hours ahead of Europe. When I was getting up my children were going to bed, and when I was going to sleep they were getting up. This oddly was quite conducive to good communication. I spoke to my children five times a week.

In the evenings I lived in a very pleasant gated community. I had a small apartment; access to a gym, a pool, and a bar; and I had my own vehicle. Nobody had a driver and to me some guy waving a knife at me, or threatening to blow my head off for my wallet was no different to being in New York. I wasn't worried. Social life was good. In Port Moresby the local yacht club was the big scene and I joined that. Most of the expats you'd come across were Australian, a lot of them colonial relics, who had lived there their whole lives. A lot of elderly Australian men married to women thirty or forty years younger than them with three or four children. The PNG women obviously looked on the older guy as a safer bet. When an expat married a Papuan woman, they were expected to support the whole extended family.

Many people in PNG drink and drive, or they did then anyway. There was no legislation prohibiting. Expats tended to socialise in the yacht club. It was there that I met Michael, a young Irish man who like me also worked for a multinational. He was a touch the worse for wear leaving the club one particular evening, although none of us really remember him going. Judging from what happened Michael was driving recklessly and probably too fast when he his car overturned at a roundabout. The car finished upside down but he had been wearing his seat belt and thankfully he wasn't really hurt. When he came around the car was surrounded by a group of people. He started to thank them profusely believing them to be coming to his aid.

"Thanks for helping me, you're lifesavers."

Unfortunately for Michael, instead of helping him out of his seatbelt they took his mobile phone, his watch, his valuables, his briefcase, his laptop. They didn't help him out of his seat belt, leaving him exactly where they found him. Weirdly he was still lucky. Lucky to be alive.

Lesson: don't drink and drive.

One of my colleagues in Bemobile at the time was another young man from Ireland. Like most young people he knew absolutely everything and could not be told anything, by anybody. He thought he was a world expert and authority on every subject. From the start we liked to call him the Walking Disaster. He had a South American girlfriend. From the beginning he began to earn his nickname.

On his second day in Port Moresby he left his laptop in the back of his car, something you would not do anywhere on earth. The laptop was stolen, oh yeah, along with his passport, which of course was in the same bag.

Next up for our hero, despite our repeated warnings that certain areas of the city were absolute no go areas, he still always knew better, he still was always right: One evening after football he went to pick up his girlfriend who'd been giving a Spanish lesson in one of the dodgiest parts of town. When he got out of the car to get her, he was approached by three men, one armed with a shot gun. They ordered him to lie on the ground while they car jacked him with a shotgun to his head, warning if he moved he was going to die. His car was used the following day in an armed robbery. They took his wallet and his phone. Then they took his vehicle, his trainers, his clothes; all they left him was his underwear. He was in a place called Six Mile in Port Moresby. We couldn't believe it. We decided it was probably better for all concerned if he left. He agreed for once.

His coup de grace, he booked his tickets to go home via Australia despite us telling him repeatedly that his girlfriend would have visa issues. Luckily for him, he was an expert on international aviation transit law and he ignored us.

He came to the office on his last day and we all wished him the best. He shook all our hands and said his final goodbyes.

Of course he was back two hours later, as he had been refused entry to the flight with his girlfriend due to visa restrictions and had lost his tickets.

We eventually managed to get them both out of the country safely and thankfully they were no longer our issue.

The road to Jalalabad 2007

With guards and Farid the day he drove the French man to the airport

Herat 2008. With two locals and a trophy from the soviet invasion

A deserted Russian airbase, this truly was a ghostly place

BAGHDAD - بەغدا
KIRKUK - کەرکوک
پارکی منارە
Minaret park
Sheki Choli - شێخی چۆلی
Media Hall - هۆلی میدیا
MOSUL
Parliament
POLICE
POLICE

Iraq 2012

The Silk road between Kabul and Jalalabad 2006

Waiting to fly home Kabul 2008

With the transporter Rafi and guard Kabul 2008

Fight Night, Stillorgan Park Hotel 2010

November 2008. My Dad, Sister and Brother

The Volcanic Island of Rabaul 2011

With Matt Geyer and Scott Hill after the game

With Shane Amian and other members of the Wanderers team Port Moresby 2011

Soloman Islands 2011

Chapter 33

Legend for one day!

Rugby league is the major sport on PNG, but there is some rugby union if you look hard enough. I started playing union with a team called Wanderers, one of the more established teams in Port Moresby. I was 46 years of age. There was an Australian and myself, the rest were Papuans. I had trained with them two or three times when they informed me of a game the following weekend against Harlequins, another local team. They asked if I would like to come and play. I said I would, but only as a sub, that if they needed me they could put me on.

The game was in the main stadium; I turned up on the Saturday and togged out. For about twenty minutes I was sitting happily on the subs bench when the coach told me I was going on. So on I went, everyone on the pitch was naturally Papuan, all Pacific Islanders. I came on at a line out, took my position at the back, and of course the ball came straight to me. I caught it and all I heard was a growl and then felt a three person strong thumping as they hammered me to the ground. All fair and proper but it was still some battering. The novelty for them was the white guy with the ball. Every time I got the ball I was the main target.

Later I went to the local nightclub, Lamana. It was a very busy place, the top floor was supposedly the VIP section where whites usually went, the bottom floor was were the Papuans tended to congregate. We were downstairs because I'd played with the team and they were treating me as if I was one of their brothers and it was better craic. Straight away both the opposition and my own team gave me their respect. Out of the blue, this aggressive Papuan stepped forward and asked me,

"Hey what are you doing down here, you should be upstairs with the rest of your white trash." Although looking back the language may have been a touch more forthright.

One of our props, Shane Amean, who played for the national team, came over and said,

"You got a problem Alan?"

"No I don't think so." I shrugged.

"No there is no problem." My questioner hurriedly answered after taking one look at the hulking Shane.

Shane looked at the man and clearly said, "That is good, because he is one of our brothers."

That evening I met Bani, the classic Pacific Island beauty. She'd represented PNG in a beauty pageant years before. Bani was incomparably beautiful, like something you would imagine in your dreams from Mutiny on the Bounty. She had long dark Pacific Island hair which made her look very alluring.

"Hey you're that crazy white guy from the match earlier?"

"Yeah"

"You looked like a white spot on a domino."

I laughed. She laughed.

We got talking. She was divorced with two children, she worked and supported her family. Her husband had run off with a younger woman. We started dating, which mostly consisted of her coming round to mine for dinner, to watch some TV and going out for drives. Bani never wanted me to go to her village as she was very protective of me. She believed her family would latch on to me and would ask for money. Her view was that it was our time together and that more than anything she needed an escape from her village life. I understood very well the need for escape. The two of us were under no illusions about a joint future. She was never going to leave her country and I was never going to settle in PNG, but we did have a lovely spark and I enjoyed my time with her. We created an island of serenity and enjoyed our time together as much as we could. She was a wonderful companion and a great friend.

I was always asking her out to dinner and she kept refusing me. I could never grasp why this was. One night I asked her.

"What's the issue? Are you embarrassed to be seen with me?"

"No no, don't be silly. You will laugh if I tell you."

She eventually told me that she'd only used a knife and fork once or twice, years before visiting Australia, but never since. Made no odds to me, we ended up going out plenty.

Rugby became a big part of my life over there. It was always played at a very fast pace, owing as much to league as to union. The only downside was we always played on a dust bowl, the ground was so hard, after playing you would be cut to ribbons. I'd come back after a game and I wouldn't be able to move at all. But I was back laughing through the pain.

A few months into my stay, I had become very good friends with one of my handset and sim suppliers Jim Qui, a very successful Malaysian businessman. Jim knew I was into my rugby. While I was over in the Solomon Islands working, he phoned to tell me he had a surprise for me. The following Saturday, 25th November 2011, I was to play for the New South Wales Legends against the Queensland Legends in the National Stadium in a Rugby League State of Origin Legends Game.

At a charity auction Jim had bid and bought the guest spot on the Legends team as a gift. A guest spot in the match with the former pros: David Peachey, Australian international fullback; Nathan Blacklock, Australian international winger; Melbourne Storm winger Matt Geyer; 2000 Rugby League World Cup Champion Scott Hill; Australian International legend Cliff Lyons; Papua New Guinea International Winger and Legend Marcus Bai and former Papua New Guinea captain John Wilshire. And Alan Barry, some Irish guy who'd just taken up rugby union and had never ever played rugby league??

Despite my trepidation bordering on complete terror, I could not say no. A week or two later I found myself in a dressing room with rugby league players who'd been amongst the best the world had ever seen. I confessed to them that I'd never played rugby league, only union. They explained they didn't know much about union, but that since it was only an exhibition they reckoned I would be fine. The only thing they did tell me was that when I got tackled not to lie on the ground, but to get up and place the ball behind me. I somewhat naively said,

"Oh just like touch rugby but with contact?"

"Don't worry mate, it's an exhibition match, it won't be tough. No worries"

I should have been really worried but by then I was too excited.

The staff got wind I'd be playing and after they'd stopped laughing they promised to attend the match. At the time I was not exactly sure why they were laughing quite so much, but then they knew a lot more about rugby league than I did. I got the joke very quickly once the game began. As soon as I was tackled in fact.

I started and straight away the ball came to me. I ran with the ball and was tackled by two Queensland Legends and completely smashed. I remember thinking I was going to die, and laughing slightly crazed. I got up because I am a glutton for punishment. As the match progressed and I got hit more and more, although still less than everyone else, I realised I was enjoying myself, broken back, lost crown and all. I kicked two conversions but I didn't score a try. The match was televised on National TV and the commentator remarked as the camera zoomed in on the unknown pasty white guest player,

"I don't know who this Number 17 Alan Barry is, the guest player, but he's certainly taken a lot of punishment out there on the field today."

As the whistle blew for the end and the crowd streamed on to try to speak to their heroes, a boy ran up to me and asked me for my boots. I explained to him I was a nobody, but he was having none of it "you kicked two conversions" was his argument, I gave him my boots. I hobbled off in that strange beautiful pain sport sometimes brings. The night out after with the team was a life memory for me. I was back in Lamana nightclub with my temporary teammates after the game, when an Australian woman came up to me,

"I watched you play today. You're a league player alright, you had a great game. You must have played in England."

I smiled and nodded. "Yeah I played for Warrington." A complete lie, but I couldn't help myself.

"What's your name?"

"Adrian Bogan. I am known as the Broganator." A friend I'd played union with back in Dublin. She assured me she would look me up when she got back to Australia. A great day.

It turned out I'd lost a cap off a tooth, and I had a massive bruise the size of a tennis ball on my back for about two years afterwards. There was a lot of scar tissue damage. It wasn't until I went to Iraq that I managed to cure that injury with a really good sports massage. Luckily the game had been casual, a relatively tame version of the real thing, which has far more blood and thunder. They were some of the soundest lads I've ever met. Total characters, made me feel like one of the team. One of them had been an Australian Gladiator after he'd retired from League: Mark McGaw. I really was in the presence of true greatness.

I was back involved in life and PNG helped me get there.

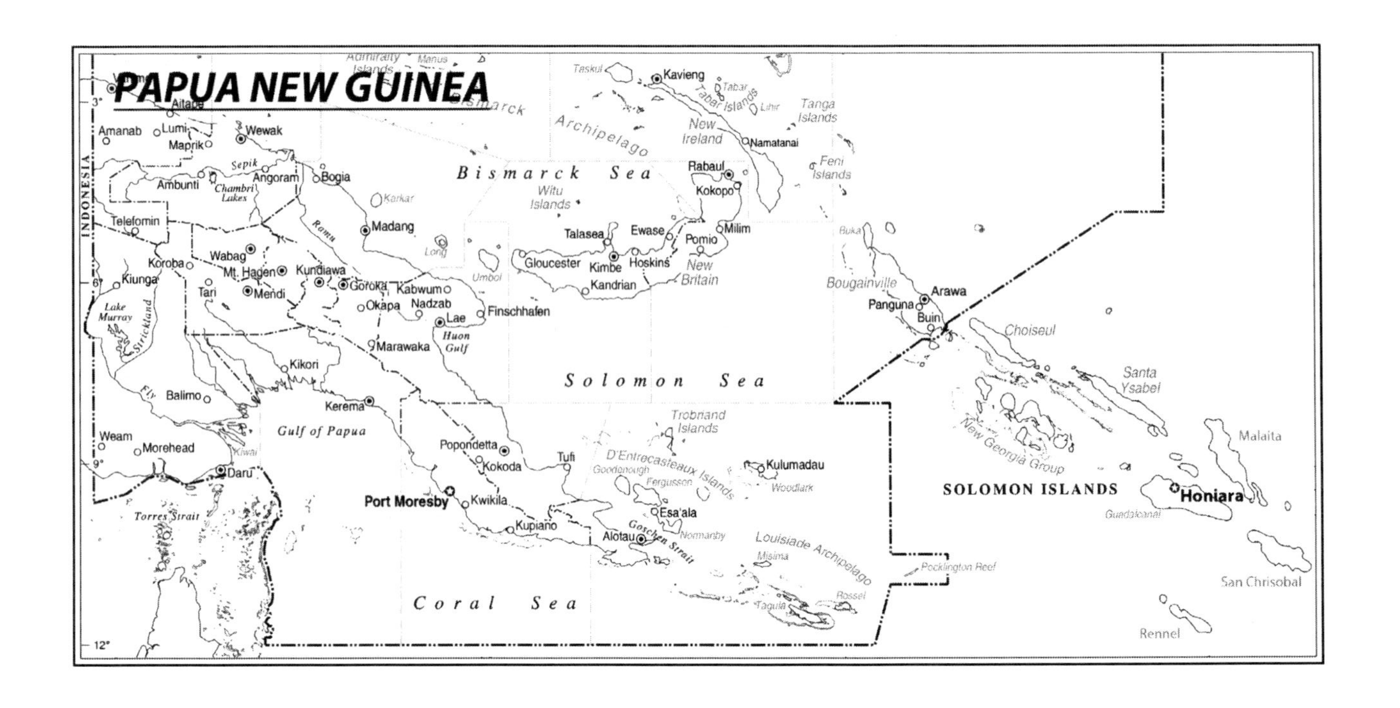
PAPUA NEW GUINEA
INDONESIA
Admiralty Islands
Manus
Aitape
Amanab
Lumi
Maprik
Wewak
Sepik
Angoram
Ambunti
Chambri Lakes
Bogia
Karkar
Ramu
Madang
Telefomin
Wabag
Mt. Hagen
Kundiawa
Goroka
Kabwum
Koroba
Kiunga
Tari
Mendi
Okapa
Nadzab
Lae
Huon Gulf
Finschhafen
Long
Umboi
Lake Murray
Strickland
Marawaka
Kikori
Fly
Balimo
Kerema
Gulf of Papua
Weam
Morehead
Kiwai
Daru
Torres Strait
Popondetta
Kokoda
Tufi
Port Moresby
Kwikila
Kupiano
Coral Sea
Bismarck Sea
Bismarck Archipelago
Witu Islands
Taskul
Kavieng
Tabar
Tabar Islands
Lihir
Tanga Islands
New Ireland
Namatanai
Feni Islands
Rabaul
Kokopo
Milim
Talasea
Ewase
Pomio
Gloucester
Kimbe
Hoskins
New Britain
Kandrian
Solomon Sea
Trobriand Islands
D'Entrecasteaux Islands
Goodenough
Fergusson
Kulumadau
Woodlark
Esa'ala
Normanby
Alotau
Goschen Strait
Louisiade Archipelago
Misima
Tagula
Rossel
Pocklington Reef
Buka
Bougainville
Arawa
Panguna
Buin
Choiseul
Santa Ysabel
New Georgia Group
SOLOMON ISLANDS
Malaita
Honiara
Guadalcanal
San Chrisobal
Rennel
3°
6°
9°
12°

Chapter 34

Bitten by the Solomon Islands

The Solomon Islands are a truly wondrous place. The people there are very different to the Papuans. They are mostly of Melanesian descent, which means they are far more laid back and easier to get along with. When you travel out to some of the remote islands, islands such as Gizo, you are in some of the most stunningly beautiful areas in the world. There is also Kennedy Island, where a young John F Kennedy was marooned for a couple of weeks during the Second World War. JFK's PT boat had been sunk by the Japanese and he and his crew faced an arduous three and a half mile swim to what at the time was known as Plum Island.

You would often clearly see planes at the bottom of the sea, all from the Second World War, perhaps a fighter bomber still visible deep down through the crystal clear water. There were many war relics on the islands, due to the number of battles between the Americans and the Japanese during the Pacific Campaign.

On the Solomon Islands, the greatest challenge for us as a business was that the company was owned by Bemobile. Amazingly and very dishearteningly, the way the business had been set up in the Solomon Islands was even more cretinous than in PNG. It was a very small market, there were only five hundred and fifty thousand people all told on the Solomon Islands. We were competing against an organisation that was in essence Cable and Wireless (Solomon Island Telecom), so there was no paddy wackery.

The Japanese had built a large airbase outside of Guadalcanal during the war. Some 70 years later while we were building our new mobile tower there, we found an old Second World War 1000lb bunker buster bomb. The authorities were called and we waited for the army to show up. Nope, two local police turned up and put it on the back of their truck using a winch and trundled off in their flatbed truck, bomb bouncing all the way. I guess it's difficult to worry about health and safety if your island is broke. Divers would pay a lot of money to dive off the islands, in and amongst the perfect, unspoilt reefs, the tropical fish and the sunken wrecks. Tourism was everything on the islands.

The flight between Port Moresby and Honiara was five hours. The only way to get around the islands themselves was by boat or light aircraft. I had a team there full time, a member of which was an alcoholic Irishman, Seamus. He used to turn up every morning for work reeking of booze. The only good news for him was that he never got malaria. I presume the mosquitos knew better than to bite him, for they'd surely have dropped dead. Seamus was another one of the feckless diaspora I have found all over the world – guys and girls squirreled away doing an awful job, but getting paid and enjoying their privilege. Seamus was the sales manager, an idiot and a raving piss artist.

The first time we worked together was a Friday up in Gizo, we decided we'd go out for a couple of drinks. We got absolutely hammered, smashed, you name it. Next day I woke up, a tomahawk hangover through my head. We both just about made it to the plane. I slept the whole way back to Honiara while Seamus drank. In Honiara he was in the accommodation beside me. I was due to fly back to Port Moresby on the Sunday morning. I was sitting out the back, facing the sea with my laptop out, doing a bit of work. As I'm listening to the sea, Seamus strolls past me with a can of beer.

"You fancy going out for a drink?"

I laughed, "Are you for real we only stopped drinking at four o clock this morning"

He was serious. "Yeah but it's the weekend." Him and his big red nose. Very few people have ever got under my skin like Seamus. I can't explain it and I am not going to attempt to, it is just one of those things. I must say he was not a bad guy and to be fair he did try his best. However, the more he tried the more irritating I found him.

When we launched 3G on the Solomon Islands, I got the worst case of malaria possible, short of dying. It was the 3rd December 2011. We'd invited the government to the launch. The deputy Prime Minister got so drunk he fell into the pool and the leader of the opposition, who was also the ex-Prime Minister, got so drunk he started abusing myself and the company secretary. The company secretary was an English man who we'd dubbed Little Britain for his resemblance to the bald headed guy on the Little Britain TV show. The leader of the opposition informed us we were white trash and were treating the Islanders like servants. In other words a truly epic night. The free bar ran from seven o clock until eternity. Pacific Islanders love to drink, so it was a match made in heaven.

I went home to bed sober as I had been working. I woke up the next day without the mosquito net and the window open, my feet were covered in bites. I should have noticed the open window going to bed but I didn't. I went back to PNG and felt fine for about two weeks. I'd almost forgotten about it. The 16th of December rolled around, the company Christmas party. I was due to fly home on the 21st. I'd arranged two days before that in Singapore for meetings with suppliers. The afternoon of the 16th, I mentioned to Little Britain that I had a very sore throat and a headache. He didn't hesitate.

"Malaria mate, I've had it twice. It's definitely malaria. Go and get yourself a testing kit."

I did and the self-testing kit came up negative. Being a malarial idiot, I naturally thought I was away with it. I went ahead and hosted the Christmas party for the staff. I felt wretched all night and I only drank tonic. I went home early enough, woke up a couple of hours later, drenched in sweat from head to foot, like I'd had a shower. I rang a friend.

"I need a doctor."

"Mate, they're not going to send a doctor out to you. You have to go and see them in a clinic."

"I cannot get out of this bed."

I have a very high pain threshold but this completely annihilated me. The doctor was eventually convinced to come and see me. She told me that on a scale of one to ten, I was ten for malaria. I had won the top prize for malaria, no mean feat on the Solomon's. The disease had incubated in my body over the two weeks since the bites. She gave me two shots and a course of anti-malaria tablets. For two days I felt like death warmed up. I still went to work though, I had too much to do and I was really conscious of wanting to get back to Ireland in time for Christmas. At least I had that Sunday free to spend all day in bed; on the Monday I went to our weekly management meeting. I wasn't hallucinating, but besides that tiny mercy I'd every other thing wrong with me that you could imagine. Horrific. The tablets helped at least.

By the time the 21st rolled around, I was well enough to get on the flight to Singapore. Our handset supplier there had planned a big Christmas party for me in what are called KTV bars in Singapore. KTV bars are karaoke bars with strippers. The last thing on earth I wanted or needed at that time was a KTV bar. I was booked into the Marina Bay Sands hotel, a really beautiful hotel overlooking the Singapore Bay. All I wanted was to relax in my room in preparation for my flight home to Ireland and spending my Christmas with my children; but I was the one being feted and even though I still had no interest in the KTV bars, I hadn't really got much of a choice as my supplier insisted I attend. I staggered through two days of meetings and celebrations. I was feeling rough after the malaria, probably more drained than anything. There was one upside though, I'd lost a lot of weight.

For Christmas in Dublin I'd decided to treat myself, so I'd booked into the Shelbourne Hotel on St Stephen's Green. I arrived home Christmas Eve 2011. It was an incredible feeling. I'd never come home so close to Christmas before. Christmas Eve is the perfect day to arrive into Dublin: truly a wonderful winter experience. I checked into the Shelbourne, into a beautiful historic room. Then I went and met my children. We all had dinner; afterwards walking down Grafton Street, nearly freezing to death creating memories I will have forever – a truly memorable day after been away from my family for the previous number of months. That evening before I went out, I heard a knock while lying on the bed in the Shelbourne. It was the staff coming around with a hamper, a real treat. That evening I went out with my friends, and although I was pretty much off the drink and food I still thoroughly enjoyed myself. I spent Christmas morning with my children. My family were happy and so was I.

I'd left Ireland and a lot of trauma behind me at the beginning of that year. I was back healed.

I was back to me.

Chapter 35

A FAMILY MAN ABROAD

There was much fun to be had in PNG, but there was also the serious side to the job and that was being up against Digicel. Our main competitor was involved in all manner of cunning activities and we had to be equally as sharp. I was enjoying myself again.

Our own network was falling apart. This was being exacerbated by a major shareholder dispute between Hong Kong Investment Company, who were milking the business dry and the government, the IPBC, who felt they were not getting anything out of it. The government could not get rid of HKIC because they were contractually bound to them but what they could do was make life difficult for them. We were all working under this completely dysfunctional board that had run out of funding.

I was blessed with an amazing team, who I'd moulded and who in turn did me proud. They'd seen all the expats come and go and they knew I was there to win, similar to how I used to work in Afghanistan. My marketing manager Judith, a Papuan, was excellent and I learnt a lot from her and, I would hope, her from me. Between Judith and my graphic designer Rasheed we came up with some great campaigns. We worked on focusing on our strengths, which were few and far between.

I had been in PNG for about a year when Andy came out of a board meeting and told me he'd been asked to resign. HKIC was not happy with Andy and got rid of him much to my disgust. Andy was a victim of boardroom politics, plain and simple. It was a crazy decision. HKIC had convinced the government to let them try one more person. I was introduced to this person from Hong Kong, who I can only describe as a complete and utter clown: a former accountant with no experience of the industry who knew nothing. He was an American who'd been living in Hong Kong. In reality he was living in a dream world – another puppet for the Hong Kong circus troop.

I tried to work with the new American CEO for around two months. By then my contract was up for renewal. Coincidentally, at this same time I received a call from Violet. It was a Saturday morning and I was still in bed. I knew it was serious when I saw her name. It had just gone 7pm back in Ireland so it was about 6am in Moresby and she was hysterical. Our youngest Connor had been hit by a car outside Wesley Youth Disco in Dublin. It wasn't clear yet the extent of his injuries. I did manage to ascertain that they were not immediately life threatening. I felt helpless. I spent an hour anxiously pacing up and down until Violet rang me back. Connor had been very lucky, his only injury was a severely fractured ankle. The doctors couldn't operate because the ankle was too swollen, they needed to reset his ankle. He was in excruciating pain. Connor has the makings of a decent rugby player and a fine athlete and I really didn't want to see that disappear, but at the time I was just thankful he was OK.

I told my new boss I needed some time off to go home to see my son. He said no, even though I'd only had around four weeks off the previous year. He said I couldn't go. I figured I could handle life without the job, as I was not particularly enjoying the new working conditions. I handed in my notice, whereupon he told me I could take my holiday. But my mind was made up. Three different CEO's was two too many. All in all, it was a lesson in how to screw up a business. My son needed me back in Ireland, but more than that I needed to be there for him.

Leaving PNG and my team was painful. We'd worked hard and the bonds had grown fast and quick, we'd come through a lot together. They came to see me off at the airport and they cried because they knew nothing good was going to come of me leaving. We'd had to put up with three CEOs in a year. For the team it was worse, they'd just lost their immediate boss and I was being replaced by an Aussie blackguard, who I'd already cautioned for groping the female staff and using one of the male staff as a tea boy.

I was leaving them to the drunken wolves no doubt. I bought them presents and whereas maybe in the past I would have stayed, I felt things more deeply now and I needed to be near my son. No bones about it though, the staff were the ones who really lost. They did not have the option to walk away, and as anyone can attest to, working in a job under those types of conditions can wear you all the way down. Digicel were the real winners, as our team was destroyed.

Personally I felt like a new man. I had a career again. I had some respect. I felt like the problems were behind me. Being an adult, you simply move on to the next challenge. Luckily, and in fairness to my former employers, they paid me the bonus I was due so the hard work had paid off.

The company went into partnership with Vodafone soon after.

As well as saying goodbye to my team, another thing I had to do was to tell Bani that I was leaving PNG for good. In the time I knew her she had never once put any pressure on me in terms of our relationship or financially. We had grown very close and I truly did care for her. Saying goodbye to someone that you care about is an exceptionally difficult thing to do. It is a credit to her that when I told her about my son, the first thing she said was you need to go home. I knew she wouldn't take any money from me, so I went out and bought a new TV and left it with a colleague on the instructions that he was to call her the following day and tell her that I had left a present in the office . I just wanted her to be able to treat herself and this was no different from any man back in Ireland wanting to treat his girlfriend with a present . When the plane took off from Port Moresby, I looked down and thought to myself, I hope one I can return as a tourist and meet up with the many friends I made, and who knows maybe even Bani.

One of my favourite stories while in PNG concerned Graham Woodruff, an English accountant in Bemobile. Graham was a character straight out of a Graham Green novel. Outwardly mild mannered, he alone out of the whole office wore a full suit and tie every day. Ah the English and their uniforms. He also used a real cup and saucer for his tea. I played golf with Graham most Sundays and we would chat about the usual fluff. He was always telling me how much he loved his wife and family. He was a skinny, very slight looking individual and looked exactly like an accountant. There were a couple of things about him that did not fit, he had a temper that would flare up from time to time, and there was always the suggestion of an unrevealed side to him. I got on well with him, despite him constantly telling me how much he loved his wife and how much he loathed Andy our CEO every single time we went golfing.

One day we were all shocked and horrified to learn that poor Graham had been kidnapped. We understood the implications. We knew that meant we all were at risk. Suddenly we were confronted with what we would do if we were kidnapped, and we all missed our family that much more. The police came and interviewed everyone, asked if any of us had noticed anything out of the ordinary, being followed or any suspicious characters. None of us had, but we were still frightened.

Next the police went through Graham's phone records, one local number showed up more than all the others. It belonged to Graham's house maid. Graham had called her an hour after he'd been kidnapped. He was a great employer, he had probably called to give her the day off once he knew he'd been kidnapped.

Frankly the cops were getting suspicious at this stage and they used the signal from Graham's phone to triangulate his whereabouts – surprisingly poor job by the kidnappers not to ditch his phone. They tracked him to a house in the middle of nowhere, off the beaten track. They found Graham alone, wearing his suit, making himself a jam sandwich, no doubt thinking about how much he loved his wife. His company car was outside the house, the house which belonged to his house maid who he may or may not have been kissing.

Weirdly the police were not satisfied with Graham's descriptions of his kidnapping ordeal. They probably roughed him up a bit during the month he spent in the PNG prison. He couldn't have held out, not Graham.

Graham had had a very strained relationship with Andy the CEO and had orchestrated a kidnapping, but unfortunately for Graham, Andy had left PNG the previous week. Graham did not have the heart to have anyone else kidnapped so he did the only honourable thing, he kidnapped himself. The police eventually let him get off with a deportation and there was never another kidnapping again.

I have spoken to him since and Graham is adamant he was framed, that the kidnappers had stolen his golf clubs. Who really knows?

Chapter 36

Bored in Iraq and smiling in Uganda

I left PNG for good just in time to get back for my son's operation. The operation was being performed by one of the best orthopaedic surgeons in Ireland.

"This is bad." The surgeon did not pull any punches, he painted a very bleak picture.

Connor's ankle turned out to be fractured and dislocated. I happily ferried him around for three months as he healed. I made sure he did not do any weight bearing and that he went in to have his dressing changed on his open wound from the surgery every 48 hours. Violet had a fulltime job so it worked out well. I was able to be there to ensure everything went smoothly. It struck me that I liked being back in Ireland. I spent three months with Connor ensuring he fully recovered. In the end he returned to rugby with both his school team and our family club, DLSP.

I updated my resume to include PNG, and alongside the Afghan adventure, I was developing a name as someone who could do a job in foreign climes, an international trouble shooter. Although I was unemployed again, this time things were not critical. Sure enough, I received another contact from LinkedIn, an email written by a man called Jihad from Iraq. Sentences you never expect to read, a man called Jihad emailed me from Iraq. It read,

"Hi Alan I've just looked at your profile on LinkedIn we are looking for an acting CEO in Iraq. I was wondering whether you would be interested?" I half thought it was a sick joke. However I knew enough to know I did not know enough, so I mailed him back, giving him my mobile number in Ireland.

Jihad phoned me back ten minutes later. He was acting on behalf of Newroz Telecom, situated in Erbil, Northern Iraq, in the semi-autonomous Kurdistan. Newroz is jointly owned by Vtel holdings, my old friends from the failed Afghan Wireless deal a thousand years ago. The other owner was a Kurdish company.

"Our CEO has to go for an operation, and he has tasked me with finding someone who could come in on an interim basis, while he is incapacitated. Would you be interested?"

"Sounds really interesting. Sure I would definitely be interested"

The following day I received an email from the secretary of the Vtel board of directors in Amman, Jordan. They flew me over to Amman for a meeting. Business class return, always a good indicator of a serious offer. I met with the Vtel board. Sure enough they remembered me from Afghanistan, which is how they found me on LinkedIn. It was not a coincidence.

"We want you." Was pretty much their approach.

They were keen for me to take the job, on condition the main local shareholder, a Kurd called Kawa who wore his heart on his sleeve, gave me his blessing, which he did. I always had a lot of time for him and I enjoyed working with him. He was really direct but a first class operator, very like Amin Ramin, my old MD in AWCC.

I was temporarily replacing a man called Abu Omar. In the Islamic world, it is considered a great honour to be called Abu followed by your eldest son's name, in this case Omar. He was a straight talker, and a Palestinian: a very pleasant man to deal with, whom I saw little of except for the handover. I started the following week. It was August 2012 when I took over.

I was acting CEO and the job was OK. I was being well remunerated, but the problem I and everyone else had was that there was absolutely nothing to do outside work. That is not exactly true; there was one thing you could do there, drink. 90% of the expats there were verging on if not complete alcoholics. Watch sport on TV, drink and eat; that was our lot. I succumbed in my own way, particularly with the eating. Try as I might, becoming an alcoholic was a bridge too far for me.

Whilst many wanted to avoid the bar, we really had very little choice. I was there all winter; the temperature dropped to a freezing –20°C. Far too bloody cold to go home, you'd freeze to death, the only way to stay warm at home was using paraffin heater death traps that were lethal if left burning overnight. Unlike in Afghanistan there were no open fires. So I, like everyone else, spent most evenings congregated in a bar or a restaurant. Everybody drank every single day, then drove home, getting into cars when they could barely stand up. I began to fall into drinking pretty heavily as well.

I lived in the Christian quarter of Erbil, in a place called Ankawa. All of the bars and restaurants were in Ankawa, as the Christians were allowed to sell alcohol. The Muslims had to come to Ankawa if they wanted a drink. The street I lived on there were mostly Iraqi Christians who had fled Baghdad to get away from the ethnic cleansing. Fascinating people. There was a Christian church on my street. I wanted to see a Christian service. One of the staff, a Kurdish Christian, took me there. They were Assyrian, Catholics who talk in the tongue of Christ, Aramaic, and are amongst the original peoples of what is now Iraq. Visiting their Chaldean Catholic church was a very spiritual experience for me.

Besides the Assyrians, Northern Iraq and Erbil is the home of the Peshmerga and the Kurds. Saladin the greatest hero of the Arab world, the most revered of all Arabic kings, was a Kurd interestingly enough – a fact very few people are aware of and certainly something I didn't know until my arrival in Erbil. Saladin was the leader of the Arab Army that captured Jerusalem in 1187 from the Crusaders. In Kurdistan Islam is mostly the Shafi'i school of Sunni Islam, one of the four schools of Sunni Islam in Islamic Law.

There were the Yazidis, ancient Christians who worship the angels and were once a considerable minority in the region. The Yazidis are regarded as devil worshippers by ISIS, the news media moniker for the so called Islamic State, and have been targeted by the group in order to cleanse Iraq of non-Muslims. Once upon a time there were also a lot of Jews in Iraq, until Saddam drove them all out. Nowadays what is left of that region's once diverse religious population is involved in a fight to the death with ISIS. The various religions are scattered. The heroic and fearsome Kurdish Peshmerga are seemingly doing most of the fighting against the forces of darkness ISIS represents.

I could have partaken more in the local carousing, but I was acting GM-CEO meaning I could not let myself go too much. Besides which, did my colleagues really want to hang around with their boss? I tended to watch a lot of TV.

Erbil was safe, probably safer than Port Moresby, but outside the city, it was a different story. ISIS had not yet reared their hydra head but Syria was fully flowing, engulfed by civil war. There were a lot of refugees in and around the city. The nightly decision to drink and eat or eat and drink was wearing me down for sure. There were no golf courses, there was the odd football pitch, and we used to play five a side in between the bouts of boozy boredom.

When it snowed, you'd wake up in the morning and breathe and the room would mist up like you'd been sleeping in a bed in the Phoenix Park all night. I couldn't leave the paraffin heater on because the fumes would kill me. My social life was a solitary chair I had placed in front of the TV and a blanket.

In the summer time it was roasting. We could go and drink outside in the German beer garden, listen to some lovely music. Then the next day you could get up, go shopping, go for a coffee, watch TV and go drink outside in the German beer garden. I didn't notice it as much in Afghanistan, as I was in a house with four others and I was not acting CEO, hence I could partake more in the nightly festivities.

Nine months of good money and boredom. Thankfully once every two months I had to go to board meetings in Amman. Those bimonthly meetings in Amman became something to look forward to, somewhat manic and angry but at least they were a change. Typically I would be there for a few days. In the meetings everyone would spend their time giving out about each other, beginning the discussions in English and then continuing on into Arabic so I couldn't understand, or more likely so they could give full vent to their expletives about whomever. Eventually I reported the figures and they would ask me various vexed questions.

On one of the trips to Amman, I was asked to remain for a further meeting the following week. This gave me a weekend to spend in Amman all to myself. Being away from Erbil was a welcome break and an opportunity to visit some of the sites in the Holy Land. This was a truly spiritual experience and something I would highly recommend. Whether you are religious or not, it's something worth seeing: a soul cleansing exercise that we could all do with. I visited the exact location that John the Baptist baptised Jesus. It was a very spiritual place, where I could sense a strange kind of peace and tranquillity, a feeling of ease and calmness that was most welcome.

I visited mount Nebo where, according to Christian tradition, Moses was buried, although his burial site is not specified. There is also a Byzantine church and monastery, which house the famous Byzantine mosaics. Again this part of the day filled me with thousands of years of history and a great feeling of serenity that was good for the soul. The final part of the day was a trip to Madaba and the Church of St George. Constructed in AD560, it is filled with mosaics of St George and the Dragon. The ancient presence of the Crusaders who battled for the Holy Land thousands of years ago was everywhere. It was a very enjoyable weekend and I feel blessed to have been given the opportunity to visit those amazing locations. This is one of the advantages of the expat experience.

The Palestinian CEO Abu Omar had gone to the States for his operation and then returned to Palestine to recuperate. When he was well enough to return to Erbil, the Israelis would not let him out of Palestine because he had so many Iraqi visas on his passport. That meant another three months on top of the contract for me. Nonetheless, it was a happy day when I left. The only thing to report from Iraq at that time was that there was nothing to report. Hard to reconcile that dull place with the hell hole it has become of late at the hands of ISIS.

I was at home in Ireland after I finished up with my Iraqi adventure when I received a call from an old friend telling me he'd recommended me for a job in Uganda. About half an hour later an email came through from a company called

Smile Communications. Smile had won a 4G LTE licence in Uganda. LTE is another phrase for 4G; it stands for long-term evolution, and is high speed connectivity on the internet. They had launched in June and this was now early July. The launch could have gone better and they needed help.

I got the phone call from HR telling me she had heard great things about me. They wanted me to come in as head of sales and marketing, but as a consultant. It was a step down but the salary was the same grade as a CEO. I agreed terms on a 6 month contract, got on a plane and flew out to Uganda.

What I arrived into was difficult to handle at first. They'd launched the new network with all of the retail outlets in the wrong place, with no footfall and no potential customers. They were even in the wrong socio-economic areas. 4G was a high end product and Smile had opened outlets in low income areas where people had little or no interest, and definitely no surplus income. The average monthly spend on the product was $100; the outlets were in areas where average wage was $100 a month. The planning had been poor, hence my predecessor being asked to fall on his sword. The search was on for a new sales and marketing director of African origin, as that was company policy.

The marketing campaign was a triumph in obscurity, nobody understood what Smile LTE 4G did. The marketing manager before me had paid an advertising agency too many dollars to come up with a billboard campaign that was confusing and nobody was able to understand. When you looked at the billboard, you couldn't make out what the overall message was. So again we needed to fix the message.

Firstly, I simplified the marketing message, so that people could understand what we did. I brought it back to basics. I had to work with the sales team to motivate them as well as closing down, repositioning and reopening retail points in the right areas.

Before I'd arrived, they'd fired half the sales team. Morale was as hard to find as the sales outlets or the marketing message. I worked with those people for a month.

For the rest of my professional career, I will always regard what I achieved in six months in Uganda as something special. Although it was only six months, I am exceptionally proud of what we achieved. Thrown in as a consultant, not an iota of support, never any recognition for what my team achieved and how we turned things around. They portrayed me as the big bad consultant sent in from head office, but in reality I was very popular with the locals. I'd been sent there to clean up management's mess. Hence management were not overly fond of me. At my very first meeting with the sales team, I gave them my usual introductory sales speech:

"I'm here to help you, I am here to work with you, I am here to help each and every one of you to succeed. But the only way that I can help you succeed is if you help yourself.

You will find me very fair. You will find me a person who can be approached, if I can coach or mentor you I will. I will help you all to be successful."

I finished with,

"I want you all to watch a famous clip of Alec Baldwin in a movie called *Glengarry Glen Ross*."

When I give my pep talk I like to quote the Alec Baldwin speech from the film based on the play by David Mamet. I played the clip on Youtube[29] of the iconic speech when he tells Jack Lemmon's character that he can't have coffee because coffee is for closers. Or the other one when Alec Baldwin puts his watch down on the desk in front of Ed Harris and says,

"See that watch, it costs more than your car."

They are both exceptionally motivational speeches and a great way to subtly get a very valuable message across, while at the same time having some fun. Fun, something that was needed to lift the doom and gloom hanging over the Ugandan sales team. The team were so into it that *Glengarry Glen Ross* became the theme of our weekly sales meeting. I'd find out who beat their target for that week and on the way to the office

29 https://www.youtube.com/watch?v=v9XW6P0tiVc

Friday morning I'd pick up whatever number of coffees I needed. The first meeting I bought coffee only for myself.

"I'm buying coffee for myself because I'm a closer, I wish I was sharing it with you," would be my opening speech every week to the sales team at our 8am meeting.

Then I had to buy two coffees, then three. I had 23 sales team members in direct sales. By the time I left I was getting everyone a coffee on the way to the Friday morning sales meeting. We'd generated a wonderful team spirit. I left a very successful sales team and a business that was increasing its revenues every month. I also handed back a highly successful marketing and commercial department, with a clearly defined marketing message. All achieved in a country I'd not known a single thing about until I landed at the start of the six months: a highly, highly enjoyable experience.

Ugandans are incredible people: very easy to get along with; slightly shy and reserved; really good to work with. Presumably a lot of their reserved nature is a learnt trait from the terrifying time of Amin. They had 15 presidents between Idi Amin and the current president Yoweri Museveni. Museveni has been in power since 1986 and although not everyone likes him he seems to have returned some measure of stability to the country. There are no civil wars and it is safe. I think if I hadn't had my children back in Ireland I might have stayed on. Kampala was a great place. From day one taking on the role full time was never on the cards. I was doing the job of head of sales and marketing, but getting the salary of a CEO. To be honest the GM was a very nice lady, but she was out of her depth. I find it difficult to suffer fools gladly. I tried my best to just ignore her.

Obviously I'd long come to realise that expats are not all great. I've come across people and I have thought to myself, how the hell did they get this job? And normally it was the old story, they just kept their head down and played politics better than they could do the job itself. A qualification that I don't have.

I have also come across some really excellent colleagues, expat or otherwise. I don't want to give the impression that I am the only person who can do the job. Politics is an important part of life and sadly it's never been my strong point. I have always tried to let my results and delivery do the talking.

The one thing that I have always prided myself on was the standard of the work that I do. When the staff found out I was leaving, they sent 38 emails asking for me to be kept on. But it was not to be and I walked away with my head held high and no regrets. Contract work can be thankless at times but that is the way of it.

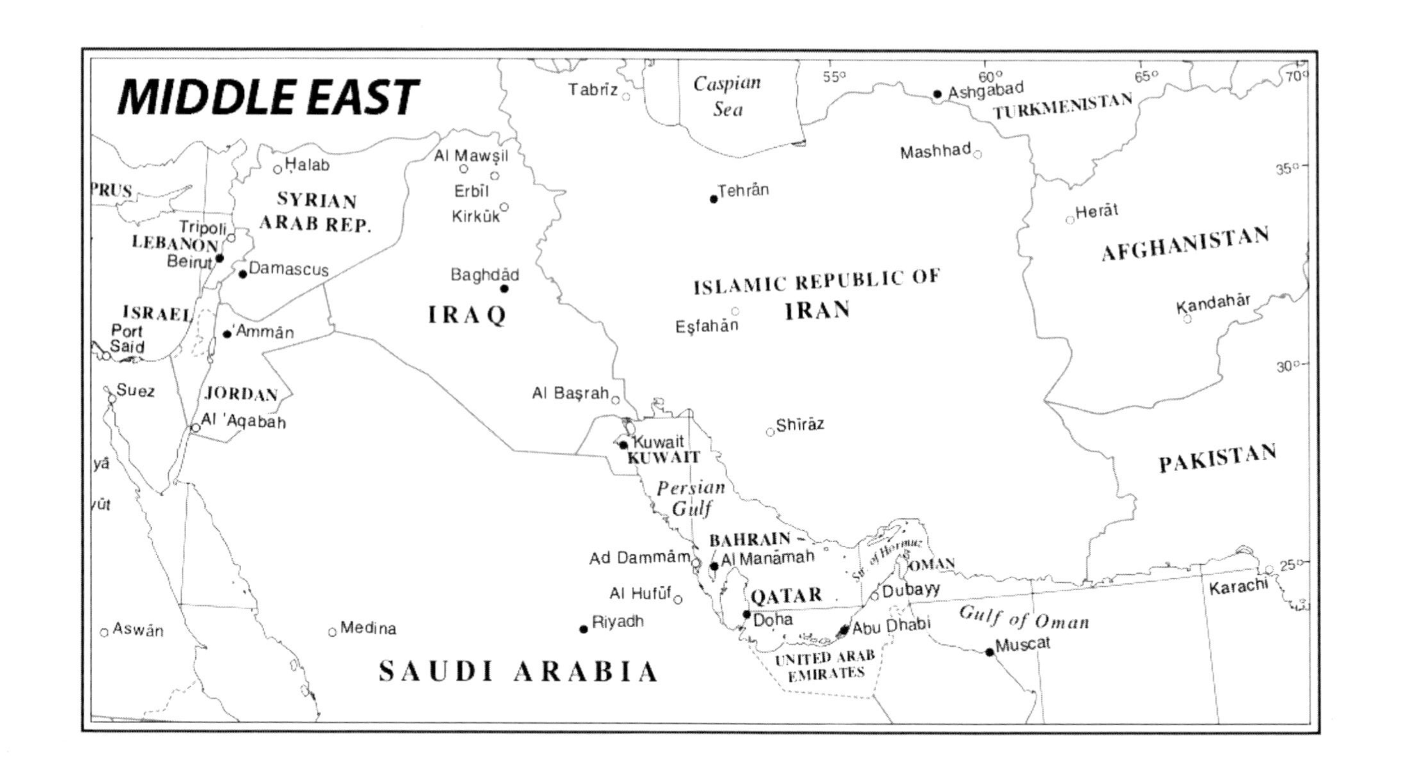
MIDDLE EAST
Tabrīz
Caspian Sea
55°
60°
65°
70°
35°
30°
25°
Ashgabad
TURKMENISTAN
Mashhad
Ḩalab
Al Mawşil
Erbīl
Kirkūk
Tehrān
Herāt
SYRIAN ARAB REP.
Tripoli
LEBANON
Beirut
Damascus
Baghdād
AFGHANISTAN
ISLAMIC REPUBLIC OF IRAN
IRAQ
Eşfahān
Kandahār
ISRAEL
Port Said
'Ammān
JORDAN
Suez
Al 'Aqabah
Al Başrah
Shīrāz
Kuwait
KUWAIT
PAKISTAN
Persian Gulf
BAHRAIN
Ad Dammām
Al Manāmah
OMAN
Al Hufūf
QATAR
Dubayy
Karachi
Doha
Abu Dhabi
Gulf of Oman
Aswān
Medina
Riyadh
Muscat
SAUDI ARABIA
UNITED ARAB EMIRATES

Chapter 37

Both sides

Twenty years ago I could not have lived openly in Ireland. Even now it's still at the back of my mind, writing this book and talking about some of my military experiences has posed some challenges. The army drummed it into us: keep a working cover story at all times. I have blown my cover story out the door in writing this book. Up until now, I had always shied away from talking about my past with any candour.

After I returned to Ireland in the late nineties, Violet came home one day and there was a car with two occupants in the driveway. She pulled in and they pulled off. She phoned me straight away, the burglaries in the UK were at the back of her mind. I phoned the local Garda station. After a couple of pleasantries,

"Oh an English accent, are you ex-military by chance?"

"Yes I am actually."

"Could you hold the line please?" A Special Branch detective came on and asked me,

"Where do you live? What time are you home at?" We arranged to meet.

Right enough he called up that evening. Violet and I stood in front of him after shaking hands and he looked at me and asked,

"Why didn't you tell us you were living here?" This was 1998. He continued,

"Do you realise there are two active service units in this area alone? One of them down the road?" It had never occurred to me. For me after the signing of the Good Friday Agreement the war was over.

The detective was not exaggerating. A few weeks later, the Real IRA tried to hold up a Securicor van in Ashford, Wicklow. Six members of a Real IRA active service unit were involved in trying to hijack the van, five were caught and imprisoned and one was shot dead. The Guards had ambushed them. So there I was, a guy who had served on all manner of operations, living pretty much down the road from two active service units. The detective was right, I should have mentioned it.

Even more incredulously, not long after the first attempted hijacking I was happily commuting back and forth to the UK. My English colleagues and friends would ask,

"Are you not worried living in Ireland, you know the IRA, bombs and the Troubles?"

I used to just laugh at them; for me Dublin was idyllic and peaceful. Nobody ever seemed overly concerned with what religion you were – a million miles from the North despite it being an hour away in the car. I was in my office one Tuesday in 1999, ignoring the TV screen on the wall. A colleague asked me as I was busying myself with paperwork,

"Where was it you said you lived again?" I was getting a bit fed up with the questions.

"Dalkey," I answered.

"Dall key?" she repeated pronouncing the silent 'L',

"Yeah" I answered a little irked.

"It's on Sky News."

I wasn't really in the humour, but I looked up and sure enough there on Sky News was a picture of Dalkey Village. I turned up the volume to listen to the report of a raid on a Brinks Allied van on Sorrento Road in Dalkey, home to some of the wealthiest people in Ireland. The Continuity IRA this time, used two vans, one fitted with an iron girder, to ram a Brink Allied cash in transit van. The gang rammed the van with the girder, giving them access to the money while the van's security guards were held at gunpoint.

Once they loaded all their loot, the gunmen armed with AK47s sped off in a Ford Granada they'd bought. Unfortunately for them, it broke down one mile away at the Dalkey Island Hotel. The raiders proceeded to hijack another car, a passing red Saab. They ordered the couple out of the car and then fired a shot, which grazed the driver, he was not seriously injured. The gang took off in the Red Saab along Coliemore Road, leaving behind most of their loot.

Neil was a British friend who lived in Dalkey around that time. Neil had been out walking his dog down Coliemore road minding his own business. He stopped to watch as the gang's Granada sped down the road, and as they piled out of it after the break down. He stood there enthralled as they waved down the red Saab and ushered the man and his partner out onto the road, firing a shot in the air that seemed to catch the innocent driver. Neil saw the gang get into the red Saab and speed off. He couldn't believe his luck getting to watch a film shoot up close, especially one that looked so realistic. He didn't find out until afterwards that he and his shih tszu Basil were witnessing a real carjacking and a robbery getaway. He'd wanted to applaud.

Of course my British colleagues watched the story unfolding alongside me, looking at me, shaking their heads,

"You must be mad living over there. It looks like chaos."

They didn't really understand how out of place this all was in Brigadoon.

Standing in my office in the UK listening to all my colleagues' advice from crime free Britain, I remember being worried that Violet would get stuck in the resulting traffic driving the kids home.

Ireland is home and home is safe, right?

I live in Ireland and it's my home, I love this country, however quite often I get comments from people I know about my past and the job I did. They see the role I performed in the North as some form of betrayal.

I don't.

I was a young man who actually discovered his own national identity as a result of being exposed to that sectarian drivel, and I am proud of the job I did.

I have never met anyone who would describe themselves as pro IRA, but the issue I constantly have thrown in my face when people discover I served in the British Army is,

"But you're Irish, how could you have done it?"

When I explain that I am also a passionate royalist and monarchist they come again at me,

"How can you be like that? You're Irish." And I feel like screaming, just like I did at that RUC officer all those years ago,

"Yeah I am, so what?"

If you look at the Royal Standard there is an Irish harp. That symbol represents the many Irish who love this country and would be happy if Ireland was still part of the Commonwealth. I personally think we wouldn't have had half the problems we have seen over the past 92 years if DeValera hadn't got such a grip back after independence in 1922.

I have more respect for men who took up arms for what they believed in than an idiot who proclaims his politics from an armchair or a bar stool. There is one acquaintance I know in particular, every time we meet he slips in remarks about the Brits and jibes about England. At first it was funny, but after 7 years of listening to him it's quite clear that he, like many others, has a real hang-up about the English. To my mind this individual is nothing more than a chocolate Republican, an armchair Provo. There are others, they harp and harp on about it. The funny thing is they have no idea. They've no idea what it was like, any of it: the North, being a soldier in the Forgotten War. I'm not sure I understand it myself, how could they?

Chapter 38

Finale

I'm pretty sure that is the end of the story. I am back to the old me or maybe it is the new me. My head is on straight and back to normal. I look forward to the future.

How do I describe my story? I was a chancer of sorts, I was someone who got through life and everything I touched turned to gold. I believed I could sell sand to Arabs and snow to Eskimos, but I learned I could never sell blarney to the Irish. I started to believe my own sales pitch, and that's when I started having problems. I was a great salesman, but like any good salesman when you start believing your own pitch you fool yourself. Why? I lost the run of myself because no matter what obstacle I was faced with, whether that be in the military on the verge of being shot, being in Afghanistan, whatever I did in life I'd always come up smelling of roses.

2010 that all stopped. 2010, the year it all started falling apart. Everything happened at once. I lost that ability to think on my feet; I lost my fighting spirit; I lost the ability to cut a deal, to hustle, to make things happen. I became a loser, and I remember being a loser for approximately twelve months. And instead of feeling positive about life, I started to feel sorry for myself. I started to think woe is me, instead of thinking of how to get myself out of my situation. The only positive I can bring out of that awful chapter, was that I came out of it a much better person. When I went into it I was a cocky arrogant jerk, when I came out of it I was humble. I now understand and believe that everyone deserves a chance, that there is an innate goodness inside everyone, even the ghouls who tried so hard to bring me low. I will never be judgemental of anyone ever again. That is my promise to myself.

I got married because it was the right thing to do. I grew to love my wife because she became my companion and my best friend. When the marriage eventually broke down in 2008, I still loved her . It was the reverse of the way it should have been.

The fact that our marriage broke up when it did was one of the reasons I found life so difficult. All of a sudden, after 22 years, I was on my own. Normally people when they split up have grown apart, for me I had grown towards her. But on reflection we had nothing left really, perhaps only an old friendship and a marriage that had zero trust both ways and absolutely no respect. I have never felt a stronger love for anyone than when she gave birth to all three of our children. For that alone I feel blessed.

Sure Violet and I have had our ups and downs – in the later years, lots of downs and very few ups – but when I look back on my life in general, I can safely say there are only three or four of those fifty years I regret. The opportunity to live and work all over the world; the people I have met who have helped and influenced me; the people I have hopefully influenced in their lives; the difference I have been able to make in distant countries; the chance to be successful; the love I have received from my family, the choices I have been able to give them in life.

On one of my final nights in the Solomon Islands as a celebration with the team, we hired a boat and went out to a lazy little perfect island. We marooned ourselves away from our lives for just one night. The island was surreal and beautiful. The delicious sweet warm air allowing us to smile and play moonlit drunken castaways. It was an uproarious bender. For some reason, everyone felt safe and let go. Sometimes you just catch the wave in this life, that night we caught it plum. Coming back to the main island through the inky black night, sea like a mirror, cigarettes bouncing around us like fireflies, the exaltation at being alive in the midst of paradise. I could see the Milky Way and all the constellations up close, the most amazing sky I had ever witnessed in my life. A year before I had been on Killiney Hill looking up at that same moon and sky.

I'll always remember that boat ride as when I finally came down off that hill.

Black, B., 2010. 'Kabul Bank: Where They Don't Fear The Regulators Enough To Even Hide The Abuses.' *Business Insider(US)*, 7 September .

Carl, A. & Garasu, L., 2002. 'Weaving consensus: The Papua New Guinea – Bougainville peace process.' *Accord,* Issue 12.

Ellis, E., 2004. 'Wireless Wars.' *Fortune International (Europe)*, 18 October, 150(7), p. 68.

Ellis, E., 2010. 'Why Farnood was Flushed Out of Kabul Bank.' *Euromoney*, 1 November.

Filkins, D., 2011. 'The Afghan Bank Heist.' *The New Yorker*, 14 February.

Freeman, M. F. & Kator-Mubarez , A., 2014. *KIRK MEYER, FORMER DIRECTOR OF THE AFGHAN THREAT FINANCE CELL.*
[Online]
Available at: https://globalecco.org/kirk-meyer-former-director-of-the-afghan-threat-finance-cell
[Accessed 29 April 2015].

Hastings, P., 2011. *Telephone Systems International and Ehsanollah Bayat Defeat US$400 Million Claim Brought by Lord Michael Cecil, Stuart Bentham and Alexander Grinling Bringing 9 Years of Litigation to a Close,* London: PR Newswire.

Kyle, T., 2013. 'Incredible Story of the British soldier who was the only survivor of a 19th century conquest – and the warnings for today's military missions.' *The Daily Mail*, 25 March.

Masterova, A., Partlow, J. & Higgins, A., 2010. 'In Afghanistan, signs of crony capitalism.' *Washington Post*, 22 February.

Morauta, T. R. H. M., 2011. *The theft and waste of public money in Papua New Guinea's Public Enterprises*, Port Moresby: The Ministry for Public Enterprises.

Quentin Sommerville, BBC, 2013. *Kabul Bank fraud: Sherkhan Farnood and Khalilullah Ferozi jailed*. [Online] Available at: http://www.bbc.com/news/world-asia-21666689 [Accessed 9 March 2015].

Rose, D., 2011. 9/11 'The Tapping Point.' *Vanity Fair*, September.

Rose, D., 2012. 'Robbed and Ruined by a British Court on the orders of the CIA...And we couldn't tell a soul: The chilling story of how secret justice cost a couple their £5m home – and £700m business.' *Mail on Sunday*, 8 April.

Wells, M., 2001. 'How smart was this bomb?' *The Guardian*, 19 November.